POLICY CHANGE, COURTS, AND THE CANADIAN CONSTITUTION

Policy Change, Courts, and the Canadian Constitution aims to further our understanding of judicial policy impact and the role of the courts in shaping policy change. Bringing together a group of political scientists and legal scholars, this volume delves into a diverse set of policy areas, including health care issues, the regulation of elections, criminal justice policy, minority-language education, citizenship, refugee policy, human rights legislation, and Indigenous policy.

While much of the public law and judicial politics literatures focus on the impact of the constitution and the judicial role, scholarship on courts that makes *policy change* its central lens of analysis is surprisingly rare. Multidisciplinary in its approach to examining policy issues, this book focuses on specific cases or policy issues through a wide-ranging set of approaches, including the use of interview data, policy analysis, historical and interpretive analysis, and jurisprudential analysis.

EMMETT MACFARLANE is an associate professor in the Department of Political Science at the University of Waterloo.

Policy Change, Courts, and the Canadian Constitution

EDITED BY EMMETT MACFARLANE

UNIVERSITY OF TORONTO PRESS
Toronto Buffalo London

Toronto Buffalo London
utorontopress.com

ISBN 978-1-4875-0412-0 (cloth) ISBN 978-1-4875-2315-2 (paper)

Library and Archives Canada Cataloguing in Publication

Policy change, courts, and the Canadian constitution / edited by Emmett Macfarlane.

Includes bibliographical references and index.
ISBN 978-1-4875-0412-0 (cloth). – ISBN 978-1-4875-2315-2 (paper)

1. Social legislation – Canada. 2. Sociological jurisprudence – Canada. 3. Constitutional law – Canada. 4. Courts – Canada. 5. Canada – Social policy. I. Macfarlane, Emmett, editor

KE3098.P65 2018 342.71 C2018-902595-6
KF3300.P65 2018

This book has been published with the help of a grant from the Federation for the Humanities and Social Sciences, through the Awards to Scholarly Publications Program, using funds provided by the Social Sciences and Humanities Research Council of Canada.

University of Toronto Press acknowledges the financial assistance to its publishing program of the Canada Council for the Arts and the Ontario Arts Council, an agency of the Government of Ontario.

For Thea

Contents

Acknowledgments

Many of the contributions in this book were first presented at a conference I hosted under the banner of the Courts & Politics Research Group (CPRG) at the University of Waterloo's Stratford, Ontario, campus in October 2016. The CPRG was established in recognition of the regional concentration of political scientists studying law and politics in southern Ontario, and it currently includes eighteen members at ten universities. This book is hopefully the first of many such collaborations.

I would like to thank the contributors to this volume for their excellent work and for their commitment to bringing a substantial volume together quickly. My thanks to the Faculty of Arts and the Department of Political Science at the University of Waterloo for providing funding for the Stratford conference.

I am also grateful to Dan Quinlan, the anonymous reviewers, and the editorial team at the University of Toronto Press for ushering the book through the editorial process. Dan was kind enough to join us at the conference to see the work presented first-hand. This is my second edited book conducted under Dan's skilful guidance, and it is a pleasure to work with him.

I would also like to thank my colleagues at the University of Waterloo for their continuous support. I offer a special shout-out to Dan Henstra for conversations that sparked ideas for this volume.

As always, this book would not have been possible without the support of my family. Thanks to my parents and sister for their continued support, and to my amazing wife, Anna.

POLICY CHANGE, COURTS, AND THE CANADIAN CONSTITUTION

Introduction: Judicial Policy Impact in Canada

EMMETT MACFARLANE

In *Canada (Attorney General) v. Bedford*,[1] the Supreme Court struck down three federal provisions criminalizing activities related to prostitution. The Court determined that those provisions, which prohibited the keeping of a bawdy house, public communication for the purposes of prostitution, and living off the avails of prostitution, violated the right to life, liberty, and security of the person under section 7 of the Canadian Charter of Rights and Freedoms. The laws effectively operated to criminalize sex work despite its status as an otherwise lawful activity. According to the Court, the prohibitions on public communication and keeping a bawdy house increased the risks of harm to sex workers in a manner grossly disproportionate to any benefit brought by the provisions. The ban on living off the avails was declared overly broad in that it prevented sex workers from employing security or drivers.

In one sense, the Court's policy impact was significant. By striking down these laws, the Court disrupted a long-standing policy status quo, compelling Parliament to craft new legislation to regulate prostitution in a manner that did not infringe sex workers' right to life, liberty, and security of the person. In another sense, however, the decision ultimately did little to change policy on the ground. First, the Court employed a remedy known as the suspended declaration of invalidity, which suspended the effects of its decision for one year in order to give Parliament time to develop a legislative response. Second, the government later successfully passed Bill C-36 through Parliament, a law that both resurrects aspects of the impugned provisions, such as a ban on public communication, and indirectly criminalizes prostitution by banning the purchase of sex. As a result, prostitution itself remains indirectly criminalized. These events make it challenging to measure policy change in this case, let alone attribute change to particular actors like courts. Further, the constitutional legitimacy of the existing policy regime remains unsettled: interest groups assert that the new law replicates the harms associated with the old provisions and have promised to bring forward a new legal challenge.[2]

What does this brief synopsis of a recent, noteworthy constitutional decision by the Supreme Court tell us about assessing the policy impact of courts or the constitution? As in many cases, policy change frequently emerges not simply from a judicial decision or the enforcement of a constitutional provision but also from the interplay between institutions within a broader policy environment. The ability of a government to respond to a court decision and protect its policy preferences, for example, might depend on the nature of the judicial remedy, the clarity of the relevant constitutional provision, and the political context, including intra-party (dis)agreement, expectations about future challenges or litigation, interest group activity, intergovernmental conflict, and public opinion.

This volume brings together a group of political scientists and legal scholars to tackle the difficult job of assessing the policy impact of courts and the constitution. While much of the public law and judicial politics literatures focus on the impact of the constitution and the judicial role, scholarship on courts that makes *policy change* its central lens of analysis is surprisingly rare in the Canadian context. In part, this may stem from a silo effect in the academic literature: neither the constitution nor the courts receive significant attention in the broader public policy/policy studies literature in Canada. Scholars who study judicial impact tend to be scholars of courts or the Charter, rather than those who might otherwise self-identify, first and foremost, as public policy scholars. A similar divide persists in the United States, despite that country's longer history of viewing courts as policymakers.[3]

This may explain, to some extent, why systematic studies of Charter of Rights outcomes, for example, tend to centre on the role of the Supreme Court or concepts relating to judicial power rather than having a more explicit policy focus. Such systematic studies debate and analyse relative rates of judicial activism[4] or the supposed inter-institutional dialogue on Charter issues.[5] Most analysis of courts and the constitution focuses on specific court cases or issue areas. Even broader works have largely focused on legal analysis rather than explicitly examining policy change.[6] The case study approach is crucial: it allows for in-depth analysis of the decision-making processes and the legal and political factors that bring about (or prevent) a change in the design, implementation, and effect of a particular policy or government program. Studies on the impact of the constitution, particularly as it regards the Charter, tend to be court-centric. This is not surprising given that courts are widely seen as the principal agents for determining the meaning of the Charter and the limitations of rights. Nonetheless, as several scholars contend, the legislative and executive branches also play an important role in scrutinizing policies for constitutional compatibility or even constitutional interpretation.[7]

Policy Change, Courts, and the Canadian Constitution aims to build on and further the development of our understanding of judicial policy impact and the constitution's implications for public policy. The contributors come together to develop new and varied ways to assess the role of courts and the constitution at various stages of the policy process and to more explicitly consider them as key players in a host of policy environments. The book adopts an explicitly multidisciplinary and methodologically pluralistic approach to examining policy change. Several chapters focus on theories of or approaches to policy change, either to examine the place of courts under those approaches or to apply specific theories to specific cases. Another set of chapters explores aspects of institutions or processes that have implications for judicially driven or constitutionally inspired policy change, including the reference procedure, executive and legislative review, the notwithstanding clause, and federalism. Finally, the largest set of contributions to this volume analyses specific cases or policy issues using a wide-ranging set of approaches, including analysing survey or interview data, applying process tracing, and adopting existing frameworks of policy analysis, historical and interpretive analysis, and jurisprudential analysis.

Although no volume of this kind can claim comprehensiveness, the chapters herein delve into a diverse set of policy areas, including health care issues, the regulation of elections, criminal justice policy, minority-language education, citizenship, refugee policy, equality and human rights legislation, and Indigenous policy. The contributions also explore various stages of the policy process, from considering judicial impact on policy in its earliest stages of development to the implementation of court decisions by front-line state actors. Further, contributors avoid treating courts in isolation, with many of the chapters considering the way judicial decisions condition, reinforce, or constrain government policy objectives or the strategies of interest groups and rights claimants. Similarly, many chapters explore how the interaction among institutions produces policy change, rather than simplistically attributing impact to solitary court decisions.

In so doing, this book aims to build on the existing literature on judicial impact. Many of the contributions hopefully serve as an important foundation for future work on policy change. As described in the next section, Canadian scholarship on the impact of courts has largely focused either on the success of litigation and legal mobilization or on broad systematic studies of government records before the Supreme Court. The Canadian literature has also been somewhat influenced by the more robust American literature on judicial impact, which is very briefly discussed below.

Existing Work on Court Impact

One of the earliest and most widely cited studies of the policy influence of the US Supreme Court is Dahl's 1957 account, which bases its assessment on instances in which the Court invalidated federal legislation.[8] Dahl concludes that the Court rarely influences policy in a manner that contradicts the wishes of the dominant national coalition (the law-making majority that passes and affirms law, comprises those voting in the House of Representatives and the Senate, and signed by the President). In fact, given the Court's institutional limitations and its role as one of the political institutions in the national "alliance," Dahl argues that, on its own, the Court "is almost powerless to affect the course of national policy."[9]

Dahl's study, however, adopts a very narrow analytical frame to assess the Court's policy influence. His analysis centres on a conception of the Court as a defender of minority interests against the majority. This places severe limits on what his empirical framework considers as policy influence. By presenting policy influence as essentially a determination of clashes between winners and losers, Dahl treats policy impact as a zero-sum game, rather than interaction among institutions.[10] Another problematic aspect of testing the Court's influence vis-à-vis a national law-making majority is the limitations this places on Dahl's case selection. Dahl limits his analysis to Court decisions striking down federal legislation *within four years of enactment*. While Dahl views this strict control on case selection as necessary to test whether a Court decision ran counter to the preferences of an *existing* law-making majority, he leaves out all the other cases in which the Court nonetheless made a determination on policy.

Studies on the impact of legal mobilization have perhaps provided the most comprehensive methodological debates about assessing the policy influence of courts. One of the most widely cited examples is Rosenberg's 1991 book, *The Hollow Hope*.[11] Rosenberg examines a range of nationally important policy issues in his analysis, including desegregation, abortion and women's rights, the environment, reapportionment, criminal law, and (in the 2008 second edition) same-sex marriage. He finds that constraints on the courts – particularly the nature of constitutional rights, limited judicial independence, and inability to implement decisions – render legal mobilization ineffective for bringing about social change. Rosenberg's analysis has been subject to much criticism, spawning epistemological and methodological debates over how to identify court influence.[12]

From the perspective of the efficacy of legal mobilization, McCann contends that Rosenberg's study ignores the symbolic impact of the law.[13] His own study on litigation surrounding pay equity finds that courts can produce important political payoffs.[14] McCann's more interpretivist approach is in line with other critics, who argue that Rosenberg's attempt to locate influence in direct and temporally sequenced ways belies the complexity of law and the policy process and, in their view, the fact that power cannot be "measured."[15] It is important to acknowledge, as Rosenberg himself points out in response to his critics,[16] that *The Hollow Hope* focuses expressly on evaluating whether litigation aimed at producing significant social reform is effective and does not argue that courts are irrelevant to social change or that they have no impact on society.

Nevertheless, Rosenberg's positivism and McCann's interpretivism offer two distinct ways of determining court impact. Rosenberg seeks evidence of direct causal influence of court decisions, and his examination focuses on discrete factors that overcome the constraints noted above. Thus, courts can be effective at creating change when there is ample legal precedent, substantial support in Congress or from the executive, and support (or low levels of opposition) among the public and when there are incentives or costs to encourage compliance and a willingness in the market or bureaucracy to implement court decisions.[17] By contrast, McCann is sceptical of linear, instrumental conceptions of causality. McCann emphasizes recognizing decision-making processes as dynamic, indeterminate, contingent, and interactive. He argues that approaches like Rosenberg's fail to pay sufficient attention to reasons and motives for action that are not "easily isolated as discrete, measurable, determinate variables."[18] McCann's work thus views the law as "constitutive" in that it shapes meaning, intent, and action in a complex, constructivist manner.

Writing in the Canadian context, Riddell notes that there is no judicial impact literature in Canada equivalent to that in the United States. Pointing to the "limited and sporadic" attempts to explain the effects of legal mobilization and judicial decisions in Canada,[19] he draws on both the Rosenberg and the McCann approaches in the context of official minority-language education policy for francophones outside Quebec. Riddell finds substantial evidence that legal mobilization brought about important changes in the policy environment and that both the factor-based, positivistic approach advanced by Rosenberg and the more interpretive perspective of McCann supported that conclusion. Riddell suggests that future work on judicial impact might incorporate a middle-ground approach that is attentive to the institutional factors that can promote or inhibit policy change, while accounting for the complex and constitutive nature of the law and the dynamic interactions that take place in the policy process.

Manfredi points out that the debate between Rosenberg and McCann demonstrates the difficulty scholars face in measuring concepts like *success* or *influence* in legal mobilization. Manfredi's work on legal mobilization in the area of women's equality rights (involving a wide range of policy issues such as abortion, sexual equality rights, employment and welfare benefits, and criminal law pertaining to sexual assault) brings to light a significant success rate in terms of advocates' ability to influence both the Supreme Court's jurisprudence and its outcomes.[20] For example, Manfredi details the sizeable policy impact of the *Morgentaler* decision on abortion, documenting a sharp rise in the number of abortions following the case (after one year, the rate of abortions per one thousand women had increased by 15.9 per cent; after ten years, it had increased by 35.3 per cent).[21] He writes that this increase "is primarily a function of an increase in the number of abortions performed in clinics rather than hospitals, a development directly traceable to *Morgentaler*."[22]

Finally, a 2001 study by Morton and Allen examining feminist litigation in both Charter and non-Charter cases elaborates on the different ways we can define litigant success (or, in broader terms, the meaning of a case outcome). The first and most obvious outcome is at the dispute level: which side, the appellant or respondent, is the "winner" of a case? The dispute in a given case may be a secondary or non-issue for third party interveners as they may be more interested in the legal outcome: does the Supreme Court adopt a set of interpretive or legal rules which would enhance later policy prospects that one side views as favourable? Morton and Allen point to the *Morgentaler* case as providing a good example of the distinction. While pro-choice advocates won at the dispute level in that case, only one judge accepted the claim that abortion was constitutionally protected under the Charter.[23]

The third indicator of success is the policy dimension, which requires a judicial remedy ordering a policy change. Morton and Allen assess whether the relevant cases altered (positively or negatively) the "policy status quo." They note that not all legal mobilization is intended to bring about policy change; interest groups sometimes litigate "defensively" to prevent what they would perceive as negative change. Partly on the basis of a low rate of judicial losses that resulted in negative policy change and a much higher rate of "offensive wins," the authors find that feminist litigation has been relatively successful in achieving significant policy change. These findings are in contrast to a more legalistic assessment of the Canadian context by Bogart, which reflects Rosenberg's view of the limited social and political change brought by the courts and the Charter.[24]

The American literature has also benefited from a focus on how that country's policies, particularly at the level of policy implementation, tend to be affected by an adversarial and legalistic dispute resolution process ("adversarial legalism"),[25] and a similar dynamic of judicialization, or "Eurolegalism," has become increasingly recognized in the European context.[26] This particular lens of analysis has only rarely been applied to the Canadian context.[27]

Beyond litigant-centred analyses are studies that examine court impact under the Charter from the broad perspective of government success. A number of early studies provide descriptive statistics of the Supreme Court's Charter record.[28] Building on this work, and writing in the context of evaluating normative claims about judicial activism, Choudhry and Hunter attempt to empirically measure judicial activism by developing a systematic, quantitative analysis of the influence of the Supreme Court.[29] Their analysis focuses on case outcomes, specifically whether a government is successful in defending its policy. Although Choudhry and Hunter do not investigate the subsequent impact of case outcomes, the framework they establish for measuring judicial activism, and the subsequent critique by Manfredi and Kelly over those measurements,[30] are illustrative of a number of relevant points. First, Choudhry and Hunter note that a strict quantitative measurement of outcomes treats all cases equally, providing no indication of those that are more important, either for the law or for their policy consequences. Second, framing an assessment of judicial influence in terms of winners and losers can mask instances where the reasons for a decision (its underlying logic) are more important than the dichotomous outcome of the case at hand. In other words, a government might lose a case on the merits, but win the overall policy argument by having the Court craft the legal rules in a particular way.

More importantly, as Manfredi and Kelly point out, "The most important question about judicial activism is not how [frequent] it is, but how judicial application of the Charter has affected the substance of public policy and the behaviour of governmental and non-governmental actors."[31] The authors note that Charter rulings have altered the legal framework for a wide range of issues, like abortion, the criminal process, same-sex marriage, and minority language education, but add, "We know far less about the practical impact of these changes."[32]

Another body of work explores the notion of a "dialogue" between courts and the elected branches of government over Charter issues. Proponents of dialogue argue that institutional mechanisms in the Canadian Charter of Rights and Freedoms, specifically the "reasonable limitations" clause under section 1 and a "legislative override" clause under section 33, allow legislatures to respond to judicial rulings striking down laws that offend its provisions. These features of the Charter are said to provide the legislatures with avenues for response, which, unlike in systems of judicial supremacy, means that courts do not always have the final word on the permissibility of the policies at stake.

Empirical, systematic studies of dialogue have produced wildly diverging assessments of just how dialogue occurs. In their original study, Hogg and Bushell count as dialogue any instance in which a legislature responded to a judicial decision striking down a law on Charter grounds through ordinary legislation (even counting instances where a legislature repeals the offending legislation), finding that dialogue occurs in 66 per cent of cases.[33] Critics argue that, for dialogue to occur, there should be some evidence that a legislative response in some way demonstrates an independent assessment of how to ensure that a given policy is consistent with the Charter. Manfredi and Kelly, for example, rightly point out that legislative responses that simply repeal offending legislation, as identified by a court, or replace entire acts should not count as dialogue. Their own analysis suggests that roughly one-third of cases are dialogic.[34]

My own study takes this analysis a step further.[35] Building on previous work by Hennigar that examines federal government responses to lower court decisions,[36] I examine all federal, provincial, and municipal government responses to Supreme Court decisions invalidating legislation under the Charter through 2009. Rather than merely cataloguing the "type" of response (such as whether a statute was repealed, replaced entirely, or amended, or there was no response), I incorporate an examination of the substance of any legislative amendment to see whether it represents an attempt to modify or avoid the Court's policy prescriptions or simply follows them. This extra stage of analysis suggests that only 17 per cent of legislative responses are truly dialogic.

Despite this range of disagreement over dialogue's empirical veracity, not to mention its conceptual utility,[37] the study of constitutional cases through the lens of inter-institutional interaction has the prospect of being an especially helpful and important way to assess judicial impact. The American political science literature has recently seen a proliferation of studies that assess judicial impact from an "interbranch perspective" in this manner.[38] Many of these studies also examine interactions between the courts and Congress or state legislatures from a dialogic perspective (some even citing the Canadian example). Given the long-held understanding of Supreme Court supremacy in constitutional interpretation, these studies forge a new path in demonstrating the willingness of the other branches of government to impose their own interpretations by responding to, avoiding, or overturning judicial rulings.

Several of the contributions to this volume explicitly or implicitly adopt an inter-institutional perspective. Others go beyond much of the extant literature by incorporating theories of policy change into their analysis or by explicitly considering the courts as but one actor in a complex institutional environment.

Outline of the Book

This volume is organized in three parts. In the first section, contributors examine and focus specifically on theories of policy change. In chapter 1, Minh Do argues that, without recourse to public policy theories, research on the role of courts as public policy actors may not reach its full explanatory potential. She examines key features of public policy studies and three broad institutionalist approaches – rational choice, historical institutionalism, and ideational – to explaining policy change.

Dave Snow and Kate Puddister apply a multiple streams analysis to medical assistance in dying policy in chapter 2. They argue that the Supreme Court was instrumental in opening a policy window for Parliament to act following its decision to invalidate the prohibition on assisted suicide in 2015. Snow and Puddister also examine the limits of judicial impact, particularly in light of the relatively restrictive legislative response passed by Parliament the following year. Applying another policy theory, Marc Zanoni explores the role of courts under a rubric of punctuated equilibrium in chapter 3. He develops a taxonomy of ways in which courts contribute to policy change or resistance, with a particular emphasis on the different constitutional remedies available to them when rendering decisions.

The second part of the book explores *institutional contexts* that have implications for how the courts or different aspects of the constitution impact policy. In chapter 4, Janet Hiebert assesses the extent to which the federal government, particularly the Department of Justice, evaluates the potential risks of constitutional challenge to legislation in development. She explores Department of Justice guidelines governing the review process and examines recent evidence indicating that political factors remain dominant, despite an increased role of government lawyers in the policy process. In chapter 5, Robert Schertzer examines the Supreme Court's impact on federalism and public policy. He argues that the Court contributed significantly to a recent shift from conflictual to collaborative federalism, pushing for intergovernmental negotiation or collaboration in many cases of policy conflict rather than setting the stage for unilateral action by either order of government. While Schertzer acknowledges other factors contributing to this shift, including institutional features as well as economic and social conditions, the Court's promotion of norms of collaboration was a necessary condition for collaborative federalism to become predominant in modern intergovernmental relations.

Kate Glover Berger examines the impact of the constitutional reference procedure on institutional reform in chapter 6. Glover Berger notes that one of the more intriguing aspects of the reference option is that governments effectively give up control over the process of reform, particularly as recent advisory opinions by the Supreme Court have effectively ended government reform efforts. She develops a framework of constitutional considerations that decision makers ought to make in the reference context, while acknowledging that ongoing reform initiatives reveal a degree of uncertainty, such as what might be considered entrenched as part of Canada's constitutional "architecture." Finally, in chapter 7, Richard Albert investigates the Charter's notwithstanding clause, which he contends is at risk of falling into desuetude. He analyses why the clause has fallen into such political disrepute and suggests ways to prevent it from becoming completely obsolete. As a provision that could help preserve legislative or government policy preferences, particularly in the face of judicial rulings that, in some contexts, are otherwise irreversible, Albert's analysis is both timely and fitting.

The third and final section of this volume contains contributions examining specific policy issues or areas. These chapters fall under a set of diverse categories, including criminal justice policy, the regulation of elections, minority-language education, citizenship, refugee policy, health policy, Indigenous policy, and equality rights.

In chapter 8, Troy Riddell and Dennis Baker examine police implementation of Charter decisions, with a focus on police responses to judicial decisions affecting civil liberties. Using a case study of a mid-sized police force in Ontario, their analysis draws on survey data, interviews, and a review of policy and training materials. Riddell and Baker note that an uneven implementation of information by front-line officers risks a similar unevenness in how Charter rights are applied day to day. Turning to another area of criminal justice policy, Kate Puddister examines the impact of section 12's right against cruel and unusual punishment on sentencing policy in chapter 9. She traces the Supreme Court's approach in the area of mandatory minimum sentences, finding that only recently has the jurisprudence evinced a growing role for section 12 in Canadian criminal justice policy. Before two recent cases, Parliament played an active role in sentencing policy under the Court's narrow reading of section 12.

Erin Crandall and Andrea Lawlor investigate the regulation of elections and third parties in chapter 10. They note that the Supreme Court's decision to uphold spending limits on third parties fundamentally shapes the policy framework surrounding non-party actors in Canadian elections. Crandall and Lawlor explore a diverse set of issues that continue to have significant implications for the regulation of elections in Canada, and they note that the courts may continue to play a role in determining the constitutional validity of policies.

In chapter 11, Stéphanie Chouinard examines the courts' impact on official-language minority education policy in Canada under section 23 of the Charter. She notes that it is a policy area in which the Supreme Court has been particularly active. Despite this, her analysis reveals that there remain many inconsistencies in access between, and sometimes within, the various provinces. In chapter 12, James Kelly also analyses the judicial impact under section 23, but his focus is specifically on access to English public education in Quebec. Kelly argues that, despite court-initiated policy change, Quebec has generally been able to retain and preserve its autonomy in language and education policy.

Megan Gaucher examines the impact of courts on policies implicating citizenship in chapter 13. She finds that the judiciary's influence on policies affecting the rights of non-citizens has been significantly limited and that the Supreme Court, specifically, has contributed to a policy environment in which parliamentary authority has been exercised to limit those rights. Gaucher analyses recent policy changes initiated by the former Conservative government under Prime Minister Stephen Harper. In chapter 14, Christopher Anderson and Dagmar Soennecken investigate the Harper government's inland refugee policy. Noting that the role of courts in relation to refugee policy is historically limited and relatively understudied, Anderson and Soennecken examine the significant mobilization on behalf of refugees following rights-restrictive policies introduced by the Harper government.

In chapter 15, Eleni Nicolaides and Matthew Hennigar examine the Supreme Court's impact on policy regarding medical assistance in dying. A key feature of their analysis is the nature of the government's restrictive policy response to the Court's invalidation of the prohibition on assisted dying in the *Carter* case. The authors map the impact of the Court's decision on the subsequent policy process, examining how Parliament and relevant interest groups characterized the legislative-judicial relationship to advance their policy preferences. Examining another contentious area of health policy, in chapter 16 Rachael Johnstone explores abortion policy in Canada in the aftermath of the Supreme Court's decision in the 1988 *Morgentaler* case. While the Court's decision had a tremendous impact on the abortion policy landscape, many provinces were able to avoid being implicated by obvious rights obligations, especially in an environment where new litigation was somewhat limited.

Michael McCrossan explores Indigenous rights and policy implicated by the "duty to consult" principle in chapter 17. His analysis finds that while the duty to consult doctrine may have initially held the promise of fundamentally altering Indigenous-state relations, existing jurisprudence has preserved and privileged non-Indigenous conceptions of land and development policy. In chapter 18, Kyle Kirkup examines significant differences in the legal activism of trans people versus that of the queer community under the Charter. Whereas the Charter became a key focal point in advancing equality rights for same-sex couples, in particular, trans activists have more readily fought discrimination before federal, provincial, and territorial human rights tribunals. Kirkup explores why these different legal strategies have emerged.

In the concluding chapter, I examine areas of agreement and divergence, particularly as they relate to the magnitude of policy change attributed to the courts or particular constitutional provisions, as well as the nature of limitations placed on change by other institutions or the litigation strategies of relevant interest groups. I then explore possible avenues for future research on courts and policy change.

NOTES

1 2013 SCC 72, [2013] 3 S.C.R. 1101.

2 Laura Stone, "Group Threatens Liberals with New Legal Challenge over Sex Work Law," *Global News*, 30 October 2015, accessed 21 January 2017, http://globalnews.ca/news/2309848/group-threatens-liberals-with-new-legal-challenge-over-sex-work-law/.

3 Scott Barclay and Thomas Birkland, "Law, Policymaking, and the Policy Process: Closing the Gaps," *Policy Studies Journal* 26, no. 2 (1998): 227–43.

4 Sujit Choudhry and Claire E. Hunter, "Measuring Judicial Activism on the Supreme Court of Canada: A Comment on *Newfoundland (Treasury Board) v. NAPE*," *McGill Law Journal* 48 (2003): 525–62; Christopher P. Manfredi and James B. Kelly, "Misrepresenting the Supreme Court's Record? A Comment on Choudhry and Hunter, 'Measuring Judicial Activism on the Supreme Court of Canada,'" *McGill Law Journal* 49, no. 3 (2004): 741–64.

5 Peter W. Hogg and Allison A. Bushell, "The *Charter* Dialogue between Courts and Legislatures (or Perhaps the *Charter of Rights* Isn't Such a Bad Thing After All)," *Osgoode Hall Law Journal* 35, no. 1 (1997): 75–124; Christopher P. Manfredi and James B. Kelly, "Six Degrees of Dialogue: A Response to Hogg and Bushell," *Osgoode Hall Law Journal*. 37, no. 3 (1999): 513–27; Emmett Macfarlane, "Dialogue or Compliance? Measuring Legislature's Policy Responses to Court Rulings on Rights," *International Political Science Review* 34 (2013): 39–56.

6 David Schneiderman and Kate Sutherland, eds., *Charting the Consequences: The Impact of Charter Rights on Canadian Law and Politics* (Toronto: University of Toronto Press, 1997); Harry W. Arthurs and Brent Arnold, "Does the Charter Matter?," *Review of Constitutional Studies* 11, no. 1 (2005): 37–117.

7 Janet L. Hiebert, *Charter Conflicts: What Is Parliament's Role?* (Montreal and Kingston: McGill-Queen's University Press, 2002); James B. Kelly, *Governing with the Charter: Legislative and Judicial Activism and Framers' Intent* (Vancouver: UBC Press, 2005); Dennis Baker, *Not Quite Supreme: The Courts and Coordinate Constitutional Interpretation* (Montreal and Kingston: McGill-Queen's University Press, 2010).

8 Robert A. Dahl, "Decision-Making in a Democracy: The Supreme Court as a National Policy-Maker," *Journal of Public Law* 6 (1957): 279–95.

9 Ibid., at 293.

10 Jonathan D. Casper, "The Supreme Court and National Policy Making," *American Political Science Review* 70, no. 1 (1976): 50–63, at 62.

11 Gerald N. Rosenberg, *The Hollow Hope: Can Courts Bring About Social Change?*, 2nd ed. (Chicago: University of Chicago Press, 2008).

12 Gerald N. Rosenberg, "Positivism, Interpretivism, and the Study of Law," *Law and Social Inquiry* 21 (1996): 435–55; Michael McCann, "Causal versus Constitutive Explanations (or, On the Difficulty of Being So Positive ...)," *Law and Social Inquiry* 21 (1996): 457–82.

13 Michael McCann, "Reform Litigation on Trial," *Law and Social Inquiry* 17 (1992): 71.

14 Michael McCann, *Rights at Work: Pay Equity Reform and the Politics of Legal Mobilization* (Chicago: University of Chicago Press, 1994).

15 David Schultz and Stephen E. Gottlieb, "Legal Functionalism and Social Change: A Reassessment of Rosenberg's *The Hollow Hope*," in *Leveraging the Law: Using the Courts to Achieve Social Change*, ed. David A. Schultz (New York: Peter Lang, 1998), 181.

16 Gerald N. Rosenberg, "Knowledge and Desire: Thinking about Courts and Social Change," in *Leveraging the Law: Using the Courts to Achieve Social Change*, ed. David A. Schultz (New York: Peter Lang, 1998), 251–91.

17 Rosenberg, *The Hollow Hope*, 36.

18 McCann, "Causal versus Constitutive Explanations," 460.

19 Troy Q. Riddell, "The Impact of Legal Mobilization and Judicial Decisions: The Case of Official Minority-Language Education Policy in Canada for Francophones outside Quebec," *Law and Society Review* 38 (2004): 583–609, at 584.

20 Christopher P. Manfredi, *Feminist Activism in the Supreme Court: Legal Mobilization and the Women's Legal Education and Action Fund* (Vancouver: UBC Press, 2004).

21 Ibid., at 180.

22 Ibid., at 181.

23 F.L. Morton and Avril Allen, "Feminists and the Courts: Measuring Success in Interest Group Litigation in Canada," *Canadian Journal of Political Science* 34, no. 1 (2001): 55–84, at 66.
24 W.A. Bogart, *Courts and Country: The Limits of Litigation and the Social and Political Life of Canada* (Oxford: Oxford University Press, 1994).
25 Robert A. Kagan, "Adversarial Legalism and American Government," *Journal of Policy Analysis and Management* 10, no. 3 (1991): 369–406.
26 R. Daniel Kelemen, *Eurolegalism: The Transformation of Law and Regulation in the European Union* (Cambridge, MA: Harvard University Press, 2011); Dorte Sindbjerg Martinsen and Juan A. Mayoral, "A Judicialisation of Healthcare Policies in Denmark and Spain? The Universalist Healthcare Model Meets the European Union," *Comparative European Politics* 15, no. 3 (2017): 414–34.
27 Michael Howlett, "Beyond Legalism? Policy Ideas, Implementation Styles and Emulation-Based Convergence in Canadian and U.S. Environmental Policy," *Journal of Public Policy* 20, no. 3 (2000): 305–29.
28 F.L. Morton, Peter H. Russell, and Michael J. Withey, "The Supreme Court's First One Hundred Charter of Rights Decisions: A Statistical Analysis," *Osgoode Hall Law Journal* 30, no. 1 (1992): 1–56; F.L. Morton, Peter H. Russell, and Troy Riddell, "The Canadian Charter of Rights and Freedoms: A Descriptive Analysis of the First Decade, 1982–1992," *National Journal of Constitutional Law* 5 (1995): 1–60.
29 Choudhry and Hunter, "Measuring Judicial Activism on the Supreme Court of Canada."
30 Manfredi and Kelly, "Misrepresenting the Supreme Court's Record?"
31 Ibid., at 748.
32 Ibid.
33 Hogg and Bushell, "The Charter Dialogue between Courts and Legislatures."
34 Manfredi and Kelly, "Six Degrees of Dialogue."
35 Macfarlane, "Dialogue or Compliance?"
36 Matthew A. Hennigar, "Expanding the 'Dialogue' Debate: Canadian Federal Government Responses to Lower Court Charter Decisions," *Canadian Journal of Political Science* 37, no. 1 (2004): 3–21.
37 Emmett Macfarlane, "Conceptual Precision and Parliamentary Systems of Review: Disambiguating 'Dialogue,'" *Review of Constitutional Studies* 17, no. 2 (2012): 73–100.
38 Mark C. Miller and Jeb Barnes, eds., *Making Policy, Making Law: An Interbranch Perspective* (Washington D.C.: Georgetown University Press, 2004);

Jeb Barnes, "Bringing the Courts Back In: Interbranch Perspectives on the Role of Courts in American Politics and Policy Making," *Annual Review of Political Science* 10 (2007): 25–43; Mark C. Miller, *The View of the Courts from the Hill: Interactions between Congress and the Federal Judiciary* (Charlottesville: University of Virginia Press, 2009); Martin J. Sweet, *Merely Judgment: Ignoring, Evading, and Trumping the Supreme Court* (Charlottesville: University of Virginia Press, 2010); Scott E. Lemieux and George Lovell, "Legislative Defaults: Interbranch Power Sharing and Abortion Politics," *Polity* 42, no. 2 (2010): 210–43.

PART ONE

Approaches and Theories of Policy Change

1 Lessons from Public Policy Theories: Ask about Policy Change First, Courts Second

MINH DO

The relationship between the judiciary and public policy is an important topic of research because cases containing fundamental questions of law can produce serious policy consequences. In Canada, the enactment of the Canadian Charter of Rights and Freedoms has focused scholarly attention on the judiciary's involvement in policy questions as a function of protecting fundamental rights. The courts' role as policymaking actors can be examined by finding the conditions under which courts can influence policy, how courts behave to influence policy when those conditions are met, and whether judicial involvement in policymaking is legitimate.

When examining the policy influence of courts, scholars often do not explicitly use theories of public policy that explain policy change. Given this lack of attention, what do public policy theories contribute to examining the role of courts in policymaking? Theories of policy change consider the entire range of actors and forces that might influence policy change and development. Therefore, public policy theories can reveal the degree to which the courts have an influence on policy change and how their influence may interact with other political actors and forces. I will argue that it may be most useful to employ public policy theories to first explain policy change in a given policy area. If the courts play an important role in producing policy change, then their role can be more closely examined to identify the *type* of influence they exercise, *how* they exercise this influence, and *why* they exercise this influence at all. Without first using public policy theories to identify the scope and nature of court influence in policy change or stability, research on the role of courts as policy actors may have limited explanatory power. For example, the courts' influence in policy change or stability may be over- or underestimated, or the nature of the influence may be inaccurately conceptualized.

This chapter will proceed in four sections to demonstrate the utility of using public policy theories to analyse the courts' policy role. The first section will provide an overview of some of the central characteristics of public policy studies and the different institutionalist explanations for policy change and development. The second, third, and fourth sections will analyse these different institutionalist approaches to explaining policy change. Each of these sections will also be accompanied by an analysis of how the existing literature on the role of the courts, and their behaviour as policy actors, can be used in combination with these institutionalist theories to reveal the relationship between courts and public policy. The chapter will then conclude with some final remarks about the advantages of using public policy theories to first explain policy change before conceptualizing the courts' policymaking role.

The Institutionalist Theories of Public Policy: Development and Change

Public policy scholarship is divided into two major research traditions. The first is policy sciences or policy analysis, which is directed at "provid[ing] knowledge and policy expertise in and for policymaking."[1] This goal is consistent with Harold Lasswell's articulation of the field of public policy, in which multidisciplinary approaches that explain the policy process can be used by decision makers to yield better outcomes to solve policy problems.[2] The policy sciences approach is advocated among some public policy scholars as they claim that there are no drawbacks to improving decision making by using knowledge of the policy process.[3] The second research tradition is policy studies, which works to "develop general theories and frameworks of the policy process explaining and predicting policy-making processes."[4] This chapter will assess institutionalist policy theories that fall within the policy studies approach.

The policy studies approach is exemplified by Richard Simeon's call to action to embrace comparative approaches; define a clear, dependent variable; and focus less attention on prescribing changes to improve decision making.[5] According to Simeon, the central task of policy studies should be to find explanations for policy changes rather than assume that decision making can be a rational process independent of "values, norms, institutions and patterns of power."[6] To this end, Simeon suggests a framework called the "funnel of causality,"[7] which identifies some key factors that may influence policy change and development. This funnel includes the role of the broader political and social environment, the distribution of power, central ideas and values, institutional structures, and the process of decision making.[8] Analysing the interactions between macro, structural forces and micro exchanges between actors in decision making leads to comprehensive explanations of policy change.

Simeon cautions that policy scholars should be attentive to the influence of the entire funnel rather than focus exclusively on one end of the funnel.[9] For instance, identifying the courts' policy influence often begins with the theoretical premise that the institution of the judiciary produces important political consequences, but there may be a larger range of actors and forces that interact with judicial institutions and also influence policy change or stability. Therefore, the focus on the institution of the judiciary should expand to include more aspects of the funnel of causality, including the role of micro-level dynamics, such as individual decision-making processes, or macro-level factors, such as the role of ideas, values, and norms.

Indeed, institutionalist theories of policy change can account for the range of actors and forces in the funnel of causality by invoking rational choice dynamics, temporality, and ideational approaches. For instance, a rational choice understanding of institutional effects posits that institutions are rules that structure interactions between utility-maximizing actors. In contrast, historical institutionalism is an institutionalist approach that emphasizes the importance of temporality in shaping policy change and development. Ideational institutional perspectives treat institutions as having the ability to transform actors' identities and preferences because institutions provide a cognitive script, or set of norms, that actors must follow.[10] It is important to note that although institutionalist approaches may stress the importance of interests, temporality, or ideas to explaining policy change, the concept of the funnel of causality is a reminder that an entire range of factors often plays a role in policy development.

The next three sections will analyse the main institutionalist public policy theories to show how they provide different explanations for policy change and development. Once an explanation for policy change is provided, the courts' role in, and influence on, politics can then be examined. Existing theories in the judicial politics scholarship are equipped to identify the conditions under which the judiciary can exercise policy influence. However, these theories must be carefully considered and may require additional refinement to ensure that they are ontologically consistent with explanations of policy change or stability.

Rational Choice Institutionalism and Courts' Policy Influence

Rational choice institutionalism places primacy on the individual actors that navigate the policy process or have decision-making power. It is assumed that actors hold agency to make decisions, are utility-maximizers, and behave strategically and instrumentally to pursue their preferences.[11] Although rational choice has its roots in economics, scholars using rational choice theories consider the role of "institutions and norms, ... the richness of context, ... questions of conflict and power, and, on occasion, ... non-egoistic motivations."[12] For instance, rational choice institutionalists treat institutions as rules or constraints that structure interactions between actors and provide more or less uncertainty for actors when they pursue strategies to attain their interests.[13] Moreover, although individual actors are often the main focus of the analysis, group dynamics, and the political outcomes that result from group actions, are also considered. Indeed, strategic interactions, whether they happen within groups or institutions or are shaped by the broader context, are considered by many rational choice theorists to be a main feature of politics.[14] For public policy studies employing rational choice institutionalism, strategic interactions are also a fundamental element in explaining policy change and stability.

An interesting application of strategic interaction to explain policy change that may involve the role of the courts comes from the work of Jacob Hacker, Paul Pierson, and Kathleen Thelen. They posit that drift and conversion are mechanisms that produce institutional change in ways that direct attention away from traditional venues of policy activity, such as legislatures.[15] It must be clarified that the authors treat public policies as types of institutions that can be explained through these mechanisms.[16] Moreover, conversion is considered a mechanism of policy change that also corresponds to the theoretical premises of historical institutionalism. Historical institutional approaches consider how temporality influences the effects of mechanisms, such that the *pace* of change may be a critical factor in explaining an outcome.[17] In the case of conversion, policy change is a product of long-term actions. Although the mechanism of change is consistent with the theoretical premises of historical institutionalism, the drivers of that mechanism, and the explanation of how that mechanism is activated, are the actors that behave strategically, as predicted by rational choice institutionalism. Due to the primary role of actors triggering the use of conversion as a temporally bound mechanism for policy change in certain institutional settings, I consider this mechanism to be compatible with rational choice institutionalism.

Conversion is a mechanism of policy change that may especially involve the influence of the judiciary. Hacker, Pierson, and Thelen describe conversion as "the transformation of an already-existing institution or policy through its authoritative redirection, reinterpretation, or reappropriation."[18] The judiciary can be a suitable venue to pursue these changes as the courts have the power to render authoritative reinterpretations of laws that have policy implications. Groups pursuing policy change through conversion can be motivated to either dismantle certain aspects of an institution or create a new institutional practice without entirely removing the institution itself.[19] The authors also note that many different groups may attempt to pursue conversion as a means of initiating policy change; these groups could be the "losers" from previous policy decisions or the "winners," who have an interest in maintaining power.[20] The strategic interaction dimension stems from the way in which actors, or groups of actors, holding distinct policy interests seek courts as a venue to pursue either policy change or stability. From this perspective, courts are part of the institutional system that self-interested actors navigate to pursue their policy preferences. In particular, the authors find that "repeat players" are the actors best equipped to engage in conversion because they are positioned to monitor the development of a policy and they have the resources to sustain their efforts to make long-term gains over a series of cases.[21]

Conversion as a mechanism for policy change is complemented by existing scholarship that explains the courts' role in policymaking as the result of interest group mobilization. Charles Epp's *The Rights Revolution* posits an argument that is highly consistent with the theoretical premises found in rational choice institutionalism. According to Epp, the judiciary promotes rights protection due to the "deliberate, strategic organizing by rights advocates," who are supported by "rights-advocacy organizations, rights-advocacy lawyers, and sources of financing, particularly government-supported financing."[22] Therefore, the resources that certain rights advocates can access help these groups sustain their mobilization efforts, increasing their likelihood of making gains through judicial decision making.[23] The actions of organized groups drive rights to the forefront of judicial decision making and encourage judges to render favourable rulings for those groups.[24] As a result, the behaviour of courts and their role in policymaking is dependent on the strength and character of groups engaging in legal mobilization. If the legal support structure is weak, then the scope conditions for judicial influence in policymaking will not be met.

In the Canadian scholarship, F.L. Morton and Rainer Knopff also examine judicial power in a manner consistent with rational choice institutionalism. Similar to Epp's observations, Morton and Knopff find that a support structure, what they call the "Court Party," is necessary to place the courts in a position to influence policy.[25] The Court Party consists of "partisans" that have an interest in increasing the judiciary's involvement in policymaking; they include social movements like "national unity advocates, civil libertarians, equality-seekers, social engineers, and postmaterialists."[26] Morton and Knopff state that "political partisans will gravitate to institutions that appear most open to their policy preferences or most closed to the preferences of their opponents."[27] Therefore, the judiciary attracts Court Party interest groups that can mobilize political resources to succeed in influencing policy change through judicial venues.[28]

It must be noted that although the legal mobilization literature emphasizes the actions of groups using judicial venues to pursue their interests, these interests are a constitutive element of broader ideas and values. Rights protections and the increased power of judicial review redistribute resources to different groups to exercise political power, but these material conditions are not the source of the groups' interests. Indeed, Mark Blyth states that "agents' interests [are] a function of their beliefs and desires rather than being simply derivative of their ostensible material positions."[29] For example, Morton and Knopff state that the Court Party is constituted of elites whose goals of socially engineering society are guided by ideas learned from the education system and knowledge-based occupations.[30] The constitutive nature of ideas and interests also demonstrates the importance of considering the entire funnel of causality to explain policy change. The political resources that interest groups use to litigate through judicial venues may be an integral component of explaining policy change, but drawing attention to the ideas underpinning those interests explains why certain interests are invoked in the pursuit of policy change.

Epp, and Morton and Knopff, direct attention to the ways in which external actors, such as organized groups, are a necessary condition for bolstering the courts' power to influence policy. However, the courts' actions in the policymaking process may also influence the decision of social movements and civil society groups to litigate for policy change. There may be a reciprocal relationship between organized groups mobilizing to encourage judicial intervention in policymaking, and the successful results of this mobilization then encourage more groups to engage in litigation. Miriam Smith addresses how gay and lesbian social movements alter their goals from achieving social and political equality to treating human rights as an element of law and public policy change due to the opportunity structure offered by litigation.[31] Thus, Smith finds that both the legal support structure for providing resources for litigation and a series of legal victories will push officials to change policy.[32]

Another dimension in these rational choice institutional approaches is the idea that once a legal support structure encourages the judiciary to take a more prominent role in policymaking, judges will be more likely to pronounce judgments that advance the interests of a mobilizing group. However, the behaviour of the courts to produce favourable rulings may depend on the judges' own policy preferences and interests. Judges themselves may be motivated by their own interests to advance certain policy preferences when given the opportunity by a legal support structure, or they may be cautious about advancing certain policy agendas because of their own stake in defending the power and legitimacy of the judiciary. This calculation shows how judicial actors may be constrained by institutional rules, even as other actors use institutional opportunities to advance policy change through the judiciary. For instance, Vuk Radmilovic finds that when courts are confronted with cases that involve politically sensitive jurisprudence, they will consider public opinion and the political context surrounding a case.[33] These measures help the courts avoid confrontation among political actors and cultivate legitimacy for themselves as an institution.[34] Similarly, Roy Flemming and B. Dan Wood find that American courts make decisions that influence policy at the margins, in a way that is consistent with public opinion and ensures that the courts remain a legitimate institution that is not usurping policymaking powers.[35] Therefore, even though the presence of a legal support structure may create the conditions whereby the judiciary can influence policy, the behaviour of judges may lead to a variation in outcomes that displays different degrees of policy influence.

There are many compelling studies consistent with rational choice institutionalism that examine court behaviour and its influence on policy change. These studies find that the conditions under which courts can influence policy lie with the actions of organized interests and a legal support structure. Moreover, the behaviour of courts as they pursue their own interests can also influence the degree to which the judiciary influences policy, even with a strong legal support structure in place. However, judicial influence as a function of the organizational capacity of groups applies only when policy change takes a particular form. Conversion may be one of these forms, whereby organized interests seek different venues to make policy change because other avenues display resistance against producing the desired change.[36] Policy change that is not related to the actions of organized interests mobilizing to access the courts may not engage rational choice institutionalism. Consequently, it is crucial to analyse the nature of the policy change first, before examining how courts exercise policy influence.

Historical Institutionalism and Courts' Policy Influence

Historical institutionalism emphasizes how power asymmetries are reflected in institutional structures and maintains that policy change occurs through temporally bound mechanisms exemplified by theories of path dependency and critical junctures. These explanations are sometimes criticized as vague[37] and overemphasizing policy stability over change.[38] In response, scholars have reacted to sharpen these two explanations. In the case of path dependency, Andrew Bennett and Colin Elman identify four main premises of the theory: causal possibility, contingency, closure, and constraint.[39] Causal possibility states that more than one path must be available to produce a variation in possible outcomes; contingency means that unintended consequences, most likely at the beginning of a path, are an important factor in influencing the causal story; closure refers to how past decisions narrow the range of future decisions and pathways; and constraint represents the "stickiness" of paths, making it somewhat difficult for paths to drastically change course.[40]

The other common explanation of policy change within historical institutionalism is critical junctures. Since institutions, which may include policies, can be difficult to change due to the enduring quality of self-reinforcing sequences found in path dependency, critical junctures are considered a means by which change can occur. Critical junctures can be identified as relatively brief moments in which powerful actors may have more options for making significant, consequential changes.[41] Scholars employing critical junctures to explain policy change should consider the problems associated with this explanation identified by Giovanni Capoccia and Daniel Keleman: the lack of specificity of the unit of analysis that constitutes a critical juncture compared to "normal" institutional change and development, the lack of clarity regarding the time horizon in which critical junctures are meant to operate, the risk of overlooking how critical junctures can produce re-equilibrium to an institutional status quo rather than trigger change, and the danger of neglecting the role of agency in favour of interpreting outcomes as merely the result of random events.[42] Consequently, policy change and development should be analysed carefully to avoid mischaracterizing an event as a critical juncture or overlooking an event that could constitute a critical juncture.

Path dependency and critical junctures can explain policy change or stability when longer time horizons are the scope of analysis and when the sequence of events that lead to a particular outcome are causally important to explaining that outcome. The judiciary may play either a significant or a minor policy role in a path-dependent explanation of policy change. For example, the judiciary may be understood as an institution that uses its powers to dramatically influence a policy's development such that other institutions, like the legislature, must adhere to a court's decision by reinforcing the policy's development on a particular path. Indeed, a legal challenge could amount to a critical juncture in which a court's decision sets a new path of policy development. In contrast, the judiciary's influence may be highly limited, enabling other institutions, such as the legislature or executive, to determine the path of policy development. In this situation, the courts play a coordinative function that rarely shifts the policy entirely from its path of development determined by other institutions.

The focus of Canadian judicial scholarship on the important effect of institutions on political outcomes should come as no surprise since the theoretical assumption that institutional roles and rules prescribe and constrain certain actions over others is widely accepted. However, despite the institutional focus of this literature, the explanations characteristic of historical institutionalist approaches are not often used to assess the courts' influence on policy change or stability.[43] Instead, this scholarship that examines institutional dynamics has focused more attention on the exchange between the judiciary and legislatures after legislative action is forwarded for judicial review; this is a narrower time frame than the scope of typical historical institutionalist studies. This emphasis on legislative and judicial interactions during judicial review processes represents the "dialogue" literature, which examines the relationship between courts and legislatures as they protect constitutional provisions that may have profound policy implications.[44] The sequence of interactions between the judiciary and legislatures is the central focus of this literature, but it has yet to directly consider how long-term, inter-institutional interactions produce patterns of policy change.

The term "dialogue" was used by Peter Hogg and Allison Bushell as they analysed the influence of courts' decisions relative to other institutional bodies by examining legislative responses to court decisions.[45] Consistent with this seminal article, the dialogue literature expanded to assess the legislatures' justification for rights violation under s. 1 of the Charter; the use of the Charter's override clause, s. 33; and the options available for legislatures to respond to court decisions.[46] There is a shared premise that the sequence of interactions between legislative and judicial behaviour in a policy area can influence policy development. However, the seemingly irreconcilable debates over what constitutes dialogue[47] create a barrier to conceptualizing the influence of institutions on patterns of policy change and stability. Moreover, the use of the dialogue literature to bolster normative arguments about the judiciary's involvement in policymaking has arguably not developed the literature to address these conceptual roadblocks.[48]

The goal of the dialogue literature is mainly to explain the effects of judicial review on various institutions' powers; this is different than examining institutions' effects on policy change and stability. As such, the debates in the dialogue literature about the nature of inter-institutional dynamics in light of enhanced judicial review are not necessarily the central focus if the goal is to explain policy development. If the dependent variable of interest is policy change or stability, then tracing the development of that policy over a longer period of time may be a better method of tracing the impact of various institutions in which policy decisions are made, which may include both legislatures and the judiciary. Once a longer time horizon is employed as the scope of analysis, it may be possible to identify whether path dependency or critical junctures can explain the nature of the policy development.

Judicial scholarship interested in identifying the influence of institutions on policy change can adopt analyses to trace a longer sequence of events beyond the exchange between judicial intervention and legislative responses. Some scholars who have contributed to the dialogue literature debate have taken on this task of analysing a longer time frame to identify the role of other institutions in the process of rights protection. For example, Janet Hiebert analyses how the Charter affects Parliament's exercise of legislative power before judicial decision making takes place. She finds that higher levels of scrutiny over bills being drafted across government departments, a more prominent role for the Department of Justice (DOJ), and a changing bureaucratic culture are some notable institutional changes to the policy process that are the result of the judiciary's ability to strike down legislation.[49] Beyond this internal review of government legislation, Parliament can play a role in providing additional oversight to ensure that any rights violations are consistent with Charter principles.

James Kelly also shifts focus from solely analysing the courts to focusing on the entire institutional system that is responsible for upholding constitutional rights and policymaking. Indeed, Kelly urges a return to a Diceyan interpretation of constitutionalism, in which political actors play a central role in policy, while judicial decision making is secondary to the actions taken by the executive or the legislature.[50] However, Kelly is more sceptical about Parliament's influence on policy as he argues that Cabinet's power has grown since the implementation of the Charter. According to Kelly, "The increased importance of the cabinet's legal advisor and the corresponding significance of the DOJ have allowed the cabinet to govern with the Charter, [and] it has occurred outside the parliamentary arena and within the machinery of government that directly supports the cabinet and its legislative agenda."[51]

Both Hiebert and Kelly examine events *before* judicial decision making to assess other institutions' influence on policy development. In the case of Hiebert, she also analyses policy responses *after* judicial decisions are made to examine how Parliament debates and contests these decisions. Building on the studies of Hiebert and Kelly, it may be fruitful to identify the range of institutional influences and the nature of their influence over time. For example, the character of Charter vetting processes by Cabinet, and to a lesser degree Parliament, may set in motion a specific pattern of inter-institutional exchanges between the courts and legislatures that influences policy development in a particular way.

Extending the time frame of analysis to consider a longer sequence of a policy's development before and after a judicial decision helps identify what inter-institutional dynamics are triggered over time and their effects. It may be uncovered that the inter-institutional exchanges involved in a policy's development resemble that of path dependency or contain moments of critical junctures.

Ideational Institutionalism and Courts' Policy Influence

Ideational institutional approaches draw attention to the influence of ideas, values, and norms within institutions and their effects on policy change and stability. Scholars adopting the ideational tradition believe that ideas are always present in policymaking as policymaking itself is "a constant struggle over the criteria for classification, the boundaries of categories, and the definition of ideals that guide the way people behave."[52] Actors may use different kinds of ideas to pursue a particular interest or act on a particular value or norm. Cognitive ideas, or causal ideas, inform people about the cause-and-effect relationships between subjects in the world. Normative ideas consist of values and norms regarding how the subjects in the world ought to be structured or what actors ought to do to improve the world. Cognitive and normative ideas operate on two levels, referred to as the background, philosophical, or paradigmatic level and the foreground level. Cognitive and normative ideas residing in the background are treated as taken-for-granted assumptions that actors rarely challenge and that operate to narrow the range of policy alternatives that actors will consider.[53] In contrast, cognitive and normative ideas in the foreground are used in everyday policymaking to justify and legitimate policy decisions.[54] Actors may even demonstrate how particular foreground ideas are consistent with the background ideas to show how a particular policy decision is more desirable than others.[55]

Institutional approaches can incorporate ideas by considering how institutions themselves reflect accepted ideas of symbolic practices that guide actors' behaviours and are also a setting that influences the degree to which ideas presented by actors are found to be persuasive. Therefore, institutions can be both the product of socially accepted behaviours and norms as well as sites for change as actors use ideas and discourse within institutional settings to challenge those institutional practices. According to Vivien Schmidt, the treatment of ideas as static and fixed, whereby institutions reflect and reproduce specific norms and behaviours that actors follow, represents sociological institutionalism;[56] in contrast, discursive institutionalism treats ideas as dynamic, with actors able to exercise agency to use discourse to change institutional settings, even as some institutional rules and practices are used and followed.[57]

Ideational institutional approaches also examine how changes in background or foreground ideas lead to policy change and to the conditions under which ideas at different levels can change. Peter Hall provides an oft-cited framework for identifying changing ideas at the foreground and background levels. First-order change involves changes in the settings of policy instruments, while second-order change requires changes in the instruments themselves as well as in the settings of those instruments.[58] According to Hall, these changes fall within "normal policymaking" as the paradigm, or world view, of the policy actors is not altered. As such, only foreground ideas are changing and being contested in first- and second-order change because actors remain reliant on background ideas to frame and challenge foreground ideas using discursive techniques.[59]

In contrast, third-order change involves changes in policy goals as well as the instruments and settings,[60] which will include changes in the way actors define policy problems and their solutions. Background ideas that make up the "policy paradigm" are contested in third-order change between competing actors attempting to replace an unstable paradigm.[61] Because third-order change is not normal policymaking, this type of change is triggered when anomalous situations arise that the previous paradigm cannot account for, leading to policy failures.[62] When policy failures occur, actors are more willing to experiment with new policies, and authority may shift towards those actors that present the policy options that address the anomalous situations.[63] Mark Blyth's findings corroborate Hall's framework as he also states that moments of great uncertainty, in which actors' interests are unclear, can trigger paradigmatic change as actors attempt to contest and institutionalize new background ideas.[64]

The ideational variant of institutional approaches has not been fully embraced by the literature addressing judicial policy influence. The judiciary is not often conceptualized as an institution that produces foreground or background ideational change in a manner that influences policy change or stability. For example, Miriam Smith analyses the discursive effects produced by the Charter rather than the judiciary, and she states that the Charter has discursively transformed how some societal actors frame policy demands as issues of human rights.[65] Scholarship addressing judicial impacts on Aboriginal law, culture, and identity more frequently adopts elements of ideational institutionalism, such as the treatment of institutions as reflections of broader norms and values. For instance, Grace Li Xiu Woo states that since the Supreme Court of Canada (SCC) is part of a colonial paradigm that is not being radically challenged and disrupted, its actions and decisions are unlikely to disrupt existing state-colonial practices.[66] Woo identifies how the judiciary maintains important background ideas or paradigms that support colonial practices and understanding of Aboriginal rights. Although not drawing directly from ideational institutional approaches, scholars commenting on the judiciary's actions in Aboriginal law cases identify those ideas and values of the courts that produce problematic assumptions about Aboriginal culture[67] and the tendency of the courts to ignore or marginalize Aboriginal legal systems and knowledge to give primacy to Canadian legal orders.[68]

More scholars are beginning to examine the ideational effects of judicial decisions to identify the judiciary's influence on policy change or stability. Robert Schertzer argues that the SCC best manages conflict in Canada's federation by upholding the legitimacy of the federal system and facilitating negotiations between contesting parties.[69] In contrast, when the SCC imposes a value or idea of federalism in its decisions, the outcome for conflict management is more problematic.[70] Similar to other authors in the judicial literature, Schertzer does not explicitly adopt an ideational institutional approach. Nevertheless, he analyses policy change related to conflict management in a federation and finds that the ideas of federalism presented in judicial decisions have some influence on certain policy areas.

When policy change can be explained using ideational approaches that emphasize the role of shifting ideas, values, and norms within institutions, the judiciary's influence should also be examined. Its decisions may create ideational effects that prompt other actors to change foreground or background ideas. For instance, it is possible that the judiciary's decisions present ideas that redefine policy problems and their solutions. Consequently, judicial decisions can narrow the range of policy alternatives that actors can pursue. However, once the judiciary presents policy ideas in its decisions, other actors can use their own discursive abilities to contest or reaffirm those ideas and values. Indeed, once an idea is communicated, actors can respond to change, or they can transform or uphold those policy ideas. Given the ability of other actors to use ideas for political purposes, it is also important to find the scope conditions under which the judiciary will use discursive abilities as a tool to influence policy. There may be certain contexts in which the courts will be more or less willing to present ideational change at the foreground or background level. These ideational dimensions of the courts' policymaking role have the potential to be explored further. Adopting ideational approaches within an institutionalist framework is a fruitful avenue for future studies if the explanation for policy change suggests that the courts produce ideational effects.

Conclusion

The role of courts in the policymaking process continues to be a major research topic occupying scholars interested in expanding knowledge about the political consequences of judicial actions. Although the relationship between the courts and policy is the focus of this literature, theories of public policy have not been fully embraced. Public policy theories explain policy change or stability by locating the range of, and interactions between, various actors and forces involved in the policy process. I argue that these policy theories can help accurately identify the nature and scope of the judiciary's policy influence, thereby improving our understanding of the courts' policymaking role. Specifically, institutionalist public policy explanations that analyse rational choice dynamics, temporality, and ideas are a fruitful way to expand the focus from just the judiciary to consider micro and macro policy processes. Existing literature on the policy role of judges can complement institutionalist public policy theories to provide a rich understanding of the complex interaction between the judiciary and policymaking.

The judicial literature that falls within rational choice, historical, and ideational institutionalism can produce more accurate and detailed findings if scholars first uncover the explanations for policy change or stability before conceptualizing the courts' role in policymaking. For instance, based on the explanation for a particular policy change, the scope conditions under which courts exercise influence can be identified. Moreover, public policy theories can help situate the courts' role in policymaking within the web of policy actors and forces that contribute to explaining policy change or stability. Understanding the courts' policy influence relative to other actors and forces will prevent overestimating or underestimating the influence of the courts. For these reasons, scholars interested in analysing the policy influence of courts should embrace public policy theories to ensure that the explanation for policy change or stability precedes the identification and analysis of the courts' policymaking role.

NOTES

1 Isabelle Engeli and Christine Rothmayr Allison, "Conceptual and Methodological Challenges in Comparative Public Policy," in *Comparative Policy Studies: Conceptual and Methodological Challenges*, ed. Isabelle Engeli and Christine Rothmayr Allison (London: Palgrave Macmillan, 2015), 2.
2 Harold Lasswell, "The Emerging Conception of the Policy Sciences," *Policy Sciences* 1 (1970): 11.
3 Michael Atkinson, "Policy, Politics and Political Science," *Canadian Journal of Political Science* 46, no. 4 (2013): 752–3.
4 Engeli and Rothmayr Allison, "Conceptual and Methodological Challenges," 2.
5 Richard Simeon, "Studying Public Policy," *Canadian Journal of Political Science* 9, no. 4 (1976): 551–4.
6 Ibid., 554.
7 Ibid., 556.
8 Ibid.
9 Ibid.
10 Peter Hall and Rosemary C.R. Taylor, "Political Science and the Three New Institutionalisms," *Political Studies* 44, no. 5 (1996): 948.
11 See Kenneth Shepsle and Mark Bonchek, *Analyzing Politics: Rationality, Behavior, and Institutions* (New York: W.W. Norton, 1997), 35; and Hall and Taylor, "Political Science," 944–5.
12 Margaret Levi, "A Model, a Method, and a Map: Rational Choice in Comparative and Historical Analysis," in *Comparative Politics: Rationality, Culture, and Structure*, ed. Mark Lichbach and Alan Zuckerman (Cambridge: Cambridge University Press, 1997), 22.
13 See Douglass North, "Institutions," *Journal of Economic Perspectives* 5, no. 1 (1991): 97; and Hall and Taylor, "Political Science," 945.
14 Levi, "A Model, a Method, and a Map," 26.
15 Jacob Hacker, Paul Pierson, and Kathleen Thelen, "Drift and Conversion: Hidden Faces of Institutional Change," in *Advances in Comparative-Historical Analysis*, ed. James Mahoney and Kathleen Thelen (New York: Cambridge University Press, 2015), 181.
16 Ibid., 183.
17 James Mahoney and Kathleen Thelen, "Introduction," in *Advances in Comparative-Historical Analysis*, eds. James Mahoney and Kathleen Thelen (New York: Cambridge University Press, 2015), 22.
18 Hacker, Pierson, and Thelen, "Drift and Conversion," 185.
19 Ibid., 195–6.
20 Ibid., 197.

21 Ibid., 201.
22 Charles Epp, *The Rights Revolution* (Chicago: University of Chicago Press, 1998), 2–3.
23 Ibid., 18.
24 Ibid., 22.
25 F.L. Morton and Rainer Knopff, *The Charter Revolution and the Court Party* (Peterborough: Broadview Press, 2000), 24–5.
26 Ibid., 28–9.
27 Ibid., 29.
28 Ibid., 59.
29 Mark Blyth, "Powering, Puzzling, or Persuading? The Mechanisms of Building Institutional Orders," *International Studies Quarterly* 51 (2007): 762.
30 Morton and Knopff, *The Charter Revolution*, 81–2.
31 Miriam Smith, "Social Movements and Judicial Empowerment: Courts, Public Policy, and Lesbian and Gay Organizing in Canada," *Politics and Society* 33, no. 2 (2005): 346.
32 Ibid., 348.
33 Vuk Radmilovic, "Strategic Legitimacy Cultivation at the Supreme Court of Canada: Quebec *Secession Reference* and Beyond," *Canadian Journal of Political Science* 43, no. 4 (2010): 844.
34 Ibid.
35 Roy Flemming and B. Dan Wood, "The Public and the Supreme Court: Individual Justice Responsiveness to American Policy Moods," *American Journal of Political Science* 41, no. 2 (1997): 494–5.
36 Hacker, Pierson, and Thelen, "Drift and Conversion," 187–8.
37 Hall and Taylor, "Political Science," 942.
38 See Kathleen Thelen, "Historical Institutionalism in Comparative Politics," *Annual Review of Political Science* 2 (1999): 388; and Vivien Schmidt, "Discursive Institutionalism: The Explanatory Power of Ideas and Discourse," *Annual Review of Political Science* 11 (2008): 313–14.
39 Andrew Bennett and Colin Elman, "Complex Causal Relations and Case Study Methods: The Example of Path Dependence," *Political Analysis* 14 (2006): 252.
40 Ibid.
41 Giovanni Capoccia and Daniel Keleman, "The Study of Critical Junctures: Theory, Narrative and Counterfactuals in Historical Institutionalism," *World Politics* 59 (2007): 343.
42 Ibid., 348.
43 Emmett Macfarlane's *Governing from the Bench: The Supreme Court of Canada and the Judicial Role* (Vancouver: UBC Press, 2013) uses a historical

institutionalist approach to understanding judicial behaviour, with particular focus on how judicial-role perceptions guide judicial actions. Nevertheless, the focus is on explaining judicial behaviour rather than identifying specific patterns of policy change or stability.

44 See Emmett Macfarlane, "Conceptual Precision and Parliamentary Systems of Rights: Disambiguating 'Dialogue,'" *Review of Constitutional Studies* 17, no. 2 (2012): 97.

45 See Peter Hogg and Allison Bushell, "The Charter Dialogue between Courts and Legislatures (or Perhaps the Charter of Rights Isn't Such a Bad Thing After All)," *Osgoode Hall Law Journal* 35 (1997): 75–124.

46 Kent Roach, "Dialogic Judicial Review and Its Critics," *Supreme Court Law Review* 23 (2004): 66.

47 Macfarlane, "Conceptual Precision," 79; and Dave Snow and Mark Harding, "From Normative Debates to Comparative Methodology: The Three Waves of Post-Charter Supreme Court Scholarship in Canada," *American Review of Canadian Studies* 45, no. 4 (2015): 456.

48 Snow and Harding, "From Normative Debates to Comparative Methodology," 456.

49 Janet Hiebert, *Charter Conflicts: What Is Parliament's Role?* (Montreal and Kingston: McGill-Queen's University Press, 2002), 7–8, 13.

50 James Kelly, *Governing with the Charter: Legislative and Judicial Activism and Framers' Intent* (Vancouver: UBC Press, 2005), 11.

51 Ibid., 7; see also James Kelly and Matthew Hennigar, "The Canadian Charter of Rights and the Minister of Justice: Weak-Form Review within a Constitutional Charter of Rights," *International Journal of Constitutional Law* 10, no. 1 (2012): 38.

52 Deborah Stone, *Policy Paradox: The Art of Political Decision Making* (New York: W.W. Norton, 2002), 13.

53 John Campbell, "Ideas, Politics and Public Policy," *Annual Review of Sociology* 28 (2002): 22–5.

54 Ibid., 26–9.

55 Schmidt, "Discursive Institutionalism," 307.

56 Ibid., 313.

57 Ibid., 316.

58 Peter Hall, "Policy Paradigms, Social Learning, and the State: The Case of Economic Policymaking in Britain," *Comparative Politics* 25, no. 3 (1993): 278–9.

59 Schmidt, "Discursive Institutionalism," 314.

60 Hall, "Policy Paradigms, Social Learning, and the State," 179.

61 Ibid., 280.

62 Ibid., 291.

63 Ibid.

64 Mark Blyth, "The Transformation of the Swedish Model: Economic Ideas, Distributional Conflict, and Institutional Change," *World Politics* 54 (2001): 3–4.

65 Miriam Smith, "The Impact of the Charter: Untangling the Effects of Institutional Change," *International Journal of Canadian Studies* 36 (2007): 32.

66 Grace Li Xiu Woo, *Ghost Dancing with Colonialism: Decolonization and Indigenous Rights at the Supreme Court of Canada* (Vancouver: UBC Press, 2011), 228–9.

67 See Caroline Dick, *The Perils of Identity: Group Rights and the Politics of Intragroup Difference* (Vancouver: UBC Press, 2011); Patrick Macklem, *Indigenous Difference and the Constitution of Canada* (Toronto: University of Toronto Press, 2001); Avigail Eisenberg, *Reasons of Identity: A Normative Guide to the Political and Legal Assessment of Identity Claims* (Oxford: Oxford University Press, 2009).

68 See John Borrows, *Canada's Indigenous Constitution* (Toronto: University of Toronto Press, 2010); Taiaiake Alfred, *Peace, Power, Righteousness: An Indigenous Manifesto* (Oxford: Oxford University Press, 2009), 95, 176; Dale Turner, "Indigenous Knowledge and the Reconciliation of Section 35(1)," in *From Recognition to Reconciliation: Essays on the Constitutional Entrenchment of Aboriginal and Treaty Rights*, ed. Patrick Macklem and Douglas Sanderson (Toronto: University of Toronto Press, 2016), 175–8; Woo, *Ghost Dancing with Colonialism*.

69 Robert Schertzer, *The Judicial Role in a Diverse Federation: Lessons from the Supreme Court of Canada* (Toronto: University of Toronto Press, 2016), 9.

70 Ibid.

2 Closing a Door but Opening a Policy Window: Legislating Assisted Dying in Canada

DAVE SNOW AND KATE PUDDISTER

As the judicial branch becomes more important in policymaking across the Western world, its role has been subject to greater scrutiny. Yet while there is no shortage of normative and empirical debates about judicial power,[1] there has been limited application of formal theories of the policy process to understand the impact of judicial power on the policymaking process. In this chapter, we argue that the multiple streams approach can provide insight into the judicial role in policy development in two specific ways. First, when courts issue suspended declarations of invalidity, they provide a precise and measurable *policy window* during which other branches of government can respond. Second, judicial decisions themselves offer influential *policy solutions* to the *policy stream*.

To demonstrate this, we apply a multiple streams analysis to the Canadian case study of assisted-dying policy, surveying attempts at policy change in the post-Charter era (1982 to the present). The policy issue remained far from the government agenda until *Carter v. Canada* (2015),[2] when the Supreme Court of Canada unanimously held that the criminal prohibition on assisted dying violated the Canadian Charter of Rights and Freedoms. We show how the Court's suspended declaration (and subsequent extension) opened a policy window that gave Parliament a specific time period to respond. Moreover, the Court constructed a category of individual – someone with "a grievous and irremediable medical condition … that causes enduring suffering that is intolerable to the individual"[3] for whom assisted dying should be legal – that constituted a powerful policy solution to the invalidated law. Coupled with the election of the pro-Charter (and pro–Supreme Court) Liberal government with a progressive ideology on social issues in October 2015, the three streams – politics, problem, and policy – seemed to align.

Yet *Carter* also demonstrates the limits of judicial impact on public policy. The Liberal government surprised many observers by passing Bill C-14, a more restrained approach (one arguably incompatible with *Carter*; see Nicolaides and Hennigar, this volume) to assisted dying than the Court's solution. Whether because of the negative public reaction to the broad access criteria proposed by the Special Joint Committee on Physician-Assisted Dying, or because of the opportunities for political manoeuvring offered by an extended policy window, the government ultimately adopted restrained legislation in the face of an ostensible opportunity for more progressive policy change.

This chapter provides several contributions and avenues for future research. First, it uses a formal theory of the policy process to explore how courts and judicial decisions can set or change a government's policy agenda, serving to bring together two related but largely separate areas in the literature. Second, highlighting courts further demonstrates the difficulty of distinguishing between *problem windows* and *political windows* in the multiple streams literature and contributes a strong argument for stream interdependence rather than independence. Finally, the multiple streams lens provides insight into why Canada's federal government responded to *Carter* as it did, showing how extended policy windows in the form of suspended declarations can paradoxically undermine the impact of judicial decisions on public policy.

Multiple Streams and Courts in Public Policy

One of the most prominent frameworks for researching the policy process is the multiple streams approach (MSA). First articulated by John Kingdon,[4] the MSA is a framework that explains how governments create policy under conditions of ambiguity and time constraints. MSA theorists posit that there are three largely independent "streams" in policy development and that major policy change occurs when these streams are coupled at critical times. The *problem* stream refers to the small number of issues that are successfully framed as requiring government action. These issues make their way to the government agenda because of a combination of reported indicators, feedback, focusing events, or crises. The *politics* stream contains political variables, such as public opinion, administrative change, and interest group campaigns, that further increase the likelihood of a policy issue making its way onto the government agenda.[5] The *policy* stream consists of the possible solutions to these problems that are available in the political system. These policy proposals are not necessarily a direct response to changes in the problem or politics stream; they are often "out there," marketed by "policy entrepreneurs," such as interest group leaders, spokespeople, researchers, and politicians.

For multiple streams researchers, changes in the politics stream or the problem stream can open a policy window, a brief period during which policy entrepreneurs can successfully attach their solutions to problems and move those issues near the top of the government agenda. Policy windows can open due to anticipated changes in the problem or politics stream (a major report, an election) or unanticipated ones (a scandal or a natural disaster). Crucially, a policy window is open only for a short time, and the "coupling" of all three streams – an available solution, a compelling problem, and political support – is required to place an item on the government agenda and produce policy change.[6]

While the MSA brings insight into the entire policy process, it is especially useful in explaining agenda setting and policy formulation.[7] Yet it has been applied only sparingly to courts and the judicial process. In the American context, Henschen and Sidlow have argued that high courts can play an important role in opening a policy window and that judicial decisions can implicate all three of the streams or even "create streams that bring non-judicial participants into the process."[8] Similarly, Lee has shown how "disruptive" precedents in the United States Supreme Court can create policy windows for lower courts to engage in policymaking.[9] However, scholarship has not systematically examined the role of high courts in opening policy windows that can facilitate policy change at the legislative and executive branches of government, particularly in Canada.

The MSA lends itself nicely to analysing the role of the judiciary. In some ways, this is obvious: when a court strikes down a statute, it clearly opens a policy window by creating a legal vacuum, to which the other branches of government might respond. However, we highlight here two additional features of high court decisions that are especially pertinent for MSA. First, when courts issue suspended declarations of invalidity – allowing an impugned law to operate for a specific period of time to enable the legislature to pass a new law tailored to a court's constitutional interpretation – this provides scholars with a finite, measurable amount of time to operationalize a policy window. Such decisions act as what Michael Howlett calls "discretionary political windows," in which "the behaviour of individual political actors" – in these cases, high courts – leads to "less predictable window openings."[10]

Second, courts rarely strike down legislation and leave the response solely to the other branches of government, particularly when interpreting constitutional bills of rights. Judicial decisions frequently offer a suggestion – a policy solution – for how a revised law might be better tailored to the constitution. Sometimes this solution can come in the form of nuanced suggestion; at other times, it can be more direct, even containing specific legal language.[11]

These two aspects of judicial decision making – the use of suspended declarations and the offering of solutions – have yet to be explored in the multiple streams literature. Our subsequent analysis uses the policy issue of assisted dying in Canada, following the Supreme Court of Canada's decision in *Carter v. Canada*, as an illustrative example.

The Post-Charter History of Assisted-Dying Policy Change in Canada

Before *Carter v. Canada*, two provisions in the Canadian Criminal Code combined to prohibit both physician-assisted dying (whereby a patient gives him- or herself a lethal medication provided by a physician) and euthanasia (whereby a physician administers a lethal injection to consenting patients).[12] Section 241(1) stated, "Everyone who (a) counsels a person to commit suicide, or (b) aids or abets a person to commit suicide, whether suicide ensues or not, is guilty of an indictable offence and liable to imprisonment for a term not exceeding fourteen years." Section 14 stated, "No person is entitled to consent to have death inflicted on him, and such consent does not affect the criminal responsibility of any person by whom death may be inflicted on the person by whom consent is given."[13]

When discussing the policy of assisted dying in post-Charter Canada, *Rodriguez v. British Columbia (Attorney General)*[14] is a natural starting point. However, before *Rodriguez*, three private member's bills were introduced in 1991, all of which attempted to legalize some form of assisted dying: Bill C-203 and Bill C-351 (sponsored by Robert Wenman) and Bill C-261 (sponsored by Chris Axworthy).[15] Wenman's bills provided for only passive euthanasia (the withholding or withdrawing of treatment), while Axworthy's bill created a more comprehensive approach to assisted dying, allowing for both passive and active euthanasia. Only Wenman's bill was referred to committee; after several hearings, the committee adjourned indefinitely, terminating the bill's progress.[16]

Due to the limited success of private member's bills in general,[17] the first probable attempt at policy change was *Rodriguez*,[18] in which the Supreme Court considered the constitutionality of the criminal prohibitions on assisted dying. Sue Rodriguez, a woman with amyotrophic lateral sclerosis (ALS), a fatal neurodegenerative disease, sought to have the courts declare section 241(1)(b) of the Criminal Code invalid so that she could pursue a physician-assisted death. Rodriguez claimed that the criminal prohibition on assisted dying violated section 7 (right to life, liberty, and security of the person), section 12 (right against cruel and unusual punishment or treatment), and section 15 (right to equality) of the Canadian Charter of Rights and Freedoms. In a 5-to-4 decision, the Court dismissed Rodriguez's application, with the majority holding that the prohibition violated neither section 7 nor section 12 and that it constituted a reasonable limit of section 15. The majority also noted that the criminalization of assisted dying was common practice in the Western world.[19]

Following *Rodriguez*, MP Svend Robinson introduced Bill C-215, *An Act to amend the Criminal Code (aiding suicide)*,[20] a private member's bill that would permit assisted dying for terminally ill individuals. In response to Robinson's bill, the Minister of Justice, Allan Rock, stated that assisted dying should be considered by Parliament, and Prime Minister Jean Chrétien also explained that when it considered the issue of assisted dying, Parliament would have a free vote.[21] Although Robinson's bill did not pass second reading, his efforts (along with similar endeavours by Sharon Carstairs in the Senate[22]) gave rise to the establishment of a special Senate committee to study the issue, which reported in 1995.[23] While members of the committee were divided on the issue of assisted dying, ultimately they recommended to maintain its criminalization. Other federal MPs advocated for policy change in the following years, including Bloc Québécois MP Francine Lalonde and Conservative Party MP Steven Fletcher, the first quadriplegic person to serve in the House of Commons.[24] In 2011, a Royal Society of Canada Expert Panel asserted that access to assisted dying was a moral right, and it recommended that the federal government amend the Criminal Code provisions prohibiting assisted dying to ensure consistency across the country.[25]

Before *Carter*, there had been sixteen attempts at legislative change to Canada's assisted-dying policy: fifteen private member's bills and one motion introduced in the House of Commons.[26] However, none of those were government bills. While Rock and Chrétien gave lip service to changing the policy and to the idea of a free vote, assisted dying remained outside the politics stream and far from the government agenda. Although other countries were beginning to legalize assisted dying, Canada lacked a feature driving the problem stream – a crisis, focusing event, policy feedback, or reported indicators – in the first three decades of assisted-dying policy under the Charter.

Defining a Problem: The Supreme Court Decision in *Carter I*

Gloria Taylor and Kay Carter provided the focusing event necessary to bring the issue to the government agenda. Carter, who had been diagnosed with spinal stenosis, was unable to access assisted dying in Canada, and in January 2010, she travelled to the DIGNITAS clinic in Switzerland, where she received medical assistance in dying. Her daughter, Lee Carter, initiated a case in the Supreme Court of British Columbia, challenging sections 14 and 241(1)(b) of the Criminal Code. She was soon joined by Gloria Taylor, who had been diagnosed with ALS. Although both Carter and Taylor died before the Supreme Court of Canada ultimately ruled in 2015, their case was taken up by the British Columbia Civil Liberties Association.

At trial, the judge found that the prohibition on assisted dying violated both section 7 (life, liberty, and security of the person) and section 15(1) (equality) Charter rights of Canadians and that it could not be saved as a "reasonable limit" under section 1 of the Charter. Specifically, it infringed the rights of "competent, fully-informed, non-ambivalent adult persons who personally (not through a substituted decision maker) request physician-assisted death, are free from coercion and undue influence and are not clinically depressed."[27] In a divided decision, the British Columbia Court of Appeal reversed the trial court, with a majority holding that the trial judge should have been bound by the Supreme Court of Canada's *Rodriguez* decision.[28]

The case was appealed to the Supreme Court of Canada, which unanimously held that the criminal provisions infringed section 7 of the Charter, could not be saved by section 1, and were of no force or effect.[29] The Court held that the prohibition could not extend to a competent adult person who "(1) clearly consents to the termination of life and (2) has a grievous and irremediable medical condition (including an illness, disease or disability) that causes enduring suffering that is intolerable to the individual in the circumstances of his or her condition."[30] This careful definition ensured that the decision would not permit medical aid for *anyone* who chose to take his or her life. In doing so, the Supreme Court offered a specific contribution to the policy stream by constructing a category of individual for whom assisted dying should be legal. If it so chose, Parliament could have used the Supreme Court's interpretation of the Charter to amend the law and ensure it would be Charter-compliant.

Because the Supreme Court is the highest appellate court in Canada, when it declares a law inconsistent with the Charter, a policy window can open. In *Carter*, the Court issued a one-year "suspended declaration" as a remedy, which gave Parliament a specific time during which the window would remain open. Yet the Court did not simply strike the law down and invite Parliament to respond; it also offered a policy solution by stipulating that a Charter-compliant criminal prohibition against assisted dying must apply to a person who "clearly consents to the termination of life" and "has a grievous and irremediable medical condition ... that causes enduring suffering that is intolerable to the individual."[31] *Carter* thus opened a one-year window for Parliament to respond and offered Parliament a specific policy solution that it could apply to fill the vacuum.

Acceptable Solutions? Surveying the Federal Government's Options

Initially, the Court's policy window gave Parliament until 6 February 2016 to respond. The federal government had many options. It could have simply repealed the law. It could also have acquiesced, adopting the Supreme Court's policy solution word for word by granting an exception for consenting adults with "a grievous and irremediable medical condition ... that causes enduring suffering that is intolerable." Yet there were other policy solutions available to the federal government that were both more restrictive and more permissive than the approach articulated in *Carter*. Here we survey four such solutions, each of which specifically addressed assisted dying, came from a Canadian political institution, and followed the *Carter* decision. As other solutions existed (produced both before and after *Carter*), this list is illustrative rather than exhaustive.

1. *External Panel on Options for a Legislative Response to* Carter v. Canada

The External Panel on Options for a Legislative Response to *Carter v. Canada* was formed under the direction of the federal Minister of Justice and the Minister of Health in July 2015. It was the federal government's first substantive step in responding to *Carter*. Originally, the External Panel was given a mandate to consult with the groups that had participated in *Carter* as third party interveners and with medical authorities, and to conduct online consultations with Canadians, with the goal of providing legislative options to Parliament.[32] However, following the October 2015 election and change in government from Conservative to Liberal, the External Panel was given a month's extension to complete its report, and its mandate was amended to provide only a summary of "results and key findings" of consultations, rather than policy options for the government.[33]

As a result, while the report canvassed a wide range of sources about the multiple issues related to assisted dying, it did not provide any specific recommendations to the government about how to proceed. The report was nevertheless supportive of the Supreme Court's decision in *Carter* and sympathetic to the adoption of a permissive policy regime for assisted dying.

2. *Provincial-Territorial Expert Advisory Group on Physician-Assisted Dying*

The Provincial-Territorial Expert Advisory Group on Physician-Assisted Dying was formed in August 2015 by all provincial and territorial governments, excluding Quebec and with British Columbia participating only as an observer. Its report provided forty-three recommendations, which largely focused on the responsibilities of the provinces and territories within their jurisdiction over health. It recommended that subnational governments create a national strategy for palliative and end-of-life care. This would include a provincial and territorial committee review system to provide oversight and to monitor cases of assisted dying, with the support and collaboration of the federal government, if possible.[34]

The Advisory Group's recommendations encouraged liberal access to assisted dying and low barriers for patients, based on competence rather than age. It advocated a streamlined approach by recommending that patients need not request the service more than once or be subject to a waiting, or "cooling-off," period.[35] Of all the policy options available to the federal government in response to the *Carter* decision, these recommendations provided the most liberal approach to assisted dying, recommending that few barriers be placed on access and that medical professionals have a clear duty to ensure access through immediate assistance, by referral or otherwise.[36] While its focus was provincial, the report urged the federal government to amend the Criminal Code to protect both individuals seeking assisted dying and the health care professionals involved.[37]

3. *Quebec's Medical Assistance in Dying Act*

Although federal MPs ultimately failed to put assisted dying on the national agenda in the 1990s and 2000s, the issue had greater success in the province of Quebec. After a task force on ethics from the Collège des médecins du Québec proposed that physician-assisted dying be included as health care in certain circumstances, Quebec's National Assembly struck a Select Committee on Dying with Dignity, which reported in March 2012. The Quebec government then appointed an expert panel to determine how to implement these recommendations, and in June 2014, the National Assembly passed An Act respecting end-of-life care, which came into force in December 2015.[38]

The Quebec law applies to insured individuals in Quebec "of full age and capable of giving consent to care," who are "at the end of life," suffering from a "serious and incurable illness," in "an advanced state of irreversible decline in capability," and experiencing "constant and unbearable physical or psychological suffering which cannot be relieved in a manner the patient deems tolerable."[39] In many ways, Quebec's legislation is similar to the Supreme Court's policy solution,[40] but it is narrower in two important ways. First, while the Supreme Court decision applied to both physician-assisted dying and euthanasia, Quebec's legislation regulates only the latter. Second, Quebec's law specifies that the person needs to be "at the end of life," whereas the Supreme Court's language applies to those suffering intolerable pain who nevertheless may have many years to live.[41]

4. *The Special Joint Committee on Physician-Assisted Dying*

Formed in December 2015, the Special Joint Committee (SJC) on Physician-Assisted Dying reviewed over one hundred written submissions, heard from over sixty witnesses, and reported in February 2016. Its majority report drew directly from the Supreme Court decision in some respects, such as its recommendation that assisted dying be available to "individuals with terminal and non-terminal grievous and irremediable medical conditions that cause enduring suffering that is intolerable to the individual in the circumstances of his or her condition."[42] In a few ways, it was more restrictive, or at least more specific, by recommending that two physicians assess the patient and that there be a waiting period.

However, the majority report also went beyond the Supreme Court in terms of access. The two recommendations that were most notable were "that individuals not be excluded from eligibility for medical assistance in dying based on the fact that they have a psychiatric condition" and that there be a "second stage" of legislation at which assisted dying would be extended to "competent mature minors."[43] The SJC report thus offered a more specific policy solution than the Supreme Court because it built on and expanded the Court's recommendations, particularly with respect to psychiatric illness and minors.

The Politics Stream: Fortuitous Timing?

The Supreme Court's one-year policy window and the multiple solutions available in the policy stream gave the federal government ample opportunity to implement new assisted-dying legislation. Yet for a policy issue to become a part of the government agenda, it also requires a responsive politics stream. In Canada's majoritarian, executive-dominated Parliament, this means buy-in from the federal government, particularly the prime minister. When the Supreme Court released *Carter* in February 2015, the politics stream did not seem amenable. Prime Minister Stephen Harper had been loath to introduce legislation on contentious moral issues that divided the socially conservative and more libertarian members of his Conservative Party caucus,[44] and an election was on the horizon. When an election was called in August 2015, six months into the Court's policy window, the federal government's main course of action had been to call the External Panel, which had yet to report.

In October 2015, Justin Trudeau's Liberal Party won a majority of seats in the House. In his November 2015 mandate letter to the Minister of Justice, Trudeau tasked her with "leading a process, supported by the Minister of Health, to work with provinces and territories to respond to the Supreme Court of Canada decision regarding physician-assisted death."[45] Compared with the previous Conservative government, the politics stream seemed far more amenable to policy change. However, the government had only three months before the policy window closed, so it asked the Supreme Court for a six-month extension to the suspended declaration in *Carter*. In a divided decision (*Carter II*),[46] the Supreme Court gave Parliament four months, which was equivalent to the length of the break that Parliament had taken before, after, and during the election. A majority of justices also created an exemption to the (now sixteen-month) suspended declaration by holding that, in the interim, affected Canadians could apply to a judge for assisted death. The policy window had been extended.

Which policy option would the Liberal government select? Certainly, one would expect that the Court's solution in *Carter* would be influential. The Liberals have long positioned themselves as the Charter party, owing to former prime minister Pierre Trudeau's initiative in incorporating the Charter into the package of constitutional reforms in the Constitution Act, 1982.[47] The juxtaposition with Stephen Harper's Conservative Party only increased this perception, particularly with respect to the judiciary. Indeed, Christopher Manfredi found that the Harper government adopted a "more consistently confrontational approach" to the Supreme Court of Canada's Charter jurisprudence than its Liberal predecessors,[48] and Harper had a much-publicized spat with then chief justice McLachlin regarding the failed appointment of Justice Marc Nadon. Justin Trudeau has presented himself as much more court-friendly, evoking the Court's authority during a 2015 federal election debate, when he accused New Democratic Party leader Tom Mulcair of "choosing to side with the separatist movement in Quebec and not with the Supreme Court of Canada."[49] The Liberals' 2015 platform also promised to "restore dignity and respect to the relationship between government and the Supreme Court."[50]

Overall, there was ample reason to suggest that the federal government's policy solution would mirror or build on the Supreme Court's solution in *Carter I*. The Liberal government was pro-Charter and, compared with its Conservative predecessor, more likely to defer to the Supreme Court. It had a majority of seats in the House of Commons and would not need opposition support. Trudeau had positioned the party as socially progressive, and a special joint committee on which it had a majority of members had recommended going further than the Supreme Court's policy solution in terms of expanding access. With the policy window fast closing, the problem (Supreme Court had struck down the law), politics (the progressive, pro-Charter, and judicially deferential Liberal party had formed government), and policy (the Supreme Court had offered a solution) streams had coupled sufficiently to expect a policy response. And, indeed, a policy response was forthcoming – just not in the manner that was anticipated.

Bill C-14: A Surprise Solution

On 14 April 2016, federal Justice Minister Jody Wilson-Raybould introduced Bill C-14.[51] The legislation's preamble quoted directly from the Supreme Court decision, noting that "the Parliament of Canada recognizes the autonomy of persons who have a grievous and irremediable medical condition that causes them enduring and intolerable suffering and who wish to seek medical assistance in dying." However, the preamble also mentioned the importance of "robust safeguards," the "inherent and equal value of every person's life," the protection of "vulnerable persons," and the fact that "suicide is a significant public health issue."[52]

The bill reasserted the Criminal Code provision "No person is entitled to consent to have death inflicted on them," but carved out an exemption for medical assistance in dying. The conditions for this exemption are enumerated in sections 241.1 to 241.4 of the Criminal Code, which stipulate that a person may receive medical assistance in dying "only" if he or she meets a number of criteria: the person must be eighteen or older, be eligible for health insurance, have a "grievous and irremediable medical condition," make a voluntary request, and provide informed consent.[53] The bill then defines what constitutes a grievous and irremediable medical condition.

> 241.2(2) A person has a grievous and irremediable medical condition only if they meet all of the following criteria:
>
> (a) they have a serious and incurable illness, disease or disability;
> (b) they are in an advanced state of irreversible decline in capability;
> (c) that illness, disease or disability or that state of decline causes them enduring physical or psychological suffering that is intolerable to them and that cannot be relieved under conditions that they consider acceptable; and
> (d) their natural death has become reasonably foreseeable, taking into account all of their medical circumstances, without a prognosis necessarily having been made as to the specific length of time that they have remaining.[54]

Many assisted-dying advocates and scholars criticized this section, with law professor Jocelyn Downie saying that the "criteria for access are not consistent with the Supreme Court of Canada's 2015 decision in *Carter*" for three reasons.[55] First is the government's use of "incurable" rather than the Supreme Court's "irremediable." While the two terms may appear similar, Downie notes that the Supreme Court held that the term "irremediable ... does not require the patient to undertake treatments that are not acceptable to the patient."[56] By contrast, Downie claims that the new law's use of "incurable ... compels patients to exhaust even treatment options they find unacceptable in order to be eligible for access to assistance in dying." Second (and third), the law stipulates that individuals be "in an advanced state of irreversible decline in capability" and that "their natural death has become reasonably foreseeable."[57] This is similar to Quebec's legislation, which states that an individual be "at the end of life." However, the Supreme Court of Canada mentioned neither foreseeable death nor irreversible decline.

As to whether the law violates the Charter, Downie is categorical. "The Bill must be amended to become *Carter* and Charter compliant."[58] Peter Hogg, Canada's pre-eminent constitutional law scholar, also testified that the new law was unconstitutional and argued that the Supreme Court would strike it down in a future Charter challenge. Other constitutional lawyers (and parliamentarians) have differed in their interpretation, with Gerald Chipeur and Tom McMorrow claiming that they would expect the Court to accord deference to Parliament (see Nicolaides and Hennigar, this volume).[59] The controversial provisions remained, and the bill received royal assent on 17 June 2016 – ten days after the Supreme Court's policy window closed. Although Prime Minister Trudeau called the law "a big first step that is going to be followed by a lot of discussions and evolution over the coming decade,"[60] the government has not announced plans to amend the law in the near future.

Discussion and Conclusion

After more than a dozen failed private member's bills and a near-miss court case in 1993, an assisted-dying policy window finally opened with the Supreme Court of Canada's unanimous *Carter* decision in 2015. With a new federal government open to progressive policy change, it seemed likely that the Supreme Court's policy solution would factor heavily into new legislation. However, the federal government surprised many observers by passing legislation that was ostensibly narrower than the Court's *Carter* decision. By giving a narrower definition of what constitutes a "grievous and irremediable medical condition," the federal government did not adopt the Court's policy solution. Moreover, by excluding minors and those with psychiatric illnesses from access to assisted dying, and by implementing a waiting period, it also rejected the broader recommendations given by the Provincial-Territorial Advisory Group and the SJC. While the streams coupled and the policy ultimately changed just after the window closed, the government's "solution" did not come from the expected sources. The latest round of litigation on assisted dying may not yet be the final word.[61]

Why did the federal government ultimately adopt a narrow solution that is arguably incompatible with the Supreme Court's approach in *Carter*? One reason might be that the SJC's recommendations swung the pendulum in the other direction. A crucial component of the politics stream in the MSA is the nebulous, difficult-to-operationalize "national mood." Clearly, Canadians support some access to assisted dying: an August 2015 poll found that 77 per cent of Canadians supported assisted dying for the terminally ill.[62] However, one poll conducted shortly after the SJC issued its report found that 78 per cent of Canadians agreed that "psychological suffering on its own should not be considered a reason to obtain doctor-assisted suicide."[63] A similar poll found that nearly 59 per cent of those polled opposed granting access to sixteen- and seventeen-year-olds, with only 36 per cent in favour.[64] Days after these polls were made public, Trudeau hinted that the forthcoming legislation might be more restrictive than the SJC report, stating that "we stand to defend individuals' rights but we also need to make sure we're protecting the most vulnerable."[65] With the policy window fast closing, the popular Trudeau government seemed averse to spending political capital on this controversial area.

Overall, the case study discussed in this chapter offers several scholarly insights. First, in the age of judicial power, it demonstrates the utility of integrating the judiciary into formal theories of the policy process, particularly those frameworks (like multiple streams) that focus on agenda setting. In particular, our analysis shows how suspended declarations can be operationalized as finite and measurable policy windows and that judicial decisions often contain concrete policy solutions in the policy stream that governments take very seriously. Even in the case of assisted dying, in which the responding law differed from the Court's policy solution, that same legislation did incorporate part of the Court's policy solution word for word.

Second, by adding another actor (the judiciary) to those offering policy solutions, this chapter highlights the difficulty of conceptualizing the problem, politics, and policy streams as being truly independent. In his classic work, Kingdon distinguishes between political windows, which open due to "a change in administration, a shift in the partisan or ideological distribution of seats in Congress, or a shift in the national mood," and problem windows, which open "because a new problem captures the attention of governmental officials and those close to them."[66] Does a judicial decision invalidating a law constitute a problem window or a political window? On the one hand, judicial decisions look like what Howlett calls "discretionary political windows," whereby decisions by "individual political actors ... lead to less predictable window openings."[67] On the other hand, the judiciary operates independently of the day-to-day politics of Parliament or Congress, and in this way, a judicial decision looks like an external focusing event, which suddenly and unexpectedly "captures the attention of governmental officials."[68]

While we define judicial decisions as political windows, we recognize that the distinction is blurry and serves to highlight how it is appropriate to speak of "stream interdependence."[69] Not only is it difficult to determine whether a judicial decision falls into the problem stream or politics stream, but the fact that judicial decisions can simultaneously open a window and offer a solution also means that "policies are not always developed in policy communities, and solutions are not developed independently of problems."[70] Moreover, in cases of constitutional ambiguity, it is likely that definitive judicial decisions can contribute to closing policy windows. A single judicial decision can simultaneously influence multiple streams, even if those streams subsequently flow along different paths.

This case study also shows that, in a federation, policy windows do not necessarily open for all jurisdictions at the same time, even in areas of shared authority. The judicially created policy window that occurred after *Carter* was explicitly open to Parliament, but because provinces have jurisdiction over the provision of health services, provincial legislatures could have responded as well (as Quebec did before the Supreme Court decision). However, because the Supreme Court had invalidated a federal law, the politics stream – public opinion, media attention, and interest group campaigns – was focused overwhelmingly on

Parliament's response, to the exclusion of provincial legislatures. The asymmetrical attention given to the *federal* response provides further evidence for Macfarlane's argument that the interaction of federalism and the Charter can lead provinces to ignore their rights obligations, leading to what Linda White calls uneven "rights implementation."[71]

The case of assisted dying can also provide theoretical guidance to the oft-criticized "dialogue" metaphor used to describe the interaction between courts and the other branches of government. By recognizing that suspended declarations constitute finite policy windows, this chapter lends further qualitative support to the notion that such declarations encourage genuine dialogue (also known as "coordinate construction"; see Nicolaides and Hennigar, this volume), whereby a legislature disagrees in some substantive way with a court's proposed policy solution. Emmett Macfarlane has shown that, from 1984 to 2009, Canadian legislatures responded with genuine dialogue in only 17.4 per cent of *all* cases, but in 36 per cent of those cases that contained a suspended declaration.[72] The federal government's response to *Carter* is yet another example of this trend. The Supreme Court's lengthy policy window, which it extended for four months, enabled the federal government to consult more widely, draw from additional reports and public opinion data, and ultimately implement a solution that may not have been available to it had the law been invalidated with immediate effect. True, a judicial invalidation without suspension also opens an immediate policy window by creating a legislative vacuum. However, the response to *Carter* suggests that a suspended declaration, by avoiding the legislative vacuum, can facilitate coordinate construction by giving the government some time to deliberate before the ruling comes into effect.

Finally, this chapter provides further evidence that judicial decisions may not have the policy impact their critics assume. Even when the Supreme Court of Canada issues a unanimous decision that has broad public support, events in the politics stream can limit its impact on the ultimate policy solution. Supreme Court decisions articulate forceful policy solutions, but courts lack the power of implementation. Even an ostensibly supportive politics stream can ultimately accept a solution that differs from that of a court, and suspended declarations seem to encourage this by extending a policy window. As such, suspended declarations might be one of those rare judicially created instruments of judicial discretion that ultimately serve to limit, rather than enhance, judicial influence on policy.

NOTES

1 See, e.g., Neal C. Tate and Torbjörn Vallinder, *The Global Expansion of Judicial Power* (New York: New York University Press, 1995); Christopher P. Manfredi, *Judicial Power and the Charter: Canada and the Paradox of Liberal Constitutionalism*, 2nd ed. (Don Mills, ON: Oxford University Press, 2001); Ran Hirschl, *Towards Juristocracy: The Origins and Consequences of the New Constitutionalism* (Cambridge, MA: Harvard University Press, 2004).

2 *Carter v. Canada (Attorney General)* [2015] 1 S.C.R. 331 ["*Carter I*"].

3 Ibid. at para. 127.

4 John W. Kingdon, *Agendas, Alternatives, and Public Policies* (Boston: Little, Brown, 1984); John W. Kingdon, *Agendas, Alternatives and Public Policies*, 2nd ed. (New York: Addison Wesley Longman, 1995).

5 Kingdon, *Agendas, Alternatives and Public Policies*, 2nd ed., 165–8; Joe Blankenau, "The Fate of National Health Insurance in Canada and the United States: A Multiple Streams Explanation," *Policy Studies Journal* 29, no. 1 (2001): 38–9; Paul Cairney, *Understanding Public Policy: Theories and Issues* (New York: Palgrave Macmillan, 2012), 271–2; Emery G. Lee III, "Policy Windows on the U.S. Courts of Appeals," *Justice System Journal* 24, no. 3 (2003): 305; Nikolaos Zahariadis, "Ambiguity and Multiple Streams," in *Theories of the Policy Process*, 3rd ed., ed. Paul A. Sabatier and Christopher M. Weible (Boulder, CO: Westview Press, 2014) , 31–4.

6 Kingdon, *Agendas, Alternatives and Public Policies*, 2nd ed., 165–6.

7 Giliberto Capano, "Understanding Policy Change as an Epistemological and Theoretical Problem," *Journal of Comparative Policy Analysis* 11, no. 1 (2009): 21.

8 Beth M. Henschen and Edward L. Sidlow, "The Supreme Court and the Congressional Agenda-Setting Process," *Journal of Law and Politics* 5, no. 4 (1988): 722.

9 Lee, "Policy Windows on the U.S. Courts of Appeals."

10 Michael Howlett, "Predictable and Unpredictable Policy Windows: Institutional and Exogenous Correlates of Canadian Federal Agenda-Setting," *Canadian Journal of Political Science* 31, no. 3 (1998): 500.

11 For example, in the 1988 *Ford* case, in which the Supreme Court of Canada struck down the province of Quebec's French-only sign law for violating freedom of expression in the Charter, the Court offered a policy solution, saying that "requiring the predominant display of the French language, even its marked predominance, would be proportional," and suggested a policy alternative: "French could be required in addition to any other language or it could be required to have greater visibility than that accorded

to other languages" (*Ford v. Quebec (AG)*, [1988] 2 S.C.R. 712 at para. 73). Although the Quebec National Assembly initially responded by using the notwithstanding clause, it eventually amended its legislation by requiring that signs give French greater visibility than other languages, just as the Court had suggested.

12 For terminology, see Jocelyn Downie, "Mind the Gap: Physician-Assisted Death in Quebec," *Impact Ethics*, 20 October 2015, https://impactethics.ca/2015/10/20/mind-the-gap-physician-assisted-death-in-quebec/.

13 Criminal Code (R.S.C., 1985, c. C-46). Before *Carter* (and notwithstanding *Rodriguez*), there were only two legal challenges to s. 241(b) of the Criminal Code, with both cases resulting in criminal convictions; see Jocelyn Downie, *Dying Justice: A Case for Decriminalizing Euthanasia and Assisted Suicide in Canada* (Toronto: University of Toronto Press, 2004), 34–5.

14 [1993] 3 S.C.R. 519 ["*Rodriguez*"].

15 Bill C-351: An Act to amend the Criminal Code (terminally ill persons), 34th Parliament, 1st session; Bill C-203: An Act to amend the Criminal Code (terminally ill persons), 34th Parliament, 2nd session; Bill C-261: An Act to legalize the administration of euthanasia under certain conditions, 34th Parliament, 2nd session.

16 Martha Butler, Marlissa Tiedmann, Julia Nicol, and Dominique Valiquet, *Euthanasia and Assisted Suicide in Canada: Background Paper* (Ottawa: Parliamentary Information and Research Services, Library of Canada, 2013), 15.

17 Kelly Blidook, *Constituency Influence in Parliament: Countering the Centre* (Vancouver: UBC Press, 2012).

18 *Rodriguez* at para. 9.

19 Ibid. at 582.

20 35th Parliament, 1st Session.

21 Butler et al., *Euthanasia and Assisted Suicide*, 17.

22 Senator Carstairs is responsible for chairing two Senate committees and authoring their reports on matters relating to assisted dying and end-of-life care: Canada, Parliament, Senate, Standing Committee on Social Affairs, Science and Technology, subcommittee to update *Of Life and Death, Quality End-of-Life Care: The Right of Every Canadian*, final report, 2000; Canada, Parliament, Senate, *Raising the Bar: A Roadmap for the Future of Palliative Care in Canada*, 2010.

23 Canada, Parliament, Senate, Special Committee on Euthanasia and Assisted Suicide, *Of Life and Death*, final report, 1995.

24 Lalonde sponsored three private member's bills that provided for access to assisted dying, only one of which made it to a vote, where it was defeated 228 to 59: Bill C-407: An Act to amend the Criminal Code (right to die with

dignity), 38th Parliament, 1st session, 2005; Bill C-562: An Act to amend the Criminal Code (right to die with dignity), 39th Parliament, 2nd session, 2008; Bill C-384: An Act to amend the Criminal Code (right to die with dignity), 40th Parliament, 2nd session, 2009. Fletcher introduced a private member's bill aimed at providing physician-assisted dying in 2014, but it did not make it to second reading: Bill C-581: An Act to amend the Criminal Code (physician-assisted death), 41st Parliament, 2nd session, 2014.

25 Udo Schuklenk et al., *The Royal Society of Canada Expert Panel: End-of-Life Decision Making*, November 2011, https://rsc-src.ca/sites/default/files/pdf/RSCEndofLifeReport2011_EN_Formatted_FINAL.pdf.

26 For a timeline and overview, see Butler et al., *Euthanasia and Assisted Suicide.*

27 *Carter v. Canada (Attorney General)* 2012 BCSC 886 ["*Carter BCSC*"] at para. 1388. Justice Smith held that the law infringed the s. 15 rights of "persons who fall under the description above and who, in addition, are materially physically disabled or soon to become so"; see ibid.

28 *Rodriguez.*

29 The Court found it unnecessary to examine whether the legislation also violated s. 15 of the Charter; *Carter I* at para. 93.

30 Ibid. at para. 4.

31 Ibid. at para. 127.

32 Canada, Parliament, External Panel on Options for a Legislative Response to *Carter v. Canada, Consultations on Physician-Assisted Dying: Final Report,* 2015, iv.

33 Canada, Parliament, "Letter from Minister Wilson-Raybould and Minister Philpott to the External Panel on Options for a Legislative Response to *Carter v. Canada,*" Backgrounders, 14 November 2015.

34 Ibid., 10.

35 Ibid.

36 Canada, Parliament, Provincial-Territorial Expert Advisory Group on Physician-Assisted Dying, *Final Report*, 2015, 9.

37 Ibid., 7.

38 C. S-32.0001, 2014, c. 1, s. 2 [End-Of-Life Care]; see also Roger Collier, "Euthanasia Debate Reignited," *Canadian Medical Association Journal* 181, no. 8 (2009): 463; Butler et al., *Euthanasia and Assisted Suicide,* 15; Downie, "Mind the Gap."

39 End-Of-Life Care at ss. 26(1–6).

40 The Supreme Court did mention the Quebec legislation in *Carter I* (at para. 7), although it did not ostensibly influence the decision directly.

41 Downie, "Mind the Gap."

42 Canada, Parliament, Special Joint Committee on Physician-Assisted Dying, *Medical Assistance in Dying: A Patient-Centred Approach*, 2016, 13.
43 Ibid., 25.
44 Dave Snow and Benjamin Moffitt, "Straddling the Divide: Mainstream Populism and Conservatism in Howard's Australia and Harper's Canada," *Commonwealth and Comparative Politics* 50, no. 3 (2012): 271–92.
45 Canada, Parliament, Office of the Prime Minister, "Minister of Justice and Attorney General of Canada Mandate Letter," http://pm.gc.ca/eng/minister-justice-and-attorney-general-canada-mandate-letter.
46 *Carter v. Canada (Attorney General)* 2016 SCC4 ["*Carter II*"].
47 In the 2004 and 2006 elections, the Liberal Party often portrayed its opponents as "anti-Charter," with former prime minister Paul Martin claiming an "unflinching allegiance to the freedoms in the Charter of Rights" as a Liberal Party value; see Rainer Knopff and Andrew C. Banfield, "'It's the Charter, Stupid!': The Charter and the Courts in Federal Partisan Politics," *Supreme Court Law Review* 45, no. 2d (2009): 43, 57.
48 Christopher P. Manfredi, "Conservatives, the Supreme Court of Canada, and the Constitution: Judicial-Government Relations, 2006–2015," *Osgoode Hall Law Review* 52, no. 3 (2015): 980.
49 Andrew Coyne, "The Moment Trudeau Had Mulcair's Number," *National Post*, 14 October 14 2015, http://news.nationalpost.com/full-comment/andrew-coyne-the-moment-trudeau-had-mulcairs-number.
50 Liberal Party of Canada, *A New Plan for a Strong Middle Class* (Ottawa: Liberal Party of Canada, 2015), 3.
51 An Act to amend the Criminal Code and to make related amendments to other Acts (medical assistance in dying), SC 2016, c. 3 [Medical Assistance].
52 Ibid.
53 Ibid.
54 Ibid.
55 Jocelyn Downie, "Bouquets and Brickbats for the Proposed Assisted Dying Legislation," *Policy Options*, 20 April 2016, http://policyoptions.irpp.org/magazines/april-2016/bouquets-and-brickbats-for-the-proposed-assisted-dying-legislation/.
56 *Carter I* at para. 127.
57 Downie, "Bouquets and Brickbats."
58 Ibid.
59 Joan Bryden, "Assisted Dying Law Unconstitutional: Expert," *Edmonton Sun*, 6 June 2016, http://www.edmontonsun.com/2016/06/06/assisted-dying-law-unconstitutional-expert.

60 Paul Wells, "'This Is a Big Step in Canadian Society and Justice,' Trudeau Says of Assisted Dying Bill," *Toronto Star*, 7 June 2016, https://www.thestar.com/news/canada/2016/06/07/trudeau-downplays-seriousness-of-missing-bill-c-14-deadline-wells.html.
61 Indeed, Bill C-14 is already the subject of a court challenge mounted by the British Columbia Civil Liberties Association; see Mike Laanela, "Assisted-Dying Legislation Faces New Legal Challenge in B.C.," *CBC News*, 27 June 2016, http://www.cbc.ca/news/canada/british-columbia/bccla-assisted-dying-legislation-1.3654220.
62 Ben Spurr, "77% of Canadians Support Assisted Suicide, Poll Shows," *Toronto Star*, 28 August 2015, https://www.thestar.com/news/gta/2015/08/28/77-of-canadians-support-assisted-suicide-poll-shows.html.
63 Sharon Kirkey, "Majority Rejects Assisted Suicide for Mentally Ill, Poll Finds," *National Post*, 1 April 2016, http://news.nationalpost.com/news/canada/majority-rejects-assisted-suicide-for-mentally-ill-poll-finds.
64 Daniel LeBlanc, "Canadians Want Restrictions on Doctor-Assisted Dying, Poll Suggests," *Globe and Mail*, 7 April 2016, http://www.theglobeandmail.com/news/politics/canadians-want-restrictions-on-doctor-assisted-dying-poll-suggests/article29548237/.
65 Ian MacLeod, "Trudeau Suggests Assisted-Dying May Be Limited to Competent Adults in New Law," *National Post*, 8 April 2016, http://news.nationalpost.com/news/canada/canadian-politics/trudeau-suggests-assisted-dying-may-be-limited-to-competent-adults-in-new-law.
66 Kingdon, *Agendas, Alternatives and Public Policies*, 2nd ed., 168.
67 Howlett, "Predictable and Unpredictable Policy Windows," 500.
68 Kingdon, *Agendas, Alternatives and Public Policies*, 2nd ed., 168.
69 See Gary Mucciaroni, "The Garbage Can Model and the Study of Policy Making: A Critique," *Polity* 24 (1992): 459–82; Scott E. Robinson and Warren S. Eller, "Testing the Separation of Problems and Solutions in Subnational Policy Systems," *Policy Studies Journal* 38, no. 2 (2010): 199–216.
70 Zahariadis, "Ambiguity and Multiple Streams," 41–2.
71 Emmett Macfarlane, "The Dilemma of Positive Rights: Access to Health Care and the *Canadian Charter of Rights and Freedoms*," *Journal of Canadian Studies* 48, no. 3 (2014): 49–78; Linda A. White, "Federalism and Equality Rights Implementation in Canada," *Publius* 44, no. 1 (2014): 157–82.
72 Emmett Macfarlane, "Dialogue or Compliance? Measuring Legislatures' Policy Responses to Court Rulings on Rights," *International Political Science Review* 34, no. 1 (2012): 40, 48–50.

3 The Supreme Court of Canada, Judicial Remedies, and Punctuated Equilibrium

MARC ZANONI

Since the constitutional entrenchment of the Canadian Charter of Rights and Freedoms in 1982, Canadian legal scholars have extensively studied how the Charter has increased the various ways that courts are able to influence government action. Through their powers of judicial review, judges have experienced an increased opportunity to perform an active policy role. And yet there have been few attempts to apply a formal policy theory that captures how such influence occurs. In other words, the literature demonstrates the policy consequences of judicial decisions, but it has yet to develop a theoretical model that adequately explains both the timing and substance of policy change when courts are more actively involved in the policy process. This chapter seeks to fill this lacuna: when and how are courts able to contribute to policy dynamics, including periods of both stability and change? And how should courts be conceptualized and situated within the broader policy context?

This chapter argues that the public policy theory of punctuated equilibrium (PE) would be very useful in answering these questions. PE allows scholars to map out the complex array of court-legislature interactions. Further, it effectively accommodates the institutional differences between legislative and court venues, which helps to explain the unique imprints that courts leave on policy issues. This argument is advanced in three stages. First, PE's analytical underpinnings are examined, followed by a brief review of its application to courts, found in the American literature. Second, it is argued that PE can be effectively applied to the Canadian context and, specifically, the Supreme Court of Canada. However, the Court's venue must be distinguished because of Canada's unique constitutional design as well as the Court's internal operations. These factors increase the likelihood that the Court is able to contribute to policy punctuations. The last stage focuses on the policy impact of judicial remedies. A PE lens is used to examine the decision of *Vriend v. Alberta* to provide an example of how PE may prove useful to judicial politics scholars. By using a remedy that read-in a provision to the impugned statute, the Court was able to punctuate the initial policy and also establish the new policy equilibrium.

Punctuated Equilibrium: A Policy Dynamics Theory

Writing in the 1990s, Baumgartner and Jones recognized that divisions were starting to form in the public policy literature.[1] Some scholars tended to gravitate towards policy issues that experienced a long duration of sustained stability, even when related policy areas were undergoing rapid change. This led scholars to study periods of incremental growth, while focusing on issues related to policy subsystems. Alternatively, other scholars were wanting to explain the causes of large changes and the conditions in which they progressed, with agenda-setting being a particularly attractive stage of the policy cycle.[2] These scholars were examining the "windows of opportunity" that led to more significant policy reforms.[3] Because of these different starting points, however, scholars could use theories to explain either incremental or large-scale changes, but struggled to incorporate both forms into one coherent theory. PE bridges this gap by explaining patterns of extended periods of stability, followed by punctuations that create rapid bursts of change. The process that leads to both stable and unstable periods, however, is the same, and this is the main strength of PE.

The initial application of PE traced nuclear energy policy developments in the United States over an extended period. Rather than targeting a specific institution, nuclear policy was the focus of the study as it made its way through the various institutions and regulatory bodies that establish safety measures and promote economic development.[4] The American system has encouraged the development of subsystems – decision-making authority is delegated to a select few actors, who dictate how an issue is framed and discussed based on their own interests. Subsystems can vary in terms of being more open or closed, but nuclear energy, which is esoteric and technocratic, became a closed system because it was monopolized and controlled by a few actors and agencies. The monopoly ensured that only incremental or very minor changes occurred, a situation that promoted the interests of the triangle in place as there were no significant shifts in actors, agencies, or framing of the policy issue. Eventually, though, the policy monopoly started to break down; those involved could no longer assume complete control of the policy debate, and this led to large-scale changes.

Baumgartner and Jones, however, point to one key idea that led to the breakdown of the policy monopoly: the policy image. A policy image refers to how the policy issue is perceived as well as the core set of symbols and values that influence how it is discussed and understood.[5] The image for nuclear policy was initially positive, focusing on the possible benefits of harnessing such an extremely powerful energy source. This image was eventually manipulated, however, focusing more on the potential for severe environmental devastation as well as the profound safety risks. Policy change, then, was caused not by a change in the governing coalition or structural reform, but was attributed to changing perceptions of the policy issue (or, a change to the policy image in PE). Consequently, rapid and successive bursts of change accumulated into significant punctuations.

When a policy image remains constant, gradual or incremental growth will persist. This lasts until a policy image manipulation creates large-scale punctuations. Image manipulation is inextricably linked to the "politics of attention."[6] Once a policy issue grabs the attention of the public, it becomes popularized. With more people focused on the details of a policy issue, the likelihood increases that governments will be willing to perceive the issue as a legitimate problem that must be dealt with, thereby securing the policy issue on its agenda. However, governments are composed of multiple venues, which often have overlapping jurisdictions. This is the complex reality of the globalized world in which we live. No institution has the information-processing capacity to handle all issues simultaneously, so governments must delegate decision-making authority to other venues for assistance. This idea is embodied by the structure of the US political system, with its federalist nature and numerous checks and balances. The fragmentation of the political system leads to multiple, overlapping venues that hold important policy debates. As previously suggested, this semi-independent nature can lead to the solidification of monopolies, whereby a few individuals can dominate and control a given policy debate. But, also, losing groups can popularize a policy issue to strategically place it on the agenda of an alternative venue.

There are three ways variables that can change a policy image: venue-shift, actors, and frames.[7] These variables are interconnected – in other words, the presence of one will reinforce the others. Venue shifts occur when actors successfully place an issue on the agenda of an alternative venue. This expands the debate into a new venue, with its own unique decision-making processes and rules. Based on its general purpose, each venue will perceive a policy issue differently. This fresh, new look offers groups an opportunity to win a policy debate. As Baumgartner and Jones observe, however, each venue has different agenda-setting properties, with its own rules for which issues it will hear. Moreover, there are variations in the information-processing habits of venues. Baumgartner and Jones observe that macro venues, such as the president, do not have the attentiveness to handle many issues at once. This limited information capacity is characterized as serial. When these macro venues do act, however, they tend to initiate large punctuations, which lead to unstable and unpredictable forms of policy change. Alternatively, the smaller venues can engage with multiple matters simultaneously – they possess horizontal attentiveness. However, these venues are not as likely to produce large punctuations; instead, they usually contribute to incremental periods of policy growth. Those groups who want to initiate significant change will attempt to expand debates into macro venues.

The recruitment of additional actors to a policy debate can also influence a policy image. Within a given venue, groups often compete for a policy outcome. Those who control how an issue is discussed, as well as the normative values and symbols attached to a given debate, will try to protect the status quo, while competing groups will try to mould the policy image in accordance with their own policy preferences. The inclusion of additional actors, each with their own individual perspective and understanding, increases the likelihood that a policy image will be destabilized. This draws increased attention to the policy debate, creating the opportunity for even more actors to become involved. Competing groups will seek to recruit members by expanding the conflict to include personnel with similar policy positions, thereby reinforcing their alliance. Moreover, an important recruitment strategy will be the framing of policy issues. Frames are composed of a series of ideological assumptions that give meaning to symbols and ideas, which will be used to discuss and promote policy positions. In a given policy debate, competing narratives will develop that influence the general perceptions of a policy issue. Strategic actors will adjust these frames based on the venue in which a debate is held. Frames can be an important mechanism for altering a policy issue, and one that draws attention to how an issue is discussed.

The policy image will dictate whether policy change will develop incrementally or whether unpredictable punctuations will occur. If actors within a given venue can consistently maintain a positive policy image, minor growth will ensue. Those who are in direct control will protect the status quo by implementing rules that privilege their positions. As a result, status quo–inducing mechanisms are installed that contribute to the activation of negative feedback processes. When a negative feedback process is present, more meaningful change is difficult to achieve, thus reflecting the incremental and stable growth periods. When a policy image is destabilized, however, it draws attention to a given policy debate. The policy issue becoming more salient further encourages other actors to get involved. As the conflict expands, macro venues are more likely to become sites of debate. The pressure accumulated from these changes will compel policymakers to adjust their decision-making habits to focus on dimensions that were previously not considered. It is the change in how these actors both understand and solve policy problems that can trigger periods of punctuation. As the attention to the policy debate dissipates, the system will absorb the shocks and establish a new status quo, including rules that protect the new policy image.

Punctuated Equilibrium: A Theory of Judicial Policy Change?

There have been very few attempts at applying PE to the judicial branch of government more generally, as noted by Robinson.[8] Since Baumgartner's early work identifies courts as a vital policymaking venue, this is somewhat surprising.[9] There is very limited literature focusing on courts as a venue, or on the various ways that policy debates have been expanded into courts, but Robinson's application of PE to the Supreme Court of the United States (SCOTUS) marks an important exception.[10] On analytical grounds, there is no legitimate reason for SCOTUS to be excluded from PE theory as the underpinnings apply relatively nicely to appellate courts. Robinson tries to explain this gap in the literature by noting that courts possess much different agenda-setting processes than other political institutions and that their heightened form of judicial independence, as well as the concealment of their internal operations, presents additional methodological obstacles.[11] Despite these factors, Robinson is optimistic about the application of PE to courts and has devised empirical research to test his claims.[12]

Robinson's work is an important starting point, but this analysis will be distinguished in important ways. Robinson's work is more court-centred; he focuses on applying PE to explain doctrinal changes that occur within a court. He uses PE to explain changes in legal precedent, focusing much more on doctrinal developments and the factors that alter established judicial decision-making patterns. This chapter applies PE to courts, but it engages with this question by focusing more on legislature-court exchanges. In addition, because PE has been tailored to the structural configurations of the US presidential system, it will have to be adapted to the Canadian context.

Policy Change and Stability in the Canadian Context

The PE literature has recently grappled with the generalizability of the theory. One major criticism of PE is that its origins are intimately tied to the US system, with its clean division of power as well as its multiple checks and balances.[13] This layout is conducive to notions of venue shifting and bounded rationality, which largely comprise the main theoretical thrust of PE. Baumgartner and Jones have responded to these criticisms by reminding scholars of the principal process of change. Separate venues are important, but PE relates to the attentiveness of governing institutions and their inability to conclude all matters simultaneously. The complexity of the globalized world in which we now live ensures that all government attentiveness is in some way bounded, regardless of the structure in place. Notwithstanding these concerns, the early PE literature dealt exclusively with the United States; however, in more recent years, scholars have illuminated its effectiveness in explaining policy change in parliamentary political systems. For example, Soroka has used aspects of the PE framework to determine how public opinion and the media influence the parliamentary agenda in Canada.[14]

There is compelling evidence to suggest that the Supreme Court of Canada can be conceptualized as a powerful policymaking venue in the Charter era. The notion of venue shopping has become attractive for political groups seeking to obtain policy victories, especially those who were unable to score similar victories in the traditional policy context.[15] Even before the Charter, the early gay movement used courts as a means of forging a separate collective identity.[16] That being said, the policy importance of the courts has been ratcheted up since the Charter. Moreover, the Supreme Court of Canada has helped to facilitate these venue shifts as it has relaxed its agenda-setting restrictions, which are normally associated with a traditional adversarial model.[17] Significant changes pertaining to standing, ripeness, and mootness have significantly increased the Court's discretion to take on policy-laden cases.[18]

Courts as Venues: Positive or Negative Feedback Mechanisms?

PE can be applied to our Canadian context, and the Supreme Court of Canada is an important policymaking venue. Although there is a significant body of literature on courts in the Charter era, very little of it tries to use policy theory to help us better understand periods of policy stability and change. The PE framework provides one explanation, which looks to the institutional features of courts and the various ways that courts can manipulate a policy image. Although such a task is difficult to measure, certain institutional features that contribute to positive feedback processes will increase a court's ability to modify a policy image. Alternatively, the presence of negative feedback mechanisms will limit a court's influence by protecting the status quo. Courts possess mechanisms that can lead to both positive and negative feedback.

Court Venues: Negative Feedback Mechanisms

As Robinson suggests, common law appellate courts possess a multitude of status quo–inducing features that encourage negative feedback.[19] More generally, judicial decision making in common law countries emphasizes applying established legal principles to the facts of a case, thereby promoting only incremental change in response to new situations. These ideas are embodied in small changes that follow doctrinal developments. Another important mechanism is the decision-making threshold that judges must satisfy to overturn precedent. Appellate court judges are unable to individually implement legal developments; they must work with their colleagues to garner a majority judgment, a process that emphasizes the importance of group dynamics. Although the Canadian literature has not been developed as much as the American literature, judges in Canada do engage in strategic bargaining to redirect the law in their desired direction.[20] This compels judges to operate within a specific institutional setting, with certain established norms and ideas, that restrict innovation and change.

The agenda setting of courts also possesses status quo–inducing attributes. Courts are often characterized as responsive institutions because they rely on external sources to place cases on their agenda. Contrary to a legislature, they are unable to independently determine the issues that they will tackle. That being said, the Supreme Court of Canada's discretion over its docket has increased in recent years. In 1975, changes made by the Department of Justice allowed the Court to limit appeals by right and focus on other applications for leave based on the "public importance" determination.[21] Nevertheless, the increased discretion does not negate the fact that the Court's agenda still relies heavily on exogenous sources. These agenda-setting factors impose additional restrictions on those judges looking to effect policy change. As a result, courts often contribute to negative feedback, which contributes to incremental and consistent growth. This process continues until a positive feedback loop becomes activated, which initiates more lasting punctuations.

Similar to SCOTUS, the Supreme Court of Canada possesses certain institutional features that can contribute to positive feedback. Before reviewing these features, however, it is important to distinguish this analysis from Robinson's work. Robinson applies the PE framework to SCOTUS, arguing that all appellate courts operate in similar ways to influence policy. However, law and politics scholars have long held that Canada's constitutional design has important distinguishing characteristics that influence how the Supreme Court interacts with the other branches of government. Although most appellate courts do have the ability to punctuate policy issues, Canada's unique constitutional design offers courts additional ways to influence policy images. In other words, the Supreme Court of Canada has additional positive feedback mechanisms that provide it with punctuating tendencies.

Canada's Constitutional Design: The Supreme Court of Canada as a Venue

Flanagan argues that Canada's constitutional scheme favours courts' ability to effectuate change.[22] Constitutions are an ensemble of rules, and Flanagan has divided Canada's constitutional history into separate periods based on how the rules either promote or overcome the status quo. Although all branches of the broader governance system do possess some status quo–inducing rules, courts can initiate change without the level of support that is required in the other branches of government. Flanagan uses ample evidence to support his claims, but two points are especially relevant. First, the Supreme Court has embraced the role of final interpreter of the constitution. Its decisions, consequently, are enshrined with an elevated constitutional status, thereby increasing its authoritative voice. Second, the Court's internal decision-making process is concealed from the public as well as the media. These factors translate into important policymaking advantages.

Flanagan's arguments can be extended to include the policy impact of courts.[23] Both the power of judicial review and the courts' internal operations provide judges with an increased opportunity to influence a policy image. The power of judicial review can influence the policy image in two ways. First, constitutionalizing a policy issue makes it extremely difficult for governments to respond to a court ruling. The stringent amending formulas make it difficult to garner enough political momentum to overrule a judicial interpretation. More recent developments in the legitimacy debate have verified that governments typically acquiesce to both the outcomes of judicial judgments and other policy formulation suggestions.[24] The notwithstanding clause was inserted into the Charter as a safeguard for judicial power; however, law and politics scholars have deemed it obsolete as it is no longer a viable option in Canada's current political landscape. Consequently, when courts decide to act, they have a lasting influence on the policy image. Second, in the eyes of the public, constitutionally enshrining any policy issue helps to legitimize it. Legal scholars have recognized the power of rights frames and legal rhetoric for shaping political culture as well as encouraging political organization and mobilization.[25] Because of the constitution's importance in the eyes of Canadian citizens, constitutionalizing a policy issue elevates its status.

A court's hidden internal operations can also influence a policy image. Because the media is excluded from the process, the public is informed only when a case enters and exits the court. When a controversial decision is released, however, all attention will be drawn to the policy issue at hand as well as the various justifications used to invalidate it. The release of a judgment reflects the potential for sudden policy change caused by a punctuation. Alternatively, when the executive is seeking to initiate important policy changes, the public is informed. Governments campaign and inform the citizenry of their actions. If they are elected, the general expectation is that these policy changes will come to fruition or that, at least, elected officials will act in some capacity to initiate them. The completion of this process is often long and drawn out. It typically involves "investigation by legislative committees, and public discussion of executive reports and draft legislation. Debate in the House of Commons and Senate generates coverage by the media."[26] As a result, the public is informed of significant changes.

Compared to other policymaking venues, the Supreme Court of Canada possesses institutional properties that allow it to influence a policy image. This is because the judges do not have to overcome the constraints that exist in the legislative venues. When Court action does influence a policy image, it increases the likelihood that a positive feedback process will become activated.

The Process of Judicial Policy Involvement

Although courts are an important policymaking venue, not all judicial action will punctuate a given policy area. When a court venue does become involved, a policy issue will be placed on the courts' agenda, and the judges activate their judicial review power by invalidating segments of legislation. Attention is drawn to the policy issue, and it is immediately sent back to the government to determine the appropriate response. In other words, the policy issue is fast-tracked, and it secures itself on the legislative agenda as the political losses incurred by having legislation deemed unconstitutional compels the government's attention. This is important because a government's agenda has limited space. Groups are struggling to have their own "problems" recognized as warranting government action. The government will not automatically respond to a court's ruling, but will survey its options to determine whether to abandon the initiative or to respond in light of the court's judgment.

Declaring legislation unconstitutional has the potential to significantly affect a policy image. A court can remove a policy initiative if it finds that the purpose or function of the legislation is unconstitutional. This would be the most blatant and extreme form of policy image change as the government will be unable to respond. Typically, however, courts do not determine whether a policy objective is compelling and necessary, but focus on the instruments and strategies used to reach a policy objective. Because judicial decisions hold such prestige in the eyes of Canadian citizens, they can influence how the public perceives a policy image. Governments that continually pass unconstitutional legislation can incur severe political losses. Drawing attention to these issues can encourage the public to organize in an effort to pressure governments for policy change.

Although court decisions can help to mobilize the public, their significance stems from their direct influence over the policymaking process. Scholars have recognized that court decisions can influence all stages of the policy cycle by imposing constraints on policymaking actors.[27] The nature and extent of these constraints will be contingent on the released judgment. Nevertheless, policymakers must consider them when legislating in the given policy area. Even if these constraints are minor, they can still lead to important policy changes. Invalidating parts of legislation compels the government to review its fundamental purpose and to draft alternative legislation that replaces the impugned sections. These new considerations have the potential to change the decision-making routines of policymaking actors, and this focuses attention on certain dimensions of a policy issue that were previously ignored. As Baumgartner suggests, all policy issues are complex and are composed of many layers and dimensions. These subtle changes, however, do possess the potential for activating positive feedback mechanisms, which develop more significant policy changes.

Judges are able to use their judicial review powers to directly influence a policy image. But judges also exert indirect influence over the policy process and outcomes. As Flanagan suggests, judicial rulings often create a legal "void," or vacuum, as different groups move to exploit this opportunity to achieve policy victories. The policy image is vulnerable during these windows of opportunities, offering groups a favourable time to mould a policy image. In an effort to parlay these opportunities into large-scale policy changes, competing sides in a policy debate employ three main techniques: venue shifts, personnel recruitment, and altering a frame.

By drawing attention to a policy issue, court decisions can create the necessary momentum for continuous venue shifts. If a group loses in the court venue, the fact that attention was brought to the issue can translate into additional venue shifts. This is not to say that strategic venue shifts will always be successful; bounded actors cannot guarantee that they will win the policy debate in an alternative venue. But each venue possesses its own internal biases, which structure the rules and procedures based on the venue's fundamental responsibility. Consequently, each venue will construct a different lens through which to perceive a similar policy issue, and it will have different rules and regulations, which will influence the debate's general trajectory. An example of a strategic venue shift occurs when governments appeal a court decision. Appellate courts operate with a different mandate than trial courts, focusing more on the development of the law as well as overseeing the conduct of trial judges. Although it is not guaranteed, governments enjoy a relatively high success rate in court venues, and this provides an incentive for them to debate a policy in a court venue.[28] This presents an opportunity for governments to salvage the policy objective.

Losing policy groups can also recruit additional participants to a debate. This idea is often intimately tied to venue shifting. Placing an issue on an agenda ensures that other actors will oversee and participate in a policy discussion. Each of these additional members has its own ideological positions and understandings, which can change the normative values attached to a policy image. The inclusion of judges can influence how other formal policy actors conduct their responsibilities. A judicialized policy, however, can benefit certain groups by providing increased access to the policy process; this was demonstrated in the Supreme Court's ruling in *R v. Morgentaler*.[29] Although the judgment did not directly favour any policy position, the pro-choice group was already organized as it was seeking to change the status quo. And while the Court's decision did not directly support this position, it did allow this group to more effectively fill the void that it generated (even though this position went contrary to public opinion at the time). This example demonstrates the indirect policy influence of courts.

Frames can also be an important way to change policy images. This speaks not so much to the general perceptions of a given policy as to the ideas and discursive practices that actors use to justify their policymaking decisions. Court involvement can have important implications for frames. Legal scholars have recognized the distinctive characteristics of rights frames and legal discourse as well as their powerful mobilization effects.[30] Under the Charter, scholars have recognized the importance of rights discourse as governments strive to ensure that legislation is Charter-sensitive.[31] Court involvement can significantly alter the ideological framework that is used to promote and justify policy decisions (see, e.g., Nicolaides and Hennigar, this volume).

A Subtler Form of Policy Influence: Issue Salience

The discussion thus far has focused on those instances when judges become directly involved in a policy area by striking down segments of legislation. Although it is not automatic, the invalidation of a law can create punctuations. The reverse is also true – when judges choose to uphold a law, this typically does not change the policy image but reinforces it. This ties into the broader negative feedback process that contributes to little or minor policy change. As a result, the general expectation is that courts contribute to more meaningful policy change only when they directly intervene in a case. Robinson's work leads to a similar conclusion. Doctrinal developments or changes to legal precedent are necessary for courts to contribute to more meaningful policy contributions. Perhaps this captures the policy influence of SCOTUS, but it does not explain all forms of policy change in Canada.

The case of *Thibaudeau v. Canada* demonstrates an important exception.[32] This case was based on the imposition of taxation for childcare payments used exclusively for the well-being and benefit of children; the plaintiff argued that the taxation was discriminatory and in violation of s. 15 (equality provision) of the Charter. The Supreme Court, however, found that no discrimination was present and dismissed the appeal. Even though the Court upheld the legislation, its involvement lent credence to the policy objective. Although it did not directly intervene and change the policy image, it illuminated a policy objective that went contrary to public opinion, which encouraged mobilization against the policy. In response to such pressure, the government reformed the policy. This case is important because it suggests that courts can influence policy even when they do not directly intervene in a case. This exemplifies the courts' power to draw attention to a given policy, thereby leading to policy change. This change is not caused by doctrinal or jurisprudential changes; the presence of a venue shift, even lacking direct judicial action, can provide enough of an impetus to contribute to change.

The Policy Impact of Judicial Remedies

In the Charter era, the Supreme Court has devised a series of innovative remedies. If a judge finds that a rights infraction is present, s. 24(2) authorizes judges to employ a remedy that they "consider appropriate and just in the circumstances."[33] This expansive provision has authorized judges to find new solutions that do not align with traditional legal remedies.[34] Although scholars have noted the important policy implications of these remedies, much of these discussions have been couched in the broader legitimacy debate, directing more attention to their impact on the broader liberal democratic system and less to their policy implications.[35] PE provides an insightful framework with which to understand the deployment of judicial remedies.

There are many judicial remedies, but much of the law and politics literature focuses on the ones used most frequently or those that allow a court to control important policy decisions. This influence occurs in two ways: each main remedy has important implications for the patterns of venue shifts. Once a court declares a ruling, the issue typically goes back on the legislatures' agenda to determine the appropriate response. Certain remedies, however, disrupt this pattern by allowing courts to assume control of law-making powers. The second factor is how a court influences a court image. Some judicial remedies are more intrusive, thereby changing how a court decision will influence a policy image. An appropriate analysis of remedies is beyond the scope of this chapter; thus, for current purposes, the discussion will focus on the reading-in remedy, while referring to the decision of *Vriend* as an example of its use. The implications of this case have received extensive scholarly attention; as a result, this analysis will not analyse the legal intricacies of the case, but will instead focus on the Supreme Court's policy impact.

The decision of *Vriend v. Alberta* involved a lab coordinator from King's College in that province who was dismissed from his job because of his sexual orientation.[36] The institution did not deny its reason for dismissal; indeed, it followed an institutional policy that was already in place. However, Vriend was unable to report his determination to the human rights board in Alberta because sexual orientation was not included in the Individual's Rights Protection Act. The Alberta government had purposely excluded it from the enumerated grounds of discrimination, thereby demonstrating a conscientious effort not to legislate in that area. Based on these issues, it seems that the Court had no legal grounds to directly intervene. The traditional role of courts is to review and impose restrictions; it is rarely to impose positive obligations on governments to act in a specific capacity. However, the Court activated its reading-in judicial remedy and compelled the government to include sexual orientation in its human rights legislation.

Perceiving these developments through the PE lens adds analytical insight into the ways that the Supreme Court controlled the policy outcome. The Court did morph into a legislature for the decision, but it did so by controlling the policy debate. As previously suggested, the more traditional judicial remedies – such as striking down – impose important constraints on policymakers. These constraints restrict choices, but they do not compel a government to act in a positive fashion according to the Court's constitutional mandate. However, the decision in this case eliminated the discretion of the policymakers by dictating both the policy goal and the tools, a result that has important implications for the general policy image. In addition, constitutionalizing the policy issue removed it from further deliberation because it remained within a court venue.

The decision attracted a large amount of media attention, but those shifts of attentiveness, either from the public or government, were unable to reverse the constitutionalized status quo. This is because the threshold for amending the constitution requires an abundance of support, which is difficult to garner in any institutional context. Using reading-in as a tool, the judges created a formidable policy subsystem by using the court venue as a shield and constitutionalizing the policy image. In other words, the judges were responsible for the initial policy punctuation, but they also established the new equilibrium.

Conclusion

The principal claim throughout this chapter is that PE is able to accommodate the complex ways that courts exert policy influence. It is argued that its theoretical underpinnings help to explain a court's involvement in the policy process and outcomes. This chapter has relied on important developments in the literature to support its main assertions, tying into the broader objective to encourage discussions between two rather isolated bodies of literature – public policy and law and politics. The courts should be considered a serious policy institution, while formal theories can be used to understand their impact.

This chapter has argued that courts offer fertile research opportunities for the PE literature. First, courts can have an impact on agenda setting, including the content and diversity of issues. Although there are few attempts in the Canadian literature, US scholars have started to delve into this area.[37] Second, scholars can trace policies as they make their way through the various venues. The law and politics literature has focused on comparing different policy venues, but Canadian scholars can also compare how a judicialized policy differs from a legislative one.[38] Third, research can focus on the conditions within a court venue that trigger transitions from negative to positive feedback mechanisms. This ties into the broader law and politics debates over the variables that lead courts to change doctrinal developments, whether they may be judicial turnover, legal factors, or changing attitudes and norms of judicial responsibilities. However, as this chapter demonstrates, scholars must be cognizant of the latent forms of judicial influence. Certain cases indicate that doctrinal changes are not a precondition for court-made policy change. Last, more research needs to consider how to operationalize and measure policy change to determine when court-initiated change should be classified as either incremental or punctuating. Certain scholars make important distinctions between policy objectives and the instruments used to attain those objectives. However, courts often focus exclusively on the justifications and strategies for obtaining a policy initiative. Focusing only on policy tools would not accurately measure the level of judicial policy influence.

Most important, the main theoretical propositions of PE must be empirically tested. This chapter has relied exclusively on theoretical points and previous research to understand how venues, actors, and frames can lead to judicial policy punctuations. Future research needs to trace these developments to determine whether these ideas accurately capture the process of change. Judicial remedies also present an interesting area of research for policy impact. Scholars should engage with the question of how these tools are able to condition government responses by determining whether a remedy can influence the initial policy punctuation or the subsequent government response that establishes a new equilibrium – or, in some cases, whether a remedy enables judges to do both.

NOTES

1 Frank R. Baumgartner and Bryan D. Jones, "Positive and Negative Feedback in Politics," in *Policy Dynamics*, ed. Frank R. Baumgartner and Bryan D. Jones (Chicago: University of Chicago Press, 2002), 1–28.
2 Ibid., 1–8.
3 John Kingdon, *Agendas, Alternatives, and Public Policies*, 2nd, Pearson new international ed. (London: Pearson, 2013).
4 Frank R. Baumgartner and Bryan D. Jones, "Agenda Dynamics and Policy Subsystems," *Journal of Politics* 53, no. 44 (1991): 1044–74.
5 Ibid., 1046–51.
6 Bryan D. Jones and Frank R. Baumgartner, *The Politics of Attention: How Government Prioritizes Problems* (Chicago: University of Chicago Press, 2005).
7 It is important to recognize that PE also considers "crisis events" as important for policy change. However, this chapter focuses on the variables that courts are capable of influencing, such as actors, venues, frames.
8 Rob Robinson, "Punctuated Equilibrium and the Supreme Court," *Policy Studies Journal* 41, no. 4 (2013): 655–82.

9 Baumgartner and Jones, "Agenda Dynamics and Policy Subsystems," 1057; see also Sarah Pralle, "Timing and Sequence in Agenda-Setting and Policy Change: A Comparative Study of Lawn Care Pesticide Politics in Canada and the US," *Journal of European Public Policy* 13, no. 7 (2006): 987–1005.

10 Rob Robinson, "Punctuated Equilibrium and the Supreme Court," 655–82; see also Brendon Swedlow, "Reason for Hope? The Spotted Owl Injunctions and Policy Change," *Law and Social Inquiry* 34, no. 4 (2009), 825–67; Frank R. Baumgartner and Jamie K. Gold, "Changing Agendas of Congress and the Supreme Court," in *Policy Dynamics*, ed. Frank R. Baumgartner and Bryan D. Jones (Chicago: University of Chicago Press, 2002), 270–90.

11 Robinson, "Punctuated Equilibrium and the Supreme Court," 657–8.

12 Rob Robinson, "Culture and Legal Policy Punctuation in the Supreme Court's Gender Discrimination Cases," *Policy Studies Journal* 42, no. 4 (2014): 555–89.

13 Frank R. Baumgartner, Bryan D. Jones, and Peter B. Mortensen, "Punctuated-Equilibrium Theory: Explaining Stability and Change in Public Policymaking," in *Theories of the Policy Process*, 3rd ed., ed. Paul A. Sabatier and Christopher M. Weible (Boulder, CO: Westview Press, 2014), 80–3.

14 Stuart Soroka, Agenda-Setting Dynamics in Canada (Vancouver: UBC Press, 2010).

15 Troy Q. Riddell, "The Impact of Legal Mobilization and Judicial Decisions: The Case of Official Minority-Language Education Policy in Canada for Francophones outside Quebec," *Law and Society Review* 38 (2004): 583–609; Christopher P. Manfredi, *Feminist Activism in the Supreme Court: Legal Mobilization and the Women's Legal Education and Action Fund* (Vancouver: UBC Press, 2004); Lisa Vanhala, *Making Rights a Reality? Disability Rights Activists and Legal Mobilization* (Cambridge: Cambridge University Press, 2011).

16 Miriam Smith, *Lesbian and Gay Rights in Canada: Social Movements and Equality-Seeking, 1971–1995* (Toronto: University of Toronto Press, 1999).

17 Roy Flemming, *Tournament of Appeals: Granting Judicial Review in Canada* (Vancouver: UBC Press, 2004), 1–18.

18 Emmett Macfarlane. *Governing from the Bench: The Supreme Court of Canada and the Judicial Role* (Vancouver: UBC Press, 2013), 15–38.

19 Robinson, "Punctuated Equilibrium and the Supreme Court," 657–8; Thomas Flanagan, "Canada's Three Constitutions: Protecting, Overturning, and Reversing the Status Quo," in *The Myth of the Sacred: The Charter, the Courts, and the Politics of the Constitution in Canada*, ed. Patrick James, Donald E. Abelson, and Michael Lusztig (Montreal and Kingston: McGill-Queen's University Press, 2002), 125–46.

20 Peter McCormick, "'Was It Something I Said?' Losing the Majority on the Modern Supreme Court of Canada, 1984–2011," *Osgoode Hall Law Journal* 50, no. 93 (2012): 93–128.
21 Flemming, *Tournament of Appeals*, 1–18.
22 Flanagan, "Canada's Three Constitutions," 125–46.
23 Thomas Flanagan, "The Staying Power of the Legislative Status Quo: Collective Choice in Canada's Parliament after Morgentaler," *Canadian Journal of Political Science* 30, no. 1 (1997): 31–53.
24 Emmett Macfarlane, "Dialogue or Compliance? Measuring Legislatures' Policy Responses to Court Rulings on Rights," *International Political Science Review* 34, no. 1 (2013): 39–56.
25 Stuart A. Scheingold, *The Politics of Rights: Lawyers, Public Policy, and Political Change*, 2nd ed. (Ann Arbor: University of Michigan Press, 2004).
26 Flanagan, "Canada's Three Constitutions," 137.
27 Janet Hiebert, *Charter Conflicts: What Is Parliament's Role?* (Montreal and Kingston: McGill-Queen's University Press, 2002).
28 Lori Hausegger, Matthew Hennigar, and Troy Riddell, *Canadian Courts: Law, Politics, and Process*, 2nd ed. (Oxford: Oxford University Press, 2015).
29 *R v. Morgentaler*, (1988) 1 SCR 30.
30 Scheingold, *The Politics of Rights*, 170–99.
31 Hiebert, *Charter Conflicts*.
32 *Thibaudeau v. Canada*, (1995) 2 SCR 627. An additional example is *Auton v. British Columbia (Attorney General)*, (2004) 3 SCR 657.
33 Canadian Charter of Rights and Freedoms, s. 24(2), Part I of the Constitution Act, 1982.
34 Robert Leckey, *Bills of Rights in the Common Law* (Cambridge: Cambridge University Press, 2016).
35 Ibid., 170–98; Dennis Baker, *Not Quite Supreme: The Courts and Coordinate Constitutional Interpretation* (Montreal and Kingston: McGill-Queen's University Press, 2010).
36 *Vriend v. Alberta*, (1998) 1 SCR 493.
37 Baumgartner and Gold, "Changing Agendas of Congress and the Supreme Court," 270–90.
38 Jeb Barnes and Thomas F. Burke, *How Policy Shapes Politics: Rights, Courts, Litigation, and the Struggle over Injury Compensation* (Oxford: Oxford University Press, 2015).

PART TWO

Institutional Contexts

4 The Charter, Policy, and Political Judgment

JANET L. HIEBERT

Most assessments of bills of rights focus on judicial rulings to analyse developments in judicial doctrine or assess what remedies are imposed when legislation is found to violate a right. Although these court-oriented approaches provide valuable insights, they offer only a partial picture of how and why judicial review affects legislation. What they cannot account for is whether and how apprehension of judicial review drives legislative decisions and, by implication, the extent to which courts influence the norms of legislative decision making. As only a fraction of legislation is ever litigated, appreciation for whether legislative decision makers integrate or reject judicial norms at the initial decision-making stages allows for a richer understanding of judicial influence than a focus exclusively on judicial decisions.

Comparative scholarly assessments suggest considerable variance in the relationship between judicial review and legislative norms. This is not simply because the codified language of protected rights varies, as does the scope of judicial remedial powers authorized (strong or weak form) or even the nature of courts themselves (i.e., constitutional versus ordinary appellate courts). Other relevant factors include the strength of support structures for social groups to use litigation to pursue social reforms,[1] the institutional setting in which a bill of rights functions, whether the prevailing political culture emphasizes juridical or political answers to rights-based disagreements, and the extent to which opposition parties are willing to focus on rights and/or have the power to force changes to proposed legislation.

In some jurisdictions, constitutional considerations are not considered a priority for legislators. This is said to be the situation in the US Congress, where decision making is dominated by other political and policy considerations,[2] and on those rare occasions when constitutional norms appear to influence decisions, most members believe Congress should form its own judgment on constitutional questions.[3] Moreover, even if a strong will emerges in Congress to use constitutional norms as a filter for assessing the merits of legislation, the separated system in the United States provides strong opportunities for political resistance.

In stark contrast to the limited effects that a bill of rights is said to have on American congressional behaviour, Alec Stone Sweet portrays European legislative behaviour as keenly sensitive to constitutional norms, particularly as articulated by courts. Thus, German, Italian, Spanish, and French decision makers are said to anticipate the likelihood of judicial censure, use constitutional rules, and engage judicially influenced modes of reasoning with the intent of insulating legislation from the prospect of a negative ruling. As Stone Sweet argues, "Governing with judges means governing like judges."[4]

That judicial influence on legislation in the European jurisdictions Stone Sweet assesses is more substantial than in the United States, and likely in Canada, is explained in part by the fact these jurisdictions use abstract review, which allows legislation to be reviewed for its consistency with rights in the absence of litigation and before legislation comes into force. Thus, opposition parties have the opportunity to exploit this opportunity to try to constrain the government's capacity to pass legislation they oppose.[5] As Stone Sweet argues, "All things being equal, systems that contain abstract review ought to experience more judicialization than systems that do not. Abstract review harnesses the (virtually continuous) struggle between parliamentary majority and opposition over policy outcomes."[6]

In Canada, Charter discourse has often made reference to the notion of "Charter-proofing" legislation, which conveys the idea of ensuring that legislation complies with judicial norms at the time of its passage. This chapter questions this perception that Charter consistency is both a strong norm for, and a regular outcome of, federal legislative decision making. It asks the following two questions: Is it appropriate to characterize federal legislative behaviour as being driven by good-faith attempts to ensure Charter compliance? And, if not, what explains why there is not a stronger adherence to judicial norms in legislative decision making?

The chapter draws on interviews conducted with (then) current and former lawyers with the Department of Justice who evaluate and advise on the relationship between proposed legislation and its potential risks of constitutional challenge.[7] It also draws on Department of Justice guidelines that govern these processes. As will be argued below, although the Charter has increased the role of government lawyers in policy processes and placed more emphasis on assessing whether legislative initiatives are consistent with judicial norms, apprehension of judicial censure has not fundamentally displaced what will be referred to as *Westminster factors* as the prominent driver of legislative behaviour.

The Charter's Impact on Legislative Decision Making

In the early years of governing under the Canadian Charter of Rights and Freedoms, department officials and ministers were resistant to Charter advice and reluctant to act on Department of Justice lawyers' recommendations about how to insulate legislation from the possibility of a negative judicial ruling.[8] However, a few early, prominent Charter rulings had sufficiently important policy implications that they increased the incentive to better integrate Charter assessments into processes for bureaucratic and executive development and evaluation.[9] This enhanced role can be traced to a decision taken in 1991, when then clerk of the Privy Council Paul Tellier alerted deputy ministers of the importance of Charter scrutiny occurring in the early stages of legislative development.[10] Acting on the request of the Department of Justice, Tellier outlined steps to ensure that Charter issues were identified and evaluated as a condition under which new policy proposals would be considered by Cabinet. This analysis was to include an assessment of the risk of successful challenge, the impact of an adverse judicial ruling, and anticipated litigation costs.[11]

Despite the significance of this focus on risk-based assessments of the Charter, it should be noted that even before the Charter was adopted, the Department of Justice evaluated whether proposed legislation implicated protected rights – in this case, the Canadian Bill of Rights. This role was precipitated by what, at the time, seemed a novel experiment (one that has been subsequently emulated and adapted in four other jurisdictions):[12] the idea of marrying a statutory bill of rights with a reporting obligation that the Minister of Justice alerts Parliament when proposed legislation is inconsistent with protected rights. This requirement, a legacy of the Diefenbaker government, reflects a different (and far more optimistic) view of how a bill of rights can function than more conventional approaches. Although a bill of rights is typically interpreted as a way of protecting rights *from* Parliament, by allowing citizens to challenge the validity of legislation, for the Diefenbaker government a principal benefit associated with adopting the Canadian Bill of Rights was the potential for protecting rights *by* Parliament.

The expectation was that a more rights-compliant culture would emerge and function as a norm for proposing and approving legislation. It arose from the hope that a reporting requirement for inconsistency would not only increase awareness within government, the bureaucracy, and Parliament about whether and how legislative bills implicated rights but also discourage the pursuit of legislation that was inconsistent with protected rights because of the assumed negative publicity and criticism such legislation would provoke. However, interviews confirm that the quality and character of the pre-legislative vetting exercise under the Canadian Bill of Rights was not particularly robust, due in large part to the weak impetus for constraining legislative choices associated with the Supreme Court's restrictive and narrow approach to rights and remedies.[13] Moreover, Parliament demonstrated little interest in questioning the infrequency of ministerial reports of inconsistency.[14]

Nevertheless, in 1985, the federal Progressive Conservative government of Brian Mulroney extended the statutory reporting obligation to include the Charter. Little is known about the reasons for this decision. The most likely explanation is that then attorney general John Crosbie and others were troubled that, despite the requirement for evaluating bills for their consistency with the Canadian Bill of Rights, no such requirement extended to the Canadian Charter of Rights and Freedoms. One way to eliminate this incongruence would have been to abolish the statutory obligation for reporting under the Canadian Bill of Rights. However, this action would likely have been considered a politically risky move by encouraging criticism that the government was insensitive to the idea of ensuring that legislation was consistent with the Charter. The other option, and the one chosen, was to create a new obligation to report incompatibility under the Charter. This was done in s. 4.1 of the Department of Justice Act.[15] No report of Charter inconsistency has ever been made.

Judicial Influence on How Legislative Initiatives Are Evaluated

As is widely recognized, the Supreme Court's approach to the Charter has been influenced by the Charter's structure and, in particular, by the general limitation clause in s. 1. The Court generally avoids imposing definitional limits when determining the scope or meaning of a protected right and instead interprets rights broadly in the first instance, subject to separate analytical consideration of whether legislation that restricts a right is justifiable. This two-stage judicial approach has led to a broader interpretation of rights than would likely have occurred had the task of interpreting rights been collapsed with the decision about whether legislation was constitutionally valid or if different levels of scrutiny were applied, depending on the perceived importance of the rights claim. Consequently, legislation has a greater chance of being held to constitute a prima facie rights infringement than had the Court adopted a more constrained interpretation of rights.

The frequency with which legislation is found to have Charter implications is significant for legislative decision making because it directs more frequent consideration to judicial norms than would otherwise be the case. Not surprisingly, the judicial approach to the Charter has provided a strong incentive for those evaluating proposed legislation to formulate advice based on how the Court interprets the Charter. In Canada, this has meant less emphasis on whether proposed legislation implicates rights and more on the considerable preoccupation with proportionality considerations that the Court associates with a s. 1 justification.[16]

James Kelly argues that the federal government has both the resources and the institutional capacity to ascertain whether legislative proposals are vulnerable to judicial censure and also to recommend changes to reduce the likelihood that legislation will be successfully challenged. By coordinating extensive Charter review at the departmental level, "and by sensitizing policy exercises to the values and purposes contained in the Charter," the Department of Justice can help reduce "judicial invalidation as a potential constraint on the cabinet's ability to achieve its agenda."[17] These resources, along with the government's domination of the executive process (a trait associated with the modern evolution of the Westminster model that Canada has inherited), combine in such a way as to ensure that the federal government is well positioned to exercise the kind of self-constraint that Stone Sweet associates with European legislative behaviour.

Uncertain Relationship between Pre-legislative Scrutiny and Decision Making

It stands to reason that senior department officials and ministers have an interest in identifying possible problems that could result in a successful Charter challenge, particularly when changes to legislative initiatives intended to minimize risk do not seriously distort or delay the government's preferred legislative agenda. This idea has almost certainly fuelled the decision, referred to earlier, to create a specific Charter filter for evaluating legislative proposals.

However, apart from the fact that the Supreme Court's emphasis on s. 1 helps structure pre-legislative Charter assessments, remarkably little is known about the extent to which apprehension of judicial censure actually influences the development and refinement of legislative initiatives in the various stages leading to their approval for presentation as bills to Parliament. For example, how often does Charter advice meet with bureaucratic and political resistance, not only because of potential delays that could arise but also because of other policy considerations or ideological resistance to the kinds of changes that are implicated by the advice received? To what extent do governments prioritize the idea of insulating legislation from a successful challenge? Stated differently, are government decision makers generally risk takers or risk avoiders when deciding whether and how to proceed with an initiative that they have been forewarned carries a relatively high degree of risk and could result in judicial censure? And over time, have the attitudes and responses of political actors influenced the bureaucratic culture and practices of how Charter evaluations are broached or how advice is framed? In short, if consistency with judicial Charter norms operates as a check, how effective is this for screening out or compelling changes to proposed legislation that is deemed to be high risk, either because of the nature of the objective itself or, more likely, the legislative means that are being used?

In addition to questions about the relative influence of Charter advice in the complex process by which a legislative initiative is formulated and approved as a legislative bill, remarkably little is known about the extent to which legislative bills are influenced by the s. 4.1 statutory reporting obligation to alert Parliament when bills are inconsistent with the Charter. For example, how robustly is the idea of Charter consistency interpreted? How frequently do Justice lawyers advise that, without changes made, they will recommend that the minister of justice report inconsistency under s. 4.1, and what influence does this advice exert? Is the advice-giving role of Justice lawyers influenced by how receptive their bureaucratic bosses or political ministers are to the advice? What standards or criteria are used by the minister of justice to be satisfied that a legislative bill does not warrant reporting Charter inconsistency to Parliament? How influential is this advice in Cabinet?

Answering either set of questions is difficult enough because of the non-transparent nature of how legislative initiatives are developed, refined, and approved as legislative bills. Adding to the difficulty is the decision to treat Department of Justice advice as confidential and therefore not subject to parliamentary or public purview. This secrecy is reinforced by the strong pressure Justice lawyers incur not to discuss Charter vetting, culminating in a refusal over the past several years to grant interviews, even upon assurance of anonymity (even when asked in a general context, without reference to any specific bill or legislative initiative). Thus, assessments of the processes and standards used for evaluating proposed legislation for Charter consistency must be inferred from information obtained from interviews that the author conducted with Justice officials about the s. 4.1 exercise more than a decade ago, from more recent interviews with former Justice lawyer Edgar Schmidt (who is willing to grant attribution) after taking his department to court for what he characterizes as using an illegal standard for determining Charter consistency for statutory reporting purposes (discussed below), from documents that the department was compelled to provide with respect to Schmidt's legal action and evidence given, and from recent interviews with former minister of justice Irwin Cotler and former Justice lawyers who wish to remain anonymous.[18]

Inferences Drawn from Interviews and an Unusual Legal Action

At this point in the chapter, it is important to acknowledge the inevitable difficulties associated with attempts to ensure that legislation is consistent with judicial Charter norms. Judgments about Charter consistency can lead to strong contestation for the following reasons. First, the relevant Charter wording in s. 1 for evaluating the justification of legislative restrictions on rights is both broad and philosophical: it refers to the values of a free and democratic society, about which reasonable people may differ when assessing the justification of a legislative restriction on rights. Second, and related, is that ideological differences among political parties can lead to contestation around core issues such as how a bill of rights implicates the role of the state, the appropriate role of Parliament when interpreting constitutional requirements (see Nicolaides and Hennigar, this volume), or what responsibility government has to pursue perceived social problems or address substantive inequality in power or resources, thus affecting assessments of Charter consistency. Third, the evolution of Charter case law and changes to the composition of the Court add an uncertain quality to interpretations of relevant judicial Charter norms. Fourth, conceiving of rational and minimally impairing ways of achieving legislative goals is prone to conflicting interpretations of scientific or other relevant information, judgments about the relevance of the experiences in other jurisdictions, incomplete information, and speculative assessments of the possible or unintended consequences of various legislative scenarios. It can also lead to differences among members of the Court and thus often account for split decisions.

For the above-stated reasons, it is far too simplistic to characterize judgment about what distinguishes consistent from inconsistent legislation as if it were analogous to a green or red light or on/off distinction. Thus, it is preferable to frame the issue as the following: *To what extent do good-faith efforts to comply with Charter norms drive how government leaders evaluate, pursue, and justify their legislative objectives?*

Is It Reasonable to Assume That Federal Legislative Processes Are Guided by Good-Faith Efforts to Ensure Charter Consistency?

Government lawyers in the Department of Justice use case-driven, risk-based assessments of the likelihood that legislative initiatives will be successfully litigated, speculate about the policy and fiscal consequences should government lose, and suggest modifications to these initiatives to lower the risk.[19]

Assessments of whether proposed legislation is consistent with the Charter occur in two separate streams. One stream functions as an advisory role for policy development purposes and is characterized as Legal Risk Management. The stated intent is to assist client departments and agencies when developing and refining legislative initiatives by identifying the risks associated with potential Charter litigation as well as the potential policy and financial impacts should the government lose. Interpretations of Charter inconsistency range from very low to manifestly unconstitutional. In circumstances of high legal risks, Justice officials are advised that if the relevant department or minister does not follow legal advice, it may be necessary to take matters to a higher level, which may include the deputy minister. Yet Justice counsel are also instructed that in cases where high levels of risk have been clearly communicated to officials in a department or agency, they should accept that the final decision ultimately rests with that department or agency in all but exceptional cases.[20] Senior officials, up to levels of the deputy minister and minister, are briefed if a proposed bill poses a significant risk. At the Cabinet level, ministers are also informed when bills have adverse implications for rights; a situation in which the minister of justice is said to perform a critical advisory role in discussions where serious Charter concerns exist.[21]

A second form of Charter assessment operates to advise whether the s. 4.1 statutory reporting obligation for Charter inconsistency is engaged. This form of assessment is said to tolerate much higher levels of Charter risk than the above-mentioned assessment when counsel are advising on whether legislation is consistent with the Charter. As mentioned earlier, not only has no report of Charter inconsistency ever been made, but the consensus among those interviewed is also that it is highly unlikely (some say completely implausible) that there will ever be a s. 4.1 report of Charter inconsistency.[22]

Some Justice officials offer pragmatic reasons for this overwhelming presumption against reporting that legislation is inconsistent with the Charter. They argue that doing so would render the legislation susceptible to public and political criticism. Equally, if not more, significant, it would almost certainly undermine the viability of the legislation in the event of litigation as it would be difficult to defend legislation that the minister of justice has already declared to be inconsistent with the Charter. Thus, some characterize this reporting obligation as a blunt instrument that is not well suited to the Charter because of its authorization of strong judicial remedial powers.[23]

One possible way of interpreting this practice of not reporting Charter inconsistency to Parliament, along with the presumption that no report will likely be made, is to assume the following: the processes for evaluating Charter issues in the legal risk-management stream involve good-faith efforts to make the necessary changes to proposed legislation and thus ensure that by the time bills are introduced to Parliament, they are indeed consistent with the judicial norms of the Charter, therefore negating the need to make a s. 4.1 report of inconsistency.

However, the cumulative weight of the following four factors makes this assumption of pre-legislative Charter compliance extremely problematic and justifies scepticism that federal legislative behaviour should be characterized as grounded in good-faith attempts to ensure that legislation complies with Charter norms.

i) Risk Tolerance

Despite the preoccupation with evaluating the prospects and consequences of legislation being declared unconstitutional, it is important to recognize that legal advice in the pre-legislative policy process is only advisory. Interviews confirm that whether legal Charter advice influences legislation often boils down to a government's risk tolerance.[24] Moreover, interviews suggest that even when lawyers propose less restrictive ways of accomplishing an objective, the amendments chosen may still embody high-risk factors that may not significantly lessen the degree of vulnerability of judicial nullification.[25] As will be discussed below, it would be naive to assume that, for government, risk-based factors focus only on the risk that legislation could result in a negative judicial ruling and the policy and fiscal consequences associated with losing. Risk-based factors almost certainly also involve political calculations about whether the perceived short-term political advantages of proceeding with risky legislation, for which the government is strongly committed, outweigh the longer-term consequences of having legislation declared unconstitutional.

ii) The Absence of a Section 4.1 Report Does Not Convey Strong Judgment of Constitutionality

Interviews confirm that it is both inappropriate and misleading to interpret the absence of a s. 4.1 Charter report of inconsistency as confidence that legislation is not vulnerable to judicial nullification.[26] Officials were also asked whether the notwithstanding clause is ever seriously considered in a pre-emptive manner, particularly in situations where government is committed to high-risk legislation and yet is reluctant to entertain more Charter-compliant changes to how objectives are conceived or the proposed legislative means to achieve them. Interviews confirm that the notwithstanding clause is not considered to be a valid policy option, even when there is little willingness to abandon or substantially alter risky legislation.[27]

Although not generally thought of in this way, the notwithstanding clause and the s. 4.1 statutory reporting obligation are conceptually linked. Arguably, both instruments have a normative element and function to impose an obligation on government to announce when it intends to promote legislation that clearly contradicts relevant jurisprudence and to explain the reasons for this. Thus, in situations where government is determined to proceed with a legislative bill that the minister of justice is fully aware is extremely vulnerable to being nullified by the Supreme Court, it is difficult to imagine how a government that is committed to good-faith efforts to abide by statutory principles and constitutional norms would tolerate a presumption against reporting under s. 4.1, regardless of the level of risk that legislation could be declared invalid, and also refuse to consider whether the notwithstanding clause should be invoked.

Either form of acknowledging that government is promoting highly risky legislation will be extremely controversial and thus will place pressure on government to defend and convince Parliament and Canadians of the merits and justification of its judgment. Politically, this task is made all the more difficult because of the Charter's popularity, public confidence in the Supreme Court's role in interpreting constitutional values, and the tendency of many to equate political judgments that differ from the Court's as ignoring or overriding rights. This difficulty explains why governments do not willingly place themselves in this difficult political position. However, this reluctance has not resulted in risk-averse behaviour, in the way Stone Sweet characterizes European legislative behaviour, of minimizing conflicts with judicial norms. Instead, it manifests itself in a different variation of risk avoidance: a refusal to acknowledge when government is aware that legislative bills seriously contradict judicial norms, and thus are vulnerable to judicial censure, and/or explaining why the government's contrary judgment is meritorious and justified. However, as this form of risk avoidance comes at the expense of a robust commitment to statutory and constitutional norms, it is difficult to characterize it as a good-faith form of Charter judgment.

iii) Weak Standards for Determining Charter Consistency

Department of Justice guidelines for assessing Charter consistency for the s. 4.1 reporting obligation raise serious doubts that this statutory requirement functions as a substantial constraint on a government's legislative agenda. The systematic use of weak standards became clear after Edgar Schmidt (then a senior lawyer in the Legislative Services Branch of the Department of Justice) took his own department to court for authorizing what he alleged was an inappropriately low standard for assessing Charter compliance (and was promptly fired). Schmidt claims that the standard for advising the minister of justice whether his or her statutory obligation is engaged to report on Charter inconsistency is so low as to be essentially meaningless.

In his legal action, Schmidt argued that the department has unlawfully transformed the standards required for fulfilling the statutory obligation that the minister of justice report to Parliament when legislation or regulations are inconsistent with the Charter. Schmidt argued that the s. 4.1 reporting obligation permits two options: either legislation is consistent with the Charter, and thus the reporting obligation is not engaged, or a bill is "more likely than not inconsistent" with the Charter, in which a s. 4.1 report is required.[28] After the Federal Court determined that the issue was justiciable (a position the attorney general strongly opposed), the Department of Justice was required to provide the guidelines and other relevant materials used for determinations of whether the s. 4.1 statutory reporting obligation was engaged.

These guidelines reveal that the department interprets Charter inconsistency for s. 4.1 reporting purposes in a manner that, arguably, bears little resemblance to what would be implied by a plain reading of the statutory reporting obligation to "report any such [Charter] inconsistency." Charter inconsistency is deemed to occur only when no good-faith, reasonable argument can be made in favour of consistency.[29] However, despite the apparent emphasis on good-faith judgments, an argument will be considered credible even when it is "reasoned with a minimum level of strength or credibility."[30] This idea characterized departmental practices between 1982 and 1991. This standard was reviewed in 1993 and involved a consultation of senior committees of the Department of Justice. Senior officials considered other options, such as "more likely than not consistent with guaranteed rights" but, in the end, maintained the "no reasonable argument standard," although they renamed it the "credible argument standard." Despite the name change, the standard embodies the same substantive idea.[31] As of the time of writing, the same standard remains in place.[32]

A core issue in Schmidt's legal challenge is that the credible argument standard is used even when arguments are highly unlikely to be accepted by courts. Instead of interpreting credibility on the basis of the likelihood of being accepted by courts and thus surviving a judicial challenge, the test used is whether a credible argument can be presented in court to justify the legislation. In defending against the Edgar Schmidt challenge, the attorney general confirmed that the appropriateness of this standard should not be equated with success in litigation. Rather, the mere fact that a court seriously considers the government's argument to defend the legislation, and does not dismiss it as frivolous, justifies use of the credible standard, even in cases where the government loses.[33]

However, this political willingness to use the credible argument standard, even if the minister of justice has serious doubts that it will be a winning argument, negates pressure on decision makers to either find more compliant ways to achieve legislative objectives or be prepared to explain and justify their reasons for not complying with judicial norms. This is significant because the original normative intent of the statutory reporting obligation was to discourage government leaders from approving legislative bills that conflict with protected rights and/or encourage Parliament to hold government to account for legislative choices that violate rights.[34]

Yet the ongoing interpretation of the reporting obligation sends a misleading message to Parliament. By interpreting this standard in a manner that operates intentionally to service the presumption against reporting under s. 4.1, even when decision makers cannot be confident that legislation will survive a Charter challenge, the absence of any s. 4.1 report routinely conveys to Parliament the following message: MPs should assume that the absence of a s. 4.1 report represents the minister of justice's judgment that legislation is consistent with the Charter. In 2013, the Harper government explicitly confirmed that this was the message MPs should draw from the absence of a s. 4.1 report (as discussed below). Yet as more than one lawyer said in interviews, it is difficult to imagine how a lawyer could fail to construct what appears to be a credible argument to justify legislation under the standard being used.[35] Not surprising in light of these criteria, Department of Justice guidelines advise Justice lawyers that the statutory reporting obligation for Charter inconsistency "will only be triggered in rare cases."[36]

There is another way in which the Department of Justice guidelines appear to confirm the basic claims that Schmidt was making about the low standard for determining Charter consistency: the tolerance level of potential judicial invalidation of legislation is so high as to virtually guarantee interpretations that the reporting obligation will not be engaged. According to the guidelines, the statutory reporting obligation for Charter inconsistency is engaged only if the level of risk constitutes the "far end" of the highest category of possible risk, so that a judicial loss is almost certain. In quantitative terms, the high-risk category identifies the likelihood of legislative defeat in the range of 81 to

100 per cent,[37] which implies that the relevant standard for risk is likely in the high-90 per cent range.

Although Schmidt was not successful in his legal action (and has appealed without success the decision), the reason does not appear to be contestation about what standard is being used. Instead, disagreement centres on what the appropriate standard should be. The Federal Court accepted the government's credible argument rather than Schmidt's "more likely than not inconsistent" standard.[38] In upholding the department's interpretation of the statutory reporting obligation, the Court rejected the idea that the minister of justice bears such strong responsibility for ensuring that legislation is consistent with the Charter. One of the many arguments the Court made was that Parliament itself must assume responsibility for ensuring that Charter rights are protected, and thus it "must not place its duties on the shoulders of the other branches, notably on those of the Minister of Justice."[39] Yet it is difficult to understand how Parliament can be expected to fulfil this role if the minister of justice's implicit claim of Charter consistency is based on questionable standards for assessing that consistency and if Parliament lacks the independent legal advice to challenge the persuasiveness of this position.

Although Justice documents suggest that reviewing Charter risks for statutory reporting obligations use different criteria than for the day-to-day Charter evaluations (the Legal Risk Management phase), the fact that such a weak standard is used for certifying that a bill is consistent with the Charter invites the following question: *If government is committed to good-faith efforts to pass Charter-consistent legislation, why is it necessary to adopt such a low standard for judgments about Charter consistency for s. 4.1 statutory reporting purposes?* If policy processes are reasonably characterized by good-faith efforts to ensure that bills are consistent with judicial Charter norms, the necessary amendments should be made to legislative initiatives to address Charter problems before bills are introduced, thus negating apprehension that a robust standard of reporting inconsistency would frequently result in s. 4.1 reports. Alternatively, the minister of justice should be prepared to issue s. 4.1 reports where appropriate and explain the government's reasons for departing from judicial Charter norms (which could trigger pressure to justify why s. 33 is not being invoked). Interviews indicate that bureaucratic attempts to clarify and/or change this standard were blocked and that pressure was placed on government lawyers not to make trouble by raising this issue.[40]

iv) Frequency of Judicial Losses despite Processes for Charter Vetting

A final factor contributing to scepticism that legislative decision making is characterized by good-faith attempts to ensure Charter consistency is the frequency with which federal legislation has been declared unconstitutional despite the various processes in place for identifying and assessing Charter problems. Between 1984 and July 2015, federal legislation or actions were declared unconstitutional on fifty-two occasions.[41] Although good-faith attempts to incorporate or respect judicial norms will not always be successful, particularly when the Court alters its own position on these norms or when case law is underdeveloped or inconsistent, the significant number of losses nevertheless suggests one or both of the following: a "relaxed" approach to how robustly judicial norms operate as constraints on legislation or weak advice.

In sum, neither the possibility of judicial nullification of legislation nor the introduction of a statutory reporting requirement for Charter inconsistency has precipitated the "governing like judges" phenomenon that Stone Sweet equates with European legislatures. At the very least, neither suggests that a high priority is given to risk-averse behaviour in the sense of insulating legislation from the threat of judicial censure. Instead, the Charter has encouraged risk avoidance in the form of refusing to acknowledge awareness when legislation is vulnerable to judicial censure. Successive ministers of justice have refused to interpret the s. 4.1 statutory reporting requirement as an obligation to inform Parliament how Charter consistency is interpreted, and instead they have endorsed weak standards intended to ensure that the reporting obligation is not engaged, no matter how serious the threat of judicial censure.

Why Apprehension of Judicial Censure Does Not Present a More Substantial Constraint on Government Behaviour

The apparent willingness of successive governments to adopt weak standards for satisfying themselves (and Parliament) that legislation is consistent with judicial Charter norms raises the following question: What explains this willingness to risk judicial censure, particularly as government has the resources and operates in an institutional setting where it dominates the legislative process? Stated differently, why do Canadian government leaders choose not to govern like judges in the way Stone Sweet characterizes European legislative behaviour?

Elsewhere, James Kelly and I have written about the importance of understanding the institutional setting in which a bill of rights functions.[42] For Canada, as in the case of similar political systems that have adopted a bill of rights, this setting is characterized by Westminster factors, which include the principle of Parliamentary supremacy;[43] executive dominance of the legislative process; and the centrality of strong, cohesive parties that organize how Parliament functions. Westminster factors function to allow the executive to dominate legislative proceedings, introduce legislation at an advanced stage of development, and regularly exert sufficient power over members of the governing party to support the government and overcome opposition attempts to defeat the government's agenda, particularly in those frequent situations where government has an electoral majority or a stable coalition.

It can be argued that the above factors accommodate integrating judicial norms into legislative decisions. If governments are committed to integrating judicial norms into legislative decision-making processes as a risk-averse strategy to protect their legislative agendas from judicial censure, they will likely encounter relatively weak pressure from parliamentary sceptics of this approach. However, these same Westminster factors can also prove detrimental to this idea if government is determined to pursue non-compliant legislation.

To return to the question of why Canadian governments are not more interested in ensuring that legislation complies with Charter norms, at least as a form of insurance against the prospects of judicial nullification, the significance of Westminster factors in how the Canadian Parliament functions points strongly to the following, blunt, explanation. Governments do not appear to equate their political interests with the goal of significantly reducing the risk of judicial censure, at least where so doing interferes with or distorts their preferred legislative agenda. Moreover, the fact that Parliament rarely addresses Charter issues, is discouraged by the current approach to the s. 4.1 reporting obligation from asking about Charter compliance, and, in any event, generally lacks the power to compel government to justify legislative choices in terms of their consistency with Charter norms, ensures that Parliament provides only a weak check on government behaviour.

The Charter has not diminished the fact that Canadian governments continue to exert strong discipline on their members, including in parliamentary committees. The Canadian Parliament has only rarely exerted sufficient influence on legislation to address Charter concerns,[44] despite having a committee in both houses that addresses legal or constitutional issues (the House of Commons Standing Committee on Justice and Human Rights and the Standing Senate Committee on Legal and Constitutional Affairs). Not only do these committees lack independent legal advice on Charter issues, but they also operate under a norm of intense partisanship and experience of government domination (particularly the Justice Committee). For example, in 2013, the Conservative government exerted substantial pressure on its members on the Justice Committee to defeat an opposition motion to conduct a study on what criteria were used for the minister of justice's determination that a s. 4.1 report of Charter inconsistency was not necessary.[45] The government subsequently tabled a document stating that the absence of a statutory report on Charter inconsistency "means that the Minister had concluded that the government bill was not inconsistent with the Charter."[46] A few months later, after Conservative committee member Brent Rathgeber resigned from the Conservative Party, he acknowledged that intense pressure had been exerted on government members to defeat the motion. Rathgeber indicated that the New Democratic Party's motion precipitated unprecedented activity between the minister of justice's staff and the party whip, with committee members informed "unequivocally that the government doesn't want the study to be done."[47]

Party voting in Canada remains extremely cohesive, reinforced by the control that party leaders exert on MPs' membership in caucus and even their ability to run in the next election. Cohesive party voting not only weakens the ability of committees to propose amendments to legislation, particularly when a government's majority status ensures a majority of members on a committee, but also influences the way issues are debated. Parliamentary debates continue to be framed in binary terms: for or against the government, in which the position that MPs take is dictated overwhelmingly by party affiliation. For whatever reasons, opposition party leaders concentrate only infrequently on Charter consistency as a key focal point in their perpetual challenge to present their party as the alternative to government. Thus, to date, governments have had little reason to fear that rights-based concerns will be regularly marshalled to defeat legislation.

For government leaders, apprehension of judicial censure may be a concern, but it appears to be a distant one. More immediate than consideration of how the Supreme Court might rule if legislation were challenged is the political interest in how to protect the government's legislative agenda from parliamentary delay, substantive amendments, or defeat. Amendments can not only undermine compromises already achieved and delay the pursuit of other goals on an often-crowded agenda but also, politically, be portrayed as a sign of weakness.

Government leaders are all too aware that in the event that legislation is subject to a Charter challenge, the process of litigating and exhausting appeal options delays the need to consider legislative changes. Thus, the task of considering revised legislation may occur several years after legislation is enacted, and this, when assessed from the perspective of the electoral cycle, is likely interpreted as being too distant a concern to be worried about and, therefore, of secondary importance to the more immediate concerns of passing the government's agenda and exploiting its accomplishments on the partisan battlefield. There is no assurance that the government responsible will actually be in office when the time comes to address the implications of a negative judicial ruling. Even if the government is required to pass revised legislation, political leaders have demonstrated their willingness not only to blame the courts for forcing them to take a position they otherwise would not but also to pursue "creative" responses to a prior negative judicial ruling so as to preserve the basic legislative goals that have been impugned, although in ways that do not necessarily comply with the spirit of a judicial ruling (or what Kelly and Hennigar refer to as "notwithstanding by stealth").[48] Although this strategy may again lead to legal challenges if individuals or groups believe it is a non-compliant response, any such challenge will be many years away, and government leaders might calculate that the possibility of this occurring will be constrained by judicial reluctance to censure legislation a second time around.[49]

Conclusions

The processes for identifying Charter difficulties as legislative initiatives are shaped and approved as bills almost certainly influence how legislative bills are framed, particularly when views of how to redress serious Charter inconsistencies do not delay or significantly alter the government's legislative agenda. However, unlike the form of risk aversion that Stone Sweet associates with European legislative behaviour, Canadian governments appear willing to be risk takers. Apprehension of judicial loss in Canada is likely only one consideration and, even at that, is likely a distant one. If characterizing Canadian government behaviour in terms of risk, the more immediate focus is likely on what factors could delay or prevent the government from passing its legislative agenda. Not only are these more politically oriented considerations than judicially influenced ones, they owe their inspiration more to Westminster factors than they do to the Charter. Thus, although it may not be constitutionally ethical behaviour to disregard both the intent of the statutory reporting obligation to report on Charter inconsistency and the constitutional mechanism in place for disagreeing with judicial norms, these practices serve government leaders' short-term interests, and the Westminster factors that shape how our political system functions allow governments to get away with this kind of behaviour.

On a final note, it should be acknowledged that the current Liberal government is rethinking how it identifies potential Charter issues. Although there is no indication that the Department of Justice is using more robust criteria for interpreting whether the s. 4.1 reporting mechanism is engaged, and the minister of justice has not issued any report of Charter inconsistency, the federal government has introduced legislation to require the minister to offer a statement to explain the considerations that support why the government believes a government bill is consistent with the Charter. The government makes clear that these statements are not intended to be interpreted as legal opinions on the constitutionality of a bill, but instead represent a "more open and transparent" way to "inform the parliamentary and public debates on a bill."[50] At the time of writing, the relevant legislation (Bill C-51) has not been passed. Although statements of Charter values are being made even without the legislation in place, it is too soon to assess whether these statements will be robust when identifying Charter problems, whether these statements have any impact on the government's legislative agenda, or what impact, if any, they have on parliamentary deliberation and voting.

NOTES

1 Charles Epp, *The Rights Revolution: Lawyers, Activists, and Supreme Courts in Comparative Perspective* (Chicago: University of Chicago Press, 1998).

2 J. Mitchell Pickerill, *Constitutional Deliberation in Congress: The Impact of Judicial Review in a Separated System* (Durham, NC: Duke University Press, 2004), 133–45.

3 Bruce G. Peabody, "Congressional Attitudes toward Constitutional Interpretation," in *Congress and the Constitution*, ed. Neal Devins and Keith E. Whittington (Durham, NC: Duke University Press, 2005), 9–63.

4 Alec Stone Sweet, *Governing with Judges: Constitutional Politics in Europe* (Oxford: Oxford University Press, 2000), 204.

5 Ibid., 44–5, 50–2.
6 Ibid., 51.
7 Interviews were conducted with several lawyers in the Human Rights Centre at the Department of Justice between 1999 and 2000, on the basis of anonymity. I also had the opportunity for repeated and candid conversations (with attribution granted) with former deputy ministers of justice John Tait (1994–95) and George Thomson (1998–99), Edgar Schmidt (2014–15), and former minister of justice Irwin Cotler (2015), and I conducted interviews on the basis of anonymity with former officials in the department (2014, 2015) (henceforth "Interviews").
8 Interviews.
9 These cases included *Singh v. Minister of Employment and Immigration,* [1985] 1 SCR 177; *Schacter v. Canada,* [1992] 2 SCR 679; and *R v. Oakes,* [1986] 1 SCR 103.
10 James B. Kelly, *Governing with the Charter: Legislative and Judicial Activism and Framers' Intent* (Vancouver, UBC Press, 2005), 232–4.
11 Mary Dawson, "The Impact of the Charter on the Public Policy Process and the Department of Justice," *Osgoode Hall Law Journal* 30 (1992): 597.
12 All statutory bills of rights in New Zealand, the United Kingdom, the Australian Capital Territory (ACT), and the Australian state of Victoria include a statutory reporting obligation to alert Parliament if legislation is inconsistent with protected rights. These reporting obligations vary. Some are made by the attorney general (New Zealand, ACT) or justice minister (Canada), whereas others are made by the sponsoring minister (United Kingdom, Victoria). Some include only government bills (Canada, United Kingdom), some require reports only for inconsistency (Canada, New Zealand), whereas others report both affirmative and negative reports of compatibility (United Kingdom, ACT, Victoria).
13 Interviews.
14 Only one statement of inconsistency was made under the Canadian Bill of Rights. This was in 1975, when an amendment made by the Senate to the Feeds Act included a provision that conflicted with the presumption of innocence. When the bill returned to the House of Commons, the minister of justice reported it as being inconsistent with the Bill of Rights, and the relevant provision was deleted. See Elmer A. Driedger, "The Meaning and Effect of the Canadian Bill of Rights: A Draftsman's Viewpoint," *Ottawa Law Review* 9, no. 1 (1977): 306.
15 In 1985, s. 4.1 was added to the Department of Justice Act by the Statute Law (Canadian Charter of Rights and Freedoms) Amendment Act. S. 4.1 states that the minister shall examine "every Bill introduced in or

presented to the House of Commons by a minister of the Crown, in order to ascertain whether any of the provisions thereof are inconsistent with the purposes and provisions of the *Canadian Charter of Rights and Freedoms* and the Minister shall report any such inconsistency to the House of Commons at the first convenient opportunity."

16 Interviews.

17 Kelly, *Governing with the Charter*, 228.

18 Interviews.

19 Ibid.

20 Department of Justice, "In Our Opinion: Best Practices for Department of Justice Counsel in Providing Legal Advice," April 2012.

21 Interviews.

22 Ibid.

23 Ibid.

24 Ibid.

25 Ibid.

26 Ibid.

27 Ibid.

28 *Edgar Schmidt v. The Attorney General of Canada*, 2016 FC 269, para. 7.

29 Ibid., para. 240.

30 Department of Justice, "In Our Opinion," 9; Federal Court, "Simplified Action, Edgar Schmidt and Attorney General of Canada, Statement of Agreed Facts."

31 *Edgar Schmidt v. The Attorney General of Canada*, 2016 FC 269, para. 243.

32 Ibid., para. 247.

33 Ibid., paras. 250, 252.

34 Janet L. Hiebert, *Charter Conflicts: What Is Parliament's Role?* (Montreal and Kingston: McGill-Queen's University Press, 2002), 4–6.

35 Interviews.

36 Department of Justice, extracts from "Effective Communication of Legal Risk," 2006.

37 Department of Justice, "Legal Risk Management in the Public Sector," 26 November 2007.

38 *Edgar Schmidt v. The Attorney General of Canada*, 2016 FC 269, para. 5.

39 Ibid., para. 276.

40 Interviews.

41 Christopher P. Manfredi, "Conservatives, the Supreme Court, and the Constitution: Judicial-Government Relations, 2006–15," *Osgoode Hall Law Journal* 52, no. 3 (2015), 956. Although the s. 4.1 reporting requirement did not come into effect until 1985, the minister of justice was still required to

report on consistency with the Bill of Rights, which includes many of the same protected rights as the Charter.

42 Janet L. Hiebert and James B. Kelly, *Parliamentary Bills of Rights: The Experiences of New Zealand and the United Kingdom* (Cambridge: Cambridge University Press 2015), 10–15, 401–3; Janet L. Hiebert, "Parliamentary Bills of Rights: Have They Altered the Norms for Legislative Decision-Making?," in *Comparative Constitutional Theory*, ed. Gary Jacobson and Miguel Schor (Cheltenham, UK: Edward Elgar Publishing, 2018).

43 Canada is the exception here. The decision to adopt a constitutional bill of rights in 1982 has effectively replaced the principle of parliamentary supremacy with constitutional supremacy as courts are authorized to interpret and impose remedies when constitutional principles are violated. Although Canadian legislatures can pre-empt or set aside the effects of a judicial ruling for most sections of the Charter for five-year periods (after which the power can be renewed), this does not displace judicial authority over the scope or interpretation of protected rights.

44 A rare exception to Parliament engaging in a robust review of whether a bill is consistent with the Charter occurred when reviewing anti-terrorist measures; see James B. Kelly, "Legislative Activism and Parliamentary Bills of Rights: Institutional Lessons for Canada," in *Contested Constitutionalism: Reflections on the Canadian Charter of Rights and Freedoms*, ed. James B. Kelly and Christopher P. Manfredi (Vancouver: UBC Press, 2010), 93.

45 In February 2013, NDP Justice critic Francoise Boivin put forth a motion to the Justice and Human Rights Committee that a "thorough study" into how s. 4.1 was being interpreted be conducted; see Canada, Parliament, House of Commons, Standing Committee on Justice and Human Rights, Evidence (no. 59, 13 February 2013), 1st Session, 41st Parliament.

46 Statement provided by the parliamentary secretary to the minister of justice, ibid.

47 "MP Brent Rathgeber's Stand Is a Principled One That Should Give the Tories Pause," http://o.canada.com/news/mp-brent-rathgebers-stand-is-a-principled-one-that-should-give-the-tories-pause, 7 June 2013.

48 James B. Kelly and Matthew A. Hennigar, "The Canadian Charter of Rights and the Minister of Justice: Weak-Form Review within a Constitutional Charter of Rights," *International Journal of Constitutional Law* 10, no. 1 (2012): 38–9.

49 These arguments are made in Hiebert, "Parliamentary Bills of Rights."

50 "Charter Statements," Department of Justice website, last modified 12 December 2017, http://www.justice.gc.ca/eng/csj-sjc/pl/charter-charte/index.html.

5 Collaborative Federalism and the Role of the Supreme Court of Canada

ROBERT SCHERTZER

The Canadian Charter of Rights and Freedoms, and its interpretation by the Supreme Court of Canada (SCC), has had a profound impact on politics and public policy in Canada. However, the bright lights focused on the Charter have cast a shadow over other important ways in which the SCC has affected public policy over the last thirty-five years – most notably, its role in the evolution of federalism and intergovernmental relations (IGR).

The goal of this chapter is to refocus on the SCC's impact on federalism and public policy. Whether an issue falls under the responsibility of the federal government or the provinces shapes its objectives and design. Where responsibility is not clear cut, or where the actions of one order of government have an impact on the interests of the other, intergovernmental negotiation and conflict can shape the eventual policy. In short, federalism is a critical contextual factor in the development and implementation of public policy in Canada.

How the orders of government have worked together to develop policy in this context has shifted over time. As is often remarked, IGR in Canada has gone through a series of phases: from initially minimal, as governments operated independently; to cooperative in the 1940s; to conflictual in the 1970s; to collaborative in the mid-1990s.[1] Understanding these approaches to IGR, and what drives the shifts from one to another, is critical to understanding public policy development. While there are many potential drivers, in this chapter, I explore the SCC's role. By focusing on the most recent shift from conflictual to collaborative federalism, we can better understand how the Court has shaped the context of public policy development in Canada.

My argument in this chapter is that the SCC has played a key role in the most recent shift from conflictual to collaborative federalism. In a number of highly contentious federalism cases starting in the 1980s, the Court introduced and reinforced an idea of the federation as an inherently contested order, urging collaborative intergovernmental negotiation over unilateral action to deal with major federal-provincial issues. It has continually reinforced this idea when the federal and provincial governments come to the Court seeking arbitration and, in so doing, has helped push IGR into a period of stable, collaborative action.

The Different Approaches to Intergovernmental Relations

It has become a staple of Canadian political science to categorize and periodize the different approaches to IGR. The scope and complexity of relations between the orders of government means that, at any given time, different IGR approaches are taking place both *across* and *within* policy sectors.[2] Accordingly, countless names describing different approaches to IGR have been coined over the years.[3]

Despite this complexity, it is still possible to identify the *dominant* approach to IGR in a period of time. Differentiation between approaches is observable using three key indicators: (1) the norms framing the federal-provincial relationship, (2) the main institutional processes used to carry out negotiations, and (3) the key outputs stemming from these negotiations.[4] Using these indicators, the principal approaches to IGR identified in the literature become clearer (see table 5.1).[5] One of the main benefits of classifying relations along this "classical-cooperative-conflictual-collaborative" spectrum is that it helps us understand the *context* that federalism and IGR provide for public policymaking in a given period (so long as it is done with conceptual clarity and a recognition of the complexity of relations that take place in and across sectors).

Given the focus in this chapter, it is important to further clarify the foundational norms, institutions, and outputs of the collaborative approach.[6] First, on norms, collaborative IGR is built upon an acceptance of the equality of the two orders of government as joint owners over a number of policy fields.[7] Stemming from this basic position is a related idea that even where governments technically hold exclusive responsibility for an area under the constitution, actions will undoubtedly affect the interest of the other order, and so intergovernmental cooperation is vital for effective and legitimate policy development. The institutions and processes of collaborative IGR reflect these norms through multilateral forums at various levels (sometimes with the participation of

Table 5.1 Overview of Dominant Approaches to IGR in Canada

Approach	Norms	Institutions	Outputs	Period
Classical	Independent orders with exclusive jurisdiction	Constitution (s. 91–92); courts (Judicial Committee of the Privy Council, or JCPC)	Expanding provincial autonomy (through JCPC)	1867–1930s
Cooperative	Overlapping jurisdiction in select areas (social union), with key role for federal government	First ministers' and ministerial meetings; federal spending power	Formal agreements and constitutional amendment (building social union)	1940s–60s
Conflictual	Mandate to protect interests of competing constituencies (national, provincial, ethnic)	First ministers' meetings; SCC	Court decisions and Constitution Act, 1982	1970s–80s
Collaborative	Equal, interdependent orders with shared responsibility in many policy areas	Multilateral, co-chaired forums (first ministers', ministerial, officials')	Non-constitutional, framework agreements (across range of policy sectors)	1990s–present

Quebec, although not always). These forums have a federal-provincial co-chair model and a mandate to carry out *joint* policy development and decision making through free and fair negotiations.[8] Outcomes indicative of the collaborative approach reflect these underlying norms and institutional process,[9] showing a demonstrable commitment to the principle of "diffuse reciprocity."[10]

A detailed account of actor adherence to collaborative federalism is beyond the scope of this chapter and is not necessary since the case has been made elsewhere.[11] While there is debate about recent IGR being truly collaborative,[12] there are many examples of a shift towards norms of shared federal-provincial ownership, the adoption of multilateral institutions, and outputs that reflect principles of diffuse reciprocity in a host of policy sectors. In brief, collaborative federalism is generally seen as emerging in the mid-1990s, with the Agreement on Internal Trade in 1994. This first milestone was followed by an extension of the approach to other key policy sectors:[13] the labour market, with active support in the form of Labour Market Development Agreements in 1996; international trade, with increasing involvement of the provinces in negotiations from 1995 forward;[14] the environment, with the Canada-wide Accord on Environmental Harmonization in 1998; the Social Union Framework Agreement in 1999; health care, with an agreement on a common federal-provincial vision in 2000, followed by the Health Care Accord in 2004; and the establishment of the interprovincial Council of the Federation in 2003.

The shift towards collaborative federalism from the mid-1990s through the early 2000s is often set against the explicit promotion of an alternative approach with the election of Prime Minister Stephen Harper. Through a series of opinion pieces in major newspapers and speeches during the 2006 federal campaign, along with the first two federal budgets in 2006 and 2007, Harper preached the virtues of "open federalism."[15] At its core, open federalism was about a more classical approach, one that stressed the autonomy of the two orders of government, allowing them to exercise their responsibilities independently and unilaterally. A series of unilateral policy changes by the federal government indicated the desire to implement this new approach, notably reforming fiscal transfers (moving towards largely unconditional grants and per capita funding models, along with the change to health care funding announced in 2011).[16] In addition, over his entire tenure as prime minister (2006–15), Harper held only two multilateral meetings with his provincial counterparts. At the same time, there has been debate about the extent to which Harper was actually able to shift approaches: many of his attempts at unilateral action ultimately failed, and considerable multilateral collaboration took place across a number of important sectors (e.g., agriculture, immigration, and labour market policy) during his time in office.[17]

There are a number of perspectives on what drives the shifts between the different approaches to IGR.[18] In this chapter, I argue that the Court plays a critical institutional role in the shifting approaches to IGR, while also recognizing the importance of ideas (particularly those related to identity and the definition of the political community). This broadly neo-institutionalist perspective is premised on the underlying argument that ideas and norms are critical factors shaping institutional dynamics.[19] Ideas and norms – particularly when they are institutionalized – are constitutive elements shaping the context of policy development. When a powerful institutional mechanism like the judiciary promotes particular ideas and norms, these ideas can both structure a legacy of policy outcomes and motivate innovations.

In the area of IGR and public policy, underlying ideas about the ideal processes for working together and the way jurisdiction ought to be shared have a direct impact on public policy outputs. For example, these ideas influence the extent to which public policy is developed and implemented, with a focus on the interests of the federal government, all provinces, particular provinces, or some combination of these parties. When looking at the role of the SCC in institutionalizing these ideas, and thus shaping the context in which IGR is carried out to develop public policy in a more collaborative manner, the key is to uncover how particular ideas related to collaborative federalism were *identified*, *established*, and *reinforced* by the SCC. And to assess the impact of these ideas on public policy development, we also need to look at how these ideas were then incorporated into the norms and institution building of IGR in subsequent periods of time.[20]

The Supreme Court's Role in Intergovernmental Relations

The Court's impact on the shifting approaches to IGR stems principally from its institutional role as the arbiter of intergovernmental conflict. In this capacity, it was particularly important in the shift from conflictual to collaborative IGR, which took place over the 1980s and 1990s.

An apex court's impact on policy development traditionally flows from three related functions: (1) its interpretive approach, (2) its dispute resolution method, and (3) its willingness to occupy a more "political role" and use its power to shape specific aspects of a public policy against the wishes of the legislative or executive branches of government.[21] In the context of the SCC's impact on IGR and how its rulings have shaped the underlying context of federalism, it is the first two of these functions that are the most applicable.

In this respect, the Court's impact on policy as it relates to federalism is a consequence of determining the constitutionality of a federal or provincial law as falling within, or outside, an order of government's jurisdiction. This act of judicial review on federalism grounds tends to involve the interpretation and application of parts VI (on the distribution of legislative powers) and VII (on the judiciary) of the Constitution Act, 1867, while at times also engaging the amending procedures in Part V of the Constitution Act, 1982. In short, federalism cases are about determining *which order of government* has the power to pass a law or take an action, not *whether any government* can pass a law (which is the question in Charter cases).

Through its federalism jurisprudence, the SCC occupies a unique institutional position in the federation: it is the final domestic forum available to manage conflicts that have not been resolved through less adversarial means (such as intergovernmental negotiation). The Court's federalism decisions have a larger effect than simply settling individual conflicts in a particular policy area. SCC decisions – as a whole – provide a framework to guide further negotiations between the federal and provincial governments to work out their respective roles in a wide set of public policy fields. In short: in federalism disputes, the Court is part of the broader institutional arrangement for the management of political conflict between the orders of government, shaping the context in which public policy is made in Canada.

There are a number of theories to explain how the SCC ought to fulfil its role as federal arbiter. The common theme running through the majority of these theories is that the Court must maintain its independence to enforce the constitutional distribution of powers.[22] On this basis, two clear roles for the judiciary are often promoted, and they are aptly captured through the use of metaphor.[23] The first frames the Court as the *umpire* of federal disputes. This is a view that asks the Court to act in a neutral fashion, adjudicating disputes in accordance with the pre-established rules set out in the constitution. It is a perspective stressing restraint as the courts are seen to occupy an important position in the development of the federation, but not the pre-eminent one.[24] The second metaphor frames the Court as the *guardian* of the federation. This view stresses the need for the Court to move beyond simply enforcing the rules to actively protecting the federal pact.[25] It is thus a much more activist position, one built upon a hierarchical understanding of the relationship between the judiciary and Parliament or the executive.[26]

Assessments against these benchmarks that unpack the SCC's effect on the federation have a long lineage in Canadian political science.[27] There are two main themes of this work. The first looks at the nature of the institution's role, with a split between those who frame the SCC as primarily a court of law and those who stress its more political nature.[28] The second theme focuses on the Court's impact on specific policy areas and the balance of power. Here there is an ongoing debate about the extent to which the Court's federal judicial review, on the one hand, is balanced or, on the other, acts as a centralizing force that favours the federal government.[29]

The analysis in the subsequent sections builds upon these two themes to highlight the Court's role in the shifting nature of IGR. In this respect, I treat the Court more as a political institution within the federal system of government than strictly as a court of law. Its place as the final domestic arbiter of intergovernmental conflict gives it the power to shape the dynamics of IGR. At the same time, I take what the SCC says in its decisions seriously. The Court exerts its power through its legal decisions: they introduce ideas, establish and reinforce norms, clarify rules, legitimize (or delegitimize) actions or particular understandings of the constitutional order, and shape the institutional structure. Accordingly, examining how the SCC has interpreted the constitution and managed disputes, paying attention to the legal doctrine, can provide insight into how it has shaped the dynamics of IGR.

To trace the Court's role in the shift from conflictual to collaborative IGR, the subsequent sections examine a number of critical federalism decisions throughout the 1980s, 1990s, and 2000s. A textual review of the decisions highlights how the Court framed the norms, institutions, and outputs of IGR, showing that the SCC was an early – and consistent – promoter of collaborative federalism in key conflicts.

Tracing the Court's Impact: From Conflict to Collaboration

The SCC's role in the turn towards collaborative federalism can be divided into three key phases. In the first phase (approximately 1980 to 1995), the Court was an early promoter of the approach, *identifying and introducing* the foundational ideas and norms. In the second phase (approximately 1996 to 2005), it handed down a number of pivotal decisions, *establishing the core framework* for these ideas and norms. In the third phase (from about 2006 forward), the SCC acted as an important protector of the approach, *reinforcing its validity* in the face of competing (unilateral) approaches.

Identifying the Norms of Collaborative Federalism

The well-documented attempts to establish a constitutional amending formula and Charter of Rights and Freedoms in the late 1970s and early 1980s were a high-water mark of intergovernmental conflict in Canada.[30] The most acute moment was the failed round of negotiations in September 1980, followed by Prime Minister Pierre Trudeau's declaration to take unilateral action by going "over the heads" of the provinces and having the United Kingdom ratify his preferred constitutional package.[31] This move led three provinces to challenge the legality of the federal government seeking an amendment to the constitution without their consent, and this led to the landmark *Patriation Reference* in 1981.[32] This was a complex decision, with two separate majorities: one on the legal right of the federal government to seek the amendment, the other on a convention requiring provincial consent.

The majority on the convention of provincial consent identified a key norm that ultimately became the foundation of the collaborative federalism approach. The clearest expression of this norm was in the framing of the constitution as a global system of rules contested by two equal orders of government. Conventions were clearly identified as part of this global system and violations of them as unconstitutional.[33] In reviewing previous successful and unsuccessful attempts to amend the constitution, the Court found that these intergovernmental negotiations had led to the development of one such constitutional convention requiring a substantial measure of provincial consent when a change engaged their interests.[34] In the Court's own words, "the reason for the rule is the federal principle."[35] Allowing the federal government to unilaterally change the federation would have run counter to the basic principles of the federal system.[36] Identifying this convention, and rationalizing its presence as protecting the federal principle, presented a powerful norm – the equality of the two orders of government in the design and functioning of the federation – that informed subsequent intergovernmental negotiation on the constitution.

This pro-provincial position must be placed in the context of the majority ruling on the legal question. Using positivist logic and textual analysis, the other majority clarified that, technically, the federal government could unilaterally seek amendments from the United Kingdom.[37] As part of this ruling, the legal majority was also clear that the Constitution Act, 1867 granted considerable power to the federal government.[38] This element of the decision thus acted as a counterbalance to the convention ruling, mitigating the possibility that subsequent negotiations would be handcuffed by provincial intransigence or insistence on unanimity to establish the constitutional amendment package. Granting validity to *both* the need for provincial consent *and* the technical ability of the federal government to move ahead with the changes was critical to setting up the conditions that would allow the orders to move beyond the previous impasse.[39]

These two features of the reference – identifying and introducing key norms of the collaborative federalism approach and facilitating the use of IGR institutions to manage conflict – were carried forward in a number of subsequent decisions in this period. Notable here is *Multiple Access* in 1982,[40] a case that upheld both provincial and federal laws regulating insider trading operating in parallel systems. The rationale for this decision highlighted the broad scope of both federal and provincial powers to regulate economic activity[41] and the idea that such overlap was an inherent part of federalism that required intergovernmental collaboration.[42] The inherent overlap of responsibilities in a federation was repeated in a number of subsequent decisions in this period.[43] And it is from this view that the Court often promoted the value and need for intergovernmental collaboration: as it said in *R. v. S(S)* in 1990, "the balancing of national interests and local concerns has been accomplished by a constitutional structure that both permits and encourages federal-provincial cooperation."[44]

In many of these decisions, the Court was doing more than introducing these norms; it was also facilitating negotiation to manage conflict. For example, in *Newfoundland Continental Shelf*,[45] the SCC ruled that the federal government had rights over natural resources, which the province was seeking control over; this seeming win for the federal government, however, was delivered in response to a Newfoundland Court of Appeal ruling that, following a heated, decades-long dispute, had favoured the province. The result was that both sides' positions were validated, and the subsequent negotiations over the management of offshore resources were productive.[46]

The sporadic identification of these norms and facilitation of IGR negotiation should not imply that these ideas were the Court's dominant view of federalism in this period. While building on earlier precedent, these ideas were still only emerging elements of the Court's federalism jurisprudence. This emergent perspective can be contrasted with the more classical notions of federalism and a tendency to favour a centralist view of the federation that were the foundation of the SCC's approach to federalism in this period. This tendency was exemplified in *Bell Canada v. Quebec*, which widened the scope of the inter-jurisdictional immunity doctrine.[47] This decision reaffirmed (and expanded) an earlier line of precedent that had rejected the value of overlapping jurisdictions in favour of protecting federal government undertakings from the effect of provincial laws.[48] Similarly, over this period, the Court handed down a number of decisions that significantly expanded the federal government's criminal law power[49] and significantly favoured a centralist view of the federation.[50] Perhaps most tellingly, in 1991, the Court explicitly allowed the federal government to unilaterally alter funding agreements related to health care and social services that it had previously negotiated with the provinces.[51]

Establishing the Norms of Collaborative Federalism

Quebec's 1995 secession referendum was a critical turning point for the SCC's approach to federalism. Following the narrow vote against secession (50.6 per cent), the federal government adopted a two-pronged strategy to combat the separatist movement (so-called Plans A and B). Plan A was showing Quebecers the promise of federalism. Plan B was taking a firm stance, showing the costs of independence. The keystone of Plan B was a reference to the SCC on the legality of Quebec unilaterally declaring independence. The Court's response, handed down in 1998, is among the most important – and widely discussed – decisions it has ever given. The *Secession Reference*[52] is simultaneously heralded and criticized for its astute political wisdom in seeking a compromise position on the secession of Quebec based on unwritten constitutional principles.[53] Setting much of this debate aside, what is critical to the argument here is how the Court conceived of the federation in this reference and how this vision became the core of its subsequent federalism jurisprudence.

In the *Secession Reference*, the Court framed the federation as a contested normative order that required collaboration and negotiation to be an effective and legitimate system. In the first part of the decision, reflecting on the nature of Canadian federalism, the SCC clearly recognized the validity of the main competing conceptions of the federation (e.g., as a centralized, pan-Canadian system; a compact among equal provinces; or an asymmetrical order stemming from a compact among nations). For example, it framed the federation as a "unified country, not a loose alliance of autonomous provinces," while also saying that "the point [of federalism] was not to weld the provinces into one" or to "subordinate" them to the federal government, and the "social and demographic reality of Quebec ... was one of the essential reasons for establishing a federal structure."[54] Critically, the Court then outlined how the federal and constitutional system incorporated these competing understandings into "a continuous process of discussion" that was built on "compromise, negotiation and deliberation."[55]

It is on this basis that the SCC constructed the main elements of its decision. Technically (under domestic and international law), a province could not unilaterally declare independence in Canada; however, the underlying principles of the constitution (federalism among them) meant that, with a clear question and a clear result, there would be a duty for all parties to negotiate independence in good faith. This rejection of a zero-sum outcome also outlined how the judiciary could explicitly facilitate negotiation through its articulation of (a free and fair) framework for the duty to negotiate following any future referendum. In this regard, the decision pushed the orders of government to manage any ongoing conflict on this issue through that framework and its related political processes.

The normative foundations of collaborative federalism established in the *Secession Reference* were further elaborated in subsequent decisions in this period. For example, in *Siemens v. Manitoba,* the Court was clear that the regulation of gambling fell under both provincial responsibilities (property and civil rights and local matters) and federal responsibilities (the criminal law).[56] The Court went on to highlight that, in cases such as this – in which the federal and provincial governments agreed to share the legislative field, and where their regulatory schemes reflected intergovernmental cooperation – deference should be shown.[57] Highlighting the shared nature of policy fields, the ability of each order to pass laws, even if they had an effect on the other's responsibilities, and placing value on federal-provincial cooperation were the hallmarks of a number of other decisions in the period.[58]

Fédération des producteurs de volailles du Québec tied many of these ideas together into a coherent vision for federalism and IGR.[59] In this case, the Court found a federal-provincial scheme on the interprovincial and international trade of poultry (particularly relating to the setting of national and provincial production quotas) constitutionally valid, even though this power should, according to the text of the constitution, reside in the federal government's domain. In reinforcing the validity of this negotiated framework for regulating the sector, the SCC framed its role in the federal system as necessarily deferring to federal-provincial schemes that allowed for a flexible operationalization of the division of powers through negotiation and cooperation.[60]

Reinforcing the Norms of Collaborative Federalism

As noted above, in 2006, Prime Minister Stephen Harper came to power explicitly promoting a shift in the approach to IGR in Canada. This approach, at its core, stressed the autonomous nature of the responsibilities of the two orders of government and, thus, an inbuilt preference for unilateral action.

It is in this context – in which a powerful actor was promoting an approach to IGR that challenged the basic tenets of the collaborative model – that the Court handed down one of the clearest expressions of the norms of collaborative federalism in its 2007 decision, *Canadian Western Bank*.[61] This decision largely rejected the idea that each order of government's jurisdiction had a "basic, minimum and unassailable" core that was immune from the application of another government's legislation (the inter-jurisdictional immunity doctrine).[62] Building on this view, the Court clearly and explicitly articulated that the "dominant tide" of constitutional interpretation recognized the overlapping nature of federal and provincial jurisdictions and "the importance of co-operation among governmental actors to ensure that federalism operates flexibly."[63] This foundational view of the federation – as a system of overlapping and shared responsibilities necessitating cooperation – was further reinforced in a series of decisions in this period that continued to narrow the application of the inter-jurisdictional immunity doctrine.[64]

The other hallmark of this period is the Court's consistent reinforcement of the validity of collaborative approaches to IGR in the face of (largely federal) unilateral action. Notable here is the 2011 *Securities Reference*, in which the Court rejected a federal plan to unilaterally establish a pan-Canadian body to replace provincial securities regulators.[65] Instead, the SCC said, "It is open to the federal government and the provinces to exercise their respective powers over securities harmoniously," urging that "a cooperative approach might usefully be explored ... to ensure that each level of government properly discharges its responsibilities to the public in a coordinated fashion."[66] Similarly, the 2014 *Supreme Court Act Reference* rejected the federal government's attempt to change the rules relating to the appointment of justices from Quebec, clarifying that such changes would affect the composition of the Court, which, under section 41(d) of the Constitution Act, 1982, required the unanimous consent of the provinces.[67] The importance of protecting provincial interests in the design of federal institutions was further reaffirmed in the *Senate Reform Reference*.[68] The rejection of a series of proposed unilateral changes to the tenure and appointment of senators in this decision was explicitly based on a view of the federation that privileged intergovernmental negotiation and cooperation.[69]

In short, in this period, the Court clearly reinforced a "modern cooperative approach to federalism" in the face of an emerging alternative approach that emphasized the autonomy and independence of the two orders.[70]

Considering the Court's Role in a Collaborative Approach to Federalism

These three phases of the Court's federalism jurisprudence have played a critical role in the transition from broadly conflictual to largely collaborative IGR. In the period from 1980 to 1995, the Court identified and introduced a set of ideas and norms regarding the equal status of the two orders of government as constitutional conventions and key considerations in the management of intergovernmental disputes through cooperation. These ideas informed the design of subsequent federal-provincial agreements that marked the transition from a conflictual to a collaborative relationship. From 1996 to 2005, the SCC further elaborated on these norms, framing the federation as a complex system of overlapping responsibilities that required intergovernmental negotiation and cooperation to maintain its legitimacy and effectiveness. These two aspects – joint federal-provincial ownership of a number of areas and the need for cooperation – were the hallmarks of the various federal-provincial agreements in this period that signalled the transition to a largely collaborative approach to IGR. From 2006 to 2015, the Court repeatedly reinforced the validity of the collaborative model when faced with arguments about the independence or autonomy of the two orders' responsibilities or federal unilateral action. These decisions were critical in heading off unilateral action in a number of areas.

This account should not be taken as saying that the Court, alone, has driven the shifts in the approach to IGR. There are numerous explanations for the changing dynamics of IGR, both external (e.g., economic and social) and internal (e.g., other institutional features). The argument here is that the Court's adoption and promotion of the norms and processes of collaborative federalism is *among the necessary conditions* for the turn towards this approach in Canada. This necessity stems from its institutional role as the federal arbiter. Its function of arbitrating intergovernmental disputes provides it with significant power to affect both the evolution of the system and the behaviour of IGR actors. Identifying collaborative norms as part of the constitutional system, establishing a coherent model for collaborative federalism, and reinforcing its validity when challenged created the framework for – and pushed IGR actors towards – a collaborative approach over the past thirty-five years. This line of jurisprudence codified the ideas and norms of IGR, while also signalling the evolving, preferred approach of the Court to managing intergovernmental disputes (further structuring the strategic calculations of IGR actors). At the same time, this role *alone is not sufficient* to bring about the shift from conflictual to collaborative IGR: the normative and institutional drivers of this shift in IGR are numerous, to say nothing of the powerful external influences.

This understanding of the Court's role – as a critical, if not ultimately *the* critical, factor in the dynamics of IGR – may also help explain why it adopted an evolving preference for the collaborative federalism model. There are different theories seeking to explain judicial behaviour, from accounts stressing the individual preferences of judges to the structuring power of the law.[71] However, seeing the SCC as an important federal institution draws attention to how this institutional role can shape its decision making: as part of the federal system of government, the Court is motivated to preserve the legitimacy of the system.[72] From this perspective, promoting a novel collaborative approach to IGR in the face of a series of legitimacy crises for the federation is a logical development in the Court's approach to managing intergovernmental disputes.

Such crises marked the outset of all three periods of the SCC's evolving jurisprudence on collaborative federalism. In the early 1980s, the long-standing impasse on adopting a bill of rights and constitutional amending formula came to a critical juncture, exposing the inability of federal and provincial officials to work together in the interests of the country without a significant push from the Court. In 1995, the near-collapse of the federation pushed the Court to find a way, when it was asked, to reimagine the system as able to accommodate the competing perspectives on its very nature through free and fair negotiation. And in 2006, after developing the norms and promoting this "dominant tide" of collaborative federalism, a new challenge emerged in the form of open federalism, with the Court continually rejecting the validity of federal unilateral action.

At the same time, a number of recent federalism decisions indicate that the Court is grappling with the limits of the collaborative model.[73] Most notable here is *Quebec v. Canada*,[74] in which Quebec attempted to stop the federal government from destroying records following the cancellation of the federal firearms registry. Quebec argued that the federal plan would violate the principles of collaborative federalism. The Court rejected this argument, saying, "The principle of cooperative federalism ... cannot be seen as imposing limits on the otherwise valid exercise of legislative competence."[75] While the Court softened its position slightly in the subsequent decision of *Rogers Communications v. Châteauguay*, it employed the line of reasoning that collaborative federalism could not override the division of powers.[76] Notwithstanding these decisions – which are as much about the enforceability of constitutional conventions overriding the text of the constitution as they are about the Court's preferred vision of federalism – the trend of the Court's federalism jurisprudence is clear. Its other most recent, and more high-profile, decisions in the *Senate Reference* and the *Supreme Court Reference* clearly reinforced the norms and institutional processes of the collaborative federalism model.

Building on this point, moving forward, we can expect that the Court will continue to reinforce the validity of the collaborative approach to IGR in its federalism jurisprudence. In this respect, its continued hostility towards unilateral action that has a significant impact on the other order of government is the likeliest manifestation of support for collaborative federalism.

At the same time, the jurisprudence discussed in this chapter has created an important legacy, one that can be expected to continue to shape actor behaviour, pushing governments away from such unilateral action. This legacy is more than a simple set of precedents that will inform future decisions of the SCC when it is called upon to intervene in a conflict (although this is one element). This jurisprudence has helped to codify the norms of collaborative federalism, establishing their place in the broader constitutional architecture of the state. This ideational force – part of the context of public policy development – can be expected to exert a pull on actors from both orders of government as they work to develop new public policies. In short, the SCC has shaped the context in which governments develop and negotiate public policies in areas of shared or intersecting jurisdictions.

Acceptance of the value of collaborative IGR is evident in the approach of Prime Minister Justin Trudeau. A number of his federal government's early, high-profile policy moves have largely been based on a collaborative approach to IGR: working with the provinces to enhance the Canada Pension Plan, developing a federal-provincial framework to deal with climate change, vowing to negotiate with Indigenous peoples on a nation-to-nation basis, and showing a broader commitment to engaging stakeholders using a seeming model of government-as-consultation. However, this early commitment to a more collaborative approach to IGR still needs to be placed in the context of a nascent pan-Canadianism, which is evident in some of the federal government's early moves. The reforms to the SCC appointment process, for example, sought to privilege a pan-Canadian identity over regional representation: the process was initially opened up to individuals from across the country for the vacant Atlantic seat, and the qualifications now include the necessity that appointments be bilingual. Similarly, the pan-Canadian agreement on climate change signed in 2016 – with its foundation of a *national* price on carbon – tested the limits of a multilateral, collaborative approach to federalism, with considerable federal-provincial conflict and a refusal from two provinces (Saskatchewan and Manitoba) to sign the initial agreement.

Even if we assume that there will be a continued commitment on both the federal and the provincial sides to a collaborative approach to IGR, the Court's role should not be minimized. The collaborative approach necessitates considerable intergovernmental interaction, negotiation, and coordination. In such an environment, even within the normative force of the broad model, conflict is inherent and unavoidable: it is wrong to assume that collaboration is all "sunny ways." Collaboration necessitates compromise and the acceptance of a measure of diffuse reciprocity on the part of both the federal and the provincial governments, which sometimes requires conflict to reach. In this regard, a collaborative era of IGR does not diminish the SCC's role: while it may result in fewer cases reaching the bench,[77] when actors do test the parameters of their allowable actions through unilateral moves, for example, it is critical that the Court exercise its power to bring them back into line with the model. Indeed, one of the observations from the analysis in this chapter is that, in the face of potential new approaches, the Court can exert its influence to reinforce the value of the collaborative model.

NOTES

1 Richard Simeon and Ian Robinson, "The Dynamics of Canadian Federalism," in *Canadian Politics,* ed. James Bickerton and Alain Gagnon (Peterborough, ON: Broadview Press, 2004).
2 Robert Schertzer, Andrew McDougall, and Grace Skogstad, "Collaboration and Unilateral Action: Recent Intergovernmental Relations in Canada," *IRPP Study* 62 (December 2016); Grace Skogstad and Herman Bakvis, "Conclusion: Taking Stock of Canadian Federalism," in *Canadian Federalism: Performance, Effectiveness, and Legitimacy,* 3rd ed., ed. Herman Bakvis and Grace Skogstad (Don Mills, ON: Oxford University Press, 2012), 340.
3 See, e.g., James Bickerton, "Deconstructing the New Federalism," *Canadian Political Science Review* 4, no. 2–3 (2010): 56–72.
4 Robert Schertzer, "Intergovernmental Relations in Canada's Immigration System: From Bilateralism towards Multilateral Collaboration," *Canadian Journal of Political Science* 48, no. 2 (2015): 383–412; Julie M. Simmons and Peter Graefe, "Assessing the Collaboration That Was 'Collaborative Federalism' 1996–2006," *Canadian Political Science Review* 7, no. 1 (2013): 25–36.
5 See, e.g., Simeon and Robinson, "The Dynamics of Canadian Federalism"; David Cameron and Richard Simeon, "Intergovernmental Relations in Canada: The Emergence of Collaborative Federalism," *Publius* 32, no. 2 (2002): 49–72.
6 See Schertzer, McDougall, and Skogstad, "Collaboration and Unilateral Action," from which this paragraph is largely drawn.
7 Cameron and Simeon, "Intergovernmental Relations in Canada," 49, 54; Harvey Lazar, "The Intergovernmental Dimensions of the Social Union: A Sectoral Analysis," *Canadian Public Administration* 49, no. 1 (2006): 28–9.
8 Cameron and Simeon, "Intergovernmental Relations in Canada," 61–3.
9 Simmons and Graefe, "Assessing the Collaboration," 30–2.
10 See Schertzer, "Intergovernmental Relations in Canada's Immigration System"; John Ruggie, "Multilateralism: The Anatomy of an Institution,"

in *Multilateralism Matters: The Theory and Praxis of an Institutional Form*, ed. John Ruggie (New York: Columbia University Press, 1993), 11.

11 See, e.g., Cameron and Simeon, "Intergovernmental Relations in Canada"; Yulia Mineava, "Canadian Federalism Uncovered: The Assumed, the Forgotten and the Unexamined in Collaborative Federalism" (PhD diss., University of Ottawa, 2012).

12 Simmons and Graefe, "Assessing the Collaboration."

13 This analysis largely draws from Cameron and Simeon, "Intergovernmental Relations in Canada," 55–61.

14 See Grace Skogstad, "International Trade Policy and the Evolution of Canadian Federalism," in *Canadian Federalism: Performance, Effectiveness, and Legitimacy*, 3rd ed., ed. Herman Bakvis and Grace Skogstad (Don Mills, ON: Oxford University Press, 2012), 207–8.

15 See James Bickerton, "Deconstructing the New Federalism"; Keith G. Banting et al., *Open Federalism: Interpretations, Significance* (Kingston: Institute of Intergovernmental Relations, Queen's University, 2006).

16 See Ken Bossenkool and Sean Speer, "How Stephen Harper's Open Federalism Changed Canada for the Better," *Maclean's* (2015); Graham Fox, "Harper's 'Open Federalism': From Fiscal Imbalance to 'Effective Collaborative Management' of the Federation," *Policy Options* (2007).

17 Schertzer, McDougall, and Skogstad, "Collaboration and Unilateral Action"; Christopher Dunn, "Harper without Jeers, Trudeau without Cheers: Assessing 10 Years of Intergovernmental Relations," *IRPP Insight* 8 (2016).

18 For an overview, see Jörg Broschek and Mireille Paquet, "Context, Mechanisms and Process-Tracing in Comparative Federalism Research: Taking Stock" (paper presented at the Canadian Political Science Association Annual Meeting, Calgary, 2016).

19 James G. March and Johan P. Olsen, "The New Institutionalism: Organizational Factors in Political Life," *American Political Science Review* 78, no. 3 (1984): 734–49.

20 I would like to thank Grace Skogstad for this insight.

21 See Malcolm Feeley and Edward Rubin, *Judicial Policy Making and the Modern State: How the Courts Reformed America's Prisons* (Cambridge: Cambridge University Press, 1999), 1–25.

22 See Daniel Halberstam, "Comparative Federalism and the Role of the Judiciary," in *The Oxford Handbook of Law and Politics*, ed. Keith Whittington, R. Daniel Kelemen, and Gregory Caldeira (Oxford: Oxford University Press, 2008).

23 Donna Greschner, "The Supreme Court, Federalism, and Metaphors of Moderation," *Canadian Bar Review* 79, no. 2 (2000): 47–76.

24 See Peter Russell, "Constitutional Reform of the Canadian Judiciary," *Alberta Law Review* 7, no. 1 (1969): 103–23; W.R. Lederman, "Unity and Diversity in Canadian Federalism: Ideals and Methods of Moderation," *Canadian Bar Review* 53 (1975): 615; Greschner, "The Supreme Court," 56–7, 61.

25 Greschner, "The Supreme Court," 54.

26 Ibid.

27 See Peter Hogg, *Constitutional Law of Canada,* student ed. (Toronto: Carswell, 2009), particularly chaps. 8 and 15; Peter Russell, *Constitutional Odyssey: Can Canadians Become a Sovereign People?* (Toronto: University of Toronto Press, 2004); Katherine Swinton, *The Supreme Court of Canada and Canadian Federalism: The Laskin-Dickson Years* (Toronto: Carswell, 1990); James Kelly and Michael Murphy, "Shaping the Constitutional Dialogue on Federalism: Canada's Supreme Court as Meta-political Actor," *Publius* 35, no. 2 (2005): 217–43; Alan Cairns, "The Judicial Committee and Its Critics," *Canadian Journal of Political Science* 4, no.3 (1971): 301–45.

28 The former position is exemplified in Hogg, *Constitutional Law of Canada;* and Gerald Baier, *Courts and Federalism: Judicial Doctrine in the United States, Australia and Canada* (Vancouver: UBC Press, 2006), while the latter perspective is exemplified in Paul Weiler, *In the Last Resort: A Critical Study of the Supreme Court of Canada* (Toronto: Carswell-Methuen, 1974); Patrick Monahan, "At Doctrine's Twilight: The Structure of Canadian Federalism," *University of Toronto Law Journal* 34, no. 1 (1984): 47–99; and Robert Schertzer, *The Judicial Role in a Diverse Federation: Lessons from the Supreme Court of Canada* (Toronto: University of Toronto Press, 2016).

29 In this debate, some authors argue that the Court is generally a balanced federal arbiter; see Peter Hogg, "Is the Supreme Court of Canada Biased in Constitutional Cases?," *Canadian Bar Review* 57, no. 4 (1979): 721–39; Baier, *Courts and Federalism;* and Gerald Baier, "The Courts, the Constitution, and Dispute Resolution," in *Canadian Federalism: Performance, Effectiveness, and Legitimacy,* 3rd ed., ed. Herman Bakvis and Grace Skogstad (Don Mills, ON: Oxford University Press, 2012), 79–95. Others argue that the SCC tends to favour the central government; see, among others, André Bzdera, "Comparative Analysis of Federal High Courts: A Political Theory of Judicial Review," *Canadian Journal of Political Science* 26, no. 1 (1993): 3–29; Jean Leclair, "The Supreme Court of Canada's Understanding of Federalism: Efficiency at the Expense of Diversity," *Queen's Law Journal* 28, no. 2 (2003): 411–53; and Eugénie Brouillet, *La négation de la nation: L'identité culturelle québécoise et le fédéralisme canadien* (Sillery, QC: Éditions du Septentrion, 2005).

30 For an overview, see Keith Banting and Richard Simeon, eds., *And No One Cheered: Federalism, Democracy and the Constitution Act* (Toronto: Methuen Publications, 1983); Russell, *Constitutional Odyssey*, chaps. 7–8.

31 See Russell, *Constitutional Odyssey*, 107.

32 *Reference re Resolution to Amend the Constitution*, [1981] 1 SCR 753.

33 Ibid. at 883–4.

34 Ibid. at 905.

35 Ibid.

36 Ibid. at 906–9.

37 On the reasoning, see *Patriation Reference* at 773–87.

38 Ibid. at 801–2.

39 Sujit Choudhry and Jean-Francois Gaudreault-DesBiens, "Frank Iacobucci as Constitution Maker: From the Quebec Veto Reference to the Meech Lake Accord and the Quebec Secession Reference," *University of Toronto Law Journal* 57, no. 2 (2007): 165–93.

40 *Multiple Access Ltd. v. McCutcheon*, [1982] 2 SCR 161.

41 Ibid. at 170, 173–4, 176–7, 179–80, 186–7.

42 Ibid. at 180–3, 187–91.

43 See, e.g., *Ontario (Attorney General) v. OPSEU*, [1987] 2 SCR 2, which was about the ability of Ontario to regulate the participation of its public servants in federal elections; see at 141, "The plain fact is that even in a federation with divided jurisdictions, the object of the political discourse, the ultimate form of political activity, remains indivisible."

44 *R. v. S.(S.)*, [1990] 2 SCR 254; see also *R. v. Furtney*, [1991] 3 SCR 89.

45 *Reference re Newfoundland Continental Shelf*, [1984] 1 SCR 86.

46 See Katherine Swinton, "Federalism under Fire: The Role of the Supreme Court of Canada," *Law and Contemporary Problems* 55, no. 1 (1992): 139; Patrick Monahan, *Politics and the Constitution: The Charter, Federalism and the Supreme Court of Canada* (Agincourt, ON: Carswell, 1987), 9.

47 *Bell Canada v. Quebec (Commission de la santé et de la sécurité du travail)*, [1988] 1 SCR 749.

48 See Hogg, *Constitutional Law of Canada*, 394–5.

49 See, in particular, *A.G. (Can) v. Can. Nat. Transportation, Ltd.*, [1983] 2 SCR 206; see also *Attorney General of Alberta et al. v. Putnam et al.*, [1981] 2 SCR 267; *Westendorp v. the Queen*, [1983] 1 SCR 43; *Bisaillon v. Keable*, [1983] 2 SCR 60; *R. v. Wetmore*, [1983] 2 SCR 284; *Skoke-Graham v. The Queen*, [1985] 1 SCR 106; *R. v. Big M Drug Mart Ltd.*, [1985] 1 SCR 295; *Scowby v. Glendinning*, [1986] 2 SCR 226; *Knox Contracting Ltd. v. Canada*, [1990] 2 SCR 338; *R. v. Swain*, [1991] 1 SCR 933; *R. v. Morgentaler*, [1993] 3 SCR 463; *RJR-MacDonald Inc. v. Canada (Attorney General)*, [1995] 3 SCR 199.

50 E.g., *Ontario Hydro v. Ontario (Labour Relations Board)*, [1993] 3 SCR 327. The majority in this case significantly expanded the scope of the declaratory power, allowing the federal government to declare a work for the general advantage of Canada (here the regulation of matters relating to atomic power generation).
51 *Reference Re Canada Assistance Plan (B.C.)*, [1991] 2 SCR 525.
52 *Reference re Secession of Quebec*, [1998] 2 SCR 217.
53 For an overview, see Schertzer, *Judicial Role in a Diverse Federation*, chap. 4.
54 *Secession Reference* at paras. 96, 58, 59.
55 Ibid. at para. 68.
56 *Siemens v. Manitoba (Attorney General)*, 2003 SCC 3, [2003] 1 SCR 6 at para. 22.
57 Ibid. at paras. 33–5.
58 See *Law Society of British Columbia v. Mangat*, 2001 SCC 67, [2001] 3 SCR 113 (on legal representation at immigration tribunals); *Kitkatla Band v. British Columbia (Minister of Small Business, Tourism and Culture)*, 2002 SCC 31, [2002] 2 SCR 146 (on provincial laws relating to Aboriginal culture); *Ward v. Canada (Attorney General)*, 2002 SCC 17, [2002] 1 SCR 569 (on the seal hunt); *Paul v. British Columbia (Forest Appeals Commission)*, 2003 SCC 55, [2003] 2 SCR 585 (on administrative tribunals and Aboriginal title); *Reference re Same-Sex Marriage*, 2004 SCC 79, [2004] 3 SCR 698 (on the effect of federal laws on provincial power over solemnization of marriage); and *Reference re Employment Insurance Act (Can.), ss. 22 and 23*, 2005 SCC 56, [2005] 2 SCR 669 (on maternity benefits).
59 *Fédération des producteurs de volailles du Québec v. Pelland*, 2005 SCC 20, [2005] 1 SCR 292.
60 Ibid. at para. 38.
61 *Canadian Western Bank v. Alberta*, 2007 SCC 22, [2007] 2 SCR 3.
62 Ibid. at para. 33.
63 Ibid. at paras. 35–42. For a similar line of analysis, focusing on the importance of this decision, see Wade Wright, "Facilitating Intergovernmental Dialogue: Judicial Review of the Division of Powers in the Supreme Court of Canada," *Supreme Court Law Review* 51, no. 2 (2010): 625–93.
64 See, e.g., *Bank of Montreal v. Marcotte* 2014 SCC 55, [2014] 2 SCR 725; *Marcotte v. Fédération des caisses Desjardins du Québec* 2014 SCC 57, [2014] 2 SCR 805; *Amex Bank of Canada v. Adams* 2014 SCC 56, [2014] 2 SCR 787. Also see *Tsilhqot'in Nation v. British Columbia* 2014 SCC 44, [2014] 2 SCR 256, where the Court rejected using inter-jurisdictional immunity to protect a broad, central government power over Indigenous peoples. See also *Marine Services International Ltd. v. Ryan Estate* 2013 SCC 44, [2013] 3 SCR 53; *Canada*

(Attorney General) v. PHS Community Services Society 2011 SCC 44, [2011] 3 SCR 134.

65 *Reference re Securities Act*, 2011 SCC 66, [2011] 3 SCR 837.

66 Ibid. at para. 9.

67 *Reference re Supreme Court Act, ss. 5 and 6*, 2014 SCC 21, [2014] 1 SCR 433 at paras. 82, 93.

68 *Reference re Senate Reform*, 2014 SCC 32, [2014] 1 SCR 704.

69 Ibid. at paras. 67, 97, 110.

70 See *Bank of Montreal* at para. 63.

71 For an overview of the main perspectives, applied to the Canadian context, see Emmett Macfarlane, *Governing from the Bench: The Supreme Court of Canada and the Judicial Role* (Vancouver: UBC Press, 2013), chap. 1.

72 Robert Schertzer, "Recognition or Imposition? Federalism, National Minorities and the Supreme Court of Canada," *Nations and Nationalism* 14, no. 1 (2008): 105–26; Schertzer, *Judicial Role in a Diverse Federation*.

73 See Eric Adams, "Judging the Limits of Collaborative Federalism," *Supreme Court Law Review* (North York, ON: LexisNexis Canada, 2016).

74 *Quebec (Attorney General) v. Canada (Attorney General)*, 2015 SCC 14, [2015] 1 SCR 693.

75 Ibid. at para. 19.

76 See *Rogers Communications Inc. v. Châteauguay (City)*, 2016 SCC 23.

77 See Baier, "The Courts, the Constitution, and Dispute Resolution," 79–95.

6 The Impact of Constitutional References on Institutional Reform

KATE GLOVER BERGER

This chapter assesses the impact of the Supreme Court of Canada's constitutional advisory opinions on the creation and reform of public institutions in Canada. Federal and provincial governments have long sought judicial opinions on the constitutionality of institutional reform policies. The resulting references have considered government plans to establish or reconfigure residential tenancies boards,[1] the Senate,[2] the Supreme Court,[3] a national securities regulator,[4] a firearms registry,[5] agricultural marketing agencies,[6] school boards,[7] courts,[8] and so on. The history of these references reveals a judiciary that is confident in its advisory role and governments that are willing, for a range of reasons, to initiate the advisory process.

Mindful of the deep history of references respecting institutional reform policy, this chapter starts from an acknowledgment of the powerful impact that reference decisions can have on government initiatives, sometimes declaring unlawful the realization of particular proposals by way of the government's preferred route. We will see this powerful effect in three of the cases explored in this chapter. And it is in appreciation of this meaningful impact that this chapter adopts a forward-looking perspective, striving to explore the relevance of present judicial "advice" to the future of institutional design and reform policy in Canada.

This chapter proceeds in two parts. In the first section, it aims to capture the current moment in the history of constitutional advisory opinions dealing with institutional reform in the federal sphere. It looks to four case studies from the current generation of references, two dealing with institutional reform (the *Senate Reform Reference* and the *Supreme Court Act Reference*) and two dealing with the creation of new entities (the *Securities Reference* and the *Firearms Reference*). As we will see, these cases reveal the significant impact that advisory opinions can have on a government's institutional reform initiatives. There is a meaningful risk for governments that test their policy preferences by way of a reference: the risk that their approach – whether already implemented or simply proposed – will be declared unconstitutional. While the cases also show that the Court turns its mind to alternative routes by which policy goals can be pursued, no government that sought a reference opinion in the four case studies has since taken up those alternatives.

In the second section, this chapter anticipates the future, offering a framework of legal considerations that should guide policymakers as they seek to create and reform public institutions in the future. This framework, which emerges from the reasoning and outcomes of the case studies, identifies constitutional aims and constraints that, from a legal perspective, govern the design of public institutions in Canada. As discussed below, these aims and constraints flow primarily from the structural dimensions of the constitution – that is, from constitutional principle, the amending procedures, the division of powers, and the overall architecture of Canada's public order.[9] While the Canadian Charter of Rights and Freedoms necessarily contributes to the framework, its guarantees have not been the basis for major disputes over institutional reform in the federal sphere.

This chapter concludes by anticipating future cases and pointing to the legal unknowns at stake therein, unknowns that may set the stage for the references of the future.

This chapter does not set out the full gamut of constitutional considerations that should guide policymakers engaged in institutional reform. Its aim is more modest: to focus only on the considerations that emerge from constitutional reference jurisprudence. Such a framework is of particular interest given that references are initiated solely at the discretion of government leaders, who also have control over the questions on which a reference opinion is sought. In this sense, references can be used as an opportunity to test the legality of policy goals and initiatives. And yet, once the questions are submitted to the Court, government control over the process – including control over the parties heard and arguments made – is lost. Indeed, this willingness to transfer control over the conversation and outcome is one of the most intriguing contextual dimensions of the reference procedure.

The Successes and Failures of Institutional Reform Policy

Reference cases are not the norm, but nor are they rare in Canada. They reach the Supreme Court by virtue of the Court's original advisory jurisdiction or its appellate jurisdiction over provincial references.[10] The advisory role facilitates judicial review of matters deemed important by government[11] and has been part of the Court's role since 1875.[12] But the advisory function has not been free from controversy.[13] One challenge contends that the advisory power undermines the separation of powers,[14] an argument that has been successful in other jurisdictions.[15] Another worries about the political character of reference cases. This critique discloses two concerns: one about the government "shunting" its responsibilities to the Court and the second about the legitimacy and capacity of the Court to deal with politically fraught matters.[16] In large measure, these concerns have been unsuccessful in disrupting the invocation of, and popular support for, the Court's reference jurisdiction. Its use is often called for, both by opposition voices seeking to constrain controversial exercises of political power and by supporters seeking to legitimize them.[17]

In the current era of constitutional references, the Court has had a significant impact on government plans to design and reform federal institutions. Over the past two decades, the Court has been asked to answer questions regarding a number of initiatives, including reform of the Senate and the Supreme Court Act, and the creation of a national securities regulator and gun registry. As is discussed below, in three of these four cases, the route by which the government sought to implement its primary policy preferences was found to be unconstitutional. In those cases, the government policy objectives could be pursued, but only by alternative, intergovernmental means.

The References

Over the past twenty years, the Supreme Court has decided a number of major reference cases. This section details the issues, reasoning, and outcomes in four of those references – namely, the most recent cases dealing with significant government initiatives regarding the design and reform of public institutions. A close study of these cases offers insight into not only shifts in the contemporary policy agenda but also the current state of constitutional law governing institutional design and reform. While the framework of considerations extracted from references decided in past eras would differ from the framework constructed from these four cases, reflecting the historical composition of the Supreme Court and past approaches to constitutional interpretation, a study of the *Senate Reform Reference,* the *Supreme Court Act Reference,* the *Securities Act Reference,* and the *Firearms Reference* offers the benefit of establishing the applicable legal parameters for implementing institutional design and reform policy today as well as in the days ahead. These cases make explicit the normative consequences of the structural dimensions of the constitution, consequences that would likely have been absent from a case study of older reference decisions. Moreover, the framework presented in this chapter also establishes a benchmark from which to clearly identify future legal changes and assess their impact on reform initiatives.

In the *Senate Reform Reference,* the Governor-in-Council referred six questions to the Court, each enquiring into the constitutionality of longstanding proposals for Senate reform. Senate reform had wide popular and political support, although agreement on the particulars remained contentious. The proposals dealt with fixed senatorial terms, advisory elections for selecting senators, the property qualifications for senators, and abolition of the Senate. The Court held that Parliament alone could not implement most of the proposals. Rather, with the exception of repealing the property qualifications for senators in all provinces outside Quebec, the proposals required some measure of intergovernmental consensus, ranging from bilateral agreement (for repealing the property qualifications for senators from Quebec) to unanimous consent (for abolition).

The Court's reasoning in the *Senate Reference* was based on its interpretation of the constitutional amending procedures set out in Part V of the Constitution Act, 1982. The guiding principle was cooperative federalism, which, in the constitutional amendment context, provides that neither Parliament nor the provinces can unilaterally reform the structure of Canada's constitutional order in a way that engages both federal and provincial interests; consensus across orders of government is required. "Parliament and the provinces are equal stakeholders in the Canadian constitutional design," the Court wrote.[18] Accordingly, "[n]either level of government acting alone can alter the fundamental nature and role of the institutions provided for in the Constitution."[19] As the government's proposals for Senate reform contemplated significant changes to the defining features of the Senate, features linked to the Senate's core constitutional role, they could not be implemented by legislative action alone. Constitutional amendments were required.

In the *Supreme Court Act Reference*, the government sought to confirm the eligibility of its most recent appointee to the Supreme Court by amending the Supreme Court Act. The appointment had been called into question because it filled one of the seats reserved for a judge chosen from among the judges of the courts of Quebec or the advocates of the Quebec bar with Justice Nadon, a current judge of the Federal Court of Appeal and a former member of the Barreau du Québec. The government responded to the controversy by introducing "declaratory" provisions into the Supreme Court Act. One such provision confirmed that current *or* former members of the Quebec bar were eligible for appointment to the Court. The government also responded by initiating the reference.

After concluding that Justice Nadon was not eligible for appointment under the unamended Supreme Court Act, the Court went on to consider whether Parliament had the authority to amend the act to allow for the appointment of former members of the Quebec bar. While section 101 of the Constitution Act, 1867 authorized Parliament to create and manage the Court, the constitutional amending procedure provided that any amendment to the Constitution of Canada in relation to the composition of the Court required the consent of both houses of Parliament and all the provincial legislatures. As the Supreme Court Act was not part of the Constitution of Canada, the issue came down to a determination of the constitutional status of the Court.

The majority held that, despite the Court's original statutory status, it had become a "constitutionally essential institution engaging both federal and provincial interests."[20] Over Canada's constitutional history, the Court had evolved into the "*final* general court of appeal for Canada, with jurisdiction to hear appeals concerning all the laws of Canada and the provinces, including the Constitution." This status was enhanced and confirmed with the adoption of the Charter and the amending procedure, which rendered the Court a "foundational premise of the Constitution" and subject to meaningful reform only by means of multilateral action.[21] Given that Parliament's reform of the Supreme Court Act would have added a new group of people eligible for appointment to the Supreme Court, it amounted to a constitutional amendment in relation to the composition of the Court. It could thus be enacted only with the unanimous consent of Parliament and the provinces.

Both the *Senate Reform Reference* and the *Supreme Court Act Reference* deal with institutions that are expressly contemplated in the constitution – the Senate[22] and the "general court of appeal for Canada"[23] – that is, the legislature and the judiciary. In both cases, the reform initiatives under scrutiny were held to be unconstitutional by virtue of the constitutional amending procedure. The next two cases – the *Securities Reference* and the *Firearms Reference* – deal with the creation of new administrative actors at the federal level. The issue in each case was whether Parliament was authorized to create these institutions under section 91 of the Constitution Act, 1867.

The *Securities Reference* was initiated as part of the federal agenda to implement a single scheme of securities regulation across the country. The proposed scheme was comprehensive, dealing with the regulation of securities dealers, disclosure requirements, duties for market participants, remedies, and offences. It was to be under the oversight of a newly created national securities regulator. The attorney general of Canada argued that this scheme was a proper exercise of Parliament's authority to regulate trade and commerce. It submitted that securities regulation had evolved into a matter of national concern. A number of provincial attorneys general and interveners opposed the proposed Securities Act, contending that securities regulation was a matter properly within provincial jurisdiction over property and civil rights.

The Court held that the proposed Securities Act was not a valid exercise of Parliament's authority over trade and commerce. It emphasized the cooperative and balanced dimensions of the current understanding of federalism in Canadian constitutional law,[24] while noting its limits.[25] "The 'dominant tide' of flexible federalism," the Court explained, "however strong its pull may be, cannot sweep designated powers out to sea, nor erode the constitutional balance inherent in the Canadian federal state."[26] It held that the proposed Securities Act would upset that balance. The thrust of the act was to regulate all aspects of securities trading in Canada; its aim was to protect investors, promote competitive markets, and ensure the integrity of the financial system. This was beyond the federal power. While the Court appreciated that the "economic importance and pervasive character of the securities market may … support federal intervention that is qualitatively different from what the provinces can do," securities regulation was ultimately a matter of primarily local concern.[27]

The Court noted, however, that the tide of Canadian federalism would be enhanced by a collaborative approach to securities regulation. It pointed out that "a cooperative approach that permits a scheme that recognizes the essentially provincial nature of securities regulation while allowing Parliament to deal with genuinely national concerns remains available."[28] After dedicating meaningful space in its reasons to comparative and historical examples of cooperative securities regulation, the Court concluded that the "common ground that emerges [from these examples] is that each level of government has jurisdiction over some aspects of the regulation of securities and each can work in collaboration with the other to carry out its responsibilities."[29]

Finally, in the *Firearms Reference*, the Court had to decide whether the Firearms Act was within the jurisdiction of Parliament.[30] It required all gun owners to license and register their guns, including long guns and shotguns. The act provided for two types of registries. The Canadian Firearms Registry, administered by the Registrar of Firearms, was to record registration certificates for listed firearms that were acquired, transferred, or possessed in Canada. In addition, the chief firearms officer designated for each province and territory was to maintain a registry of the issuance and revocations of firearms licences and authorizations. The Attorney General of Canada argued that the Firearms Act was valid under Parliament's authority over criminal law. Alberta opposed the law, arguing that the act was outside Parliament's authority because it was regulatory legislation in relation to property and civil rights in the provinces, rather than an exercise of criminal law. Further, Alberta argued, the act interfered with provincial powers such that its operation would upset the balance of federalism.

Writing per curiam, the Court concluded that the Firearms Act was valid federal legislation under Parliament's criminal law power. According to the Court, the act was aimed at promoting public safety and possessed the three features of a valid criminal law: a criminal law purpose backed by a prohibition and a penalty.[31] The creation of the registries and the registrar and officer roles was constitutionally valid, the Court held, because the contemplated registries and roles were manifestations of Parliament's aim to promote public safety. This was evident from the scope of the institutions' design – the registrar and officers were empowered to act in ways consistent with public safety (e.g., by implementing licensing criteria, background checks, and safety course requirements), but not to regulate insurance or the price or manufacture of weapons. "What the law does not require," the Court reasoned, "also shows that the operation of the scheme is limited to ensuring safety."

> For instance, the Act does not regulate the legitimate commercial market for guns. It makes no attempt to set labour standards or the price of weapons. There is no attempt to protect or regulate industries or businesses

> associated with guns. ... Unlike provincial property ... schemes, the Act does not address insurance. In short, the effects of the law suggest that its essence is the promotion of public safety through the reduction of the misuse of firearms, and negate the proposition that Parliament was in fact attempting to achieve a different goal such as the total regulation of firearms production, trade, and ownership.[32]

The Court rejected Alberta's claims of provincial jurisdiction and interference. In particular, it rejected the claim that the administrative offices created by the act rendered it regulatory. While the chief firearms officer and registrar were given discretion under the act, this discretion was sufficiently constrained by statute so as not to be undue.[33] Further, the design of the statute revealed the integrated character of the licensing and registration schemes, both serving the purpose of public safety. The Court reasoned that the "interconnections demonstrate that the registration and licensing portions of the Firearms Act are both tightly linked to Parliament's goal of promoting safety by reducing the misuse of any and all firearms. Both portions are integral and necessary to the operation of the scheme."[34] Finally, the Court was not persuaded that the act would upset the balance of federalism. Upholding the spirit of the incidental effects and double aspect doctrines, the Court affirmed the multiple legal dimensions of the complex social issue of gun control and the broad areas in which the provinces could legislate, including regulation of hunting, discharge of firearms within municipal boundaries, labour standards in weapons production, and all other aspects of gun control that implicated property and civil rights.[35]

The Reference Landscape

The references discussed above provide a snapshot of the terrain on which judicial advisory opinions regarding institutional design and reform are decided. They demonstrate the direct impact that judicial references can have on government policy initiatives to create and reform public institutions in Canada. In this collection of recent opinions, the Court held that the federal government could lawfully pursue its reform objectives by its preferred route in only one case, the *Firearms Reference*. In the remaining cases, the government's objectives could be pursued only by other means, that is, only in cooperation – or, at a minimum, coordination – with the provinces. We will return to this cooperative dimension in greater detail in the next section.

Beyond the outcomes for specific policy initiatives, the reference opinions discussed above also highlight the modern Court's posture towards its advisory function. In its advisory opinions, the Court repeatedly gestures to the limits of its role. It points out that the extent to which it can contribute to the often-fraught and polycentric circumstances in which references arise is necessarily constrained by concerns about institutional capacity and legitimacy. In so doing, the Court emphasizes that what it can offer to any conversation about policy initiatives leaves much, if not most, of the important decision making regarding institutional reform to political actors and the public.

For example, in the *Firearms Reference,* the Court noted that its task was not to opine on the advisability, effectiveness, or access issues at stake in the creation of the gun registries; these were matters of policy. The legal issue, the Court wrote, "is not whether gun control is good or bad, whether the law is fair or unfair to gun owners, or whether it will be effective or ineffective in reducing the harm caused by the misuse of firearms. The only issue [for the Court] is whether or not Parliament has the constitutional authority to enact the law."[36] The Court was similarly emphatic in the *Senate Reform Reference,* reminding its audience that the Court's "proper role ... in the ongoing debate regarding the future of the Senate is to determine the legal framework for implementing the specific changes contemplated in the questions put to us. The desirability of these changes is not a question for the Court; it is an issue for Canadians and their legislatures."[37] In other words, the Court reserved its role to answering the legal questions; the policy inputs and outcomes extended beyond the law.

These gestures towards the limits of resolving legal issues must not obscure the meaningful impact that references have on policy agendas that extend well beyond declarations of constitutional invalidity. The cases discussed above demonstrate that the Court is confident in the exercise and legitimacy of its advisory role. The judgments show that, in some cases, the Court has held that the constitution grounds positive obligations of institutional creation and maintenance on government actors. For example, in the *Supreme Court Act Reference,* the majority concluded that the permissive language in section 101 of the Constitution Act, 1867 must now be read as requiring Parliament to "maintain – and protect – the essence of what enables the Supreme Court to perform its current role."[38] Such was also the case in the *Remuneration Reference,* in which a majority of the Court held that the demands of judicial independence entailed that the provinces create independent bodies to oversee and report on the salaries and benefits of provincial court judges.[39]

Similarly, the Court pushes the limits of its advisory role by going beyond noting the availability of alternative routes of achieving policy goals to endorsing particular choices. For example, as discussed above, in the *Securities Reference*, the Court gestured towards cooperative, intergovernmental schemes as a route by which the federal government could pursue its aims of regulating securities. The Court noted that it was "open to the federal government and the provinces to exercise their respective powers over securities harmoniously, in the spirit of cooperative federalism."[40] It went on to advise on the cooperative option, noting that a "cooperative approach might usefully be explored" in light of comparative and historical experience.[41]

> It is not for the Court to suggest to the governments of Canada and the provinces the way forward by, in effect, conferring in advance an opinion on the constitutionality [of] this or that alternative scheme. Yet we may appropriately note the growing practice of resolving the complex governance problems that arise in federations, not by the bare logic of either/or, but by seeking cooperative solutions that meet the needs of the country as a whole as well as its constituent parts.
>
> Such an approach is supported by the Canadian constitutional principles and by the practice adopted by the federal and provincial governments in other fields of activities. The backbone of these schemes is the respect that each level of government has for each other's own sphere of jurisdiction. Cooperation is the animating force. The federalism principle upon which Canada's constitutional framework rests demands nothing less.[42]

A reference opinion that is unfavourable to the implementation of a particular policy on constitutional grounds need not be a death sentence to a reform agenda, despite interpretations to the contrary. The Court's reasoning in cases dealing with institutional reform demonstrates an attentiveness to the availability of alternative routes by which policy goals can be pursued. Yet this awareness reflects a structural tension at the heart of many references – the boundaries of legitimacy in reasoning and role. The Court cannot reasonably claim that its hands are completely tied by the constitution when faced with questions of interpretation; similarly, the Court should not be made to bear full and final responsibility for failed intergovernmental relations or stymied policy agendas. It is not the Court's role to ensure that governments can achieve all their policy goals or to defer to the government's preferred means. While the Court must not be blind to the context in which its decisions are made or the force that they carry, it is equally unreasonable to invoke the Court's advisory opinions as the perpetual scapegoat for policy failures.

The Goals and Limits of Institutional Design

The impact of the Supreme Court's constitutional reference jurisprudence dealing with institutional reform has not been limited to the validation or invalidation of specific initiatives. A deep look at the case studies also reveals that this jurisprudence advances the law on matters of institutional design and reform more generally, contributing additional considerations to the broader constitutional framework governing the setting and execution of government policy goals. Indeed, this generation of cases has been particularly expansive in its reach. In this way, the institutional reference jurisprudence has a broader effect on policymaking than any individual case suggests. By adding to the legal framework, these cases help to set the broad parameters within which political actors exercise their discretionary and policymaking functions.

There are three areas of particular significance for future cases of institution making and reform: constitutional architecture, constitutional amendment, and the demands of cooperative federalism.

Constitutional Architecture

An exercise of institutional design or reform within the public sphere should be guided by an understanding of the architecture of the constitution. The notion of constitutional architecture is not new to Canada's constitutional lexicon or imagination,[43] but it was a particularly powerful analytical vehicle in both the *Senate Reform Reference* and the *Supreme Court Act Reference*. In those opinions, not only are we reminded that the constitution has "an architecture, a basic structure,"[44] but we also learn more about the legal understanding and obligations that flow from this architecture. The "basic structure" of the constitution speaks to Canada's fundamental institutions and their design. It captures the allocations of power to those institutions, their interactions, and the relationships between "individuals and ... cultural groups to one another and to the state."[45] In short, the architecture of the constitution is the manifestation of the "structure of government" that the constitution "seeks to implement."[46] In this sense, constitutional architecture is encompassing – it captures not only the institutions of the constitution but also the principles, assumptions, traditions, and purposes that animate and enliven them.

It is within the architecture of the constitution that the foundational institutions of Canada's public order are imbued with an internal morality. The expectation is that the core institutions of the constitution will embody, respect, and be animated by the foundational principles of the constitution – the principles of democracy, federalism, judicial independence, constitutionalism and the rule of law, respect for minorities, constitutional integrity, and so on.[47] As the Court noted in the *Secession Reference,* these principles "dictate major elements of the architecture of the Constitution itself," including its central institutions, and are therefore its "lifeblood."[48] This "lifeblood" not only animates the operation of institutions that fit into existing policy agendas but also gives rise to obligations to create, protect, and maintain certain institutions, regardless of executive intent. According to the jurisprudence, these institutions include, at a minimum, the Supreme Court, the provincial superior courts, judicial salary review bodies, and democratically elected legislative bodies.[49]

The reform of these bodies, and the creation of new bodies that might bear on their work, must be pursued with a keen understanding of the structure of the constitution as a whole. Qualitative assessments of architecture, in both its material forms and its interpretive demands, are required. This can be a challenging exercise as the extent of the constitutional architecture and its normative force are still being worked out in the courts. Further, the *Supreme Court Act Reference* confirms that architecture can change over time and through the operation of history. The challenge is amplified as the *Senate Reform Reference* confirms that parts of the constitution's architecture are entrenched and protected from unilateral legislative reform.[50] Thus, an intentional or unintentional reconfiguration or shift of constitutional architecture draws a boundary between the legislative reform initiatives that can be pursued unilaterally by Parliament and those that trigger the multilateral procedures of constitutional amendment. Ultimately, the current state of the law on constitutional architecture entails that care be taken when plotting out the route by which institutional reform initiatives can be pursued.

The Amending Procedure

The second consideration that must guide policymakers in their endeavours to design and reform public institutions in Canada is the constitutional amending procedure, as set out in Part V of the Constitution Act, 1982.[51] Part V establishes a general rule – that amendments to the constitution of Canada require the consent of Parliament and the provincial legislatures in significant measure – and several exceptions. The exceptions are triggered by virtue of the subject matter of the amendment, whether in relation to, for example, the composition of the Supreme Court, the powers of the Senate, or the office of the Queen.[52]

The *Supreme Court Act Reference* and the *Senate Reform Reference* represented the Court's first opportunities to interpret and apply the amending procedures, and they have significantly advanced our understanding of the legal approach to amendment. These cases and the interpretation and limits of Part V have now been the subject of much commentary and scrutiny.[53] But in the moments of policymaking, of particular assistance may be the guiding principles that emerge from these two reference opinions, principles that coalesce into a general posture towards the process of pursuing institutional reform in the public realm.

First, as an overarching guide, "Parliament and the provinces are equal stakeholders in the Canadian constitutional design."[54] Accordingly, the boundary between multilateralism and unilateralism in the design and reform of constitutional institutions is constructed by federalism and, more specifically, by a cooperative understanding of federalism.[55] It follows that "neither level of government acting alone can alter the fundamental nature and role of the institutions provided for in the Constitution."[56] Beyond the realm of "housekeeping" and routine matters of organizational administration, the reform and design of constitutional institutions is an exercise calling for multilateralism.[57]

Second, understanding the operation of Part V assists in identifying the configuration and demands of the constitutional architecture. The *Supreme Court Act Reference* suggests that the subject matters mentioned in Part V may have normative force, signalling an entrenchment of elements and institutions of the constitution as they existed and were configured in 1982.[58] In the exercise of qualitative assessments of the constitution to establish the baselines for reform and design, Part V thus serves as one source of insight into questions about which institutions and which of their features are constitutionally entrenched.

Finally, Peter Oliver has written that the politics of constitution making and amending tend to be very revealing as they "expose the stress spots and irregularities in a country's overall political structure." But, he notes, a constitutional amending formula is usually "unforthcoming."[59] Canada is an outlier in this sense. Given the federal nature of the country, the differences among the provinces, and the difficulty of entrenching an amending procedure, Canada's amending formula is ultimately an explicit expression of some of the country's long-standing stress spots, vulnerabilities, and irregularities. It is revealing of the issues that have plagued and troubled and divided the country. Both the *Senate Reform Reference* and the *Supreme Court Act Reference* confirm this.

As a result, and as Canada's constitutional history establishes, embarking on reform that triggers the amending formula necessarily opens difficult, long-standing political conversations and negotiations. As F.R. Scott explains, "Changing a constitution confronts a society with the most important choices, for in the constitution will be found the philosophical principles and rules which largely determine the relations of the individual and of cultural groups to one another and to the state."[60] But Part V was intended not only to shield the status quo from unilateral action but also to channel and structure intergovernmental relations in moments of constitutional stress. The obligations of Part V are facilitative; they are "designed to foster dialogue between the federal government and the provinces on matters of constitutional change."[61] When this position is the starting point for a general attitude towards constitutional amendment, institutional reform in the constitutional realm can become more aspirational than confrontational, and the conception of policymaking as an exercise in designing routes around the amending formula becomes less pressing.

Federalism

The final consideration is an understanding of the legal implications of cooperative federalism. Assessing the constitutionality of legislative initiatives through the lens of the division of powers is the bread and butter of the Supreme Court, whether in a reference or otherwise. But the *Firearms Reference* and the *Securities Reference* suggest that trends towards cooperative federalism outside the reference context are well entrenched in the current judicial approach to the application of sections 91 and 92. The Court explains in the *Securities Reference* that it has "rejected rigid formalism in favour of accommodating cooperative intergovernmental efforts."[62] As a result, initiatives to create or reform public institutions that deal in areas implicating matters of both provincial and federal jurisdiction will fit within current legal conceptions of the division of powers when they do not exhaust the field, when they leave open the possibility of an intergovernmental cooperative scheme, or when they are part of an interlocking federal-provincial scheme. The Court's reasoning in both the *Securities Reference* and the *Firearms Reference* manifested this commitment to coordinated schemes. The exhaustive character of the securities regime proposed in the *Securities Reference*, and the opportunity for the provinces to regulate firearms in a variety of ways in the *Firearms Reference*, were persuasive in the result of each case.

That said, while the spirit of cooperative federalism runs deep in the *Securities Reference* and the *Firearms Reference*, the demands of cooperation have limits, at least for now. In the *Securities Reference*, the Court explained the limits of cooperative federalism. "While flexibility and cooperation are important to federalism," the Court wrote, "they cannot override or modify the [division] of powers."[63] Federalism imagines coordinated efforts, but the space for cooperation cannot undermine the division of powers or the "maintenance of a constitutional balance between federal and provincial powers."[64] These limits to cooperative federalism were recently invoked in follow-up litigation to the *Firearms Reference*. In assessing the obligations attendant upon the dismantling of the firearms registry, the Court held that cooperative federalism could not "impos[e] limits on the otherwise valid exercise of legislative competence."[65] It could not, in other words, be the basis of Quebec's claim of entitlement to the data in the registry or of obligations on Parliament in enacting legislation dismantling the registry scheme. The majority explained that cooperative federalism could not hinder Parliament from exercising legislative authority that it otherwise had.

> Neither this Court's jurisprudence nor the text of the *Constitution Act, 1867* supports using that principle to limit the scope of legislative authority or to impose a positive obligation to facilitate cooperation where the constitutional division of powers authorizes unilateral action. To hold otherwise would undermine parliamentary sovereignty and create legal uncertainty whenever one order of government adopted legislation having some impact on the policy objectives of another.[66]

Moreover, the Court was reluctant to impose obligations on unilateral legislative authority that might undermine cooperative efforts. Such would be the case with attaching conditions to the dismantling of an existing institution. "Paradoxically," the Court held, attaching conditions "could discourage the practice of cooperative federalism for fear that cooperative measures could risk diminishing a government's legislative authority to act alone."[67] Thus, while cooperative federalism remains as strong in principle, its use does not extend to positive obligations to cooperate in the exercise of otherwise valid legislative authority. The order of government that creates an institution thus has jurisdiction to dismantle it.

Conclusion

The *Senate Reform Reference*, the *Supreme Court Act Reference*, the *Securities Reference*, and the *Firearms Reference* comprise a significant era of references dealing with federal institutional design and reform policy. They show the meaningful impact that a reference can have on specific initiatives, marking the end of some projects even when alternative routes exist for political actors to pursue substantive goals. Further, they have contributed to developments in the law, adding to the framework of constitutional considerations (and confusion) that sets parameters within which decisions about institutional reform should be made. These references highlight, in particular, the impact of cooperative federalism and multilateralism in the constitutional assessment of institutional initiatives.

Questions remain, of course. Reform initiatives currently being debated and pursued reveal the uncertainties in the existing constitutional framework. The case of electoral reform, for instance, exposes the difficulty of identifying what is entrenched in the architecture of the constitution and thus subject to the multilateral provisions of the amending formula. In what contexts would electoral reform trigger Part V? Are there other procedural obligations emerging from the architecture of the constitution that bear on the implementation of electoral reform?

These questions and others also emerge from the recent reform to the process of appointing judges to the Supreme Court. Part V provides that amendments to the constitution in relation to the composition of the Supreme Court require the consent of Parliament and all the provincial legislatures;[68] all other amendments trigger the general 7/50 rule.[69]

Apart from these amending requirements, Parliament alone has the authority to legislate in relation to routine matters of maintenance and administration of the Court.[70] This unilateral legislative authority ends where reform to the constitutionally protected features of the Court begins.

In this constitutional context, what does the amending procedure entail for the Supreme Court appointment process? On the one hand, it has facilitated keeping the appointment process a matter of executive policy rather than a process articulated in statute or the constitution. There is some virtue in this approach as it allows for flexibility and innovation over time and between governments. It has also allowed, however, for long-standing practices of appointment that are opaque, unilateral, and ad hoc. At what point, though, if any, does executive policy trigger the amending formula? In working through the types of action that can constitute an amendment to the constitution, it is well established that legislative action falls within that category. For the most part, it is accepted that matters of executive decision making would not meet the threshold to trigger the formal consent requirements, thus rendering the changing appointment policies "safe" from the amending procedures. The question remains open, though, as to whether this distinction between legislative and executive action is the meaningful distinction to rely on and whether there are executive policies that could make such a qualitative difference to the constitutionally protected features of the institution that it would rise to the level of a constitutional amendment.

Given the extensive resources involved in establishing new institutions and reforming existing ones, it might be that this is an area particularly ripe for the use of the Supreme Court's advisory function. But the unknowns are also matters with which the law is comfortable and perhaps politics less so. Indeed, this might be the ultimate tension at play in any future choice to pursue a reference on matters of institutional design and reform.

NOTES

1 *Re Residential Tenancies Act*, [1981] 1 SCR 714; *Reference re Amendments to the Residential Tenancies Act*, [1996] 1 SCR 186.

2 *Reference re Senate Reform*, 2014 SCC 32 [*Senate Reform Reference*]; *Re Authority of Parliament in relation to the Upper House*, [1980] 1 SCR 54.

3 *Reference re Supreme Court Act, ss. 5 and 6*, 2014 SCC 21 [*Supreme Court Act Reference*].

4 *Reference re Securities Act*, 2011 SCC 66 [*Securities Reference*].

5 *Reference re Firearms Act (Can)*, 2000 SCC 31 [*Firearms Reference*]. Subsequent litigation regarding the dismantling of the gun registry also reached the Supreme Court: *Quebec (AG) v. Canada (AG)*, 2015 SCC 14 [*Quebec (AG)*].

6 *Reference re Agricultural Products Marketing*, [1978] 2 SCR 1198.

7 See, e.g., *Reference re Education Act (QC)* [*Education Reference*], [1993] 2 SCR 511; see also *In re The Brothers of the Christian Schools in Canada* (1876) Cout. Dig. 1.

8 *Reference re Young Offenders Act* (P.E.I.), [1991] 1 SCR 252.

9 Questions dealing with the Charter have been deployed with greater frequency in disputes over institutional reform and design in the provincial realm, as we see in references dealing with minority language rights in education, the impact of same-sex marriage on religious actors, and the reduction of salaries of provincial court judges: *Education Reference*; *Reference re Same-Sex Marriage*, 2004 SCC 79 [*Same-Sex Marriage Reference*]; *Reference re Remuneration of Judges of the Provincial Court* (PEI), [1997] 3 SCR 3 [*Remuneration Reference*].

10 Supreme Court Act, RSC 1985, c. S-26, ss. 36, 53.

11 Barry Strayer, "Constitutional References," in F.L. Morton, ed., *Law, Politics and the Judicial Process in Canada*, 3rd ed. (Calgary: University of Calgary Press, 2002), 265 at 265–8.

12 Charles Feldman, "Parliament and Supreme Court of Canada Reference Cases," Briefing Paper Publication No. 2015-44-E, 12 August 2015, http://www.lop.parl.gc.ca/content/lop/ResearchPublications/2015-44-e.html#ftn24.

13 See, e.g., *Ontario (Attorney General) v. Canada (Attorney General)*, [1912] AC 571; *Reference re Secession of Quebec*, [1998] 2 SCR 217 [*Secession Reference*].

14 The argument is that this advisory function is not a judicial one because the questions considered do not arise in the context of adversarial litigation and the executive's legal advisers are the Crown legal officers in the Department of Justice; see, e.g., *Secession Reference*.

15 See, e.g., Australia and the United States. Note, however, that the argument regarding the Supreme Court of the United States is tied to the "case" and "controversy" language in the American constitutional definition of judicial power: Peter W. Hogg, *Constitutional Law of Canada*, student ed. (Toronto: Carswell, 2010), 8–17, citing *Re Judiciary and Navigation Act*, (1921) 29 CLR 257 (Australia); and Note, "Advisory Opinions on the Constitutionality of Statutes," *Harvard Law Review* 69, no. 7 (1956): 1302–13 (U.S.).

16 Strayer, "Constitutional References." As Bateman et al. note, the Court's advisory role "provides governments the opportunity either to avoid deciding a contentious political issue themselves or to use the authority of the Court to support a policy position they already hold. It may be too much to say that the reference procedure facilitates an abuse of judicial authority, but certainly the procedure often inserts the Supreme Court into salient political issues of the day": Thomas M.J. Bateman, Janet L. Hiebert, Rainer Knopff, and Peter H. Russell, *The Court and the Charter: Leading Cases* (Toronto: Emond Montgomery, 2008), 12. In addition to concerns about the government referring to the Court inappropriately political questions, the Court has been criticized for improperly engaging not merely in policy choice or policy framing but also in policy design: see, e.g., Adam M. Dodek, "Chief Justice Lamer and Policy Design at the Supreme Court of Canada," in *The Sacred Fire: The Legacy of Antonio Lamer*, ed. Adam Dodek and Daniel Jutras (Markham, ON: LexisNexis, 2009), 93; Pierre Patenaude, "The Provincial Court Judges Case and Extended Judicial Control," in *Judicial Power and Canadian Democracy*, ed. Paul Howe and Peter H. Russell (Montreal and Kingston: McGill-Queen's University Press, 2001), 99.

17 Such was the case with respect to the *Senate Reform Reference*, submitted to the Court on 1 February 2012; see, e.g., Postmedia News, "Harper Government Asks Supreme Court to Rule on Legality of Senate Reform," 1 February 2013, http://nationalpost.com/news/politics/harper-government-asks-supreme-court-to-rule-on-legality-of-senate-reform; Minister of State for Democratic Reform, "Harper Government Advances Senate Reform," news release, 1 February 2013, https://www.canada.ca/en/news/archive/2013/02/harper-government-advances-senate-reform.html?=undefined&wbdisable=true; Gloria Galloway, "Ottawa Asks Supreme Court for Opinion on Senate Reform," 1 February 2013, https://www.theglobeandmail.com/news/politics/ottawa-asks-supreme-court-for-opinion-on-senate-reform/article8123417/.

18 *Senate Reform Reference*, para. 48.

19 Ibid.

20 *Supreme Court Act Reference*, para. 87.

21 Ibid., paras. 89–95.

22 Constitution Act, 1867, 30 & 31 Vict., c. 3, ss. 17, 21–36.

23 Ibid., s. 101.

24 *Securities Reference*, paras. 6–10, 54–61.

25 Ibid., paras. 61–2.

26 Ibid., para. 62.

27 Ibid., para. 128.

28 Ibid., para. 130.
29 Ibid., para. 131.
30 The *Firearms Reference* came to the Court by way of appeal. The provincial government in Alberta had submitted a reference to the Alberta Court of Appeal, which was then appealed to the Supreme Court.
31 *Firearms Reference,* paras. 24, 27–35.
32 Ibid., para. 24.
33 Ibid., para. 37.
34 Ibid., para. 47.
35 Ibid., paras. 50–2.
36 Ibid., paras. 2, 56–7.
37 *Senate Reform Reference,* para. 4.
38 *Supreme Court Act Reference,* para. 101.
39 *Remuneration Reference.*
40 *Securities Reference,* para. 9.
41 Ibid.
42 Ibid., paras. 132–3.
43 See, e.g., *Ontario (AG) v. OPSEU,* [1987] 2 SCR 2 and *Secession Reference.*
44 *Senate Reform Reference,* para. 27.
45 Ibid., para. 26; Frank R. Scott, *Essays on the Constitution: Aspects of Canadian Law and Politics* (Toronto: University of Toronto Press, 1977), ix.
46 *Senate Reform Reference,* para. 26.
47 See, e.g., *Secession Reference,* paras. 49–82; Robin Elliot, "References, Structural Argumentation & the Organizing Principles of Canada's Constitution," *Canadian Bar Review* 80 (2001): 67–142.
48 *Secession Reference.*
49 *Supreme Court Act Reference; Remuneration Reference; Senate Reform Reference.* The references, and the concept of constitutional architecture in particular, have been the subject of much criticism; see, e.g., Emmett Macfarlane, "Unsteady Architecture: Ambiguity, the *Senate Reference,* and the Future of Constitutional Amendment in Canada," *McGill Law Journal* 60, no. 4 (2015): 883–903; Dennis Baker and Mark D. Jarvis, "The End of Informal Constitutional Change in Canada?," in *Constitutional Amendment in Canada,* ed. Emmett Macfarlane (Toronto: University of Toronto Press, 2016), 185; Paul Daly, "Supreme Court's Place in the Constitutional Order: Contrasting Recent Experiences in Canada and the United Kingdom," *Queen's Law Journal* 41, no. 1 (2015): 1–40.
50 *Senate Reform Reference,* para. 26.
51 Constitution Act, 1982, Part V, being Schedule B to the Canada Act 1982 (UK), 1982, c. 11.

52 Ibid., ss. 41(a), (d), 42(1)(b).
53 For a collection of commentary on constitutional amendment in Canada, see Emmett Macfarlane, ed., *Constitutional Amendment in Canada* (Toronto: University of Toronto Press, 2016).
54 *Senate Reform Reference*, para. 48.
55 Kate Glover, "Structural Cooperative Federalism," *Supreme Court Law Review* 76, 2D (2016): 45–66; see also Carissima Mathen, "The Federal Principle: Constitutional Amendment and Intergovernmental Relations," in Macfarlane, *Constitutional Amendment in Canada*, 65.
56 *Senate Reform Reference*, para. 48.
57 Ibid.; *Supreme Court Act Reference*, para. 101; *Re: Authority of Parliament in relation to the Upper House*, [1980] 1 SCR 54, 65.
58 *Supreme Court Act Reference*, paras. 90–1.
59 Peter Oliver, "Patriation and Amendment of the Constitution of Canada" (unpublished PhD diss., University of Oxford, 1992), 180.
60 Scott, *Essays on the Constitution*, ix.
61 *Senate Reform Reference*, para. 31.
62 *Securities Reference*, para. 58.
63 Ibid., para. 61.
64 Ibid.
65 *Quebec (AG)*, para. 19.
66 Ibid., para. 20.
67 Ibid.
68 Constitution Act, 1982, s. 41(d).
69 Ibid., s. 42(1)(d).
70 Constitution Act, 1867, s. 101; *Supreme Court Act Reference*, para. 101.

7 The Desuetude of the Notwithstanding Clause – and How to Revive It

RICHARD ALBERT

The Supreme Court of Canada recently invalidated the Criminal Code prohibition on physician-assisted dying in *Carter v. Canada (Attorney General)*.[1] The Court concluded that the prohibition deprived those "suffering from grievous and irremediable medical conditions" of the right to life, liberty, and security of the person, at variance with the principles of fundamental justice,[2] and that the prohibition could not be saved by the limitations clause in the Charter of Rights and Freedoms.[3] The judgment was controversial. It provoked strong reactions on both sides,[4] as was perhaps to be expected from a ruling on any matter of deep moral contestation like this one, let alone one on which the Court reversed its decision from a generation earlier.[5]

The Court's controversial judgment was met with the equally controversial suggestion that the government should re-enact the prohibition using the notwithstanding clause retrospectively.[6] The Harper government of the day rejected that suggestion. "Don't count on it," was how the justice minister responded to the question whether the government would invoke the clause.[7] After the Trudeau government was elected with a decisive majority in October 2015, the question arose whether the government would resort to a retroactive or pre-emptive use of the notwithstanding clause to pass its new law on physician-assisted suicide. Many suggested that the government could or should take this course.[8] But the government declined when it passed its new law[9] – a law that has its share of critics.[10]

The notwithstanding clause, entrenched in the Charter, authorizes Parliament or a provincial legislature to "expressly declare in an Act ... that the Act or a provision thereof shall operate notwithstanding a provision included in section 2 or sections 7 to 15 of this Charter."[11]

To translate this formal legal authority into practical political reality, the notwithstanding power gives legislatures the ultimate trump card over courts in the interpretation of the Charter rights and freedoms entrenched in section 2 and sections 7 to 15. We can understand this power as the "final word" or, alternatively, as a legislative veto. This notwithstanding power gives federal and provincial legislatures a veto over policy changes that are made, induced, accelerated, reversed, or retarded by courts – any changes that are not the legislatures' own. We can conceive of this power neither as extraordinary nor as exceptional but simply as a vehicle for legislatures to enact and preserve their policy objectives. The notwithstanding power rests on an unspoken but critical precondition: popular consent. It gives a government acting with the democratic legitimacy of a legislative majority the capacity both to return to the policy status quo ante in the face of a judicial decision that undermines or nullifies the policy choice and to pre-emptively insulate its policy choice from a real or imagined judicial threat to its policy preferences. The competing interests are sharp, and the stakes are high.

If ever there had been a moment ripe for invoking the notwithstanding power, it was in the aftermath of *Carter*. The Harper government, known for its confrontational approach to the Court,[12] faced the prospect of entering the then-upcoming federal general election with the albatross of yet another loss on its judicial scorecard – this one on an important values-based law that its partisans strongly supported. But the Harper government chose against taking the route offered by the notwithstanding clause. The new Trudeau government similarly opted against invoking it. When the use of the notwithstanding power was suggested in the *Carter II* hearing at the Supreme Court of Canada – Justice Russell Brown asked why "can't the minister ask Parliament effectively for a suspension by way of exercise of the override?" – counsel for the attorney general of Canada replied that "the government has said nothing other than that it will respect this Court's judgment."[13]

It should come as no surprise that the Harper and Trudeau governments took the same view of the notwithstanding clause. The notwithstanding power has become politically toxic. Governments use the power at their own risk, and even merely considering its use entails political risk for a government. Since patriation, the notwithstanding power has travelled a path towards illegitimacy as a result of its non-use and political repudiation. There is a name for this phenomenon: constitutional desuetude. A textually entrenched constitutional rule may fall into desuetude when political actors no longer see it as politically viable, despite there being no legal prohibition on its use. Today, the notwithstanding power is at risk of constitutional desuetude. It is important to stress here that the *provincial* notwithstanding power appears for now to be both legally and politically viable. The *federal* notwithstanding power may be viable strictly as a matter of law, but in politics it is nearing the point where it might as well be repealed from the constitution.

Many scholars have suggested that the notwithstanding power has fallen into desuetude, but none has theorized how this condition develops.[14] In this chapter, I explain why the federal notwithstanding power is at risk of desuetude, how this came to be, and also how to halt its decline towards obsolescence to make it more likely that Parliament will, in the future, have a real choice to exercise the policymaking power the clause confers upon it – rather than being compelled to accept the rulings of the Supreme Court of Canada as final and irreversible. If indeed the federal notwithstanding power has fallen into desuetude, or eventually does, serious implications will follow for policymakers: legislatures will be sidelined as courts take centre stage on many of the high-salience matters of public policy implicating the Charter.

How a Power Falls into Desuetude

The condition that threatens to afflict the federal notwithstanding power is constitutional desuetude. We can define *constitutional desuetude* as the present state of an entrenched constitutional provision that has lost its constraining force on political actors as a result of its conscious, sustained non-use and public repudiation.[15] In the case of the federal notwithstanding power, we cannot yet make the claim that it has fallen into constitutional desuetude, although we can observe that it is presently at risk of falling into constitutional desuetude as a result of its conscious, sustained non-use and public repudiation by a long string of political actors. The potential desuetude of the federal notwithstanding power is not without consequence: it would deny Parliament a legitimate policymaking power that the Charter has legally conferred upon it.

Reservation and Disallowance

To understand how a power falls into desuetude, consider the British and Canadian reservation and disallowance powers, two pairs of powers that have lived different histories but suffered the same fate. Reading the Constitution Act, 1867 would suggest that the powers of reservation and disallowance – both textually entrenched – may today be validly exercised by both the British and the Canadian governments.[16] The constitutional text authorizes the British government to assent, or not, to a bill of the Canadian federal Parliament that has been "reserved" by the governor general; and the Canadian federal government may likewise assent, or not, to a bill of a provincial assembly that has been reserved on its behalf by the lieutenant governor of a province. The same is true of the disallowance power: the constitutional text authorizes the British government to "disallow," as in repeal, a law passed by the Canadian federal Parliament, a power the Canadian federal government possesses in respect of a law passed by any provincial assembly.

And yet, both pairs of powers are today invalid and unusable despite their textual entrenchment, the British powers as a result of subsequent, constitution-level enactments and the Canadian powers as a consequence of the evolution of Canadian federalism.

The first and only time the British government disallowed a law was in 1873, over 140 years ago. The most recent use of its reservation power was almost as long ago in 1878, the last of the twenty-one times it reserved a law.[17] The beginning of the end for the reservation power came when the British government changed its instructions to the governor general for when to reserve a bill.[18] It had initially authorized the governor general in 1867 to reserve Canadian bills on eight specifically designated subjects,[19] but it then removed these grounds altogether in 1878.[20] Both reservation and disallowance were effectively repealed by the 1931 Statute of Westminster, which removed the power of the Parliament of the United Kingdom to legislate for Canada without consent.[21] The statute reflected an agreement struck the year before that neither power would again be used in Canada.[22]

The desuetude of the Canadian powers of reservation and disallowance is a more recent development. Since Confederation, the Canadian government has used its power of disallowance 112 times, most recently in 1943; the power of reservation has been used sixty-nine times, most recently in 1937.[23] Both powers were still valid when they were last used before the end of the Second World War, as the Supreme Court of Canada confirmed unanimously in its 1938 reference on their usability.[24] But since then, federalism has evolved to delegitimize their use, although both powers remain textually entrenched. Provinces are now seen as coordinate partners in the project of Confederation, not as subordinate bodies subject to the whims of Parliament. The use of reservation and disallowance reflects the old framework of provincial subordination – a framework that has long been rejected by the provincial rights movement[25] and that today makes little sense politically insofar as its use would have consequences in federal electoral politics.[26] To the extent that the desuetude of the Canadian powers of reservation and disallowance has created a void in federal-provincial relations, the rise of the reference procedure has filled that void as a functional analogue. Instead of exercising the reservation or disallowance powers, as it might have ordinarily done before, the federal government today refers what would have previously been reserved or disallowed to the Supreme Court for its opinion on the matter.[27] The point is that both powers are today effectively unusable despite their textual entrenchment.

The Life Cycle of Constitutional Desuetude

The mechanism that gives rise to constitutional desuetude is a constitutional convention. Ivor Jennings theorized that a convention develops when practice establishes precedent, when political actors feel themselves bound by the precedent, and when the precedent is supported by good reason.[28] Practice alone is insufficient to establish precedent. Political actors must "believe that they ought"[29] to conform their conduct to the practice, which itself must be "desirable in the circumstances of the constitution"[30] and not just a matter of convenience or narrow self-interest. The interaction between convention and constitutional text is quite complex as the former can incorporate new and unwritten rules into the latter, just as it can repudiate the latter's written rules. In the case of constitutional desuetude, a constitutional convention does not formally repeal, but it does functionally remove a provision from a codified constitution, leaving a void in its place.

We can identify with greater specificity the life cycle of an entrenched constitutional provision that has fallen into desuetude.[31] The first stage occurs over a significant period of time, during which the provision remains unused. There is such sustained non-use of the provision that we can identify a constitutional reordering in formation. The provision features less and less in constitutional law and politics, and it finds itself pushed to the outskirts of the constitution. The second stage follows from the first: as a result of the provision's sustained non-use, it approaches irrelevance and may come to clash with the existing constitutional framework. It is at this point that the provision becomes expressly repudiated by political actors as unusable.

At the same time, a third stage of the sequence begins: a new non-constitutional rule informally replaces the repudiated rule and becomes accepted as the standard for the conduct of political actors. The fourth stage in the sequence of constitutional desuetude is norm generation: the new non-constitutional rule that replaces the repudiated textual rule exercises a binding effect on political actors, so that it approximates the effect of a formal constitutional amendment, even though the new rule has emerged informally. Fifth, political actors begin self-consciously to follow the new rule, discarding the old textually entrenched one because they no longer believe themselves bound by it. Here the previously non-constitutional rule transforms itself into a constitution-level obligation. The sixth stage is permeation: the new constitutional rule permeates the elite understanding of the constitution, of what it allows and how it functions. The seventh stage is the recognition of a paradox: the repudiated rule remains textually entrenched, despite the system-wide recognition and acceptance of a new rule that is contrary to the old.

There is an eighth stage in the life cycle of constitutional desuetude, although this final stage bleeds into the first. At the eighth stage, it is possible, although not necessary, that a new non-constitutional norm will emerge to reverse the non-use of the textually entrenched provision. This new non-constitutional norm could develop over time to breathe new life into the repudiated provision to re-establish it as a textually entrenched power that may be legitimately invoked after years of non-use, perhaps even decades. Where a textually entrenched provision reaches this eighth stage, the constitutional convention operates in a manner directly contrary to its operation in the creation of constitutional desuetude: rather than slowly establishing a norm of non-use over time, a norm of valid use emerges over time to re-legitimate the provision.

This sequence helps explain the constitutional desuetude of the Canadian disallowance power. After its last use in 1943, the federal government turned away from the power for a significant period of time. This extended non-use eventually prompted observers and political actors to repudiate the power as an antiquated relic,[32] and today it is obsolete,[33] defunct,[34] illegitimate,[35] and nullified by a convention against its use.[36] A new constitutional rule developed while the old rule was expiring: the disallowance power would no longer be used, and federal political actors would instead have recourse to other devices to police the boundary between federal and provincial jurisdiction. In the place of disallowance, the reference power was deployed to test provincial laws whose constitutional validity was in doubt. Political actors internalized this norm as though the disallowance power had been formally repealed, even though it remains to this day textually entrenched in the Constitution Act, 1867. This new rule has permeated the elite understanding of the constitution, and, thus far, the disallowance power has yet to begin to make its way out of desuetude. The power may never reach the eighth stage in the sequence.

A Tale of Two Powers

The notwithstanding clause may be on the same path towards desuetude travelled by the reservation and disallowance powers. But we have to distinguish between two notwithstanding powers. The Charter confers the power upon both Parliament and the provincial legislatures. The power authorizes a legislature to expressly declare in an act that the act, or one of its provisions, "shall operate notwithstanding a provision included in section 2 or sections 7 to 15" of the Charter.[37] Such a declaration expires no later than five years after it is made, although the enacting legislature may renew it for subsequent terms no longer than five years.[38] At bottom, this notwithstanding power authorizes Parliament and provincial legislatures to suspend a court judgment in connection with a right found in section 2 or sections 7 to 15 of the Charter. The reason why we must distinguish the two powers is because one is at risk of desuetude, and the other is not.

The Provincial Notwithstanding Power

In what is probably a surprise even to scholars of constitutional law, the provincial notwithstanding power has been used many times since its creation in 1982. Tsvi Kahana reports that legislatures in Alberta, Quebec, Saskatchewan, and Yukon have used the notwithstanding power sixteen times,[39] not including its controversial omnibus use by Quebec between 1982 and 1985 as a protest against both the process and the outcome of patriation.[40]

There have also been threatened uses of the notwithstanding power across the provinces on subjects of serious controversy. For instance, Pauline Marois, leader of the Parti Québécois, said she was willing to invoke the notwithstanding power to protect the Charter of Quebec

Values,[41] Saskatchewan Premier Brad Wall expressed his willingness to do the same in connection with a labour law the Supreme Court had ruled was contrary to the Charter,[42] and Alberta's justice minister suggested that the province would consider invoking the power to protect officials from having to solemnize same-sex marriages when their religious beliefs would not allow it.[43] In the end, none of these threats came to pass, but their very mention as possibilities by high-visibility public officials confirms that the notwithstanding power is today usable at the provincial level.

The Federal Notwithstanding Power

The same cannot be said of the federal notwithstanding power. Not once since patriation has the power been used. It was mentioned in connection with the Court's same-sex marriage reference and later its ruling on the sex workers law,[44] but there has never been any real possibility that Parliament would use it either retrospectively or pre-emptively.

Peter Russell has identified a number of Charter decisions where he believes use of the notwithstanding power would have been appropriate.[45] One concerned the power of courts to review their remuneration, as determined by an independent compensation commission – a case in which Russell believes the justices of the Supreme Court were conflicted by self-interest.[46] Another was the tobacco advertising case, in which the Court invalidated a federal law prohibiting tobacco advertising and requiring health warnings on tobacco-product packaging.[47] And a third was the Court's decision on private medicine in Canada – a decision about national health policy that Russell believes is best made by Parliament.[48]

None of these constitutional controversies provoked Parliament to use the notwithstanding power. Parliament instead deferred to the Court, as it had done in the past.[49] And it remains unlikely that Parliament will in the near to medium term consider using the notwithstanding power. The federal notwithstanding power has not yet reached the point of desuetude, but it is close.

Reviving Notwithstanding

The main purpose of the notwithstanding power was to preserve parliamentary sovereignty in the new era of Charter constitutionalism.[50] Yet no one today could reasonably claim that Canada is a parliamentary supremacy. It is true that a plain reading of the constitutional text could suggest that ultimate power rests with legislative actors – not only through the notwithstanding power but also through the amending formula – yet political reality teaches us otherwise. For better or worse, Canada is much closer to what Ran Hirschl has described as a "juristocracy."[51]

Today, the final word on constitutional rights interpretation in connection with section 2 and sections 7 to 15 of the Charter belongs to the Supreme Court. But this is not what the authors of the Charter had in mind. The power was intended to guarantee the final word to Parliament. As the federal minister of justice at the time explained, the notwithstanding power was created to "ensure that legislatures rather than judges have the final say on important matters of public policy."[52]

Nor has the purpose retrospectively attributed to the notwithstanding power been fulfilled: to foster an institutional dialogue between Parliament and the Supreme Court.[53] The true engine of Charter dialogue is the limitations clause, as Kent Roach has explained.[54] Successful uses of the notwithstanding power could, in theory, promote a dialogic relationship between Parliament and the Supreme Court, but we have yet to see any evidence of its possibility – precisely because the power has not once been used by Parliament since its entrenchment in 1982.

All these purposes of the notwithstanding power remain unmet. If the power continues on its path towards desuetude, it will become unlikely that any of its purposes will ever be fulfilled. Our challenge, then, is to solve a puzzle: how may we revive the possibility of using the notwithstanding clause in order to save it from desuetude?

Rewriting Section 33

One suggestion is to rewrite the text of the notwithstanding power. As it currently reads, the text presupposes that courts are Charter-enhancing and legislatures are Charter-undermining. The very text of the clause conveys the false impression that the use of the notwithstanding power violates the Charter. Consider its key passage: "Parliament or the legislature of a province may expressly declare in an Act of Parliament or of the legislature, as the case may be, that the Act or a provision thereof shall operate *notwithstanding a provision included in section 2 or sections 7 to 15 of this Charter*."[55]

What in fact happens when a legislature invokes the notwithstanding power retrospectively is altogether different from what the text suggests: the legislature formalizes its disagreement with a previous judicial interpretation of a Charter right.[56] The notwithstanding power is neither Charter-enhancing nor Charter-undermining; it is Charter-neutral and is instead concerned with making it possible for legislatures to have a voice in the interpretation of constitutional rights.

We could rewrite the text of the notwithstanding power to make clear that legislatures are not Charter antagonists. One way to rewrite it is to replace the italicized words in the passage quoted above with the following: "Parliament or the legislature of a province may expressly declare in an Act of Parliament or of the legislature, as the case may be, that the Act or a provision thereof shall operate *notwithstanding an inconsistent judicial interpretation of* a provision included in section 2 or sections 7 to 15 of this Charter." This would reposition legislatures as advocates for their own rendering of Charter rights rather than as opponents of the Charter.

But rewriting the text of the notwithstanding power is not a productive avenue for reviving it. For one thing, it would require a formal constitutional amendment using the general amendment formula – a threshold of agreement that has proved impossible to satisfy since 1983. We know from the failures of the Meech Lake and Charlottetown Accords that mega-constitutional changes on this scale are, for now, realistically beyond the reach of political actors.[57]

More important, even if the text were somehow formally amended as suggested, the amendment is unlikely to have its intended effect because the only way to promote the use of the federal notwithstanding power is to make a bigger change to our constitutional culture. This is the kind of change that cannot be achieved simply by a formal textual amendment. It must come from a change to how political actors understand their function and how they carry it out.

Transforming Political Culture

The notwithstanding power can be redirected from its path towards desuetude only if Canadian constitutional politics develops a culture of what Joshua Braver has called "counter-interpretation."[58] Political actors engage in counter-interpretation when they "interpret the Constitution independently of, and sometimes in opposition to, the Supreme Court."[59] Counter-interpretation does not undermine the constitution; on the contrary, it strengthens it because "it ensures that when the legislature disagrees with a court decision, the legislature speaks through the Constitution rather than against it."[60] The core aim of counter-interpretation is not to provoke conflict with courts and legislatures. It is instead to make clear that courts and legislatures may have reasonable disagreements about the constitution – and that it should be open to legislatures to express that disagreement in the transparency and contestability of the legislative process.

There is presently no culture of counter-interpretation in Canada. Were there such a culture, it would be possible for Parliament to invoke the federal notwithstanding power without prompting the charge that Parliament was violating the constitution. In that world, we would accept Parliament's use of the power as a valid and legitimate exercise of its institutional right of coordinate constitutional interpretation.[61] Whose interpretation carried the day would depend on a number of factors, not the least of which would be Parliament's appetite to incur the political risk of taking a view contrary to the Supreme Court.

We cannot transform Canadian political culture overnight into one that embraces counter-interpretation. But two legislative strategies can slowly help move Canada in that direction. Neither is uncontroversial, and both would require Parliament to expend political capital in the near term to create the conditions that would allow Parliament in the medium to long term to use the notwithstanding power in the normal course of its legislative deliberations.

One suggestion is for Parliament to engage in what Adrian Vermeule has described as the "pointless exercise" of a power at risk of atrophy as a way of setting a precedent that its use is acceptable.[62] Vermeule suggests how Parliament could revive its notwithstanding power.

> Where it is politically feasible to do so, institutional actors may do well to engage in deliberate precedent-setting by taking actions that may quite possibly be unnecessary or even undesirable, according to the actors' first-order policy preferences. A wise legislature concerned to promote its institutional interests over the long run will occasionally override or conspicuously ignore a court decision, even if – by virtue of the law of anticipated reactions – the court issues only decisions that comport with the legislature's first-order policy preferences. Conspicuous, publicly visible exercises of power will preserve the power for the future, preventing the gradual growth and hardening of a constitutional norm that the legislature always – at least as far as the public observes – complies with judicial decisions and thus should continue to do so.[63]

Vermeule's roadmap counsels Parliament to exercise its notwithstanding power occasionally in a publicly visible way – even when the outcome is insignificant or undesirable – to prevent the formation of a constitutional convention against its use. This strategy could have been usefully deployed at patriation – but not now, thirty-five years later, when a constitutional convention against the use of the federal notwithstanding power is already in formation. It would be unlikely, but also ill advised, for Parliament today to use the power in a publicly visible way that could in any way be perceived as overruling the Court's interpretation of the Charter.

This concern, coupled with Vermeule's suggestion of pointless exercises of power, generates an alternative strategy for Parliament to redeem the notwithstanding power: to use the power pre-emptively in low-stakes cases where there is likely to be no disagreement about the constitutional validity of the law passed by Parliament. These low-stakes laws would be shielded from judicial review, even though a constitutional challenge would be unlikely in any case since the laws passed with pre-emptive recourse to the notwithstanding power would have been chosen precisely because of their constitutional validity. These would be pointless exercises of the power in the sense described by Vermeule, and they would have the effect of normalizing its use.

Parliament would in the near term suffer a political cost for using the notwithstanding power pre-emptively in this way. Critics would argue that Parliament should not shield the laws from review, nor should it spend parliamentary resources on such low-stakes laws when those resources could have been directed to more pressing matters. These would be legitimate concerns, but they would in the end be neutralized by the banality and clear constitutionality of the low-stakes laws that had been passed using the notwithstanding power. As it became more frequent, this strategy would eventually make it possible in the medium to long term for Parliament to use the power in cases where the stakes were much higher. In the best-case scenario, Parliament's use of the notwithstanding power in a high-stakes Charter case would provoke resistance not for its actual use but rather on the merits of Parliament's interpretive disagreement with the Court.

Conclusion: Constitutional Design and Political Reality

The risk that the federal notwithstanding power might fall into desuetude has significant consequences for constitutional law and politics in

Canada. Most important, the desuetude of the federal notwithstanding power would frustrate the design of the Constitution Act, 1982, which was intended to strike a balance between Parliament and the Supreme Court.[64] Over thirty-five years later, we know from our lived experience under the Charter that no such balance exists and that the Court is the dominant institution in Canada.

We are fortunate that our post-Charter Supreme Court has been staffed by extraordinarily intelligent and compassionate jurists whose judgments have made Canada the envy of constitutional democracies around the world. But our pride in the Supreme Court should not blind us to the reality that despite its success in enhancing rights for increasingly more classes of Canadians, the Charter today is not functioning the way it was intended. This is no fault of the Court. Fault rests fully with Parliament for its reluctance to invoke the notwithstanding power. Parliament's lament about its loss of any measure of policymaking power should not be directed at courts; it should point the finger back at itself. The notwithstanding clause gives Parliament the legal power to reclaim its policymaking dominance – but it must first muster the political will to do so.

Canada can, of course, survive without a fully deployable federal notwithstanding power, but the possible desuetude of the power highlights a problematic feature of the constitution of Canada: the growing disjunction between our constitutional text and our political reality.

The reservation and disallowance powers are not the only ones that remain textually entrenched in the constitution despite their informal repeal. There are too many similar provisions to list that are now spent, or very likely so, yet still appear in the codified portions of our constitution. The constitutional rules creating electoral districts have since been superseded by law,[65] and so have the constitutional rules governing elections and the eligibility requirements for parliamentary office.[66] The constitution still today contains rules about legislatures for Ontario and Quebec, but these are, of course, no longer valid.[67] We can even today still read in the codified constitution spent provisions involving penitentiaries,[68] the division of debts and credit between Ontario and Quebec,[69] and federal power to mandate the production of books and records from Ontario to Quebec and from Quebec to Ontario.[70]

Were the federal notwithstanding power to fall into desuetude, it would therefore have company. Yet this mismatch between the codified rules of the constitution and the practice of constitutional law and politics poses a problem for the rule of law. A constitutional culture rooted in the rule of law requires respect for what is formally codified. In Canada, the Court has recognized that it has a duty to "give effect to the Constitution's text"[71] and that political actors should not "trivialize or supplant the Constitution's written terms."[72] A codified constitution whose rules are superseded by law or convention therefore undermines the very purpose of codification. The duty on political actors is to narrow as much as possible the gap between the constitutional text and political reality, whether by updating the codified constitution to reflect new social and political realities or conforming their conduct to the codified rules that are meant to govern their actions.

The entrenchment of the notwithstanding power does not entail a requirement that Parliament invoke it always, sometimes, or even at all. But it does mean that the power should be a real option when the circumstances warrant. Today there is no genuine possibility that Parliament would have recourse to the notwithstanding power to assert its interpretation of the Charter over the Court's own reading. If this persists any longer, the power should be removed from the Charter rather than keeping the false appearance that Parliament actually has the institutional capacity to exercise it. My preferred outcome, however, is for Parliament to have no hesitation to invoke the power and to treat it as a valid and legitimate device in its policymaking toolkit.

NOTES

1 2015 SCC 5.

2 Ibid., paras. 70–92.

3 Ibid., paras. 94–123.

4 See, e.g., Amir Attaran, "Unanimity on Death with Dignity – Legalizing Physician-Assisted Dying in Canada," *New England Journal of Medicine* 372, no. 22 (2015): 2080; Stephanie Palmer, "'The Choice Is Cruel': Assisted Suicide and Charter Rights in Canada," *Cambridge Law Journal* 74, no. 2 (2015): 191. For a useful collection of perspectives, consult the *Saskatchewan Law Review*'s symposium on *Carter*: Janelle Souter and Amanda Zalmanowitz, "Symposium: *Carter v. Canada (Attorney General)*: Introduction and Background to Symposium," *Saskatchewan Law Review* 78, no. 2 (2015): 197; Sarah Burningham, "A Comment on the Court's Decision to Suspend the Declaration of Invalidity in *Carter v. Canada*," *Saskatchewan Law Review* 78, no. 2 (2015): 201; Mark Carter, "*Carter v. Canada*: Societal Interests under Sections 7 and 1," *Saskatchewan Law Review* 78, no. 2 (2015): 209; Dwight Newman,

"Judicial Method and Three Gaps in the Supreme Court of Canada's Assisted Suicide Judgment in *Carter*," *Saskatchewan Law Review* 78, no. 2 (2015): 217; Doug Surtees, "The Authorizing of Physician-Assisted Death in *Carter v. Canada (Attorney General)*," *Saskatchewan Law Review* 78, no. 2 (2015): 225; Barbara von Tigerstrom, "Consenting to Physician-Assisted Death: Issues Arising from *Carter v. Canada (Attorney General)*," *Saskatchewan Law Review* 78, no. 2 (2015): 233.

5 See *Rodriguez v. British Columbia (Attorney General)*, [1993] 3 S.C.R. 519.

6 See, e.g., Pete Baklinski, "Canada's Top Court Rules Doctors Can Help Kill Patients; Overturns Assisted Suicide Law," *Life Site*, 6 February 2015, accessed 15 September 2016, https://www.lifesitenews.com/news/breaking-canadas-top-court-rules-doctors-can-help-kill-patients; Conrad Black, "Supreme Court on the Loose," *National Post*, 14 February 2015, accessed 15 September 2016, http://news.nationalpost.com/full-comment/conrad-black-supreme-court-on-the-loose; Deborah Gyapong, "Canada's Bishops Urge Invoking Notwithstanding Clause on Assisted Suicide," *Catholic Register*, 18 September 2015, accessed 15 September 2016, http://www.catholicregister.org/item/20910-canada-s-bishops-urge-invoking-notwithstanding-clause-on-assisted-suicide; Mark Penninga and André Schutten, "Euthanasia Q&A: Where the Supreme Court's Decision Leaves Canada," *Association for Reformed Political Action*, 18 February 2015, accessed 15 September 2016, https://arpacanada.ca/news/2015/02/18/euthanasia-q-a-where-the-supreme-court-s-decision-leaves-canada.

7 Stephanie Levitz, "Government Unlikely to Invoke Notwithstanding Clause over Assisted Suicide Ruling: Peter MacKay," *National Post*, 10 February 2015, accessed 15 September 2016, http://news.nationalpost.com/news/canada/canadian-politics/government-not-likely-to-invoke-notwithstanding-clause-over-assisted-suicide-ruling-peter-mackay.

8 See, e.g., Catholic Civil Rights League, "The Catholic Civil Rights League (CCRL) Opposes Bill C-14," news release on its submission to the Standing Committee on Justice and Human Rights regarding Bill C-14, 2 May 2016, accessed 15 September 2016, https://ccrl.ca/2016/05/billc-14submission; James Bezan, House of Commons, Debates, 42nd Parl., 1st Sess., vol. 148, no. 062, 31 May 2016; Kelly Brock, House of Commons, Debates, 42nd Parl., 1st Sess., vol. 148, no. 062, 31 May 2016; Dianne Pothier, House of Commons, Standing Committee on Justice and Human Rights, Evidence (Issue no. 013, 4 May 2016), 42nd Parl., 1st Sess.; Hon. Candice Bergen, House of Commons, Debates, 42nd Parl., 1st Sess., vol. 148, no. 047, 3 May 2016; Phil McColeman, House of Commons, Debates, 42nd Parl., 1st Sess., vol. 148, no. 047, 3 May 2016; Brad Trost, House of Commons, Debates, 42nd Parl., 1st Sess., vol. 148,

no. 047, 3 May 2016; Cathay Wagantall, House of Commons, Debates, 42nd Parl., 1st Sess., vol. 148, no. 047, 3 May 2016; Bob Zimmer, House of Commons, Debates, 42nd Parl., 1st Sess., vol. 148, no. 047, 3 May 2016; Harold Albrecht, House of Commons, Debates, 42nd Parl., 1st Sess., vol. 148, no. 046, 2 May 2016; Todd Doherty, House of Commons, Debates, 42nd Parl., 1st Sess., vol. 148, no. 046, 2 May 2016; Hon. Michelle Rempel, House of Commons, Debates, 42nd Parl., 1st Sess., vol. 148, no. 046, 2 May 2016.

9 *An Act to Amend the Criminal Code and to Make Related Amendments to Other Acts (Medical Assistance in Dying)*, S.C. 2016, c. 3.

10 See, e.g., André Picard, "We Can't Debate the Assisted Dying Law without Data," *Globe and Mail*, 13 September 2016, accessed 15 September 2016, http://www.theglobeandmail.com/opinion/we-cant-debate-the-assisted-dying-law-without-data/article31837713; Joana Baron and Geoff Sigalet, "The Liberal Government Is Rediscovering the Role of Parliament in Articulating the Meaning of Charter Rights," *Policy Options*, 8 September 2016, accessed 8 September 2016, http://policyoptions.irpp.org/magazines/september-2016/the-charter-partys-new-dance-with-the-judiciary; Joan Bryden, "Assisted Dying Bill C-14 Is Unconstitutional: Leading Expert," *Huffington Post*, 6 June 2016, accessed 15 September 2016, http://www.huffingtonpost.ca/2016/06/06/leading-constitutional-expert-says-assisted-dying-law-unconstitutional_n_10317512.html.

11 The notwithstanding clause is entrenched in s. 33 of the Canadian Charter of Rights and Freedoms, Part I of the Constitution Act, 1982, being Schedule B to the Canada Act 1982, 1982, c. 11 (U.K.) (hereinafter "Charter").

> 33. (1) Parliament or the legislature of a province may expressly declare in an Act of Parliament or of the legislature, as the case may be, that the Act or a provision thereof shall operate notwithstanding a provision included in section 2 or sections 7 to 15 of this Charter.
>
> (2) An Act or a provision of an Act in respect of which a declaration made under this section is in effect shall have such operation as it would have but for the provision of this Charter referred to in the declaration.
>
> (3) A declaration made under subsection (1) shall cease to have effect five years after it comes into force or on such earlier date as may be specified in the declaration.
>
> (4) Parliament or the legislature of a province may re-enact a declaration made under subsection (1).
>
> (5) Subsection (3) applies in respect of a re-enactment made under subsection (4).

12 See Christopher Manfredi, "Conservatives, the Supreme Court of Canada, and the Constitution: Judicial-Government Relations, 2016–15," *Osgoode Hall Law Journal* 52, no. 3 (2015): 951.

13 *Carter v. Canada (Attorney General)*, Docket no. 35591, Transcription, 11 January 2016, at pp. 63 (21–5)–pp. 64 (1–5).

14 See, e.g., Jeffrey Goldsworthy, *Parliamentary Sovereignty: Contemporary Debates* (Cambridge: Cambridge University Press, 2010), 217–22; Thomas Flanagan, "Canada's Three Constitutions: Protecting, Overturning, and Reversing the Status Quo," in *The Myth of the Sacred: The Charter, the Courts, and the Politics of the Constitution in Canada*, ed. Patrick James, Donald E. Abelson, and Michael Lusztig (Montreal and Kingston: McGill-Queen's University Press, 2002), 125 at 136; Scott Stephenson, "Constitutional Reengineering: Dialogue's Migration from Canada to Australia," *International Journal of Constitutional Law* 11, no. 4 (2013): 870 at 880; Ming-Sung Kuo, "Discovering Sovereignty in Dialogue: Is Judicial Dialogue the Answer to Constitutional Conflict in the Pluralist Legal Landscape?," *Canadian Journal of Law and Jurisprudence* 26, no. 2 (2013): 341 at 349.

15 See Richard Albert, "Constitutional Amendment by Constitutional Desuetude," *American Journal of Comparative Law* 62, no. 3 (2014): 641 at 643–4.

16 See Constitution Act, 1867, 30 & 31 Victoria, c. 3 (U.K.), Part IV, ss. 55–7; Part V, s. 90 (hereinafter Constitution Act, 1867).

17 See Peter W. Hogg, *Constitutional Law of Canada*, 5th ed. (Toronto: Carswell, 2015), 3–2n5.

18 J.E.C. Munro, *The Constitution of Canada* (Cambridge: Cambridge University Press 1889), 165–6.

19 "Draft of Instructions to Be Passed under the Royal Sign Manual and Signet to Viscount Monck, Governor General of Canada," *Sessional Papers of the Parliament of the Dominion of Canada*, vol. 7, no. 22, art. VII.1–8 (1867–68).

20 "Draft of Instructions to Be Passed under the Royal Sign Manual and Signet to the Governor-General of the Dominion of Canada, 1878," *Sessional Papers of the Parliament of the Dominion of Canada*, vol. 7, no. 13 (1877).

21 See Statute of Westminster, 1931, 22 Geo 5, ch. 4, ss. 2, 4.

22 Report of the Conference on the Operation of Dominion Legislation and Merchant Shipping Legislation 1929, at 16 (1930); Balfour Declaration, Imperial Conference, Inter-Imperial Relations Committee, Part II, at 2 (1926).

23 See Gerard V. La Forest, *Disallowance and Reservation of Provincial Legislation* (Canada: Department of Justice, 1955), 83–115.

24 See *Reference re The Power of the Governor General in Council to Disallow Provincial Legislation and the Power of Reservation of a Lieutenant-Governor of a Province*, [1938] SCR 71.

25 *See* Robert C. Vipond, *Liberty and Community: Canadian Federalism and the Failure of the Constitution* (Albany: State University of New York Press, 1991), 113–50.

26 See Garth Stevenson, *Unfulfilled Union: Canadian Federalism and National Unity*, 5th ed. (Montreal and Kingston: McGill-Queen's University Press, 2009), 214–15.

27 As of 1990, 84% of all references had involved federalism disputes, precisely the kind of matter that would prompt the federal government to reserve or disallow a provincial bill or law; see James L. Huffman and MardiLyn Saathoff, "Advisory Opinion and Canadian Constitutional Development: The Supreme Court's Reference Jurisdiction," *Minnesota Law Review* 74, no. 6 (1990): 1251 at 1290 n214.

28 Ivor Jennings, *The Law and the Constitution*, 5th ed. (London: University of London Press, 1967), 136.

29 Ibid., 135.

30 Ibid., 136.

31 This sequence builds on Stephen Griffin's five-part framework for identifying an informal constitutional amendment; see Stephen M. Griffin, "Constituent Power and Constitutional Change in American Constitutionalism," in *The Paradox of Constitutionalism: Constituent Power and Constitutional Form*, ed. Martin Loughlin and Neil Walker (Oxford: Oxford University Press 2008), 49–66.

32 Gérald A. Beaudoin, "La Loi 22: À propos du désaveu, du référé et de l'appel à l'Exécutif fédéral," *Revue générale de droit* 5, no. 2 (1974): 385 at 386 (describing disallowance in French as "d'une autre époque").

33 Standing Senate Committee on Legal and Constitutional Affairs, *Report to the Senate of Canada on Certain Aspects of the Canadian Constitution*, November 1980, 7.

34 Richard Simeon, "Canada: Federalism, Language, and Regional Conflict," in *Federalism and Territorial Cleavages*, ed. Ugo M. Amoretti and Nancy Bermeo (Baltimore: Johns Hopkins University Press, 2004), 93 at 100.

35 R. Kent Weaver, "Political Institutions and Canada's Constitutional Crisis," in *The Collapse of Canada?*, ed. R. Kent Weaver (Washington, DC: Brookings Institution, 1992), 7 at 44–5.

36 Andrew Heard, *Canadian Constitutional Conventions: The Marriage of Law and Politics* (Toronto: Oxford University Press, 1991), 103.

37 Charter, s. 33(1).

38 Ibid., ss. 33(3)–(4).

39 Tsvi Kahana, "Legalism, Anxiety and Legislative Constitutionalism," *Queen's Law Journal* 31, no. 2 (2006): 536 at 555.

40 As Kahana explains, Quebec's *Act Respecting the Constitution Act, 1982*, S.Q. 1982, c. 21, repealed all Quebec's laws and re-enacted them using the notwithstanding power. For all laws passed in the subsequent three years, Quebec's National Assembly resorted to the notwithstanding power. Tsvi Kahana, "The Notwithstanding Mechanism and Public Discussion: Lessons from the Ignored Practice of Section 33 of the Charter," *Canadian Public Administration* 44, no. 3 (2001): 256 at 281 n1.

41 See Rhéal Séguin and Daniel Leblanc, "PQ Vows to Use Charter Protection for Religious Ban," *Globe and Mail*, 31 March 2014, accessed 15 September 2016, http://www.theglobeandmail.com/news/politics/pq-would-use-notwithstanding-clause-to-protect-charter-from-challenge-marois/article17737134.

42 See "Brad Wall Open to Using 'Notwithstanding Clause' over Labour Ruling," *CBC News*, 4 February 2015, accessed 15 September 2016, http://www.cbc.ca/news/canada/saskatchewan/brad-wall-open-to-using-notwithstanding-clause-over-labour-ruling-1.2945304.

43 See "Alberta May Invoke Notwithstanding Clause over Same-Sex Marriage," *CBC News*, 27 July 2005, accessed 15 September 2016, http://www.cbc.ca/news/canada/alberta-may-invoke-notwithstanding-clause-over-same-sex-marriage-1.528949.

44 See *Canada (Attorney General) v. Bedford*, [2013] 3 SCR 1101; *Reference re Same-Sex Marriage*, [2004] 3 SCR 698.

45 Peter Russell, "The Notwithstanding Clause: The Charter's Homage to Parliamentary Democracy," *Policy Options*, 1 February 2017, accessed 15 September 2016, http://policyoptions.irpp.org/magazines/the-charter-25/the-notwithstanding-clause-the-charters-homage-to-parliamentary-democracy.

46 *Reference re Remuneration of Judges of the Provincial Court of P.E.I.; Reference re Independence and Impartiality of Judges of the Provincial Court of P.E.I.*, [1997] 3 SCR 3.

47 *RJR-MacDonald Inc. v. Canada (Attorney General)*, [1995] 3 SCR 199.

48 *Chaoulli v. Quebec (Attorney General)*, [2005] 1 SCR 791.

49 There is some evidence of "notwithstanding by stealth," the practice of reversing judicial decisions by simple statute without following the publicity requirements required by the Charter. See James B. Kelly and Matthew A. Hennigar, "The Canadian Charter of Rights and the Minister of Justice: Weak-Form Review within a Constitutional Charter of Rights," *International Journal of Constitutional Law* 10, no. 1 (2012): 35.

50 R. Roy McMurtry, "The Creation of an Entrenched Charter of Rights – A Personal Memoir," *Queen's Law Journal* 31, no. 2 (2006): 456 at 466–7.

51 Ran Hirschl, *Towards Juristocracy: The Origins and Consequences of the New Constitutionalism* (Cambridge, MA: Harvard University Press, 2004).
52 Hon. Jean Chrétien, House of Commons, Debates, 32nd Parl., 1st Sess., vol. 12, no. 062, 20 November 1981, at 13042.
53 See Peter W. Hogg and Allison A. Bushell, "The *Charter* Dialogue between Courts and Legislatures (or Perhaps the *Charter of Rights* Isn't Such a Bad Thing After All)," *Osgoode Hall Law Journal* 35, no. 1 (1997): 75 at 79–83.
54 Kent Roach, *The Supreme Court on Trial: Judicial Activism or Democratic Dialogue* (Toronto: Irwin Law, 2001), 156, 176.
55 Charter, Part I, s. 33(1) (emphasis added).
56 Jeffrey Goldsworthy, "Judicial Review, Legislative Override, and Democracy," *Wake Forest Law Review* 38, no. 2 (2003): 451 at 467.
57 For an explanation of why major formal amendment in Canada is today virtually impossible, see Michael Lusztig, "Constitutional Paralysis: Why Canadian Constitutional Initiatives Are Doomed to Fail," *Canadian Journal of Political Science* 27, no. 4 (1994): 747.
58 Joshua Braver, "Exporting U.S. Counter-Interpretation: Redeeming Constitutional Supremacy in the U.K.," *Georgetown Journal of International Law* 47, no. 3 (2016): 867.
59 Ibid., 869.
60 Ibid.
61 See Dennis Baker, *Not Quite Supreme: The Courts and Coordinate Constitutional Interpretation* (Montreal and Kingston: McGill-Queen's University Press, 2010).
62 Adrian Vermeule, "The Atrophy of Constitutional Powers," *Oxford Journal of Legal Studies* 32, no. 3 (2012): 421 at 441.
63 Ibid., 439.
64 A. Wayne MacKay, "The Legislature, the Executive and the Courts: The Delicate Balance of Power or Who Is Running This Country Anyway?," *Dalhousie Law Journal* 24, no. 2 (2001): 37 at 56.
65 Constitution Act, 1867, Part IV, s. 40.
66 Ibid., Part IV, s. 41.
67 Ibid., Part V, ss. 70–1.
68 Ibid., Part IX, s. 141.
69 Ibid., Part IX, s. 142.
70 Ibid., Part IX, s. 143.
71 *British Columbia v. Imperial Tobacco Canada Ltd*, [2005] 2 SCR 473, at para. 67.
72 Ibid.

PART THREE

Policy Issues

8 The *Charter* Beat: The Impact of Rights Decisions on Canadian Policing

TROY RIDDELL AND DENNIS BAKER[1]

In October 2013, a judge in Ontario excluded thousands of images of child pornography because they were the product of an illegal search of a "thumb drive" by police "due to carelessness, negligence and/or a willful or flagrant disregard for the law and established *Charter* standards."[2] In commenting on the case, lawyer Michael Spratt wondered whether this case had resulted from poor police training in the latest developments in the case law or "rogue" police officers.[3] Although such cases provide anecdotal information about police responses to jurisprudence resulting from the Canadian Charter of Rights and Freedoms, we have very little systematic evidence about how frequently, and to what extent, police do not follow Charter requirements and a lack of theory, at least in the Canadian context, to help us predict and explain police responses to judicial decisions affecting civil liberties. As discussed below, American research in this area points to possibly more complex, institutional reasons for police deviating from constitutional requirements than simply the existence of rogue police officers. But to what degree would these theories hold in the Canadian context? In the *Dufaure* case noted above, the trial judge speculated that there was a "systemic problem,"[4] which suggests that organizational factors contributed to the Charter violations. Unfortunately, however, we lack systematic study of police responses to the Charter to help answer such questions.

It is well known that the Charter and judicial decisions have significantly altered the constitutional rules surrounding police investigative practices, but very little is known about the effects of such rule changes on police policy and practices. In 1994, Peter Russell noted that "until the appropriate kind of empirical research is carried out, we will not know the extent to which the Supreme Court's Charter jurisprudence is actually modifying police behaviour."[5] Nevertheless, eleven years later, law professor Alan Young was still lamenting that "we can only speculate whether or not the police are trying to live up to the constitutional obligations imposed upon them by the Charter."[6] This remains largely true even today. More generally, how judicial decisions are implemented (or not) and how they influence policy remain among the most understudied dimensions of judicial politics.

This chapter begins to fill these empirical and theoretical gaps by presenting the results of a case study of one southern Ontario police service's response to the Charter – in particular, recent decisions involving search and seizure and investigative detention.

Existing Research

The policy impact that a court decision or series of decisions will have is rarely straightforward and is dependent on numerous factors. Although the literature on judicial impact is replete with various analytical frameworks, several broad factors are routinely considered significant with respect to how individuals and organizations implement judicial decisions (or not): incentives or disincentives for promoting compliance, the alignment of court decisions with individual attitudes and organizational goals, the clarity of the judicial decisions, and how decisions are communicated to implementers. How other actors (such as bureaucratic agencies, politicians, lower court judges, the media, and so on) respond to judicial decisions is also important as they can influence individuals and organizations directly charged with implementing decisions.[7]

There have been numerous US studies investigating the impact of constitutional rules on policing. Such studies rarely use theoretical frameworks developed by judicial-impact scholars explicitly, but their analyses often reflect the general factors identified throughout the impact literature. Insights into the police implementation of constitutional rules differ somewhat among studies, as do the methodological techniques used to study the implementation and policy impact of decisions. Some researchers observed the police in action to assess the effects of constitutional rules on police behaviour.[8] Others, looking to avoid potential problems with non-participant observation, used data on arrest rates, amount of seized goods, motions to suppress evidence, and/or search warrant requests, before and after key judicial decisions on search and seizure had been handed down, to assess the impact of search and seizure rules and the exclusionary rule on police behaviour.[9]

However, these data (such as arrest rates) are all influenced by a host of factors, such as crime rates. Moreover, many police encounters with citizens in which the police violate the constitutional rights of a suspect will not be captured by any statistic. Some studies have tried to overcome these problems by supplementing the data analysis with interviews of police officers and others in the legal community.[10] Others have studied the effects of judicial decisions on police behaviour primarily by interviewing or surveying police officers as well as lawyers and judges.[11]

How did police policies and practices change, if at all, after Supreme Court decisions about rights, and what explanations were given for these findings? The literature suggests that, after an initial period of adjustment, police forces adapted to the requirement set out in the Supreme Court's decision in *Miranda v. Arizona* that suspects in custodial detention be provided with a warning that they had the right to counsel and could remain silent.[12] Researchers suggest that there is high police compliance with *Miranda* because (a) the rule is easy to understand, (b) police do not want confessions excluded at trial, and (c) police use interrogation techniques that often result in confessions, regardless of whether a suspect is told about his or her Miranda rights.[13]

The American research on police compliance with constitutional rules, particularly in the realm of search and seizure, has revealed that organizational norms and institutional priorities can shape individual police behaviour.[14] If police organizations emphasized getting drugs off the street, for example, or if police officers supported their organization's efforts to rid the community of drugs and drug dealers through community policing, officers were less likely to adhere to the constitutional rules regarding search and seizure.[15] Alternatively, police officers might unwittingly break the law if they were not properly trained in what the law required.[16] Other researchers have found a calculated effort on the part of some police to engage in deceptive practices to obtain a search warrant or conviction.[17] In their interviews, Godschmidt and Anonymous found that these officers were motivated by personal and organizational pressures to be effective in spite of the formal operation of the criminal justice system, with subcultural forces (such as peer pressure) playing some motivating role. The lack of disincentives was also considered to be a factor that influenced behaviour.[18]

Compared to the United States, little work has been done in Canada to assess the impact of the Charter judgments on police policy and behaviour. Moore undertook case studies of the responses of the RCMP and the Halton (Ontario) Regional Police Force to the Supreme Court decisions[19] in *Brydges*[20] – wherein the Court held that a detainee should be informed of the availability of duty counsel and legal aid in the jurisdiction – and *Duarte*[21] – wherein the Court held that participant or consent surveillance by an agent of the state without prior judicial authorization was unconstitutional. Based on an unspecified number of interviews with government officials and members of the two police organizations, Moore reported that the implementation of *Brydges* was relatively straightforward, but implementation of *Duarte* was longer and more complicated. Moore argued that strong communications systems, especially those found in the RCMP, facilitated implementation, as did the number of resources at the disposal of the police. The complexity of the *Duarte* decision did not seem to be raised by interviewees until they were prompted, while attitudes towards the Charter tended to be generally positive and were thought not to be a "significant impediment to implementation."[22] However, Moore argued that "organizational complexity" could hamper implementation based on frustration expressed by those members of the Halton police force who stated that it was unclear what organization would take responsibility for drafting new policy in response to Court decisions.

Devonshire's study suffers from some of the same defects as Moore's since it does not specify the number of interviews conducted and focuses more on policy than activity "on the ground."[23] For his study, Devonshire interviewed a deputy chief, a hold-up squad detective, the breathalyser field coordinator, and (an unspecified number of) drug squad members, and he analysed various policy and training materials to gauge the response to over fifty Charter decisions. According to Devonshire, the Charter has been beneficial because, in response, organizations like the Metro Toronto Police have altered investigative methods and procedures and thoroughly trained its members about Charter procedure. Investigations are more thorough and professional, cases are more solid, and the police now help legislators and the courts in protecting rights. Devonshire also noted, however, that investigations are more time-consuming and expensive, that some criminals will go free, and that some officers express frustration over various effects of Charter decisions. While Devonshire suggested that, "with some possible exceptions, police circumvention of Supreme Court decisions does not appear to have occurred,"[24] he provided no empirical evidence about how often or why officers might skirt Charter decisions or whether training is indeed adequate when officers are confronted with various scenarios in the course of their duties.

Methodology

In this chapter, we build on Moore's and Devonshire's work using a case study of a mid-sized police force in Ontario (such forces have between approximately 450 and 750 officers). The study consists of a survey that was posted on the organization's intranet, interviews with four officers and one civilian in the organization, and a review of policy and training materials that were provided to us. To make the project more manageable, we were particularly interested in how the organization responded to relatively recent Supreme Court decisions in the areas of search and seizure[25] and investigative detention.[26]

The survey was designed to probe various dimensions of the impact of Charter decisions. Fifty-seven individuals responded to our survey – primarily constables and sergeants, but also a handful of staff sergeants and senior officers. A third of the respondents had been in policing between eleven and fifteen years; 19 per cent had between zero and ten years' experience, and 47 per cent had sixteen or more years' experience. The vast majority had either a college degree (43 per cent) or a university degree (43 per cent). The respondents came from various units in the organization, from patrol to drugs and major crimes. As reported below, some questions asked about training and communications; others probed attitudes towards the Charter and Charter decisions; and still others attempted to delve into the difficult area of the degree to which decisions are followed and why. These latter questions, in particular, did more to probe perceptions of actual, "on-the-ground" implementation than either Moore or Devonshire was able to do.

Nevertheless, there were limitations to the methodology. For example, to encourage police department cooperation and to avoid any potential legal complications, we did not ask respondents directly whether they had violated the Charter and, if so, why; instead, we couched these questions in more general terms and also asked scenario questions, which tried to examine issues of knowledge and what officers would do in certain situations. Nor did we observe officers in action. In terms of training materials, we were not given access to information disseminated in specialized training seminars or verbally at meetings. Finally, there were the usual difficulties with trying to create generalizable, causal inferences from a case study. Despite these limitations, the case study provided important insights, including those that can drive future research. We discuss three major themes from our findings: perceptions about the Charter and Charter decisions; communication, training, and knowledge surrounding Charter decisions; and, more generally, implications for on-the-ground implementation of Charter rights.

Findings and Discussion

Perceptions of the Charter of Rights and Charter Decisions

All survey respondents and interviewees reported that the Charter of Rights and Charter decisions played an important role in policing. Over half of our survey respondents (56 per cent) indicated that the Charter and Charter decisions "play a large role in [their] day-to-day work activities," with another 30 per cent indicating that they played "some role" in their day-to-day activities. A strong majority of respondents indicated that they thought that the Charter "strongly encourages" (32 per cent) or "somewhat encourages" (35 per cent) professionalism. An overwhelming number of respondents, however, argued that the "balance between protecting the rights of the accused and controlling and investigating crime" has shifted "much too far towards benefiting the accused" (51 per cent) or "somewhat too far towards benefiting the accused" (44 per cent). One interviewee told us that criminal trials are now all about the actions of the police rather than the accused. Not surprisingly, a clear majority of respondents also indicated that the Charter and Charter decisions made it "much more difficult and time-consuming to investigate crime" (47 per cent) or "somewhat more difficult and time-consuming to investigate crime" (35 per cent); only 16 per cent indicated that Charter decisions had only a "marginal" impact or no impact.

When given the option to elaborate on the impact of the Charter on investigations, a few respondents argued that the effects were positive. For example, one respondent indicated, "If it makes our job more difficult then I'm fine with that. It slows us down and compels us to think critically. It makes me more comfortable with the idea that when someone is found guilty in a Canadian court, that they are truly guilty. My job was never meant to be easy." Another respondent stated, "Having noted it was much more difficult does not necessarily mean it's a bad thing. The Charter and its principles are fundamental to our way of life. It is just a fact that the Charter tips the scales to the favour of the accused, and investigating crime becomes a more time-consuming and difficult task."

However, the majority of respondents took the opportunity to highlight how Charter decisions have made investigations lengthier, more difficult, and uncertain. One survey respondent indicated that courts did not consider limited police resources when making decisions, and others noted the lack of consistency in courts' interpretation of the Charter. One survey respondent and a couple of our interviewees also identified instances in which the Crown seemed to be interpreting the Supreme Court decisions more restrictively than the Court itself may have intended.

A number of respondents provided specific examples of the difficulties that some decisions have caused. The expanded requirements for search warrants generated by the *Feeney*,[27] *Spencer*,[28] and *White*[29] decisions were often highlighted. One respondent, for instance, stated that

> *R. v. Spencer* has been interpreted by large corporations to apply to any information regarding clients in any circumstance as opposed to just the anonymous nature of accessing the Internet. As a result, corporations are refusing to provide any information about accounts without a judicial authorization. This is true even in cases where there is no expectation of privacy in the information sought. Often there are insufficient grounds to seek an authorization or no authorization available to obtain the information. The investigation is stymied before it even begins.

Another respondent wrote,

> Look at [the] *Feeney* decision [SCC] and most recently *R v. White* [ONCA]. We have to be able to put someone "physically or visually" into a place before warrant will be granted (assuming grounds to do so of course) yet now cannot go into an apartment building/condo without prior judicial authorization? So we now need a "warrant" (to trespass into the building to confirm the unit) before we can get a "warrant" (to search that unit). AND, the trespass is done by way of a General Warrant which has to go to a Judge. AND, in order for us to do that, the warrant has to be read and approved by a Crown. Terribly time-consuming in a ruling that extends a person's REOP [reasonable expectation of privacy] to hallways/common areas of buildings.

A number of our interviewees argued that *Feeney* and *Spencer* also made it more difficult to undertake investigations. One interviewee reinforced the perception that *Spencer* was being interpreted so broadly that some corporations would refuse to provide information, even when it would help (and was requested by) the person whose privacy was ostensibly being protected (such as in the case of cell phone account fraud). One interviewee also highlighted how right-to-counsel decisions, particularly those to do with "choice of counsel," made investigations more difficult, especially in drinking and driving cases, where the accused had obvious trouble exercising that choice and required extraordinary help from the officers to do so.

When respondents were given the opportunity to comment on whether there were Charter rules that they would like to see "modified to better balance protecting rights of the accused and the controlling and investigation of crime," a number of them also mentioned right-to-counsel decisions. They raised concerns about how soon the caution had to be read (including before an investigative detention) and the need to delay questioning if an accused requested a specific counsel. Not surprisingly, the *Feeney* and *Spencer* rules were mentioned, as were very onerous warrant requirements in general. Investigative detentions and changes to the "street checks" rules were also raised.

Our case study suggests that Charter decisions play a key role in day-to-day policing and that officers see the Charter as contributing to the professionalization of policing. At the same time, however, frustration arises from perceptions that Crowns and courts are inconsistent in interpreting the Charter and that some decisions push individual rights too far at the expense of investigating crime.

Communication, Training, and Knowledge

Our study indicates that there is considerable desire for additional training with respect to the Charter and its impact on police practices. An overwhelming majority of 77 per cent of respondents stated that they would like to receive more information and training (with 40 per cent asking for "much more"), and only 21 per cent thought that the current level of information and training was sufficient. This desire arises even when it is clear that officers are receiving some training already: 68 per cent reported that they were receiving "some" (47 per cent) or "a lot" (21 per cent) of information and training. In their open-ended feedback, respondents tended to refer to their initial training at the Ontario Police

College (OPC), which required specific courses on the Charter. This suggests that the desire for more training is really a desire for ongoing training. Indeed, several respondents emphasized keeping current with the changing demands of the law: one noted, "Every police officer is well versed in Charter rights. … The problem is keeping up to date with the judicial interpretations of police actions"; another suggested that "periodic refresher training" would be welcome. Given the constantly evolving nature of Charter jurisprudence, the assumption that the training received at the outset of a police career – which might easily stretch over several decades – is sufficient for the entire career can be a cause of considerable dysfunction unless there are mechanisms to keep officers current.

There is some variation in how new information and training reaches the officers, but it is clear that most of the instruction comes from within the service itself. When asked to identify the primary source of information about the Charter and judicial decisions, 60 per cent of respondents indicated that they learned from bulletins and other communications from police leadership (30 per cent) or through discussion with colleagues (30 per cent). These discussions took a myriad of forms; they included calls to sergeants when there might be a Charter-related question (if time permitted) as well as more experienced officers providing mentorship to more junior officers through the Field Development Officer program.[30] Only a small percentage (11 per cent) reported "classroom training" as a primary source, which supports the notion that formal training is infrequent after the initial OPC training. We did hear about Charter cases being part of mandatory training programs for officers moving into specialized units, such as drugs. A significant number – 16 per cent – of respondents reported that their primary source of information was the news media. Given that such reporting is often overly general and occasionally inaccurate, the reliance on such sources for police information could be worrying. Text responses to this question are more reassuring, however, as respondents reported relying on professional police publications (such as *Blue Line Magazine*, which routinely provides detailed articles on case law), and many reported reading full decisions themselves through CanLII and QuickLaw.

Further investigation revealed that the primarily in-house sources of information were actually much more varied and self-initiated than one might have suspected. In terms of top-down distribution of information about changing case law, the primary vehicle is the "bulletin." Police leadership distributes information to all members of the force using electronic bulletins, which are posted on the organization's intranet. More formal bulletins are prepared by the force's Legal Services branch, but with some input from and coordination with the force's Training branch. (During our study, the force was transitioning to making this exclusively the role of Legal Services; we wonder whether unclear demarcations between the Training and Legal Services branches might contribute to less effective communication on other police forces.)

We reviewed two bulletins: one on *R. v. Vu*,[31] which the force claimed represented the old approach (where there was an unclear division between Legal Services and Training), and one on *R. v. Fearon*,[32] which represented the new approach (where Legal Services would be more clearly responsible). The revised approach appears to have yielded positive results. In terms of timeliness, *Vu* was decided on 7 November 2013, and the bulletin was issued on 12 February 2014 (thirteen weeks later); *Fearon* was decided on 11 December 2014, and the bulletin was issued on 18 December 2014 (seven days later). The *Vu* bulletin contained little information about the facts of the case or the reasoning behind the decision; instead, it provided terse instructions for police in rather technical legal jargon. By contrast, the much longer *Fearon* bulletin gave the facts of the case, presented a summary of the Court's reasoning, and clearly set out the four conditions to be met for a police search to be constitutional. In addition, the bulletin offered three plausible scenarios (two where the search would be warranted and one where it would not) to give officers a good sense of how the rule could be applied prospectively. It is very readable and blunt in its advice ("Do not go on unfettered fishing expeditions and try to hide behind this ruling because it will not stand up in court").

While the new bulletins reflect a clear improvement – and suggest "best practices" for other forces – we question whether they, no matter how well crafted, will have an impact on individual police behaviour. In an interview, a constable on the force continued to think of the bulletins as "out of date" and infrequent. There are no measures to ensure that individuals read a bulletin, and they are not required to acknowledge that they have received it. It may be left to a few careful readers to disseminate the information more broadly throughout the force.

Much of the information that ultimately arrives at an officer's ears or eyes takes a more chaotic and ad hoc route. Respondents and interviewees told us that some information is passed along to them at platoon meetings before a shift, but the informality of that mechanism makes it difficult to track the accuracy and efficacy of such communications. At the force we studied, several vehicles for better communication emerged organically in response to perceived needs. The warrant writer, for example, has a blog on the organization's intranet – his "pet project" – that he updates to include key decisions. This has decreased the amount of time he needs to spend answering emails and allows him to direct interested parties to the blog. While he liaises with the Legal Services branch, his additional sources of information include British Columbia Crown counsel Henry Waldock's blog and QuickLaw alerts on new decisions. The warrant writer notes that he is not himself a lawyer, has no formal training on case law, and, for these reasons, is careful not to "interpret" the law for others. Other specialized branches of the force reportedly have people who also take it upon themselves to research and disseminate information. They may create an internal "network" of information gatherers and providers who can supplement the information provided by more formal sources. The danger, of course, is that there may be considerable gaps in this network; indeed, the constable we interviewed had no idea that the warrant writer's blog existed, even though it contains information directly related to the policing activities he engages in.

What is not shared broadly throughout the force are the electronic bulletins created by the Ministry of the Attorney General's Crown Law Office – Criminal. These timely and frequent summaries *are* produced by legal experts ("one of the premier criminal law offices in Canada," according to its website) and contain clear information on the impact that decisions might have on police practices. At the force we studied, the Legal Services branch was included on this email distribution – once it had learned that it existed and, even then, only after it had obtained internal ministry approval. The Crown Law Office considers this its "work product" and thus restricts distribution. It now provides access to the Police Legal Advisors Committee of the Ontario Association of Chiefs of Police, but this includes less than 20 per cent of the police forces in Ontario. It is hard to justify the limited distribution of this useful information since it was produced for the benefit of the state. Because public resources are used to creating these bulletins, a proactive distribution to police organizations is surely warranted.

At the local level, as discussed further below, there is only sporadic feedback or information from Crowns to the police organization about Charter requirements. Many respondents expressed a desire for more regular feedback from Crowns in general and particularly in cases where evidence was excluded by the judge or deemed too risky for Crowns to use at trial. One respondent, for instance, wrote that

> a simple email from a Crown would be very appreciated. For example: In the case you submitted before the courts, R. v. XXXXXX, the result was _____. The following are considerations we used. … It would be helpful in the future if you. … I am aware that many cases get plead out [*sic*] because of other circumstances, but it would be helpful to know if it was something we did incorrectly or could refer to case law to improve upon.

While too much communication between police and a Crown could impair the independence of each, it is difficult to see how such a debriefing – if it were after the fact and strictly informative – would be problematic. It would also have the potential to significantly improve police conduct and Charter compliance.

On-the-Ground Implementation

The question of how knowledge and training as well as attitudes towards the Charter, along with other factors, might influence the degree to which police officers do or do not follow Charter decisions is, of course, very difficult to trace. It is challenging even to gauge the degree to which organizations and individual officers follow Charter decisions, let alone to untangle reasons for compliance, evasion, or non-compliance. Nevertheless, in our survey and interviews we tried, however imperfectly, to begin generating data about compliance and what might explain whether police are complying with decisions.

We attempted to discover issues of implementation and compliance using different kinds of questions in the survey. A few questions asked about compliance, but from different angles. One question asked generally about compliance. When asked about the frequency with which Charter violations occur in general in Canadian policing, a plurality (45 per cent) suggested that they occur "occasionally," but 20 per cent responded "frequently," and 25 per cent chose "infrequently." Only 8 per cent of respondents thought that violations occurred only "rarely." Another question probed the issue of deliberate evasion of constitutional rules by referencing two cases – *R. v. Panjak Bedi*[33] and *R. v. Jinje*[34] – in which judges found that there were conscious attempts to construct evidence to justify searches. No respondents described this behaviour as "frequent," and most (58 per cent) described it as occurring only

Table 8.1 Factors Explaining the Implementation of Charter Rights

Factor	Mean (out of 5)
Knowledge and training about Charter decisions	4.45
The extent to which judicial Charter decisions provide clear guidelines for police behaviour	4.25
The degree to which police organizations and leadership stress following Charter rights	4.20
The importance and severity of the crime being investigated	3.63
Personal attitudes of individual police officers	3.27

"rarely" (14 per cent thought it occurred "occasionally," and 22 per cent thought it occurred "infrequently").

To better understand what might help to explain the implementation of Charter rights and the degree to which decisions are followed (deliberately or not), we asked respondents to rate the importance of potential explanatory factors on a scale of 1 (not very important) to 5 (very important). Most of the factors we chose are commonly cited as important in the judicial-impact literature discussed earlier:[35] the attitudes of individual implementers, communication and training, organizational leadership, and clarity of the rules. We also added a question about the importance of the crime being investigated to assess whether that influenced officers' decisions. The results are set out in table 8.1, ranking the factors from those that generated the highest average score to those that generated the lowest.

Although all the factors were deemed to be at least somewhat important, the institutional-level factors involving communication, leadership, and clarity of judicial decisions were considered to be more important than the micro-level factors of individual attitudes and type of case being investigated. This suggests that respondents believed that, overall, police were committed to following Charter rules regardless of their individual opinion or the case they were working on, but also that they believed they could do so more effectively if the rules were clear and clearly communicated by a supportive police leadership.

To help us gauge the impact of some of these factors, particularly clarity of the rules and communication and training, we asked respondents to read two scenarios. The first is a clear-cut scenario about computer searches that has been definitively settled by the Supreme Court (*R. v. Vu*).

> Police officers were executing a warrant to search the basement of a home for a meth lab. The warrant authorized the officers to search "the premises

> of 99 Hypothetical Way, Anyplace, Ontario, for any equipment related to the manufacture of crystal meth." During their search, the officers found the lab along with a desk with a computer on it. The officers believed that the computer may have information about drug transactions. The officers searched the computer and found evidence of various transactions.

The results were promising: 85 per cent correctly answered that the search of the computer was unconstitutional, including 55 per cent who were certain of their answer. In another, less clear scenario, the responses were much more divided on whether a Charter violation had occurred. The scenario is based on a possible arbitrary detention, followed by a search and seizure.

> Two police officers in a city in Ontario spotted a young black man, Smith, walking down the street. As part of a proactive policing policy of engaging individuals in high-crime neighbourhoods in conversation, one police officer shouted out of the patrol car's window to Smith. THE OFFICER: Smith, come here. What's going on, man? Which one are you? Come here, I have got to talk to you. THE ACCUSED: What do you want? THE OFFICER: Which one are you? THE ACCUSED: Smith. THE OFFICER: I know. Are you – there are two brothers. Keep your hands down. Which one are you? What's your first name? Smith gave his first name, and in a brief conversation, the police officer realized that it was Smith's brother who had outstanding warrants. As the police officer was filling out a card with details of Smith's name, address, and race, a second man appeared near the police car and started shouting. The man startled everyone, and Smith went into a "blading" posture, with his body turned sideways and his left arm pinned against his left side. When the police officer saw the blading posture, he asked Smith to show his hands – Smith did not comply – the officer reached out to check Smith's side for weapons and felt what he suspected was the handle of a gun. The officer shouted "Gun!" – Smith ran but was apprehended and arrested. The officers searched Smith and found a gun along with his cell phone. The officers then searched through Smith's email, texts, pictures, and Facebook and Instagram apps on the phone to see whether there was any information associated with his possible use of the gun.

The results reported in table 8.2 as to whether the suspect was arbitrarily detained reveal large discrepancies in opinion.

In the qualitative comments, the respondents were similarly divided, although united in some frustration with the unclear rules emanating

Table 8.2 Was the Suspect Arbitrarily Detained?

Response	N	%
Yes, definitely	7	14
Yes, probably	13	25
Uncertain	3	6
No, probably	9	18
No, definitely	19	37

from the judiciary ("As to what a judge would say, flip a coin," noted one respondent). In general, our survey suggests that the clarity of the judicial rule affects its dissemination to police organizations; perhaps unsurprisingly, "black-and-white" rules have a much better chance of being received and understood by police officers than murky, "contextual" ones.

The search of the cell phone in the investigative-detention scenario generated a more clear-cut response, but still almost a quarter of the sample did not indicate that an in-depth search of the phone without a warrant violated the guidelines set out by the Supreme Court in *R. v. Fearon*.

We also asked interviewees directly about issues related to implementation. One experienced officer noted that, in specialized training seminars (involving various police forces), "Often some guy in the room says, 'But I always do that,'" when a particular unconstitutional technique was identified, perhaps pointing to haphazard training and dissemination affecting implementation (but hopefully addressed in the subsequent seminar discussion). As for conscious efforts to circumvent Charter decisions, this officer thought that there might be some police officers who would stretch grounds for justifying a search on occasion, but his impression was that the appetite for taking such risks was low owing to the possibility of a lawsuit or disciplinary action. A constable whom we interviewed also indicated that the prospect of disciplinary proceedings under the Police Services Act, or even criminal prosecution, helped deter deliberate Charter violations. However, this constable argued that, in day-to-day police operations, there was often ambiguity about how the Charter applied. And, the constable noted, most cases end with a plea bargain, with very little feedback from prosecutors unless one is the lead on a major case.

This echoes the responses that we received on the survey to an open-ended question inviting participants to describe what happens (formally or informally) after evidence has been excluded. Most commentators stated that they usually received no feedback whatsoever about what happened to the evidence or the case: officers were left wondering whether the Crown proceeded with the case, whether the evidence collected was used or avoided because of a potential Charter problem, or, if the case ended with a plea bargain, what role their behaviour and work played in the plea negotiations. Only in an exceptional case – perhaps a major crime in which key evidence was excluded – would officers be made aware of any mistakes they might have made. Minor transgressions were likely to go unidentified and uncorrected.

A handful of commentators, though, mentioned that serious Charter breaches could lead to disciplinary proceedings or other legal action. For example, one respondent indicated an awareness that "on occasion, court cases have been directed to Professional Standards to investigate for misconduct. Officers have been disciplined for Neglect of Duty or Discreditable Conduct under the Police Services Act for serious Charter breaches." From the survey and interviews, it becomes apparent that feedback about Charter violations to the force and to individual officers is ad hoc and inconsistent. Some Crowns appear more willing to provide feedback to the force than others. When willing, the Crowns will most often liaise with Legal Services, but sometimes an officer's commander or court police officers will be contacted. One survey respondent stated that sometimes a Crown will initiate a process of review of an officer if the behaviour was "egregious" or if prompted by media reports.

Overall, the picture painted by our case study is that deliberate evasion of clear Charter rules is likely to be relatively infrequent, perhaps owing to the threat of possible legal sanctions, internal commitments to following law and procedure, and a desire not have evidence excluded, but that good-faith mistakes might happen somewhat more often because of a lack of knowledge and training. There is also a considerable amount of police activity about which it is not necessarily clear how the Charter rules apply and about which reasonable people, even those well versed in criminal law, may disagree. All survey respondents and interviewees suggested that there was a fair degree of variation in how local judges and Crowns interpreted the Charter.

Conclusions

A large proportion of Charter cases decided by the Supreme Court and other appellate courts in Canada involve whether police activity violated the Charter. However, very little work has been done to examine the implementation of these decisions. Our case study suggests that these decisions, particularly those with the highest profile, do have an impact on police policy and behaviour, but that implementation is uneven in Ontario and on individual police forces. The only real standardization at the provincial level comes from training modules developed by the OPC, not from the provincial government. As a result, interpretation of Charter rules by local forces, local Crowns, and local judges can vary. In the organization that we studied, which appeared to have a leadership committed to following constitutional rules, efforts are made to communicate these decisions to officers, but it appears that ongoing training in Charter decisions is lacking.

Insufficient systematic feedback from Crowns to police organizations exacerbates this problem. Although many officers may be frustrated by Charter decisions that they perceive fail to appreciate the difficult realities of policing and are overly generous to suspects (judicial decisions often do not align with individual and organizational goals of investigating and stopping crime), it appears that the threat of disciplinary action (an incentive to comply) and a commitment to professionalism (including the belief that judicial Charter decisions are legitimate and encourage professionalism overall) are enough to dissuade most deliberate, egregious violations of the Charter. Yet poor training and communication, and the lack of clear-cut rules in certain situations, create a degree of unevenness in how Charter decisions are applied day to day. This highlights the importance of communication and training identified in the more general literature on policy implementation and impact.

More work, of course, remains to be done. In the jurisdiction that we studied, we hope to also interview actors external to the police force, particularly defence counsel, Crowns, and judges, to assess their perception of how the police implement Charter decisions. And we wish to conduct studies of other jurisdictions in Ontario; this would not only give us much-needed empirical data but also enable us to begin making limited causal inferences as to what factors may be more important than others in explaining the implementation of the Charter. At the same time, we wish to explore in greater detail the initial training the OPC provides to all officers and the modules it develops for training for specialized units. If time and resources allow, we will then extend the research to organizations outside Ontario. It would be especially interesting to assess whether other provinces rely on local jurisdictions to obtain and communicate information about Charter decisions to the same degree that Ontario does. Comparisons could then also be made to the findings in the more extensive literature on the impact of constitutional rights on policing in the US literature.

NOTES

1 The authors would like to thank the Ontario Bar Association Foundation for research funding assistance for this project. The authors would also like to thank Sarah Cahill for her research assistance. The findings and conclusions herein are solely those of the authors.

2 *R. v. Dufaure* (2014) 294 C.R.R. (2d), 182, 243.

3 Michael Spratt, "Poor Training or Rogue Police?," blog post, 10 October 2013, http://www.michaelspratt.com/law-blog/2013/10/10/1ix55czvughklaxssnw2fptf7cus1t.

4 *R. v. Dufaure* (2014) 294 C.R.R. (2d), 182, 223.

5 Peter Russell, "Canadian Constraints on Judicialization from Without," *International Political Science Review* 15 (1994): 170.

6 Allan Young, "Search and Seizure in 2004 – Dialogue or Dead-End?," *Supreme Court Law Review* 29 (2005): 351–84.

7 See, e.g., Stephen L. Wasby, *The Impact of the United States Supreme Court* (Homewood, Il: Dorsey Press, 1970); Bradley C. Canon and Charles A. Johnson, *Judicial Policies: Implementation and Impact*, 2nd ed. (Washington, DC.: CQ Press, 1999); Gerald N. Rosenberg, *The Hollow Hope: Can Courts Bring About Social Change?* (Chicago: University of Chicago Press, 1991); Malcolm M. Feeley and Edward L. Rubin, *Judicial Policy Making and the Modern State: How the Courts Reformed America's Prisons* (Cambridge: Cambridge University Press, 1998).

8 Jerome Skolnick, *Justice without Trial: Law Enforcement in Democratic Society*, 3rd ed. (New York: Macmillan, 1994); Richard A. Leo, "The Impact of *Miranda* Revisited," *The Journal of Criminal Law and Criminology* 86 (1996): 621–92; Jon B. Gould and Stephen D. Mastrofski, "Suspect Searches: Assessing Police Behaviour under the US Constitution," *Criminology and Public Policy* 3 (2004): 316–62.

9 James E. Spiotto, "Search and Seizure: An Empirical Study of the Exclusionary Rule and Its Alternatives," *Journal of Legal Studies* 2 (1973): 243–78; Bradley C. Canon, "Testing the Effectiveness of Civil Liberties Policies at the State and Federal Levels," *American Politics Quarterly* 5 (1977): 57–82.

10 "Comment: Effect of *Mapp v. Ohio* on Police Search and Seizure Practices in Narcotics Cases," *Columbia Journal of Law and Social Problems* 4 (1968): 87–104; Dallin H. Oaks, "Studying the Exclusionary Rule in Search and

Seizure," *University of Chicago Law Review* 37 (1970): 665–757; Craig D. Uchida, Timothy S. Bynum, Dennis Rogan, and Donna Murasky, "Acting in Good Faith: The Effects of *United States v. Leon* on the Police and Courts," *Arizona Law Review* 30 (1988): 467–95.

11 Myron W. Orfield, Jr., "The Exclusionary Rule and Deterrence: An Empirical Study of Chicago Narcotics Officers," *University of Chicago Law Review* 54 (1987): 1016–69; Myron W. Orfield, Jr., "Deterrence, Perjury, and the Heater Factor: An Exclusionary Rule in the Chicago Criminal Courts," *University of Colorado Law Review* 63 (1992): 75; William C. Heffernan and Richard W. Lovely, "Evaluating the Fourth Amendment Exclusionary Rule: The Problem of Police Compliance with the Law," *University of Michigan Journal of Law Reform* 24 (1991): 311–69; Victoria M. Time and Brian K. Payne, "Police Chiefs' Perceptions about *Miranda*: An Analysis of Survey Data," *Journal of Criminal Justice* 30 (2002): 77–86.

12 *Miranda v. Arizona*, (1966) 384 U.S. 436.

13 George C. Thomas, III, and Richard A. Leo, "The Effects of *Miranda v. Arizona*: 'Embedded' in Our National Culture?," vol. 29, *Crime and Justice* (Chicago: University of Chicago Press, 2002), 203–71; Time and Payne, "Police Chiefs' Perceptions about *Miranda*"; Leo, "The Impact of *Miranda* Revisited"; Heffernan and Lovely, "Evaluating the Fourth Amendment Exclusionary Rule."

14 Skolnick, "Justice without Trial"; Orfield, Jr., "The Exclusionary Rule and Deterrence"; Orfield, Jr., "Deterrence, Perjury, and the Heater Factor"; Gould and Mastrofski, "Suspect Searches."

15 Orfield, Jr., "The Exclusionary Rule and Deterrence"; Gould and Mastrofski, "Suspect Searches."

16 Heffernan and Lovely, "Evaluating the Fourth Amendment Exclusionary Rule."

17 Orfield, Jr., "Deterrence, Perjury, and the Heater Factor"; Jona Goldschmidt and Anonymous, "The Necessity of Dishonesty: Police Deviance, 'Making the Case,' and the Public Good," *Policing and Society* 18 (2008): 113–35.

18 Goldschmidt and Anonymous, "The Necessity of Dishonesty."

19 Kathryn Moore, "Police Implementation of Supreme Court of Canada Charter Decisions: An Empirical Study," *Osgood Hall Law Journal* 30 (1992): 547–77.

20 *R. v. Brydges*, [1990] 1 S.C.R. 190.

21 *R. v. Duarte*, [1990] 1 S.C.R. 30.

22 Moore, "Police Implementation of Supreme Court of Canada Charter Decisions," 572.

23 Reginald A. Devonshire, "The Effects of Supreme Court Charter-Based Decisions on Policing: More Beneficial Than Detrimental?," *Crim. R. (4th)* 31 (1994): 82–99 (1–17 from LawSource).

24 Ibid., 11 (from LawSource).
25 *R. v. Vu*, [2013] 3 S.C.R. 657; *R. v. Fearon*, 2014 SCC 77.
26 *R. v. Grant*, [2009] 2 S.C.R. 353.
27 *R. v. Feeney*, [1997] 2 S.C.R. 13.
28 *R. v. Spencer*, 2014 SCC 43.
29 *R. v. White*, 2015 ONCA 508 (CanLII).
30 The Field Development Officer program – known before 2016 as the Coach Officer Program – pairs a more experienced officer, who has undertaken mentorship training, with a group of junior officers. One interviewee noted that this was one method by which Charter knowledge was imparted throughout the organization. The training to become a mentor includes a very short module on new legal and Charter issues (as well as workplace standards and so on). However, the program is geared towards how to be an effective mentor and assumes that field development officers have the knowledge of legal issues that is expected of them.
31 *R. v. Vu*, [2013] 3 S.C.R. 657.
32 *R. v. Fearon*, 2014 SCC 77.
33 *R. v. Panjak Bedi*, 2014 ONSC 4392 (CanLII).
34 *R. v. Jinje*, 2015 ONSC 2081 (CanLII).
35 Stephen Wasby, *The Impact of the United States Supreme Court*; Canon and Johnson, *Judicial Policies*; Rosenberg, *The Hollow Hope*.

9 Protecting against Cruel and Unusual Punishment: Section 12 of the Charter and Mandatory Minimum Sentences

KATE PUDDISTER

In *R. v. Lloyd*,[1] the Supreme Court of Canada struck down a one-year mandatory minimum sentence of imprisonment, provided in the Controlled Drugs and Substances Act (CDSA),[2] as a violation of section 12 of the Canadian Charter of Rights and Freedoms, the right not to be subject to "cruel and unusual punishment."[3] The Court found that while the punishment was appropriate when applied to the particular case of the appellant, the mandatory minimum could be grossly disproportionate and a violation of section 12 when applied to another, hypothetical offender who might be charged under the same provision of the CDSA, but engaged in less blameworthy conduct. The dissent in this case noted that the majority's approach to reviewing the mandatory minimum sentence set by Parliament was a "departure from the Court's jurisprudence, which has consistently maintained that mandatory minimums are not *per se* unconstitutional."[4] Along with *R v. Nur* (2015),[5] in which another mandatory minimum was struck down by the Supreme Court, *Lloyd* appears to signal that Parliament's ability to create sentencing policy and mandatory minimums with little interference from section 12 and the courts is coming to an end. Until *Lloyd* and *Nur*, the Supreme Court had not struck down a mandatory minimum set by Parliament since 1987, and the protection against cruel and unusual punishment has had a limited impact on criminal justice policy compared to other Charter-protected legal rights. Yet the sentencing of offenders is the most visible and heavily scrutinized aspect of the criminal justice system and one area of criminal justice policy in which Parliament is willing to play an active role.

Within the realm of sentencing policy, one tool favoured by policymakers of all political stripes is mandatory minimum sentences.

Although mandatory minimums have been highly criticized by scholars and practitioners alike for being ineffective in reducing crime, having disproportionate effects on marginalized populations, and being an affront to judicial discretion,[6] this has not curbed Parliament's appetite for introducing more mandatory minimums into Canadian criminal law. Mandatory minimum sentences create a role for elected policymakers in the sentencing of the criminal offenders, while, at the same time, constraining judicial discretion; thus, they serve as an interesting area for carrying out a case study to examine the impact of the Charter on criminal justice policymaking.

A minimum sentence set by legislators allows parliamentarians to create a sanction that prioritizes the sentencing objectives of denunciation, retribution, and general deterrence over other sentencing objectives, such as rehabilitation.[7] However, when legislators play a larger role in the sentencing process, it limits the discretion of the judiciary to craft a sentence that is proportionate and individualized to the particular circumstances of the offender. Using mandatory minimums, Parliament can actively limit judicial discretion and the power of the courts in the criminal law context, an area of law that can be understood as the natural domain of the judiciary and where judicial decision making is more likely to be audacious. As a result, examining the mandatory minimum sentences set by Parliament and subject to review (and implementation) by the judiciary provides an interesting case study of the dynamics between the courts and the executive.

The present chapter examines these trade-offs in light of the Supreme Court's approach to mandatory minimums and section 12 of the Charter. In an effort to understand the impact of section 12 on criminal justice policy, this chapter is guided by the central question, What has been the effect of section 12 on mandatory minimum sentences in Canada? In addressing this case study, this chapter traces the Supreme Court's interpretation of section 12 as applied to mandatory minimum sentences. It will demonstrate that, after the invalidation of a mandatory minimum in the 1987 case *R. v. Smith*, the Court generally moved towards a narrow view of section 12; this created the space for Parliament to play an active role in sentencing policy, leading to a steady increase in the number of mandatory minimums in Canadian criminal law. The final section of the chapter considers the future of mandatory minimum sentences of imprisonment in light of the Supreme Court's recent section 12 jurisprudence in *Nur* and *Lloyd*, and it suggests that section 12 will be a growing area of importance for Canadian criminal

Table 9.1 Key Developments in Mandatory Minimum Policy and Section 12[8]

Mandatory minimum policy	Year	Application of section 12
6 offences carrying MMS[a] introduced into Canadian criminal law with the enactment of the Criminal Code	1892	
13 offences carrying MMS in Canadian criminal law	1927	
First MMS repealed[9]	1931	
Last MMS repealed[10]	1969	
Death penalty abolished; creation of MMS for high treason and first- and second-degree murder	1976	
	1987	*Smith*: s. 5(1) of the Narcotics Control Act violates s. 12
	1990	*Luxton*: MMS for first-degree murder does not violate s. 12
Enactment of the Firearms Act creates 18 additional offences carrying MMS	1995	
Principles of sentencing codified in the Criminal Code	1996	
29 offences carrying MMS in Canadian criminal law	1999	
	2000	*Morrisey*: s. 220(a) of the Criminal Code does not violate s. 12
	2001	*Latimer*: MMS for second-degree murder does not violate s. 12
40 offences carrying MMS in Canadian criminal law	2006	
	2008	*Ferguson*: s. 236(a) of the Criminal Code does not violate s. 12
An estimated 80 offences carry MMS or minimum fine in Canadian criminal law	2015	*Nur*: s. 95(2) of the Criminal Code violates s. 12
	2016	*Lloyd*: s. 5(3)(a)(i)(D) of the CDSA violates s. 12

[a]Mandatory minimum sentence.

justice policy. For an overview of the key developments in the relationship among mandatory minimums, Parliament, and the Supreme Court discussed in this chapter, please refer to table 9.1.

Sentencing Policy and Section 12

In Canada, although both provincial and federal governments have a role to play in criminal justice policy,[11] the authority for sentencing policy falls under the jurisdiction of the federal government, flowing from its constitutional power over criminal law and procedure. The federal government creates sentencing policy largely through the Criminal Code. Broad sentencing principles are found in part XXIII and section 718 of the Code, which provides the overarching goal of proportionality in sentencing, along with the other objectives of denunciation, deterrence, separation, rehabilitation, reparation, and responsibility.[12] Policy choices over sentencing must accord with the Charter, specifically section 12, which provides "the right not to be subjected to any cruel and unusual treatment or punishment." The Supreme Court has found that section 12 guarantees that punishments under criminal law must not be "grossly disproportionate" and that sentences cannot be "so excessive as to outrage the standards of decency," as defined by the Court in *R. v. Smith*.[13]

Gross disproportionality sets a high bar for violations of section 12 and is best explained by the Supreme Court in *Steele v. Mountain Institution*: "It will only be on rare and unique occasions that a court will find a sentence so grossly disproportionate that it violates the provisions of s. 12 of the *Charter*. The test for determining whether a sentence is disproportionately long is very properly stringent and demanding."[14] The requirement of gross disproportionality invokes a sentence that is not merely harsh but also so egregious that would offend community standards.

In interpreting section 12, the Supreme Court has found that it applies not only to a specific sentence imposed by a court but also to the effects of the sentence. In *Smith*, the Court explained that section 12 protections could be invoked to challenge the treatment and disciplinary measures in correctional institutions, such as the practice of solitary confinement and the frequency of searches.[15] However, this expansive view of section 12 has not materialized in section 12 jurisprudence. For example, courts have found that the administrative segregation of an inmate for five years did not violate section 12[16] and that indeterminate detention of individuals held under the dangerous offender label,[17] even when the initial offence had been removed from the Criminal Code, did not offend section 12.[18] Section 12 protections have been narrowed in relation to jurisdiction regarding *habeus corpus* as the Supreme Court has explained that challenges to parole decisions must be made through the parole board, not through the courts.[19] In *United States v. Burns*,[20] the Supreme Court found that, in extraditing Canadians to the United States, the minister of justice must seek assurance that the death penalty will not be imposed through section 7 "fundamental justice," while refusing to decide this case under section 12. Although the Court found that the death penalty "engages the underlying values of the prohibition against cruel and unusual punishment," it did not clearly indicate that capital punishment would violate section 12 in the very unlikely event that Canada reinstated this punishment.[21]

In applying section 12 to mandatory minimums, courts must consider first whether the sentence imposed against an individual offender is grossly disproportionate as applied to the immediate offender and offence committed. However, if the punishment is not considered grossly disproportionate in the immediate case, a court ought to consider whether the sentence would be grossly disproportionate when applied to "reasonable hypothetical circumstances."[22] In other words, a sentence can violate section 12 if a court is presented with a hypothetical case of another person, who may not be the intended target of the law, who would be subject to the same mandatory sentence, resulting in gross disproportionality. Although courts can consider a hypothetical and more sympathetic case, the threshold for protection is relatively high, and its application is narrower when compared with other criminal rights sections of the Charter.[23]

The effect of section 12 has been limited when applied to mandatory minimums because courts tend to defer to Parliament in sentencing policy. The Supreme Court has explained the need for deference in reviewing mandatory minimums to respect Parliament's role in sentencing and its choice to include a mandatory sentence for a particular offence. As the Supreme Court explained in several cases (quoting the Ontario District Court),

> It is not for the court to pass on the wisdom of Parliament with respect to the gravity of various offences and the range of penalties which may be imposed upon those found guilty of committing offences. ... While the final judgement as to whether a punishment exceeds constitutional limits set by the *Charter* is properly a judicial function, the court should be reluctant to interfere with the considered views of Parliament.[24]

This consideration for Parliament's preferences acknowledges that the majority of criminal offences do not carry a mandatory minimum sentence, and, as such, Parliament must have a legislative purpose for creating a minimum for a particular offence.

While Parliament can use its broad criminal law power to enact a wide range of sentencing provisions, one tool favoured by governments of all political stripes is mandatory minimum sentences. Mandatory minimums have been a part of the Criminal Code since it came into force in 1892, when six offences carried minimum sentences of incarceration.[25] However, until the late 1920s, mandatory minimums found in the Criminal Code remained an exception to the norm, with only thirteen offences carrying a mandatory term of incarceration.[26] Following the late 1920s, Parliament began to rely more often on this sentencing tool and sought to implement more mandatory sentences to counteract judicial discretion.[27]

Mandatory minimum sentences have proved to be ineffective as a means of controlling crime by a deluge of social science research, and they are subject to criticism from a wide range of scholars. Although it is beyond the scope of this chapter to detail the volume of research on mandatory minimums in Canada, it is useful to review the central criticisms of this sentencing policy choice. First, mandatory minimums pose a problem for the administration of justice because they can transfer discretion over sentencing, the sole prerogative of judges, to the prosecution. The existence of a mandatory minimum can result in evasion by criminal justice actors because it encourages police and prosecution to avoid charging individuals with offences that carry mandatory sentences that they perceive as disproportionate, thereby effectively subverting Parliament's intentions.[28] Second, not only do mandatory minimums encourage plea bargaining, a practice that is subject to a great deal of criticism,[29] but they also give the prosecution an unfair advantage in inducing a plea agreement. Most disturbing is that a mandatory minimum can encourage an innocent individual to plead guilty to a lesser offence to avoid the possibility of conviction under an offence carrying a significant minimum penalty.[30]

Third, research on the impact of mandatory minimums finds that there are disproportionate consequences for those who are already vulnerable and overrepresented in the criminal justice system.[31] In terms of effectiveness, mandatory minimums appear to have little impact on deterrence, which is explained in part by the fact that the public is often unaware of which crimes carry a minimum penalty.[32] Finally, mandatory minimums demonstrate what Benjamin Berger explains is an a priori determination by legislators regarding proportionality in sentencing.[33] More specifically, in creating a minimum penalty, policymakers must be able to articulate an appropriately proportionate sentence for all offenders, from all backgrounds, in all situations, and in all contexts – arguably an impractical feat.

Yet the weight of the social science evidence that undermines the usefulness of mandatory minimums has done little to quell the political appetite for adding mandatory minimums to Canadian criminal law. The political attraction to minimum penalties is easy to understand. Enacting a mandatory minimum allows political actors to signal to the public that they take crime seriously, appealing to the sentiments of victims' rights and "tough-on-crime" policy. Conversely, those who publicly oppose mandatory minimum penalties can be easily portrayed as soft on crime and a threat to the safety of law-abiding citizens, demonstrating the effectiveness of "penal populist" rhetoric.[34]

The Promise of Section 12: Initial Reactions to the Charter and *Smith*

The first section 12 challenge considered by the Supreme Court, in 1987, concerned mandatory minimums. In *R. v. Smith*, the appellant pleaded guilty to importing seven and a half ounces of cocaine into Canada, contrary to section 5(1) of the Narcotics Control Act (NCA).[35] Importing narcotics carried a mandatory minimum sentence of seven years; however, Smith was sentenced to eight years in custody. In reviewing the minimum sentence set by Parliament, the Court held that the mandatory correctional term of seven years violated section 12 and was of no force or effect. The Court found that the sentence was unconstitutional when applied to another hypothetical case, rather than applied to the immediate facts of the appellant, Smith. The wording of the NCA was indiscriminate and would apply to both significant instances of drug trafficking, like Smith, and to other, more trivial cases, such as a hypothetical first-time offender importing one joint of marijuana into Canada after spring break.[36] The Court found that a seven-year sentence applied to the hypothetical first-time offender would be grossly disproportionate, violating section 12, in a manner not saved by section 1 reasonable-limits analysis.

Although the Supreme Court struck down the minimum sentence set by Parliament and allowed for the use of reasonable hypothetical analysis, it made it clear that mandatory minimums were not per se unconstitutional. Instead, Justice Lamer, writing for the majority, explained that "a minimum mandatory term of imprisonment is obviously not in and of itself cruel and unusual. The legislature may, in my view, provide for a compulsory term of imprisonment upon conviction for certain offences without infringing on the rights protected by s. 12

of the *Charter*."[37] The central concern with section 5(1) of the NCA was that it did not specify the quantity or the substance to which the mandatory minimum penalty would apply; instead, the provision applied to *all* quantities of *any* narcotic. The Court made it clear that although Parliament had a legitimate role to play in setting sentencing policy, it must act within the parameters of section 12 and could not create sentences that were grossly disproportionate and offended community standards.

On the whole, *Smith* was a victory for the due process rights of the accused. The Court was unwilling to rely on prosecutorial discretion to ensure that future offenders, like the example provided by the reasonable hypothetical case, would not be subject to the mandatory minimum provided in the NCA. When engaging in section 1 analysis, the Court placed very little weight on the government's claims regarding deterrence, finding that the minimum of seven years was simply too high. "We do not need to sentence the small offenders to seven years in prison in order to deter the serious offender."[38] Perhaps the most important finding in *Smith* was the Court's willingness to allow appellants to argue that courts should look beyond the facts of the immediate case to consider how the minimum sentence would affect another, more sympathetic, hypothetical future case.

If one were to assume that a robust approach to section 12 would follow from *Smith*, he or she would be met with disappointment. In a series of decisions, the Supreme Court narrowed the application of section 12, maintaining a deferential approach to Parliament's role in sentencing policy. The Court upheld the mandatory minimums set by Parliament for both first- (*R. v. Luxton*)[39] and second-degree murder (*R. v. Latimer*),[40] regardless of the very sympathetic appellant in the latter case. *Luxton* challenged the minimum punishment of twenty-five years without eligibility for parole for first-degree murder. In upholding the mandatory minimum, the Court was not concerned with the effect of the punishment on the individual offender, finding that the minimum sentence was not disproportionate to the gravity of the offence and that it would not offend societal standards of decency.[41] In *Latimer*, the Supreme Court upheld the mandatory minimum for second-degree murder, again relying on the gravity of the offence committed, regardless of the fact that the sentencing principles of rehabilitation and public protection (separation), which are often of concern in homicide cases, were not relevant to the appellant in this particular case and context.

The reach of section 12 was further limited by the Supreme Court through its narrow approach to reasonable hypothetical analysis in decisions since *Smith*. In *Morrisey*,[42] the Court was asked to consider the mandatory minimum sentence of four years for the offence of criminal negligence involving the use of a firearm. In this case, the appellant urged the Court to follow the approach set out in *Smith*, that even though the sentence was appropriate in the immediate case, it would violate section 12 when applied to a hypothetical case. The Supreme Court was not sympathetic to the appellant's argument and responded by limiting the approach to reasonable hypotheticals. For a hypothetical case to apply, a court must consider only "imaginable circumstances which could commonly arise with a degree of generality appropriate to the particular offence."[43] In this case, the Court rejected the lower court's approach of relying on reported cases to construct a reasonable hypothetical, explaining that the facts in such cases would reflect only what could be deduced in court and would be inherently related to the specific idiosyncrasies of each case.[44]

For the offence in this case, the Supreme Court upheld the mandatory minimum, finding that Parliament was justified in sending a strong message regarding the care of firearms and the serious nature of the offence, a message that effectively demonstrated the legitimate sentencing principles of denunciation, deterrence, and retribution. In his commentary on *Morrisey*, Peter Sankoff explains that the Court's decision had the effect of virtually eliminating any arguments concerning the over-breadth of an offence by requiring that abnormal scenarios, which may be caught by an offence carrying a mandatory minimum, must actually materialize in court rather than provide the basis for reasonable hypothetical arguments.[45]

The narrow approach to section 12 demonstrated by the Supreme Court in *Morrisey* was continued in *R. v. Ferguson*.[46] *Ferguson* concerned the mandatory minimum of four years for manslaughter with a firearm in a case in which an RCMP officer had shot and killed a detainee in police custody. The appellant in this case did not challenge the mandatory minimum on the basis of a reasonable hypothetical analysis as this option had been largely eliminated by *Morrisey*. Instead, he argued that the mandatory minimum violated section 12 and the appropriate remedy should be constitutional exemption provided by section 24(1) of the Charter. The appellant urged the Court to use its remedial power to exempt him from the mandatory minimum, while leaving the section in place, thereby allowing for continued deference to Parliament's sentencing policy agenda. A unanimous Supreme Court found that the mandatory minimum of four years did not violate section 12 and rejected arguments regarding constitutional exemptions. The Court explained that although the exemption power in section 24(1) was less intrusive to Parliament than striking a law down, it was not an acceptable way to proceed with mandatory minimums:

> In granting a constitutional exemption, a judge would be undermining Parliament's purpose on passing the legislation: to remove judicial discretion and to send a clear and unequivocal message to potential offenders ... they will receive a sentence equal to or exceeding the mandatory minimum specified by Parliament. The discretion that a constitutional exemption would confer on judges would violate the letter of the law and undermine the message that animates it.[47]

The Court explained that dealing with mandatory minimums in such a way would undermine the rule of law. In the Court's opinion, if a judge were to grant a constitutional exemption to a mandatory minimum, the effect would be to leave the law uncertain and unpredictable; in the Court's words, "The law is on the books, but in practice, it may not apply."[48] Finding the unpredictability and uncertainty that would result from a constitutional exemption unacceptable, the Court made it clear that the section 24(1) remedial power was not applicable to mandatory minimums; this effectively shut the door on another possible argument for defence counsel to use to challenge existing mandatory minimums.

Writing in 2008, Jamie Cameron describes the Supreme Court's approach to section 12 as providing only a "faint hope" to defendants, one that appears to be of assistance only in the "clearest of cases."[49] Indeed, since the groundbreaking case in *Smith*, the Court has routinely found that the threshold for engaging section 12 is high, that reasonable hypotheticals are limited in applicability, and that other mechanisms for limiting the reach of mandatory minimums, such as constitutional exemptions, are unavailable. Unlike other legal rights provided in the Charter, notwithstanding *Nur* and *Lloyd*, the reach of section 12 can be characterized as minimalist and underwhelming. This narrow approach to applying section 12 has created space for Parliament to play an important role in sentencing policy, thus allowing for the rapid growth of mandatory minimums in the post-Charter era.

Mandatory Minimums in the Charter Era: Parliament Takes the Lead

As mentioned above, mandatory minimum sentences have always been a part of Canadian criminal law; however, it is only in recent decades that we have witnessed a significant reliance on this tool as part of a government's sentencing policy agenda. Not only have governments steadily increased the number of mandatory minimums in Canadian statutes, but Parliament has also not repealed a minimum penalty since 1969.[50]

The year 1995 marked the modern era of mandatory minimum sentences, when the Chrétien government enacted the greatest number of mandatory minimums in a single bill by passing the Firearms Act.[51] Although the central purpose of the legislation was to implement gun control and to create a national firearms registry, the bill included eighteen new mandatory minimums, with a minimum penalty for certain violent offences when carried out with a firearm. In an important step, the government incorporated the minimum penalty directly into the offence provision itself, a change from previous enactments of minimum sentences.[52] This was aimed at ensuring that the mandatory minimum would apply consistently across cases, thereby limiting both judicial discretion in sentencing and prosecutorial discretion in plea negotiations.

Various mandatory minimums were added by governments over the years, and, by 2006, it was estimated that there were over forty offences that carried a mandatory minimum sentence.[53] The appetite for mandatory minimums did not diminish with the change in government from Liberal to Conservative. Indeed, David Paciocco estimates that, by 2015, there were approximately eighty offences that carried a mandatory minimum sentence, including both minimum imprisonment terms and mandatory fines.[54] Throughout the years of the Harper government (2006–2015), there was a great flurry of activity in criminal justice policy and in the specific domain of sentencing policy. During almost a decade in office, the Conservative government passed forty-two crime bills that consistently emphasized a punitive, or tough-on-crime, approach to criminal justice.[55] A large number of these bills were concerned with sentencing policy, shown in the enactment of the Truth in Sentencing Act,[56] aimed at limiting the pretrial credits that judges routinely gave at sentencing, the elimination of the "faint hope" clause,[57] and the imposition of an increased mandatory victim fine surcharge.[58] The government increased the number of minimum penalties across a variety of acts, including the Criminal Code and the CDSA. The Harper government not only created new mandatory minimums but also increased the length of existing minimum sentences.[59]

Writing in 2018, it is too early to fully appreciate the effects of the Harper government's approach to sentencing policy on the criminal justice system and the impact of the added mandatory minimum sentences on Canadian imprisonment rates. However, early evidence demonstrates that, in some respects, the effects have been much less powerful than expected. First, during the Harper government, the rates of incarceration remained relatively similar, ranging from 115 to 120 per 100,000 of the general population.[60] The second explanation for the muted impact (thus far) likely reflects judicial decisions that have circumscribed the effects of the Harper government's sentencing policy. Indeed, as will be discussed below, the Supreme Court has already invalidated two of its mandatory minimums provisions in *Nur* and *Lloyd*. Similarly, the government's approach to limiting increased credit for pretrial custody was moderated by the Supreme Court in *R. v. Summers*[61] and *R. v. Safarzadeh-Markhali*.[62] Finally, the limited impact of the Harper government's criminal justice policy may also be evidence of evasion or a change in behaviour by criminal justice actors to either avoid or limit the effect of these policy changes. While the immediate, system-wide effects of the Harper government's approach to criminal justice policy may be limited, one future effect of its particular focus may be to encourage an increased number of challenges made under section 12, thus reinvigorating this Charter section.

The current Liberal government under Prime Minister Justin Trudeau has made some legislative changes in relation to criminal justice policy (notably the decriminalization of doctor-assisted dying), but there has been limited implementation of significant criminal justice system reform. That being said, it appears that change may be coming with respect to mandatory minimums. Indeed, the Department of Justice has recently begun a review of the criminal justice system, with a specific focus on the reforms implemented by the previous government, including a review of mandatory minimums.[63] A report that the department prepared for the government suggests that one strategy for softening the rigidity of mandatory minimums would be to create exceptions to a mandated minimum sentence that would apply when certain facts were present in a case, such as a guilty plea.[64] Creating a statutory "escape valve" for mandatory minimums would provide the opportunity for individualization in sentencing and might limit the blunt aspect of mandatory sentences of incarceration, thereby possibly avoiding future challenges under section 12.

Nur and *Lloyd*: The New Normal?

When assessing the impact of section 12 on mandatory minimums and the sentencing policy agenda of governments, from 1982 to 2014 two broad trends emerge. First, the impact of section 12 as interpreted by the courts has been limited (with the exception of *Smith*). The Supreme Court has made several decisions that demonstrate a narrow approach to section 12; this is explained by the high threshold set by gross disproportionality and a deference to the sentencing policy decisions of Parliament. The second trend is that this approach has allowed Parliament to pursue a sentencing policy agenda with little interference from the courts, resulting in an increased number of mandatory minimum sentences of incarceration in Canadian criminal law. With the many aforementioned drawbacks to a mandatory approach to sentencing, a great deal of academic commentary has been critical of both the courts and Parliament, often suggesting a return to the original understanding of section 12 in *Smith*.[65] If the present chapter had been written in 2014, the story of section 12 and mandatory minimums would end here. However, the recent Supreme Court decisions in *Nur* (2015) and *Lloyd* (2016) appear to signal a critical juncture in section 12 and sentencing policy, and this could promote a reinvigoration of section 12 and a diminished capacity for mandatory minimums in Canadian sentencing law.

In *Nur*, the Supreme Court was asked to review section 95 of the Criminal Code, which makes it an offence to possess a prohibited or restricted firearm loaded with ammunition, or with readily accessible ammunition, without a licence or registration certificate, and carries a mandatory minimum sentence of three years' incarceration when preceded by indictment.[66] Originally, the mandatory minimum was one year, but this was increased to three years in 2008 through the Tackling Violent Crime Act.[67] In *Nur*, the appellant argued that a mandatory minimum penalty for an indictable conviction was a violation of section 12, when applied to a reasonably foreseeable hypothetical case rather than the immediate case.[68] The majority in *Nur* found that the mandatory minimum set in section 95 would be grossly disproportionate and a violation of section 12 when applied to the hypothetical case of an absent-minded hunter who had stored her firearm in a second residence without the proper paperwork.[69] The Court found that this mandatory minimum was not saved by section 1 of the Charter and struck it down.

In *Nur*, the Court provided a strong critique of mandatory minimum sentences, demonstrating a departure from the deferential approach of previous section 12 jurisprudence. The Court found that the government had not convincingly established that mandatory minimum sentences provided deterrence and that, in fact, empirical evidence suggested otherwise.[70] Instead, the Court suggested that a more narrowly tailored offence, which specifically targeted those engaged in criminal activities, might survive constitutional scrutiny. In addition, the majority strongly rejected the argument that Crown discretion to proceed by summary or indictment would prevent disproportionality in sentencing by protecting the judicial role in sentencing. Chief Justice McLachlin, writing for the majority, explained, "It is the courts that are directed by Parliament to impose a mandatory minimum term of imprisonment, and it is the duty of the courts to scrutinize the constitutionality of the provision."[71] In responding to this argument, the Court articulated one of the criticisms of mandatory minimums, discussed above – that the assignment of discretion from the judiciary to the Crown through mandatory minimums was problematic due to the weaker accountability measures placed on the prosecution.

Nur can be sharply contrasted with the previous section 12 jurisprudence, most notably with *Morrisey,* in which the Court had rejected a similar argument based on a reasonable hypothetical account of a careless hunter. For the Court, it was unacceptable for a gun owner to be careless in discharging a firearm in *Morrisey* because individuals with firearms must be especially cautious.[72] In *Nur,* this same requirement of care was not extended to the storage of ammunition for the "absent-minded hunter," who was deemed to be less morally blameworthy for violations of the firearms provisions in the Criminal Code. To be fair, in *Morrisey* the Court had been concerned with conduct that resulted in death, while this was not at issue in *Nur*. That being said, in *Morrisey* the Court had made it clear that firearms posed a significant danger and that extra care was necessary, providing justification for Parliament to set stiff mandatory penalties for firearms offences.

It is reasonable to assume that this rationale, which had led the Court to defer to the policy preferences of Parliament in *Morrisey,* would also apply to the care of storage of ammunition in *Nur*. Furthermore, Peter Sankoff argues that the reasoning in *Morrisey* appeared to rely on the discretion of the Crown to not proceed on charges in which the individual conduct did not constitute the moral blameworthiness required of the offence carrying the mandatory minimum.[73] Yet for the Court in *Nur*, relying on Crown discretion not to proceed by indictment in cases where the mandatory minimum would be inappropriate was not an acceptable remedy for preventing constitutional violations.

The Court's approach to mandatory minimums in *Nur* does not appear to be an aberration from recent section 12 jurisprudence. Instead, in *Lloyd*, the Court again took a critical approach to mandatory minimum sentences, marking another clear departure from the previous approach to section 12. *Lloyd* concerned a mandatory minimum sentence of one year, associated with section 5(3)(a)(i)(D) of the CDSA, which applied to individuals who had been found guilty of trafficking or possessing a controlled substance and had a previous conviction (within ten years) of a "designated substance offence."[74] As in *Nur*, the appellant argued that the mandatory minimum was not grossly disproportionate when applied to his case, but that it was a violation of section 12 when applied to another reasonably foreseeable offender. The majority in *Lloyd* found that provision to be a violation of section 12 due to the fact that it applied to an indiscriminate quantity of illicit substances, it relied on a broad definition of trafficking, and the included list of prior offences had not been narrowly tailored.[75]

In reaching this conclusion, the majority decision issued a rather scathing critique of Parliament's reliance on mandatory minimums:

> The reality is this: mandatory minimum sentences that, as here, apply to offences that can be committed in various ways, under a broad array of circumstances and by a wide range of people are vulnerable to constitutional challenge. ... If Parliament hopes to sustain mandatory minimum penalties for offences that cast a wide net, it should consider narrowing their reach so that they only catch offenders that merit the mandatory minimum sentences.[76]

This passage marks a clear departure from the narrow approach to reasonable hypothetical analysis demonstrated in *Morrisey*. In *Morrisey*, the Court explained that "unusual" cases, which may be caught by broad provisions, should not form the basis of a reasonable hypothetical; instead, if not diverted through Crown discretion, such cases should be addressed by a court only when they materialized. The Court explained that a reasonable hypothetical must not be a "marginal" case, but rather a case that "could commonly arise with a degree of generality appropriate to the particular offence."[77] Yet in *Lloyd*, the Court explained that any broad offence that carried a mandatory minimum would "inevitably include an acceptable reasonable hypothetical."[78] The Court did not provide the *Morrisey* caveat that the hypothetical must arise from routine application of the law; instead, it simply explained that, for almost every offence carrying a mandatory minimum, there was the potential for the disproportionate application to arise in a hypothetical scenario.

This departure from the Supreme Court's previous approach to mandatory minimums was noted and criticized by the dissent in *Lloyd*. The dissent noted that the majority's interpretation of section 12 stood in contrast to the Court's previous decisions and found that the majority's section 12 analysis undermined Parliament's role in sentencing policy.[79] In finding that the mandatory minimum in *Lloyd* did not violate section 12, the dissent questioned whether any mandatory minimum could survive the majority's scrutiny. Indeed, in the majority's reasoning, any provision that was found to have a broad application could be struck down by the precedent set in *Lloyd*. In *obiter*, the majority recommended that one way to avoid the invalidity of mandatory minimums in the future was to enact a statutory safety valve, allowing for judicial discretion to exempt a mandatory minimum that would be disproportionate in the immediate case.[80] This suggested that if the current government were to go forward with creating an escape clause for mandatory minimums, it would respect the constitution.

It is possible that the Supreme Court is signalling that, in the future, it will take a less deferential approach to section 12, one that goes beyond just sentencing policy and mandatory minimums. Indeed, trial courts have begun to take a more expansive approach to applying section 12 to the rights of prisoners in Canadian correctional facilities. Until very recently, much like the previous approach to mandatory minimums, the courts have held a narrow application of section 12 to the rights of prisoners.[81] In the past, courts have been reluctant to intervene in the decisions made by correctional authorities and administrative bodies in relation to the rights of incarcerated individuals.[82] However, like the Supreme Court's decisions in *Nur* and *Lloyd*, this deference appears to be waning, and courts are becoming more willing to intervene in cases involving correctional institutions.

Recently, an Ontario judge awarded two inmates at Maplehurst Correctional Complex $85,000 as compensation for the facility's excessive reliance on lockdowns, which was found to be a violation of the inmates' section 12 rights.[83] In *Bacon v. Surrey Pretrial Services Centre (Warden)*, the British Columbia Supreme Court found that the conditions of pretrial administrative segregation had constituted a violation of an accused's section 12 rights and constituted cruel and unusual treatment or punishment.[84] Finally, and most recently, a class action lawsuit involving former inmates of an Ontario correctional facility alleging violence and overcrowding was certified by an Ontario court.[85] It appears that if recent trends persist, section 12 will no longer be a faint hope that applies in the rarest of cases; rather, it may have an important purposive impact on sentencing policy, including mandatory minimums, and the treatment of incarcerated individuals in Canadian correctional facilities.

With the recent decisions in *Nur* and *Lloyd*, the Supreme Court has departed from its previous approach to section 12, and this has the effect of potentially reinvigorating the protection against cruel and unusual punishment. The critical evaluation of mandatory minimums by the Court in *Lloyd* makes it possible that many mandatory minimums will be vulnerable to challenge under section 12, a clear break with the Court's previous approach. The effect of recent section 12 jurisprudence on future sentencing policy remains to be seen. However, it is clear that the Court is willing to eschew its previously minimalist approach and is intent on limiting Parliament's choices in creating sentencing policy, thereby potentially increasing the importance of section 12 of the Charter.

NOTES

1 [2016] 1 S.C.R. 130.

2 S. 5(3)(a)(i)(D), Controlled Drugs and Substances Act, S.C. 1996, c. 19.

3 The full provision reads, "Everyone has the right not to be subjected to any cruel and usual treatment or punishment."

4 *R. v. Lloyd*, at para. 106.

5 *R. v. Nur*, [2015] 1 S.C.R. 773.

6 Benjamin L. Berger, "A More Lasting Comfort? The Politics of Minimum Sentences, the Rule of Law, and *R. v. Ferguson*," *Supreme Court Law Review* 47, no. 2D (2009): 1–25; Anthony N. Doob and Carla Cesaroni, "The Political Attractiveness of Mandatory Minimum Sentences," *Osgoode Hall Law Journal* 39, no. 2/3 (2001): 287–304.

7 This effect is also noted by the dissenting opinion in *Lloyd*. S. 718.2 of the Criminal Code of Canada sets out the purposes and principles of sentencing.

8 Data adapted from Nicole Crutcher, "Mandatory Minimum Penalties of Imprisonment: A Historical Analysis," *Criminal Law Quarterly* 44 (2001): 279–308; Wade R. Raaflaub, "Mandatory Minimum Sentences," Library of Parliament, Parliamentary Information and Research Service, 2006: 1–3; Lincoln Caylor and Gannon G. Beaulne, "Parliamentary Restrictions on Judicial Discretion in Sentencing: A Defence of Mandatory Minimum Sentences" (research paper, Macdonald-Laurier Institute, Ottawa, May 2014): 1–30; and David Paciocco, "The Law of Minimum Sentences: Judicial Responses and Responsibility," *Canadian Criminal Law Review* 19, no. 2 (2015): 173–229.

9 Bill 113: an Act to Amend the Criminal Code of Canada, 6th Sess., 17th Parl., 1931. According to Crutcher, "Mandatory Minimum Penalties of Imprisonment," this bill repealed the minimum penalty of one-month incarceration for the offence of conducting an insurance business without a licence.

10 Bill C-150 repealed the seven-day minimum for driving while intoxicated and the minimum sentence of three months for the offence of theft from mail, see ibid.

11 The provincial role in criminal justice is outlined in s. 92(14), which provides the power to make laws for "the administration of justice." Federal power over criminal justice policy flows from s. 91(27), which provides jurisdiction over "the criminal law ... including the procedure in criminal matters"; see Constitution Act, 1867 (30 & 31 Vict.) c. 3, s. 91(27) and s. 92(14).

12 See s. 718, Criminal Code of Canada, R.S.C. 1985, c. C-46.

13 [1987] 1 S.C.R. 1045.

14 [1990] 2 S.C.R. 1385, at 1417.

15 *Smith*, at para. 204.

16 *R. v. Olson* (1987), 38 C.C.C. (3d) 543 (Ont. C.A).

17 *R. v. Lyons*, [1987] 2 S.C.R. 309.

18 *R. v. Milne*, [1987] 2 S.C.R. 512.

19 Don Stuart, *Charter Justice in Canadian Criminal Law*, 5th ed. (Toronto: Carswell, 2010), 482.

20 *United States v. Burns*, [2001] 1 S.C.R. 283.

21 Ibid., at para. 78.

22 *R. v. Goltz*, [1991] 3 S.C.R 485.

23 See Kent Roach, "Searching for *Smith*: The Constitutionality of Mandatory Sentences," *Osgoode Hall Law Journal* 39 (2001): 367–412; Lisa Dufraimont, "*R. v. Ferguson* and the Search for a Coherent Approach to Mandatory Minimum Sentences under Section 12," *Supreme Court Law Review* 42, no. 2D (2008): 459–78.

24 *R. v. Guiller* (1985), 48j C.R. (3d) 226 (Ont. Dist. Ct).
25 Crutcher, "Mandatory Minimum Penalties of Imprisonment," 280.
26 Ibid., 286.
27 Ibid., 293; Caylor and Beaulne, "Parliamentary Restrictions on Judicial Discretion in Sentencing."
28 Dufraimont, "*R. v. Ferguson* and the Search for a Coherent Approach to Mandatory Minimum Sentences," 465; Doob and Cesaroni, "The Political Attractiveness of Mandatory Minimum Sentences," 291; Berger, "A More Lasting Comfort?," 110.
29 Joseph Di Luca, "Expedient McJustice or Principled Alternative Dispute Resolution? A Review of Plea Bargaining in Canada," *Criminal Law Quarterly* 50 (2005): 14–66.
30 Dianne L. Martin, "Distorting the Prosecution Process: Informers, Mandatory Minimum Sentences, and Wrongful Convictions," *Osgoode Hall Law Journal* 39 (2001): 513–27.
31 Faizal R. Mirza, "Mandatory Minimum Prison Sentencing and Systemic Racism," *Osgoode Hall Law Journal* 39 (2001): 491–512; Thomas Gabor and Nicole Crutcher, "Mandatory Minimum Penalties: Their Effects on Crime, Sentencing Disparities and Justice System Expenditures" (Ottawa: Department of Justice, Research and Statistics Division, 2002), 22–3.
32 Doob and Cesaroni, "The Political Attractiveness of Mandatory Minimum Sentences," 291; Roach, "Searching for *Smith*," 389.
33 Berger, "A More Lasting Comfort?"
34 Julian V. Roberts, Loretta J. Stalans, David Indermaur, and Mike Hough, *Penal Populism: Lessons from Five Countries* (Oxford: Oxford University Press, 2003).
35 S. 5 of the Narcotics Control Act read, "(1) Except as authorized by this Act or the regulations, no person shall import into Canada any narcotic. (2) Every person who violates subsection (1) is guilty of an indictable offence and is liable to imprisonment for life but not less than seven years." The Narcotics Control Act has been superseded by the Controlled Drugs and Substances Act (S.C. 1996, c. 19).
36 *Smith*, at 1057.
37 Ibid., at 1077.
38 Ibid., at 1080.
39 [1990] 2 S.C.R. 711.
40 *R. v. Latimer*, [2001] 1 S.C.R. 3. This case involved the "mercy" killing of Tracy Latimer, a twelve-year-old girl suffering from severe cerebral palsy, by her father, Robert Latimer.
41 Stuart, *Charter Justice in Canadian Criminal Law*, 485.

42 [2000] 2 S.C.R. 90.
43 Ibid., at para. 50.
44 Ibid.
45 Peter Sankoff, "The Perfect Storm: Section 12, Mandatory Minimum Sentences and the Problem of the Unusual Case," *Constitutional Forum* 22, no. 1 (2013): 5.
46 *R. v. Ferguson*, [2008] 1 S.C.R. 96.
47 Ibid., at para. 55.
48 Ibid., at para. 71.
49 Jamie Cameron, "Fault and Punishment under Sections 7 and 12 of the Charter," *Supreme Court Law Review* 40, no. 2D (2008): 583.
50 Crutcher, "Mandatory Minimum Penalties of Imprisonment," 301.
51 Ibid., at 302. The full title of the Firearms Act is An Act respecting firearms and other weapons, S.C. 1995, c. 39.
52 Crutcher, "Mandatory Minimum Penalties of Imprisonment," 302.
53 Raaflaub, "Mandatory Minimum Sentences." 1.
54 Paciocco, "The Law of Minimum Sentences," 177.
55 Anthony N. Doob and Cheryl M. Webster, "Weathering the Storm? Testing Long-Standing Canadian Sentencing Policy in the Twenty-First Century," *Crime and Justice* 45, no. 1 (2016): 359–418.
56 Truth in Sentencing Act, S.C. 2009, c. 29.
57 An Act to amend the Criminal Code and another Act, S.C. 2011, c. 2.
58 Increasing Offenders' Accountability for Victims Act, S.C. 2013, c. 11.
59 Ibid.
60 Doob and Webster, "Weathering the Storm?"
61 [2014] 1 S.C.R. 575.
62 [2016] 1 S.C.R. 180.
63 Jim Bronskill, "Liberals Eye Exceptions to Mandatory Minimum Sentences," *Globe and Mail*, 21 August 2016, http://www.theglobeandmail.com/news/national/liberals-eye-exceptions-to-mandatory-minimums-championed-by-conservatives/article31481108/.
64 Ibid.
65 E.g., Benjamin L. Berger, "A More Lasting Comfort?," 1–25; Doob and Cesaroni, "The Political Attractiveness of Mandatory Minimum Sentences"; Kent Roach, "Searching for *Smith*"; Dufraimont, "*R v. Ferguson* and the Search for a Coherent Approach to Mandatory Minimum Sentences."
66 It is important to note that another central issue of *Nur* was the gap between the maximum summary penalty and the minimum indictable penalty. Under s. 95 of the Criminal Code, when the Crown proceeds summarily, the maximum penalty is one year, which creates a gap of two

years between the maximum penalty for a summary conviction and the minimum penalty for an indictable conviction. This two-year gap was also challenged by *Nur*, but under s. 7 of the Charter: "Everyone has the right to life, liberty and security of the person and the right not to be deprived thereof except in accordance with the principles of fundamental justice."

67 S.C. 2008, c. 6, s. 8.

68 *Nur*, at para. 78.

69 Ibid., at para. 83.

70 Ibid., at para. 114.

71 Ibid., at para. 87.

72 *Morrisey*, at para. 53.

73 Sankoff, "The Perfect Storm," 5.

74 S. 5(3)(a)(i)(D), Controlled Drugs and Substances Act, S.C. 1996, c. 19.

75 *Lloyd*, at paras. 29–31.

76 Ibid., at para. 35.

77 *Morrisey*, at para. 50.

78 *Lloyd*, at para. 35.

79 Ibid., at paras. 106–7.

80 Ibid., at para. 36.

81 Debra Parkes, "The Punishment Agenda in the Courts," *Supreme Court Law Review* 67, no. 2D (2014): 589–615.

82 Ibid., 605.

83 *Ogiamien v. Ontario* 2016 ONSC 3080.

84 [2010] B.C.J. No. 1080.

85 Canadian Press, "Ontario Inmates' Class-Action Lawsuit over Jail Conditions Gets Green Light," *Toronto Star*, 24 August 2016, https://www.thestar.com/news/canada/2016/08/24/ontario-inmates-class-action-lawsuit-over-jail-conditions-gets-green-light.html.

10 Third Party Policy and Electoral Participation after *Harper v. Canada*: A Triumph of Egalitarianism?

ERIN CRANDALL AND ANDREA LAWLOR

Third parties (or independent parties) include persons or groups, other than a political candidate, registered political party, or constituency association, that participate in elections. Their participation in elections matters, particularly when considering one of the most cited metrics of campaign success: money spent. This is especially apparent in the United States, where third parties play a prominent role in federal election campaigns. It is estimated that nearly $1.1 billion was spent by political action committees (Super PACs) during the 2016 election cycle, nearly twice the amount of independent spending that took place during the 2012 campaign.[1] This astounding level of spending was made possible by the US Supreme Court's 2010 decision in *Citizens' United vs. FEC*, which ruled that spending limits on third parties constituted an undue restriction on freedom of expression. The content of the decision notwithstanding, *Citizens' United* illustrates a second common feature of election finance regulations: the role of the judiciary in (re)defining campaign spending laws.

As in the United States, the regulations that currently govern third parties in Canadian federal elections were reviewed in a recent Supreme Court decision, *Harper v. Canada (AG)*, [2004] 1 S.C.R. 827. However, unlike in the United States, this case upheld the constitutionality of spending limits. This decision, coupled with four major legislative changes to election laws from 2000 to 2014, have fundamentally altered the policy framework of non-party actors in Canadian federal elections. Yet we have little empirical knowledge of how the legislation that precipitated the *Harper* case and the legislation that emanated from the Court's decision have changed the campaign behaviour of third parties. Whether the relatively low visibility of third parties in Canadian federal elections can be attributed to the policies that arose from the Supreme Court's rulings has, to date, not been closely examined.[2] To address these ambiguities, this chapter sets out to evaluate the policy impact of the Court's rulings with regard to third party election regulations and the policy outcomes that have followed.

Before launching into our analysis, it is helpful to address two questions particular to judicial review and election law: (1) What role should Canadian courts play in regulating election law? and (2) Do the courts' decisions matter to policymaking and, subsequently, political behaviour? To the first question, the issue of how the judicial branch should navigate its policymaking role is a long-standing topic of political debate. In Canada, the Supreme Court's status as an unelected branch of government capable of overriding the policy choices of legislatures has sometimes been touted as an unwelcome constraint on Canadian democracy.[3] This debate is an inevitable, necessary, and very likely perpetual one for any democracy that exercises judicial review. However, even within this wide-ranging debate, there appear to be features unique to election law that arguably make it well suited for judicial review.

In terms of protecting the interests of democratic governance, one of the biggest challenges in the design of election laws is that of partisan self-dealing. This is where incumbent political actors, who are by nature self-interested, implement election laws designed to entrench their own power and disadvantage their political rivals.[4] In the political science literature, partisan-self dealing has been tested using a number of theories, including the cartel thesis[5] and electoral economy model.[6] While these theories differ as to what policy measures should be expected, they are united in their view that political incumbents will design election laws in a manner that is observably self-interested. In Canada, changes in federal election law over the past decade and a half have been investigated most extensively by Lisa Young and Harold Jansen, who have, unsurprisingly, found evidence of partisan self-dealing, although not always through the commonly anticipated approach of maximizing the revenues of entrenched parties.[7] Once it is recognized that the electoral laws governing voting, the administration of elections, political parties, electoral boundaries, and campaign finance are frequently constructed so as to serve the interests of incumbents, the potential use of judicial review as a check on these partisan motivations becomes clear. Even those who are otherwise highly sceptical of the courts' exercise of judicial review in rights cases[8] can recognize the value of judicial intervention into election law policies that could otherwise stymie the practice and legitimacy of democratic processes.[9]

To the second point, even if it is accepted that courts should play a role in regulating the design of election policy, does this type of policy intervention matter to campaign behaviour? This, too, is a complex question, and the ways in which changes to election policy can matter, and for whom, need to be specified so that the question can be answered properly. For example, although we know that the US Supreme Court's decision in *Citizens' United* opened the floodgates to higher spending by Super PACs, it is less clear how money actually affects election outcomes in US elections.[10] However, even if we acknowledge that the effects of election policies – specifically, the different electoral outcomes they produce – can be difficult to measure, it remains the case that judicial decisions on election law are generally acknowledged to matter to the composition of actors who are participating in campaigns and to the potential scope of that participation. The next section of this chapter will consider in detail how the Supreme Court's rulings on third party regulations have had a measurable policy impact; however, it is also important to acknowledge at the more abstract level how cases that ask courts to choose between competing rights (e.g., freedom of expression versus equitable political participation) may act to entrench or uproot a certain approach to election administration.

On the issue of election finance in Canada, debate has centred around two competing approaches to electoral regulation: the egalitarian and libertarian models.[11] In brief, the *egalitarian model* is rooted in the idea that all individuals and groups should have relatively equal and meaningful opportunities to participate in the political process. Because private wealth may provide a more influential voice (e.g., with the purchase of well-publicized advertising), the egalitarian model argues that the influence of money should be constrained by spending limits to facilitate a political environment in which all voices have a relatively equal opportunity to meaningfully participate.

In contrast, the *libertarian approach* stresses democracy's liberty dimension and, in practice, calls for virtually no regulation of political spending. For many proponents of the libertarian model, the spending limits advocated by the egalitarian model are criticized for increasing the risk of incumbent entrenchment, or "political lockup," by elected elites.[12] As explained by Yasmin Dawood, the competing views of these two approaches highlight a paradox embedded in the regulation of election finance: "An unregulated marketplace of ideas may result in the entrenchment of the wealthy, while a regulated marketplace of ideas may result in the entrenchment of the powerful."[13]

This type of fundamental disagreement about how elections should be regulated is not one that the courts, or any other actor, can fully resolve. However, that Canada's courts have been tasked with addressing this debate means that their decisions play an important role in shaping the fundamental contours of election policy and, in turn, public confidence in the legitimacy of these processes. As will be explored in the section that follows, for election policy concerning third party advertising, the Supreme Court's decisions in *Libman v. Quebec (Attorney General)*, [1997] 3 S.C.R. 569 and *Harper v. Canada* both informed and secured the entrenchment of the egalitarian model in federal election policy. While the actual impact of these regulations on the behaviour of third parties is less clear, the Supreme Court's rulings on the constitutionality of election policy matter because they function as a check on partisan self-dealing, while also serving to articulate the values that are recognized and entrenched in the regulations themselves.

Data and Methods

This chapter takes a multi-method approach to answering the abovementioned questions, incorporating a process tracing of the development of policy alongside the judicial decision making of the courts. This is coupled with an analysis of the composition of third parties in federal election campaigns from 2000 to 2015 and their expenditures, which are provided in detail by Elections Canada. While the composition and spending analysis is necessarily at the macro or election level, we supplement this analysis with responses from a short survey of third parties that participated in elections between 2004 and 2015; the survey was conducted in the fall of 2015 ($N = 33$).

A survey on the role of third parties was sent to over 150 third parties who had participated in one or more federal election campaigns. The survey had a response rate of 19 per cent; therefore, it should not be considered a representative sample of third parties across Canada, nor should the data be considered suitable for disaggregation by third party type (individual, corporation, union, interest group) or region. Rather, it is useful as a descriptive commentary of third party opinions. This combination of data sources helps triangulate whether legislative changes to third party policy have had any meaningful impact on third party behaviour and whether we can find evidence in support of the claim that the way third parties participate in federal campaigns reveals a demonstrable link among judicial decision making, regulatory frameworks designed by policymakers, and outcomes.

The Development of Third Party Regulations: Legislation and Litigation

Regulation of third party advertising is distinguished for being one of the most legally contested election policies in Canada. This constitutional back-and-forth began soon after the entrenchment of the Canadian Charter of Rights and Freedoms in 1982, when the interest group National Citizens' Coalition (NCC) launched the first of a series of constitutional challenges to regulations that effectively banned the participation of third parties in federal election campaigns. Arguing that spending restrictions on third party advertising amounted to an unreasonable encroachment on groups' and individuals' freedom of expression under section 2(b) of the Charter, the NCC was twice successful at the Alberta Court of Appeal in having federal regulations struck down (*National Citizens' Coalition Inc. v. Attorney General of Canada,* [1984] 32 Alta. L.R. (2d) 249; *Somerville v. Canada (Attorney General),* [1996] 184 A.R. 241). These decisions meant that, with the exception of a few short-lived policy interventions by the federal government, third parties were able to participate in federal elections without spending restrictions from 1984 to 2000.

This policy vacuum may have very well continued were it not for the Supreme Court's unexpected contribution to the third party debate in *Libman v. Quebec (Attorney General),* a case that dealt with challenges to parts of Quebec's referendum law. While the Alberta Court of Appeal had, in its earlier decisions, stressed that the objective of limiting third party spending was inconsistent with the Charter because it gave preferential treatment to the expression of candidates and political parties,[14] in *Libman* the Supreme Court noted how spending limits for all participants in elections, including third parties, were needed to preserve the fairness of elections.[15] The Court went on to explain, rather bluntly, "that we cannot accept the Alberta Court of Appeal's point of view because we disagree with its conclusion regarding the legitimacy of the objective of the provisions."[16] Instead, the Court approvingly cited the 1991 report by the Royal Commission on Electoral Reform and Party Financing, which recommended that election expenses incurred by a third party during the campaign period should not exceed $1,000.[17]

Interestingly, the federal government essentially adopted this recommendation in 1993 by introducing a $1,000 spending limit for partisan advocacy (while imposing no restriction on issue advocacy). It was this $1,000 spending limit that the NCC had challenged successfully in the Alberta case and that the Supreme Court referenced with disapproval in *Libman*.

The importance of the Supreme Court's reasoning in *Libman* cannot be overemphasized in that the federal government relied on it to justify its renewed efforts to regulate third party spending. While recommendations to place spending limits on third parties had been made by Canada's chief electoral officer before the *Libman* ruling,[18] when regulations were proposed as part of Bill C-2: the Canada Elections Act, 2000, *Libman* emerged as the "go-to" explanation for why limits on third party spending were both needed and constitutional.

The Liberal minister responsible for overseeing Bill C-2 and leader of the government in the House of Commons, Don Boudria, was an ardent supporter of spending limits for third parties. While the proposed third party regulations in the bill were extensive, spending limits were, unsurprisingly, the topic of greatest interest during parliamentary debate and study. Whereas under the status quo third parties were unencumbered by spending limits, the proposed legislative measures capped spending limits on election advertising at $150,000 in relation to a general election, of which no more than $3,000 could be used to promote or oppose the election of one or more candidates in an individual constituency (indexed to inflation[19]). During consideration of Bill C-2, some members of the Reform Party pushed on the issues of whether spending limits were warranted, desirable, or constitutional. In responding to their questions at the House of Commons Standing Committee on Procedure and House Affairs, Boudria made repeated reference to the Supreme Court's ruling in *Libman*. Boudria used this example to explain the rationale of spending limits to the committee.

> On the third-party expenses, we're all aware of the *Libman* decision of 1997 … the court said, at page 601: "While we recognize their right to participate in the electoral process," – "their right" meaning the right of third parties – "independent individuals and groups cannot be subject to the same financial rules as candidates or political parties and be allowed the same spending limits. Although what they have to say is important, it is the candidates and political parties that are running for election." So says the Supreme Court in *Libman*. The court also says: Limits on independent

> spending must therefore be lower than those imposed on candidates or political parties. So the court was quite clear on that: it's not that limits on third parties "should" be lower or greater or "perhaps should" be lower or greater, but that they "must therefore be lower than those imposed on candidates or political parties." So there's no doubt.[20]

On whether the proposed $150,000 spending limit would be found to be a reasonable limitation on a third party's right to political expression, Boudria responded, "Now, the Supreme Court tells us that $1,000 was okay, and if we increase it 150 times it must be at least equally okay."[21] We can clearly see, then, a direct and explicit link between the Supreme Court's *obiter* in *Libman* in 1997 and the reforms to third party regulations introduced by the Liberal government with Bill C-2.

Once these regulations received royal assent in 2000, the NCC, unsurprisingly, moved to challenge these third party spending limits and was once again successful in having them struck down at the Alberta Court of Appeal. The case was appealed to the Supreme Court, which rendered its decision in *Harper v. Canada* in 2004. Here the Court itself recognized its part in the formation of the challenged legislation, noting, "The current third party election advertising regime is Parliament's response to this Court's decision in *Libman*."[22] Not surprisingly, then, the legislation was upheld, with a divided Court (6–3) finding that the spending restrictions set out in the Canada Elections Act were a reasonable limit on a person's right to freedom of expression under section 2(b).

The federal government's victory in *Harper* means that the last five federal elections (2004 to 2015) have operated with these third party spending limits in place (see table 10.1). This brief tracing of the legislation's genesis illustrates how this policy stability can be directly attributed to *Libman* and *Harper*: the *obiter* in *Libman* was used by the federal government in the design of and justifications for the third party spending limits introduced in the Canada Elections Act in 2000, and these same regulations were upheld by the Supreme Court in *Harper*.

Third Party Spending Behaviour

Looking at the behaviour of actors directly affected by policy changes is particularly useful in evaluating how legislators respond to judicial decision making. As observed above, in the case of third party legislation, policymakers faced the challenge of articulating a new

Table 10.1 Judicial and Policy Developments with Regard to Third Party Expenditures

Year/date	Event	Implications
1984	*National Citizens' Coalition Inc. v. Attorney General of Canada,* [1984]	Federal elections held in 1984, 1988, and 1993 without third party spending limits
1996	32 Alta. L.R. (2d) 249; *Somerville v. Canada (Attorney General),* [1996] 184 A.R.	Federal election held on 2 June 1997 without third party spending limits
9 October 1997	*Libman v. Quebec (Attorney General),* [1997] 3 S.C.R. 569	Decision creates potential policy space for third party spending limits
31 May 2000	Bill C-2, amendments to Canada Elections Act passed	Maximum spending limit of $150,000 for a national third party campaign, of which no more than $3,000 can be spent in a riding to promote or oppose a candidate Federal election held on 27 November 2000, with third party spending limits in place for only a portion of the campaign (10–27 November) due to court injunction
19 June 2003	Bill C-24, An Act to amend the Canada Elections Act and the Income Tax Act (political financing) passed	Corporate and union donations to parties reduced to a maximum of $1,000; individual donations limited to $5,000
18 May 2004	*Harper v. Canada (AG),* [2004] 1 S.C.R. 827	Federal election held on 28 June 2004 with third party spending limits
12 December 2006	Bill C-2, Federal Accountability Act (S.C. 2006, c. 9) passed	Federal election held on 23 January 2006 with third party spending limits Corporate and union donations to parties and candidates banned
19 June 2014	Bill C-23, Fair Elections Act passed	Federal elections held in 2008, 2011, and 2015 with third party spending limits Spending formula adjusted to allow for higher third party spending for campaign periods extending beyond thirty-seven days

regulatory framework that would enhance an egalitarian approach to third party participation, while still holding parties and candidates to be the primary actors in election campaigns. Assessing whether the effects of these judicial decisions on third party policy have fundamentally altered third parties' campaign behaviour is a difficult task. Any observed behavioural change related to campaign advertising is unlikely to come from policy modifications alone; after all, there are a great many political factors, including local riding competitiveness, the timing of an election, and possible fatigue with incumbent leaders or candidates, that may affect if and how a third party will choose to participate.

The notable uptick in third party participation and spending in the 2015 federal election, which will be discussed in more detail below, is a good demonstration of how regulations alone do not control behaviour. That said, we anticipate that the regulations now governing third party spending do have some effects on third party behaviour, if for no other reason than that they prohibit third parties from advertising with the same resource intensity as political parties and candidates. Observing the reactions of third parties can help to determine whether the concerns of policymakers have been borne out by the actual patterns of third party behaviour. Two types of information are used here to assess the effects of third party policy on third parties' campaign behaviour: what they did (e.g., how much they spent in federal election campaigns) and what they said about their experiences under the current regulatory framework.

First, we concentrate on what third parties did – in other words, how many third parties participated in election campaigns and how much money they spent under the new regulatory framework. While all six elections between 2000 and 2015 were contested with spending limits in place, looking exclusively at the post-regulatory environment over time still helps us evaluate how third parties have behaved following the *Harper* decision. Looking first at the composition of third parties in each federal election campaign in table 10.2, we observe that political participation reveals a surprising preservation of the status quo.

Table 10.2 lists the number of third party participants by year as well as the total amount spent by third parties combined in each election. Considering the aforementioned changes in the policy framework brought about by court decisions and the direct policy changes instituted by Bill C-2 (2000), we might expect that the policy stability created by the *Harper* decision would have created a more robust change in the number of participants and their financial activity. However, we see only a nominal increase in overall spending (less than a 10 per cent increase from 2000 to 2004) and a slight decrease in the number of third party participants (2000: $N = 50$; 2004: $N = 47$). Furthermore, although one third party (Canadians Against Bilingual Injustice) spent to the prescribed limit in the 2000 election campaign, the highest-spending third party in 2004 was more than $40,000

Table 10.2 Spending by Third Parties in Federal Elections, 2000–15

Third parties	2000	2004	2006	2008	2011	2015
Number	50	47	66	57	55	114
Total spent, all parties	$678,193	$721,078	$1,045,985	$1,260,482	$1,258,245	$6,027,256
Largest expenditure made by	Canadians Against Bilingual Injustice	Fédération des travailleurs et travailleuses du Québec	Responsible Firearms Owners Coalition of BC	Canadian Labour Congress	The Professional Institute of the Public Service of Canada	United Steelworkers
Largest overall expenditure	$150,000	$110,661	$126,788	$179,936	$166,162	$431,640

under the spending limit, suggesting that the new regulatory environment did not unduly constrain third parties. Similarly, in the four subsequent elections, we see small increases in the amount of money spent by third parties and only a nominal increase in the number of participants.

While third party spending limits have not changed since 2000, a number of other changes to election financing have had the potential to affect the behaviour of third parties (see table 10.1). Donations to political parties by corporations and groups were first significantly reduced in 2003 (Bill C-24) and then banned altogether in 2006 (Bill C-2). An unintended consequence of these legislative changes may have been a move by corporations and unions to offset the closing of one avenue of political participation by increasing their participation in another: as third parties. However, we do not observe a major change in third party behaviour over this period.

The 2015 federal election campaign, on the other hand, was a tremendous departure from the trends we observed in third party behaviour in previous years. Not only did the number of third parties more than double from 2011, the amount of money they collectively spent increased by nearly 500 per cent (see table 10.2). Three factors may help to explain the 2015 campaign's departure from the established trend of low participation. First, the theme of "change" appeared to take hold of voters and third parties alike, creating an impetus for enhanced advertising as a change from the status quo (see also below for evidence from third parties to corroborate this assumption).

Second, the length of the campaign (78 days)[23] allowed third parties to spend up to approximately $430,000 thanks to changes introduced in 2014 by Bill C-23, the Fair Elections Act. Even so, this level of aggregate third party expenditures represents only 5 per cent of the amount spent by parties and candidates in the same campaign. Finally, the fixed election date, even though it was accompanied by an unusually long campaign period, may have encouraged greater participation since third parties were aware of the time frame in which they would be able to participate. By contrast, the previous four elections did not follow fixed election dates, thereby preventing third parties from mobilizing in advance of the writ drop.

Another way in which we might consider the impact of the *Harper* decision on public policy outcomes is by examining whether the expectations of the egalitarian model have been actualized in the behaviour of third parties – for example, by determining whether there is a preponderance of organizations with greater means outspending smaller third parties. The classification of actors eligible to participate as a third party (individual, union, corporation, and interest group) suggests that, even with spending caps, some voices might displace others by virtue of how much advertising they are able to afford. For example, unions and corporations tend to have sustained funds to direct to government relations or political advocacy, while individuals are more likely to be paying for expenses out of pocket or through comparatively limited fundraising.

Interest groups could fall into either group: larger, established interest groups, such as the NCC, which had enough capital to fund a series of court challenges against the law, may very well have a formidable budget for political advocacy. Smaller interest groups or those that are struck only for the purpose of an election (e.g., Citizens for Trustworthy Government) may have limited funds and fundraising capacity. Similarly, larger organizations have existing infrastructure to deal with the regulatory environment (administrative forms, audit requirements, etc.) in a way that smaller groups do not. One possible limitation of the *Harper* decision, therefore, is that, even in a regulated environment with modest third party spending limits, some third parties will inevitably be better able to capitalize on the regulation than others.

Looking at the breakdown of spending by third parties in figure 10.1, we can observe whether the trend across elections was for larger organizations to dominate the playing field, as cautioned against by the Supreme Court. The first observation comes from the mean expenditures themselves: they are, without question, small. The mean expenditure in 2000 amounted to only $13,563.86, with incremental changes up until 2011, when the mean expenditure by a third party totalled $25,043. Only in 2015 do we see a larger average mean expenditure, with an increase to $53,057 – but still well below the limit of $430,000. Furthermore, across all elections, more than 70 per cent of third party participants were spending below the average amount, suggesting that the majority of third parties were not using this channel to maximize the potential impact of their advertising. Of the 20 to 30 per cent of high spenders per election, 42 per cent were unions, 53 per cent were interest groups, and the remaining 5 per cent were individuals or corporations. Note that unions were also the single highest spenders in all elections but 2000 and 2006. Therefore, there is some evidence that, even within an egalitarian framework, some interests are better represented than others.

Figure 10.1. Number of Below-Average and Above-Average Spenders, by Election, 2000–15

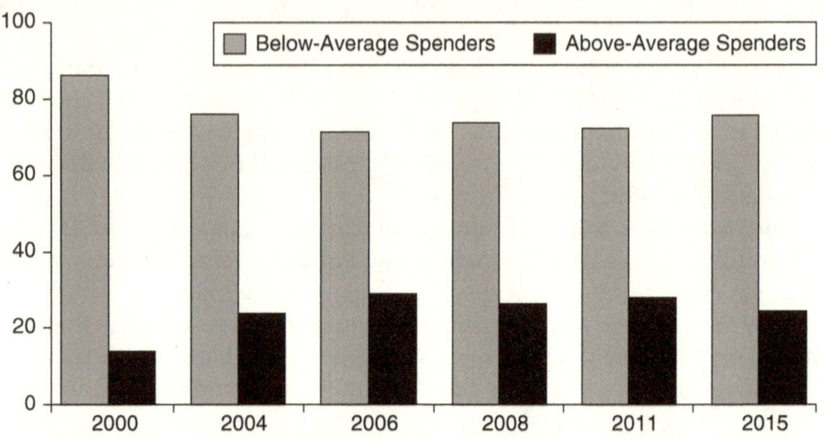

Note: Mean expenditures by year: $13,563.86 (2000); $13,592 (2004); $15,042 (2006); $21,367 (2008); $25,043 (2011); $53,057 (2015).

A second way in which we can consider the chapter's core questions about the impact of the courts' decision making on policy outcomes is by soliciting the opinions of third parties about the regulatory process designed by policymakers to meet the courts' rulings. Here a number of indicators are of interest: first, why individuals and groups become involved in federal campaigns as third parties; second, their perspectives on the imposition of spending limits; and third, whether the accompanying administrative changes brought in under the new regulatory framework have created any unintended consequences for the egalitarian model.

To the question of participation motivations, all but one third party surveyed responded that their involvement in an election campaign stemmed from a lack of attention from parties and candidates to an issue of importance. They therefore thought that it was necessary to engage the public separately from party- and candidate-issue advertising to bring the issue to light. Similarly, 70 per cent of respondents noted that even when their issues were brought to bear in a campaign, their position on a particular issue was underrepresented and therefore required independent advocacy. Motivations for participation were, for most third parties, explicitly non-partisan: only one-third of respondents noted that they engaged in third party advertising specifically to oppose or support a particular party or candidate. On the question of effectiveness, over 60 per cent of third parties rated this channel of participation as somewhat or very effective in promoting political change (with another 20 per cent of respondents reporting that they found it to be neutral). Therefore, there was reasonable consensus that, even with the constraints of spending limits, third parties found value in this avenue of participation in election campaigns.

Third parties' perspectives on spending limits themselves showed a considerable degree of support for the contemporary policy framework. When asked whether individuals and organizations should be free to advertise as third parties without limits, only 11 per cent of respondents suggested that third party spending limits should be abolished altogether, with another 10 per cent reporting that third parties should be allowed to spend freely, but only on a narrow set of subjects (e.g., policy, rather than partisan, issues). The vast majority of respondents supported the use of spending limits, and, on a separate indicator, they reported that they had designed their third party advertising campaign to be non-partisan and issue-focused to make clear to the public that they were participating as an independent third party rather than as a surrogate for a political party. Similarly, on the subject of whether they or their organization would have donated to a party or candidate if it were still permitted, only one respondent replied Yes and thought that the current ban on donations should be repealed. The remainder expressed a lack of interest in reopening the debate on corporation, union, and interest group contributions to parties and candidates, and they supported the view that third party spending limits were a reasonable limit on freedom of expression.

Finally, as suggested above, policy changes – initiated by courts or legislators – could have unintended consequences for the realization of the egalitarian model insofar as they may risk overburdening participants with regulatory requirements. In the case of third party regulation, the accompanying administrative changes brought in under the new regulatory framework have set out specific reporting and auditing requirements to ensure that third parties are compliant with spending limits and that their advertising expenditures are wholly transparent to voters following an election campaign. Here respondents indicated some dissatisfaction with the current regulatory regime. When asked whether the election regulations set out by Elections Canada created confusion over what spending should be included in the reporting, respondents were evenly split. However, while only 20 per cent stated that reporting regulations were a burden on their campaign activities, over 55 per cent of respondents reported that they believed such requirements had discouraged some independent groups from participating in campaigns as third parties. These results suggest a trade-off between the desired outcome of levelling the playing field by imposing transparency requirements and encouraging democratic participation from a broad variety of actors.

This combination of spending data and third party opinion on the subject of regulation provides a great deal of insight into how well third party limits, as prescribed by courts and legislators, meet their stated goals. On the surface, it would be easy to suggest that third party spending regulations are working simply by virtue of the fact that they are keeping election advertising spending below the threshold. However, that does little to shed light on the impact of the courts' push towards the egalitarian model and legislators' decision to keep the role of third parties minimal when compared with that of candidates and parties. In examining the policy outcomes by looking at the actions and perspectives of third parties, we are able to provide some evaluation from the viewpoint of those electoral actors who are being regulated. While evaluations of the policy may differ when consulting other stakeholders (e.g., legislators, regulators, voters), these data answer a number of critical questions about the link between judicial decision making, policy development, and outcomes.

Looking to the Future

While there are currently no pending cases concerning third party spending, this remains a policy area rife for constitutional challenge, especially given the recent wave of policy changes at the provincial level and proposed federal changes introduced in 2018. Indeed, while spending limits are unlikely to be challenged in the same fashion as they were in *Harper*, issues related to third party regulations may nonetheless arise. Concerns over advertising spending are increasingly being pushed to the background by those related to the use of new communications techniques, particularly the trend towards low- or no-cost technologies, and increasing tendencies by third parties to circumvent third party regulations by advertising outside the writ period. All these considerations can be illustrated by the 2015 election campaign.

While candidates and parties in previous campaigns embraced the use of new communications techniques, such as robocalls and automated email management using purchased list services, third parties were typically excluded from using these outreach tools precisely because of the costs associated with rolling them out. The use of these communications tools may act to widen the gulf among parties, candidates, and third parties even further than policymakers originally intended. At the opposite end of the spectrum, low- or no-cost technologies, including social media platforms and other forms of free communications management, have become widely available (and are often cited to be useful) to third parties. It could be argued that these types of communications tools level the playing field even further than the policy measures endorsed by the *Harper* decision. This trend allows communications teams and professional marketing strategists to be replaced by a single social media user with a powerful network. During the 2015 campaign, small groups of active citizens were not only communicating their own political preferences widely but also leveraging these sorts of approaches to push issues that were, arguably, underrepresented in party platforms. For example, Canadian Veterans ABC 2015, a third party formed for the 2015 election, used both Twitter and Facebook extensively to criticize the record of the Conservative government on veterans' affairs.

However, low- or no-cost technologies present a very specific problem for third party regulation: they have the potential to have a large impact on issue awareness, voter mobilization, and, indeed, voter outcome, but they are effectively non-monetary contributions and therefore not measured by current regulations. This separation between spending and political expression made possible by new technologies has led some to speculate that current third party regulations are no longer sufficient to maintain political parties' privileged position in election campaigning.[24] The advent of new technologies brings at least two further challenges to the regulation of third parties: first, despite the fact that these new technologies are seemingly egalitarian, some third parties will be able to leverage them more fully and with more professional results because they can afford to hire experts to deploy them to their advantage; and second, if the federal government does eventually choose to regulate social media advertising, the courts may be presented with the question of whether such restrictions on political expression can be justified, a question that will likely require judges to consider the non-monetary value of these communications tools – an inherently subjective matter. If the use of digital technologies remains unregulated in the campaign context, governing parties may have an increasingly difficult time using the logic set out in *Libman* to justify their preferential status vis-à-vis third parties.

Finally, the 2015 campaign also challenged the existing policy's approach to regulating spending exclusively during the official campaign period. In the lead-up to the 2015 election, a number of third party actors circumvented spending regulations by engaging in advertising outside the writ period.[25] Some speculated that this was what pushed Stephen Harper into calling an early – and lengthy – general election.[26] Advertising in the pre-writ period is attractive to many prospective third parties precisely because it is not subject to regulations. This strategic workaround received considerable attention in the media – and was effective enough that some organizations that operated before the writ was dropped, such as Engage Canada, chose not to advertise during the regulated writ period.[27] Concern over the strategic use of the pre-writ period by third parties has led some provinces to consider introducing spending limits in the months before the official campaign period, something made feasible by the move to fixed election dates in Canada.[28] However, two attempts in British Columbia to introduce spending limits in the period preceding the official campaign period were quickly challenged and struck down by the BC Supreme Court as an unreasonable limitation on third parties' freedom of expression under section 2(b) of the Charter.[29]

All three issues pose potential questions for constitutional law and public policy scholars, jurists, and legislators alike. At a minimum, each of these issues engages questions of freedom of expression and the rights of democratic participation – areas rife for judicial intervention. Because election campaigning will inevitably evolve with the introduction of new technologies, and because such political communication is unquestionably protected under the Charter, this is a policy field that is likely to continue to face legal challenges. Moreover, given the risks of partisan self-dealing, as discussed earlier in the chapter, election law is arguably not an area to which the courts owe governments special deference when exercising judicial review. That said, the difficulties of anticipating how election campaigning will evolve, as illustrated by the example of third parties, suggest that courts should be cautious in offering their own policy solutions because they are at risk of becoming rapidly outdated.

NOTES

1 Opensecrets.org (Centre for Responsive Politics), "2016 outside Spending, by Super PAC," https://www.opensecrets.org/outsidespending/summ.php?cycle=2016&chrt=V&disp=O&type=; Opensecrets.org (Centre

for Responsive Politics), "2012 outside Spending, by Super PAC," http://www.opensecrets.org/outsidespending/summ.php?cycle=2012&chrt=P&disp=O&type=S.

2 For reviews of how third parties have advertised in the federal elections since the *Harper* decision, see Erin Crandall and Andrea Lawlor, "Third Party Election Spending in Canada and the United Kingdom: A Comparative Analysis," *Election Law Journal: Rules, Politics, and Policy* 13, no. 4 (2014); Andrea Lawlor and Erin Crandall, "Understanding Third-Party Advertising: An Analysis of the 2004, 2006 and 2008 Canadian Elections," *Canadian Public Administration* 54, no. 4 (2011).

3 Frederick Lee Morton and Rainer Knopff, *The Charter Revolution and the Court Party* (Toronto: University of Toronto Press, 2000); Christopher P Manfredi, *Judicial Power and the Charter: Canada and the Paradox of Liberal Constitutionalism*, 2nd ed. (Don Mills, ON: Oxford University Press, 2001).

4 Yasmin Dawood, "Electoral Fairness and the Law of Democracy: A Structural Rights Approach to Judicial Review," *University of Toronto Law Journal* 62, no. 4 (2012): 500.

5 Richard S. Katz and Peter Mair, "Changing Models of Party Organization and Party Democracy: The Emergence of the Cartel Party," *Party Politics* 1, no. 1 (1995).

6 Susan E. Scarrow, "Explaining Political Finance Reforms: Competition and Context," *Party Politics* 10, no. 6 (2004).

7 Lisa Young, "Shaping the Battlefield: Partisan Self-Interest and Election Finance Reform in Canada, 2003–2014," in *The Deregulatory Moment? A Comparative Perspective on Changing Campaign Finance Laws*, ed. Robert G. Boatright (Ann Arbor: University of Michigan Press, 2015); Harold J. Jansen and Lisa Young, "Cartels, Syndicates, and Coalitions: Canada's Political Parties after the 2004 Reforms," in *Money, Politics, and Democracy: Canada's Party Finance Reforms*, ed. Lisa Young and Harold J. Jansen (Vancouver: UBC Press, 2011), 82–103.

8 See, e.g., John Hart Ely, *Democracy and Distrust: A Theory of Judicial Review* (Cambridge, MA: Harvard University Press, 1980).

9 For a discussion of how the Supreme Court of Canada may act to provide oversight of the democratic process, see Dawood, "Electoral Fairness and the Law of Democracy."

10 Steven D. Levitt, "Using Repeat Challengers to Estimate the Effect of Campaign Spending on Election Outcomes in the US House," *Journal of Political Economy* (1994); Adam R. Brown, "Does Money Buy Votes? The Case of Self-Financed Gubernatorial Candidates, 1998–2008," *Political Behavior* 35, no. 1 (2013).

11 Colin Feasby, "*Libman v. Quebec (A.G.)* and the Administration of the Process of Democracy under the Charter: The Emerging Egalitarian Model," *McGill Law Journal* 44 (1999); Janet L. Hiebert, "Money and Elections: Can Citizens Participate on Fair Terms amidst Unrestricted Spending?," *Canadian Journal of Political Science/Revue canadienne de science politique* 31, no. 1 (1998); Christopher P. Manfredi and Mark E. Rush, "Electoral Jurisprudence in the Canadian and U.S. Supreme Courts: Evolution and Convergence," *McGill Law Journal* 52, no. 3 (2007): 457–93.
12 Manfredi and Rush, "Electoral Jurisprudence in the Canadian and U.S. Supreme Courts," 465.
13 Yasmin Dawood, "Democracy, Power, and the Supreme Court: Campaign Finance Reform in Comparative Context," *International Journal of Constitutional Law* 4, no. 2 (2006): 290.
14 *Libman*, para. 55.
15 Ibid., para. 56.
16 Ibid., para. 79.
17 Canada, *Reforming Electoral Democracy: Final Report* (Ottawa: Royal Commission on Electoral Reform and Party Financing, 1991).
18 Chief Electoral Officer of Canada, "Report of the Chief Electoral Officer of Canada on the 36th General Election" (Ottawa: Elections Canada, 1997).
19 Because spending limits are indexed to inflation, a third party who participated in 2016 in a federal election campaign lasting thirty-seven days could spend up to $208,200 and $4,164 in an individual constituency.
20 Don Boudria, House of Commons, Standing Committee on Procedure and House Affairs, Evidence (24 November 1999), 36th Parl., 1st Sess.
21 Ibid.
22 *Libman*, para. 63.
23 The base limits of $150,000 nation-wide and $3,000 per riding are multiplied by the inflation adjustment factor and for any election period beyond thirty-seven days. If a campaign extends beyond thirty-seven days, limits are increased by 1/37th for each additional day.
24 Léonid Sirota, "'Third Parties' and Democracy 2.0," *McGill Law Journal* 60, no. 2 (2015).
25 Andrea Lawlor and Erin Crandall, "Third Parties in the 2015 Federal Election: Partying Like It's 1988?," in *Canadian Election Analysis 2015: Communication, Strategy, and Democracy*, ed. Alex Marland and Thierry Giasson (Vancouver: UBC Press, 2015).
26 Stephanie Levitz, "Federal Election 2015: Timing of Election Call a Political Calculus for Conservatives," *CBC News*, 19 July 2015.
27 Lawlor and Crandall, "Third Parties in the 2015 Federal Election."

28 Erin Crandall and Andrea Lawlor, "When More Isn't Better: Regulation of Third Parties in Ontario Elections," IRPP, http://policyoptions.irpp.org/magazines/july-2016/when-more-isnt-better-regulation-of-third-parties-in-ontario-elections/.

29 Jennifer Smith and Gerald Baier, "Fixed Election Dates, the Continuous Campaign, and Campaign Advertising Restrictions," in *From New Public Management to New Political Governance: Essays in Honour of Peter C. Aucoin*, ed. Herman Bakvis and Mark D. Jarvis (Montreal and Kingston: McGill-Queen's University Press, 2012).

11 Section 23 of the Charter and Official-Language Minority Instruction in Canada: The Judiciary's Impact and Limits in Education Policymaking

STÉPHANIE CHOUINARD

This chapter takes an in-depth look at the evolution of official-language minority education – that is, full English-language instruction in Quebec and French-language instruction in the rest of Canada[1] – through the interpretation that the Supreme Court of Canada (SCC) has given to section 23 of the Canadian Charter of Rights and Freedoms (Charter). In the last thirty-five years, the SCC has paid a lot of attention to this question as it has been called upon many times to clarify the meaning and the extent of these rights. The evolution of Canada's language regime has, since then, been driven by the courts rather than the legislatures.[2] The SCC has had to interpret the provisions contained in section 23, while attempting to steer away from interference from provincial jurisdictions. The policy of the SCC towards official-minority language education has, therefore, had a substantial impact, but has contained enough flexibility to be adapted by the provinces.

In 1982, section 23 of the Charter entrenched in the constitution a new provision guaranteeing, for the children of parents whose first language was the minority official language in their province of residence, access to instruction in that language. This section entailed obvious new duties for provincial governments everywhere in the country, education being an area of provincial jurisdiction. It also demonstrated a blatant jurisdictional encroachment of the federal government on the provinces – and many provinces responded by openly admitting that they would disregard section 23 since it was not available to dismissal through the notwithstanding clause. The provincial backlash against this new provision was such that every province in the country has, since 1982, been found in disrespect of its section 23 obligations at least once by Canadian courts. The SCC has been particularly active in this area, handing down ten decisions since 1982 that have gradually clarified the provinces' obligations and elaborated a liberal and generous interpretation of the extent of section 23.

Three and a half decades later, one could believe that these numerous cases of jurisprudence regarding the provincial governments' official-language education obligations would have led to a normalization of the conditions of access to minority official-language schools and to a standardization of the quality of instruction provided in those institutions throughout the federation – especially since provincial education policies, with the exception of Quebec, have significantly converged in the last decades.[3] And yet, still today, many inconsistencies and inequalities persist among different provinces and sometimes within them. As this chapter was being written, nearly half the provinces and territories of Canada were facing a constitutional challenge brought forward by francophone minority communities, which were accusing the provincial and territorial instances of failing to fulfil their section 23 obligations. According to the newspaper *Le Devoir*, "Never in Canada's history have so many legal cases in the domain of official-language minority education concurrently ended up in the higher courts."[4]

It thus appears that court intervention in official-language minority instruction does not constitute a panacea for official-language minority communities. While the SCC has certainly done its part to enforce the respect of section 23 since 1982, it is clear that case law has a limited impact on provincial implementation of said obligations. This chapter will aim to demonstrate that these policy outcomes are the result of power relationships, both between the two parties involved in each case (the minority communities and the provincial governments) and between the SCC and the legislatures that are responsible for implementing the policy changes following a decision.

In the first case, the adversarial nature of litigation systematically disadvantages the non-state actors as they have limited means and can rarely present an adequate and complete record of evidence – an issue already highlighted in the works of Marc Galanter[5] and demonstrated in other non–section 23 language rights cases by Power, Larocque, and Bossé.[6] The burden of evidence being thrust on the shoulders of official-minority communities in these cases creates a clear advantage for the state actor, who has virtually unlimited resources and who is a "repeat player"[7] in the judicial system, with a sophisticated knowledge of said system. In the second case, and as will also be highlighted in James B. Kelly's findings in the following chapter, the SCC relies on the provincial legislative assemblies to enact language policy changes – changes that they might be reluctant to make[8] for electoral and/or ideological reasons.

This chapter will begin with a brief overview of the historical and political reasons behind the entrenchment of section 23 rights in the 1982 constitution and the population to whom these rights apply. It will then present, chronologically, an analysis of the ten SCC section 23 decisions to highlight how the Court has read into this provision since 1982. It has notably clarified and extended the minority communities' right to manage their own educational institutions as well as highlighted the importance of these institutions being granted the resources necessary to ensure that they can provide an education of the same quality as the majority institutions. This second part will set out the "state of affairs" in the jurisprudence. Finally, the chapter will shed light on some of the SCC's limits regarding official-language minority education policymaking. The adversarial aspect of litigation, the federal division of powers, and the courts' jurisdictional limits on the implementation of positive rights are three issues that will be discussed.

Historical Context

The issue of minority education rights has been at the forefront of political debate in Canada since before Confederation. It is also an issue with which courts have had to grapple for almost as long. Originally, the debate regarding access to education in French or in English in Canada was closely intertwined with another important divide in Canadian society: the religious divide between Catholics and Protestants. As early as 1864, the legislature in Nova Scotia, a province where schooling in French and in Gaelic had been recognized for decades, voted to implement an English-only, non-confessional school system[9] – legislation that was only partly repealed in 1902. In 1867, the Fathers of Confederation decided to grant provinces jurisdiction over education, but to constitutionalize a universal guarantee of access to "separate or dissentient schools" – a guarantee found in section 93 of the British North America Act (BNA Act). Back then, religious cleavages mostly followed linguistic ones, with the majority of the anglophone population being Protestant and the francophone population Catholic; these provisions were thus also assumed to protect access to schools in both those languages, where one or the other would be the language of the minority.

However, this belief was proved wrong a few short years following Confederation. The Irish Catholic clergy quickly proved reluctant to provide French-language education outside Quebec. Moreover, more provinces passed legislation to abolish the right to separate schools – legislation that, despite being unconstitutional, was never disavowed by the federal government. This situation led to a number of "school crises."[10] Catholic schools were abolished in New Brunswick in 1871, leading to the 1875 Caraquet riot, after which the provincial government retracted its legislation. The Manitoba government abolished public funding of confessional schools as well as the bilingual status of the province in 1890 – just two decades after entering Confederation. The federal government refused to disavow these legislative moves, preferring to let the courts intervene. Franco-Manitobans went all the way to London to see these provisions abolished – at that time, the Judicial Committee of the Privy Council (JCPC) was the highest court in Canada – first, to no avail; then, three years later, they were granted a recognition of prejudice towards Catholics in the province. Following the 1896 "Greenway-Laurier compromise," Catholic instruction would be re-established for up to an hour a day, but French would continue to be forbidden as a language of instruction until 1947.[11]

Finally, following the adoption of Regulation 17 by the Ontario Department of Education in 1912, French-language education was abolished and forbidden throughout that province past second grade.[12] Members of the Franco-Ontarian community, with the help of a newly founded community organization, the Association canadienne-française d'éducation en français de l'Ontario, went to the JCPC and argued that section 93 of the BNA Act also protected the language of education; they lost that legal battle.[13] Regulation 17 was eventually repealed in 1927.

In short, following Confederation, and for many decades, most French Canadians outside Quebec had limited, if any, access to instruction in their mother tongue, and this instruction was often provided in English schools as an addendum to the regular curriculum. Meanwhile, the government of Quebec never threatened English-language education in that province, where English schools flourished, from first grade to university.[14]

In 1969, the final report of the Laurendeau-Dunton Commission (Royal Commission on Bilingualism and Biculturalism) rang an alarm bell: access to education in French outside Quebec was still dismal, and the quality of instruction provided in existing schools was unsatisfactory, especially when compared to the quality of English schools. The commissioners recommended that parents whose first language was the minority official language have access to public schools in which the language of instruction would be theirs in areas where the demand was sufficient.[15] In 1977, the Quebec government began to restrict access to English schools in the province through provisions found in the Charter of the French Language, commonly known as Bill 101. René Lévesque's government's plan was to limit the anglicization of newcomers, who almost systematically sent their children to the province's English schools,[16] rather than to limit access to those schools for the children of Anglo-Quebecer parents.[17] Nevertheless, this legislation was coldly received by his provincial counterparts. In August 1977, all premiers of Canada, with the exception of Lévesque, signed the St. Andrews Declaration, in which they vowed to "make their best efforts to provide instruction in English and French wherever numbers warranted."[18] The Council of Ministers of Education, Canada was also to conduct a review of the state of minority-language education in each province.

The premiers reiterated and clarified their engagement the following year in the Montreal Accord, which stated that each "child of the French-speaking and English-speaking minority is entitled to an education in his or her language in the primary or the secondary schools in each province wherever numbers warrant. The implementation of this principle will be as defined by each province."[19] Provincial governments were looking to regularize official-language minorities' situation in education; but despite these good intentions, there still existed, at the end of the 1970s, significant disparities among the provinces in the conditions of access to instruction in the minority language. Moreover, as was made explicit in the 1978 accord, provinces still retained full discretion over the implementation of these policies, and official-language minorities had no legal recourse should a provincial government refuse to respect its obligations.

A second series of school crises hit French Canada in the same period, notably in Ontario, where many English school boards refused to create French-language classes and schools, despite numbers widely warranting such measures. Confrontations took place in many localities: Ottawa, Elliot Lake, Cornwall, Sturgeon Falls, Burlington, Kirkland Lake, East York, Windsor-Essex, and, finally, Penetanguishene (Penetang).[20] The "Penetang crisis," in particular, gained momentum through political and media attention across the country as it unfolded during the Quebec referendum campaign – during which Premier Bill Davis campaigned for the No camp.[21]

The Adoption and Entrenchment of Section 23 and Its Subsequent Interpretation by the Supreme Court of Canada

This series of events, followed by the victory of the federalist camp during the 1980 Quebec referendum, set the scene for engagement by the federal government – an actor that, until then, had decided not to intervene – in the debate on official-language minority education. This engagement was reflected in section 23 of the Canadian Charter of Rights and Freedoms.

Minority Language Educational Rights

Language of instruction

23. (1) Citizens of Canada

(a) whose first language learned and still understood is that of the English or French linguistic minority population of the province in which they reside, or

(b) who have received their primary school instruction in Canada in English or French and reside in a province where the language in which they received that instruction is the language of the English or French linguistic minority population of the province,

have the right to have their children receive primary and secondary school instruction in that language in that province. (93)

Continuity of language instruction

(2) Citizens of Canada of whom any child has received or is receiving primary or secondary school instruction in English or French in Canada, have the right to have all their children receive primary and secondary school instruction in the same language.

Application where numbers warrant

(3) The right of citizens of Canada under subsections (1) and (2) to have their children receive primary and secondary school instruction in the language of the English or French linguistic minority population of a province

(a) applies wherever in the province the number of children of citizens who have such a right is sufficient to warrant the provision to them out of public funds of minority language instruction; and

(b) includes, where the number of those children so warrants, the right to have them receive that instruction in minority language educational facilities provided out of public funds.

Seeing a lack of strong commitment on the part of the provinces, Prime Minister Pierre Elliott Trudeau sought to enshrine these rights in the constitution.[22] According to James Kelly, "Trudeau considered judicial activism necessary to ensure greater protection for language rights and 'long realized that he would need to enlist the courts as allies.'"[23] Official-language education rights had, therefore, been deliberately removed from the political arena by the Charter masterminds and put in the hands of the judges. Jean Chrétien, minister of justice at the time, corroborated this strategy. As he explained himself,

> The courts will decide and it would be out of the political arena, where the matter is sometimes dealt with by some people who do not comprehend or do not want to comprehend.
>
> I think we are rendering a great service to Canadians by taking some of these problems away from the political debate and allowing the matters to be debated, argued, coolly before the courts with precedents and so on.
>
> It will serve the population, in my judgement very well.[24]

The point of this legislation was to guarantee the same level of access to schools for all official-language minorities in Canada. It is worthy of note that Charter language rights were also not available for derogation; provincial governments could, therefore, not make use of the notwithstanding clause to circumvent their section 23 duties. However, the text of section 23 actually fell quite short of what minority official-language communities, especially francophone minority communities, had been expecting from the new constitution. Indeed, they had been very vocal during the constitutional renewal process, requesting not only a right to schooling in their own language but also a right to the management and control of their own educational institutions.[25] The vagueness of the text of this section of the Charter meant that to reveal its true extent, it would need to be interpreted by the courts. The implementation of the Court Challenges Program, created in 1978 by the federal government to give Anglo-Quebecers and francophones outside Quebec the financial means to challenge their respective provincial governments' linguistic laws and policies, would subsequently help minority communities make their way before the judges through hefty financial contributions.[26]

As is also noted in James Kelly's chapter in this volume, official-language minorities did not delay in making use of this new legal tool:

the SCC heard its first section 23 challenge in 1984. In *Attorney General of Quebec v. Quebec Protestant School Boards*,[27] the SCC deemed sections 72 and 73 of Bill 101, which set out the conditions of access to English-language minority schools, overly restrictive. The Quebec provisions created stricter conditions than those found in section 23 and were not justifiable under section 1 of the Charter, as proved by the *Oakes* test. They were therefore struck down. The SCC justices went so far as to argue that the language of section 23 was perhaps chosen by the legislators to object to Bill 101's provisions.

> This set of constitutional provisions was not enacted in a vacuum. When it was adopted, the framers knew, and clearly had in mind the regimes governing the Anglophone and Francophone linguistic minorities in various provinces in Canada so far as the language of instruction was concerned. They also had in mind the history of these regimes. ... Rightly or wrongly, – and it is not for the courts to decide, – the framers of the Constitution manifestly regarded as inadequate some – and perhaps all – of the regimes in force at the time the Charter was enacted, and their intention was to remedy the perceived defects of these regimes by uniform corrective measures.[28]

The next case to make its way to the SCC, *Mahe v. Alberta*,[29] called on the judges to determine whether section 23 rights included a right to facilities that belonged to the minority community – and that would be managed and controlled by the minority community rather than, in the case at stake here, an English school board. This case was brought forward by a group of francophone parents from Edmonton, who wished to obtain their own school board to manage the existing French schools in the area. The SCC read section 23 in a generous and liberal manner, in line with what the justices believed was the remedial nature of those rights. In other words, section 23 had been entrenched to remedy historic wrongs suffered by official-language minority communities, notably regarding instruction in their own language. This generous interpretation was meant to guide the determination of the extent of the rights enshrined in section 23.

To settle the issue regarding the management and control of minority institutions, the justices first turned to the wording of subparagraph 23(3)(b), which states, in English, the right to "minority language educational facilities" and, in French, "*des établissements d'enseignement de la minorité linguistique.*" Confirming a prior decision from the Ontario

Court of Appeal, the SCC justices decided that while the English text of the law might seem ambiguous, the French text suggested that "the facilities belong to the minority and hence that a measure of management and control should go to the linguistic minority in respect of educational facilities."[30] They then explained that this measure of management and control required a sliding-scale approach, which relied on the number of potential pupils in a given region: the greater the number of potential students, the more autonomy the minority community would be granted in the area of education. The justices focused on clarifying the upper echelons of this scale, determining that where the numbers warranted, section 23 might go as far as granting the minority its own school board to manage its own homogeneous, government-funded schools – the optimal situation for a given minority community.

The SCC did not specify how many students would be required to trigger this superior echelon of obligations. However, it did decide that, in the case at hand, in Edmonton the number of francophone pupils was not sufficient to mandate the creation of a school board. Nevertheless, those pupils' parents should be granted some power of control over their schools in the English school board's governance system, in the form of a number of seats on the board at least proportional to the percentage of their children in the school board's population. It is worthy of note that the provincial government went ahead and created a homogeneous French-language school board in 1993, following further negotiations with the francophone community (and a pending threat of litigation before the United Nations' Human Rights Committee), therefore going beyond its section 23 obligations as interpreted by the SCC.

The SCC had a chance to substantiate the position it had taken in *Mahe* with the *Manitoba Public Schools Reference*[31] case in 1993. The justices determined that "minority language educational facilities" could mean facilities distinct from those of the majority or, at the very least, a demarcation in the physical spaces between minority and majority schools. Chief Justice Lamer added that it was of the utmost importance that minority language parents participate in assessing the educational needs of the children attending minority schools as well as in determining the structures and services necessary to respond to those needs. The reference case therefore clarified the Court's position in *Mahe* regarding the right of minority communities, flowing from section 23, to educational facilities that they owned, managed, and controlled, adding that these should be in separate locations from the majority's facilities – all within the frame of the sliding-scale approach, relying on the size of the minority-language pupil population.

Next, the SCC's *Arsenault-Cameron*[32] decision in 2000 was the result of the legal mobilization of a group of parents from Summerside, Prince Edward Island, formed in 1982 to build a French school in their town. In this case, the SCC re-evaluated section 23 rights through the notions of *substantial equality* and *differential treatment*. According to the justices, implementing policies following a pattern of formal equality between majority and minority communities in education would entail a failure by governments to take into account the purposive, remedial nature of section 23. Policies should therefore follow a pattern of substantive equality, which meant that different measures might need to be taken for a minority community to achieve equality with the majority. For example, the pedagogical needs of a minority could not be the same as those of the majority, and the provincial government, while retaining the power to implement universal standards and to expect that they be met in all the province's public schools, had an obligation to take these different needs into account. Moreover, the SCC's decision recognized the role of minority community organizations (in this case, minority school boards) as legitimate spokespersons.

> Where a minority language board has been established in furtherance of s. 23, it is up to the board, as it represents the minority official language community, to decide what is more appropriate from a cultural and linguistic perspective. The principal role of the Minister is to develop institutional structures and specific regulations and policies to deal with the unique blend of linguistic dynamics that has developed in the province.[33]

The SCC therefore explicitly restricted the power of the provincial government in favour of the minority communities in the area of education.

The next decision, *Doucet-Boudreau*,[34] handed down in 2003, is probably the most fascinating of all SCC decisions from the standpoint of section 23. After the government of the province of Nova Scotia had failed for many years to begin the construction of homogeneous French high schools in five districts where the number of potential pupils warranted such facilities but none existed, a group of francophone parents from those districts appealed to the Supreme Court of Nova Scotia to direct the ministry of education to answer its constitutional obligations. Not only did Justice LeBlanc find that the parents were within their right to demand these new facilities and that the government had failed, but he also found that the government "had not given sufficient attention to the serious rate of assimilation among Acadians and Francophones in Nova Scotia."[35] He therefore decided to remain seized of the case after he rendered his decision, setting a number of deadlines by which those facilities and programs should be provided as well as a series of follow-up meetings with the applicants and respondents to make sure that reasonable advancement was made to respect these deadlines.

The government appealed the remedial part of this decision. The Nova Scotia Court of Appeal effectively struck it down on the basis that "the trial judge, having decided the issue between the parties, had no further jurisdiction to remain seized of the case."[36] This decision was again appealed by the Association of Parents. The SCC agreed to hear the case despite the fact that the issue at stake had become a theoretical one, as the French-language schools and programs had by then been put in place. The Court confirmed Justice LeBlanc's 2003 ruling and thus created an important precedent for future cases in which provincial governments have an obligation, by virtue of section 23, to fulfil their obligations in a timely manner.

The *Solski*[37] and *Nguyen*[38] cases, brought to the SCC in 2005 and 2009, respectively, called into question the admission criteria to English-language public schools in Quebec, set out in Bill 101, in the wake of the debate on "bridging schools" in that province. As is also discussed by James Kelly in the next chapter, this debate concerned the practice of expanding access to minority schools in Quebec to children of parents who were not rights-bearers, according to section 23, through their temporary registration in unsubsidized private schools. These parents

> were enrolling their children in [unsubsidized private schools] for short periods so that they would be eligible – on a literal reading of s. 73 CFL and in light of the administrative practice of the Ministère de l'Éducation – to attend publicly funded English schools. In the government's view, parents who did so were circumventing all the rules relating to the language of instruction.[39]

The National Assembly of Quebec had amended sections 72 and 73 of Bill 101 in 2004 in an attempt to curb this phenomenon. As was the case in 1984, the SCC found the legislation to be overly restrictive; it struck down the two sections as unconstitutional and gave the Quebec government a year to revise its provisions. The National Assembly responded by adopting Bill 115 in 2010. This new bill created a points-based system allowing non-rights-bearing children, under certain circumstances, to attend bridging schools – a system that did not respect either "the letter or the spirit of the judgment of the Supreme Court,"[40] according to lawyers involved in the *Nguyen* case. However, at the time this chapter was written, no further legal challenge to the provisions enacted by Bill 115 had been brought forward.

Meanwhile, the *Gosselin*[41] case was brought to the SCC in 2005 by a number of Quebec-born francophone parents, who argued that section 23 of the Charter as well as sections 72 and 73 of Bill 101 were unconstitutional, according to equality rights found in section 15 of the Charter and sections 10 and 12 of the Quebec Charter of Human Rights and Freedoms. The SCC rejected their claim, stating that there was no hierarchy of Charter rights. The justices also reiterated that the purpose of section 23 was "the protection and promotion of the minority language community in each province,"[42] a purpose that could not be respected if minority schools were accessible to members of the linguistic majority. Moreover, in Quebec, access to English schools for everyone would go against the legislature's intent of protecting and favouring the French language: the language of the majority in that province, but that of the minority in the rest of the country.[43]

Finally, in 2015, the SCC was seized with two section 23 cases: *Rose-des-Vents*[44] and *Yukon Francophone School Board*.[45] In *Rose-des-Vents*, a group of francophone parents in Vancouver claimed that the province was acting in an unconstitutional manner by denying their children access to a school equivalent in quality to that of the majority in the same part of the city, a practice that had been going on for a number of years. The French-language school had been operating over capacity for many years, and basic facilities were not available to their children. The SCC sided with the francophone parents, reminding the province that its section 23 obligations were time-sensitive, a point it had already made in *Doucet-Boudreau*. The justices also clarified that substantive equality in education should be applied to facilities, a finding that responded to the principle of "substantive equivalence."[46] They explained this new principle as follows:

> When assessing equivalence, a purposive approach requires a court to consider the educational choices available from the perspective of s. 23 rights holders. Would reasonable rights-holder parents be deterred from sending their children to a minority language school because it is meaningfully inferior to an available majority language school? If so, the purpose of this

> remedial provision is threatened. If the educational experience, viewed globally, is sufficiently superior in the majority language schools, that fact could undermine the parents' desire to have their children educated in the minority language, and thus could lead to assimilation. The inquiry into equivalence should thus focus on comparisons that would adversely affect the realization of the rights under s. 23 of the *Charter*.[47]

In the *Yukon Francophone School Board* decision, the SCC had to decide whether the minority community had the right to unilaterally extend the conditions of admission to its schools beyond section 23 obligations so that they could take in pupils who were not rights-bearers under the Charter. In this instance, the school board had admitted children whose parents did not speak French into its own schools and argued that decision making over admissions was one of the powers granted to it by section 23. The justices sided with the territorial government in the case, stating that it was up to the Department of Education to decide whether section 23 principles for admission could be extended to admit non-rights-bearers to francophone schools, not up to the school board. However, following further negotiations with its francophone community, the Yukon government accepted in August 2016 to delegate to the Francophone School Board control over its admissions through a territorial regulation.[48]

It is clear from this review of the jurisprudence that the SCC has had a notable influence on policymaking regarding official-language minority instruction since 1982, gradually clarifying the provincial governments' obligations and restricting their discretionary powers, while empowering minority communities and imposing on provinces a duty to consult the community representatives in areas of cultural and linguistic relevance in education. It has expressed and enhanced a policy of substantive equality and substantive equivalence between the minority and majority school systems – where numbers warrant – and has reminded the provinces, on many occasions, to fulfil their duties in a timely manner to combat assimilation. However, it is also worth noting that the justices have attempted to preserve the separation of powers between the judiciary and legislatures so as not to impose remedies that would encroach on the provinces' prerogatives in their own areas of jurisdiction, leaving as much room for provincial policymaking as possible within the framework built around section 23 obligations. In many instances, the SCC did not have the last word in implementing provincial minority-language education.

Limits on the Impact of the SCC on Minority Official-Language Education Policymaking

Flowing from these SCC decisions, as well as the myriad lower court jurisprudence that could not be discussed here, one could believe that the provinces would now be keenly aware of their section 23 obligations and that minority official-language education policies would have been standardized across the country. However, such is not the case, as demonstrated by the overwhelming number of francophone minority communities that currently find themselves in litigation processes against their respective provincial governments. I would like to offer three hypotheses to explain why such standardization has not happened since 1982 and why legal mobilization is still so prevalent today.

First, to understand the challenges to the creation of a clear and standardized regime of minority official-language education, one needs to look to the vehicle through which it developed – that is, the repeated use of judicial recourse. Not only is this recourse symptomatic of continuous failures by provincial governments to adequately live up to their constitutional responsibilities, but it is also an adversarial system in which governments and communities repeatedly butt heads. One of "the inefficacies of the adversarial system in Canada from an evidentiary perspective [is] the near impossibility, for disadvantaged parties, to present an adequate and complete evidence record."[49] From the cases described above, it is clear that the organization or community members pleading their case, who have to rely on fundraising and underfunded "legal aid and access-to-justice programs,"[50] such as the Court Challenges Program and Language Rights Support Program, are at a disadvantage when they face provincial attorneys general or departments with in-house counsels and potentially limitless resources. Provincial justice departments, unlike community organizations, have "advance intelligence"[51] of the legal system, with expertise at the ready.

Moreover, some observers of francophone minority communities, such as Joseph Yvon Thériault and Linda Cardinal, are wary of the "perverse effects"[52] of Supreme Court decisions on the political relationship of these minorities with their provincial majorities. As Thériault explains, "Law ... steers the involved parties away from any spirit of dialogue, of mediation, or in other words, of political compromise."[53] He continues, arguing that legal mobilization "could turn the majority against the minority in other cases where law can't be mobilized"[54] to protect the latter. However, Pierre Foucher points out that official-language minorities have time and time again used legal mobilization precisely because mediation and attempts at dialogue with their respective majorities have proved unsuccessful.[55]

In sum, according to these authors, legal mobilization puts minority communities at a disadvantage when they bring forward constitutional litigation against their governments, but it is also, because of its adversarial nature, a political strategy like no other. Beyond those victories obtained through legal recourse, there can be deleterious effects on the relationship between minority and majority, which may be counterproductive in the long run. Courts' decisions could be subsequently used against minorities, or used as "ceilings" to the rights granted to minorities, even after their situation has changed.

Second, federalism places limits on the power of justices to outline a complete regime of minority-language education. Education is a provincial jurisdiction, and the SCC has been sensitive enough in its decisions to leave as much room as possible for the provinces to adapt to the duties bestowed upon them by section 23. Provinces have enacted official-language minority education schemes without much consultation with one another, which would have fostered an apt environment for policy learning and convergence. These differences are also exacerbated by the sliding-scale approach found in the SCC's interpretation of section 23, which entitles each province to adapt its duties on a case-by-case basis. It is, however, worthy of mention that one province, New Brunswick, has gone beyond the sliding-scale approach with regard to minority-language education, implementing a dualist structure in its Department of Education in 1981.

Finally, it is inherently difficult for a judge to force a government to fulfil its duty when that duty flows from positive rights – that is, rights that can be fulfilled only with governmental action (and spending of public funds). While most provinces will abide by court decisions in a timely manner, some provincial governments will delay their actions as long as possible, even after they have been ordered to act by a court, for either ideological or electoral reasons. As Hall underscores, courts constantly face "the counter-majoritarian difficulty"[56] – that is to say, judicial review can be unpopular with the majority of the people and appear undemocratic because it exercises control *against* the majority. When a ruling goes against public opinion or interest, as it often does in minority-language cases, legislative assemblies are less likely to enact a policy change prescribed by a court. Such a situation is presently unfolding in British Columbia. It has been three years since the SCC, in the

Rose-des-Vents case, found that the province had failed to fulfil its section 23 duties towards francophone students in West Vancouver by failing to provide teaching facilities of equivalent quality to those of the majority. The school was recently granted access to a trailer to alleviate the issue of overcrowding; no further proposal for an upgrade of existing facilities or for the construction of a new school has been put forward.[57]

Remedies such as the one used by Justice LeBlanc in *Doucet-Boudreau* to ensure proper implementation of section 23 duties are exceptional, and it would be surprising if they became the norm. However, in the area of minority-language education, time is of the essence: assimilation is a threat in every minority community. In many of them, school is the only public space where the minority language is spoken. Moreover, school is the quintessential place for inter-generational cultural transfer and identity building. When governments unduly delay fulfilling their section 23 duties, effects on these communities may be dire.

As previously mentioned, positive rights also entail financial investment by governments. Money forms the sinews of war, it is often said, and "[t]he courts control neither the 'sword' nor the 'purse.'"[58] More and more section 23 litigation deals with the issue of insufficient funding of the minority official-language school system – and the unequal quality of education that flows from those budgetary restrictions. However, it is not the courts' place to decide on public spending, and justices are often quite wary of writing decisions that restrain legislators' public spending choices. This limits the extent to which they can push governments in any policy direction.

Conclusion

The aim of this chapter was to demonstrate the profound influence that the SCC has had in the evolution of the minority official-language education system in this country since the adoption of the Charter, but it also set out to shed light on some of the limits on this influence. Indeed, the SCC has elaborated a liberal and generous interpretation of section 23 constitutional guarantees since 1982. However, these legal advances have been undermined by a lack of adequate funds and, at times, blatant ill will by provincial legislators to fulfil their duties. The issue of education is, as explored above, one of the most important historical battles fought by official-language minorities, especially francophone minorities, throughout Canada, and one for which the federal government has granted them an important legal tool.

As a result, it appears certain that the courts will continue to be thoroughly involved in policymaking in this area, but that their influence will remain limited. Justices will likely continue to be called upon to remind legislators of their duties as well as to further clarify their extent – by recognizing both the processes of community decision making and the significance of the principles of *substantive equality* and *substantive equivalence* – in the policymaking and budgetary processes. These decisions will continue to act as a frame of reference for provincial policymaking; however, the provinces will not always subsequently enact adequate policy changes, as is also highlighted by James Kelly's analysis in the following chapter. Consequently, we are likely to see further litigation in the area of official-language education rights, although the effect of this litigation on provincial policy change remains uncertain.

NOTES

1 This excludes immersion programs, which are part of the language majority's school system in each province.

2 Linda Cardinal and Selma Sonntag, *State Traditions and Language Regimes* (Montreal and Kingston: McGill-Queen's University Press, 2015), 35.

3 Jennifer Wallner, *Learning to School: Federalism and Public Schooling in Canada* (Toronto: University of Toronto Press, 2014), 28.

4 *Le Devoir*, "La francophonie à rude école," author's translation, accessed 18 September 2016, http://www.ledevoir.com/societe/actualites-en-societe/431164/la-francophonie-a-rude-ecole.

5 Marc Galanter, "Why the 'Haves' Come Out Ahead: Speculations on the Limits of Legal Change," *Law and Society Review* 9, no. 1 (1974): 95–160.

6 Mark C. Power, François Larocque, and Darius Bossé, "Constitutional Litigation, the Adversarial System and Some of Its Adverse Effects," *Review of Constitutional Studies* 17, no. 2 (2012): 1–40.

7 Galanter, "Why the 'Haves' Come Out Ahead," 98.

8 Matthew E.K. Hall, *The Nature of Supreme Court Power* (Cambridge: Cambridge University Press, 2011).

9 Marcel Martel and Martin Pâquet, *Langue et politique au Canada et au Québec: Une synthèse historique* (Montreal: Boréal, 2010), 66.

10 Michel Bock and François Charbonneau, eds., *Le siècle du Règlement 17: Regards sur une crise scolaire et nationale* (Ottawa: Prise de parole, 2015).

11 Ibid., 73.

12 Ibid., 77–8.

13 *Trustees of the Roman Catholic Separate School for the City of Ottawa c. Mackell* (1916), [1917] A.C. 62, 32 D.L.R. 1 (P.C.).
14 McGill University (Montreal) was founded in 1821, Bishop's University (Sherbrooke) in 1843.
15 Martel and Pâquet, *Langue et politique au Canada et au Québec*, 158.
16 Ibid., 140.
17 For a broader discussion of the adoption of the Charter of the French Language, see Kelly, this volume.
18 St. Andrews Declaration, quoted in Matthew Hayday, *Bilingual Today, United Tomorrow: Official Languages in Education and Canadian Federalism* (Montreal and Kingston: McGill-Queen's University Press, 2005), 104.
19 Montreal Declaration, quoted in ibid., 105.
20 Martel and Pâquet, *Langue et politique au Canada et au Québec*, 206–7.
21 On this subject, see Michael D. Behiels, *Canada's Francophone Minority Communities: Constitutional Renewal and the Winning of School Governance* (Montreal and Kingston: McGill-Queen's University Press, 2004).
22 Here I respectfully disagree with Kelly (this volume) regarding Trudeau's intent in drafting section 23. While the Charter of the French Language was certainly targeted by this new constitutional provision, the overturning of the Quebec legislation was not its sole objective: access to minority-language schooling was a country-wide issue and was more acute outside Quebec than in that province.
23 James B. Kelly, *Governing with the Charter: Legislative and Judicial Activism and Framers' Intent* (Vancouver: UBC Press, 2005), 12.
24 Jean Chrétien, quoted in Kelly, ibid., 94.
25 Martin Normand, "De l'arène politique à l'arène juridique: Les communautés francophones minoritaires au Canada et la *Charte canadienne des droits et libertés*," in *Un nouvel ordre constitutionnel canadien: Du rapatriement de 1982 à nos jours*, ed. François Rocher and Benoît Pelletier (Quebec: Presses de l'Université du Québec, 2013), 179–203, 187–8.
26 Linda Cardinal, "Le pouvoir exécutif et la judiciarisation de la politique au Canada: Une étude du Programme de contestation judiciaire," *Politique et sociétés* 19, no. 2–3 (2000): 43–64.
27 *Attorney General of Quebec v. Quebec Protestant School Boards*, [1984] 2 S.C.R. 66.
28 Ibid., 79.
29 *Mahe v. Alberta*, [1990] 1 S.C.R. 342.
30 Ibid.
31 *Reference re Public Schools Act (Man.)*, s. 79(3), (4) and (7), [1993] 1 S.C.R. 839.
32 *Arsenault-Cameron v. Prince Edward Island*, [2000] 1 S.C.R. 3.

33 Ibid., 33.
34 *Doucet-Boudreau v. Nova Scotia (Minister of Education)*, [2003] 3 S.C.R. 3.
35 Ibid., at para. 6.
36 Ibid., at para. 9.
37 *Solski (Tutor of) v. Quebec (Attorney General)*, [2005] 1 S.C.R. 201, 2005 SCC 14.
38 *Nguyen v. Quebec (Education, Recreation and Sports)*, [2009] 3 S.C.R. 208, 2009 SCC 47.
39 Ibid., at para. 7.
40 Canadian Broadcasting Corporation, "Quebec Liberals Push Language Law Through," 19 October 2010, accessed 30 November 2016, http://www.cbc.ca/news/canada/montreal/quebec-liberals-push-language-law-through-1.969976.
41 *Gosselin (Tutor of) v. Québec (Attorney General.)*, [2005] 1 S.C.R. 238.
42 Ibid., at para. 28.
43 Ibid., at para. 31.
44 *Association des parents de l'école Rose-des-Vents v. British Columbia (Education)*, [2015] 2 S.R.C. 21.
45 *Yukon Francophone School Board, Education Area #23 v. Yukon (Attorney General)*, [2015] 2 S.C.R. 282.
46 *Association des parents de l'école Rose-des-Vents v. British Columbia (Education)*, at para. 33.
47 Ibid., at para. 35.
48 Canadian Broadcasting Corporation, "Yukon's Francophone School Board Gains Power over Admissions," 31 August 2016, accessed 30 November 2016, http://www.cbc.ca/news/canada/north/yukon-francophone-school-board-admissions-1.3743310.
49 Power et al., "Constitutional Litigation, the Adversarial System and Some of Its Adverse Effects," 1.
50 Ibid., 38.
51 Galanter, "Why the 'Haves' Come Out Ahead," 98.
52 Linda Cardinal, "La judiciarisation de la politique, les droits des minorités et le nationalisme canadien," author's translation, *Forum constitutionnel* 13, no. 3 / 14, no. 1 (2005): 62.
53 Joseph Yvon Thériault, *Faire société: Société civile et espaces francophones*, author's translation (Sudbury: Prise de parole, 2007), 293.
54 Ibid., author's translation, 293–4.
55 Pierre Foucher, "Les gardiens de la paix: La Cour suprême du Canada et le contentieux des droits linguistiques; Montée en puissance des juges, pourquoi?," author's translation, in *La montée en puissance des juges: Ses*

manifestations, sa contestation, ed. Mary Jane Mossman and Ghislain Otis (Montreal: Éditions Thémis, 2000), 129–60.

56 Hall, *The Nature of Supreme Court Power*, 4.

57 Radio-Canada, "École surpeuplée: une annexe pour Rose-des-Vents," 4 May 2017, accessed 26 February 2018, http://ici.radio-canada.ca/nouvelle/1031847/ecoles-surpeuplees-vsb-annexe-csf-rose-des-vents-megaproces-sylvain-allison-vancouver.

58 Hall, *The Nature of Supreme Court Power*, 3.

12 The Charter of the French Language and the Supreme Court of Canada: Assessing Whether Constitutional Design Can Influence Policy Outcomes

JAMES B. KELLY

The entrenchment of minority-language education rights as section 23 of the Canadian Charter of Rights and Freedoms was designed by the Liberal government of Pierre Elliott Trudeau to achieve a specific political objective – to overturn section 73 of the Charter of the French Language.[1] Section 23 is therefore a unique constitutional provision.[2] It is the only part of the Charter that directly applies to an area of provincial jurisdiction (language and education policy),[3] targets a specific province (Quebec), and was drafted with a clear, remedial *policy* intention by the national government.

This chapter focuses on a key provision of Bill 101, section 73, which regulates access to English public education in Quebec. It assesses whether judicial invalidation has produced consequential policy changes in an area considered by the National Assembly to be vital for Quebec's cultural and linguistic survival. Have the policy preferences of the Trudeau Liberals been realized in regard to Bill 101? Alternatively, has the Quebec National Assembly been able to defend its sovereignty by amending section 73 to offset judicial invalidation? These are the essential questions that inform this chapter and its consideration of constitutional design, judicial invalidation, and the subsequent amendments to Bill 101 introduced by the Quebec National Assembly.

To assess the relationship between judicial invalidation and statutory amendment of the Charte de la langue française, this chapter considers the following landmark cases: *Attorney General of Quebec v. Protestant School Boards* [1984], *Solski (Tutor of) v. Quebec (Attorney General)* [2005], and *Nguyen v. Quebec (Education, Recreation and Sports)* [2009]. It also analyses the subsequent amendments to section 73 in response to these landmark invalidations.

Invalidation did produce policy change, but, as this chapter will argue, it resulted in short-term, unstable changes. The Quebec National Assembly responded by amending section 73 to reassert its autonomy in language and education policy. While the National Assembly did comply with elements of these judicial decisions, the amendments ultimately preserved Quebec's policy autonomy. What explains this phenomenon – the instability of judicial review – which Mark Tushnet has referred to as "weak-form" judicial review,[4] despite the Charter's notwithstanding clause not applying to minority-language education rights?

The occurrence of weak-form review suggests that the power of Supreme Courts, and, by extension, the ability of constitutional design to effect policy change, may not be as straightforward as previously contended. As Matthew Hall suggests, the traditional approach to courts and policy does not capture the complexity of the judicial-political relationship. According to Hall, "The critical question is not 'How powerful is the Court?' but rather 'Under what conditions is the Court powerful?'"[5] To understand the power of the Court, Hall makes an important point regarding appellate courts, such as the Supreme Court of Canada and the United States Supreme Court. He states that Supreme Courts are "implementer-dependent institutions" as they must rely on other political actors – be it lower courts or non-judicial actors such as legislatures – to implement their rulings.[6]

To understand the conditions under which the Court can be powerful, Hall makes a further distinction between vertical and lateral issues. Vertical issues are decisions that are implemented by subordinate judicial actors, whereby a Supreme Court can be confident that the ruling will be complied with and fully implemented.[7] By contrast, lateral issues are judicial decisions implemented by non-judicial actors such as Congress or Parliament, whereby compliance may be conditional on the popularity of a judicial ruling. These issues involve statutory frameworks that authorize public policy on behalf of Congress or Parliament, such as the Charter of the French Language. Hall contends that a popular judicial ruling in a lateral issue generally results in legislative compliance as "elected officials may be unwilling or unable to resist the Court when it is supported by strong public opinion."[8] However, the possibility of non-compliance increases when a Court issues an unpopular ruling in a lateral issue: Congress or Parliament may pursue its own policy preferences if a consensus forms against the judicial ruling.[9]

This chapter employs Hall's framework to evaluate judicial invalidation of the Charter of the French Language and to explain Quebec's ability to defend its policy preferences despite the remedial intention of section 23 of the Charter of Rights and Freedoms. Language and education policy represents a lateral issue, and in the context of Bill 101, the Supreme Court of Canada has delivered decisions that are highly unpopular in Quebec. While judicial victories involving section 23 have been popular with Quebec's anglophone and allophone communities, they have not been popular with the majority francophone population or with the political actor required to implement these judicial decisions, the Quebec National Assembly. Opposition to judicial invalidation of the Charte de la langue française has transcended the party/political, federalist/sovereigntist divides in Quebec. Similar to the findings in Stéphanie Chouinard's chapter in this volume, this has allowed the Quebec National Assembly to pursue policy preferences largely (but not completely) independent from judicial decisions.

To demonstrate that constitutional design may not have produced consequential policy changes involving access to English public education in Quebec, this chapter begins with a discussion of Bill 101, which was enacted in 1977, and the purpose of section 23 of the Charter of Rights implemented by the Trudeau Liberals in 1982. Once having identified the remedial intention of section 23, this chapter will consider the invalidation of section 73 of the Charter of the French Language before turning to an evaluation of the 1993, 2002, and 2010 amendments passed by the Quebec National Assembly.

Language of Instruction in Quebec: Bills 63, 22, and 101

The status of Quebec was the core political question that motivated both Pierre Trudeau and Réné Lévesque. For instance, Trudeau introduced the Official Languages Act in 1969, which established Canada as an officially bilingual country, where citizens were guaranteed federal government services in either French or English. This statutory policy would be constitutionalized in 1982, when official bilingualism was entrenched as sections 16 to 22 of the Canadian Charter of Rights and Freedoms.

In contrast, Lévesque introduced the Charter of the French Language in 1977; it built on Bill 22, introduced by the Liberal government of Robert Bourassa in 1974: Bills 22 and 101 declared French as the only official language of Quebec in government and business.[10] However, on the issue of language of instruction in public schools, Bill 101 was a significant departure from previous attempts to navigate this sensitive issue in Quebec. In 1969, the Union Nationale government introduced Bill 63, which allowed parents to choose the language of instruction in public education for their children.[11]

Liberal Premier Robert Bourassa introduced Bill 22 (Official Language Act) in 1974, which attempted to appease both the francophone demand for limited choice of instruction and, for anglophone and allophones, the demand for unlimited choice in public education. Although Bill 22 did not remove the choice regarding language of instruction, it did establish under section 41 that "pupils must have a sufficient knowledge of the language of instruction to receive their instruction in that language" and, further, "pupils who do not have a sufficient knowledge of any of the languages of instruction must receive their instruction in French."[12] The intention of section 41 was to limit access to English education to the existing anglophone community and to direct the growing allophone community towards French instruction.[13]

The election of the Parti Québécois in 1976 saw the abandonment of incrementalism in education policy[14] as English language instruction became the historical right of Quebec's anglophone community, to the exclusion of allophones.[15] Under section 73, request for public instruction in English was restricted to the children, or siblings, of those educated in English in Quebec on or before Bill 101 came into force in 1977. Therefore, section 73 of Bill 101 had two objectives: prevent the integration of the allophone community into the anglophone community through parental choice in public education and narrow accessibility to English education to simply Quebec anglophones.

Pierre Elliott Trudeau and the Charter of the French Language

Recognizing that it could not directly challenge Bill 101 because of the Parti Québécois' commitment to a referendum on Quebec's constitutional future during its first mandate,[16] the Trudeau government introduced the Court Challenges Program in 1978. This program provided funding to anglophone groups to challenge the constitutionality of Bill 101.[17] The significance of the Court Challenges Program would be realized once the Trudeau government's *constitutional* response to Bill 101 was entrenched as section 23 of the Charter of Rights.

Whereas Bill 101 established in statutory form English instruction as a historical right of Anglo-Quebecers, section 23 of the Charter of Rights constitutionalized the right to minority-language instruction for the children and siblings of Canadian citizens educated in English in

Canada, provided they were members of official-language minority communities. Finally, it provided a remedial power for the Supreme Court of Canada to determine the level of minority-language education rights to provide. In this respect, section 23 was drafted with a clear, remedial policy intention – to subject the *statutory* Charter of the French Language to *constitutional* review to ensure its invalidation by the Supreme Court of Canada under section 52 of the Constitution Act, 1982.

Attorney General of Quebec v. Protestant School Boards [1984]

The right to minority-language education in section 23 outlines several conditions that must be met before the child of a Canadian citizen is entitled to its provision out of public funds: first, a parent must have received his or her primary or secondary school instruction in English in Canada, or a sibling must have "received or [be] receiving" his or her education in English in Canada; second, the public provision is provided "where numbers warrant." As a result, section 23 does not specify the length of time of English instruction or the type of educational institution (public or private) providing English instruction to be satisfied. It simply requires that Canadian citizens have "received or [are] receiving" language instruction in either official language to ensure that their children or a sibling has access to minority-language education services.

As also discussed by Stéphanie Chouinard in this volume, the first constitutional challenge to section 73 of Bill 101 was launched by Quebec's anglophone community and funded under the Court Challenges Program. In *Protestant School Boards,* the Supreme Court of Canada sided with the anglophone community and declared section 73 of Bill 101 unconstitutional because of its incompatibility with section 23 of the Charter. In reaching this decision, which was in the name of "The Court," this unanimous judgment considered the political intention of this Charter provision and concluded that it had been drafted with the explicit intention of invalidating section 73.

> By incorporating into the structure of s.23 of the *Charter* the unique set of criteria in s.73 of *Bill 101,* the framers of the Constitution identified the type of regime they wished to correct and on which they would base the remedy prescribed. The framers' objectives appear simple, and may readily be inferred from the concrete method used by them: to adopt a general

> rule guaranteeing the Francophone and Anglophone minorities in Canada an important part of the rights which the Anglophone minority in Quebec had enjoyed with respect to the language of instruction before *Bill 101* was adopted.[18]

The Court also stated what provincial governments could not do in regard to section 23: "In our opinion, a legislature cannot by an ordinary statute validly set aside the means chosen by the framers and affect this classification. Still less can it remake the classification and redefine the classes."[19] The Court was clear that provincial governments could not legislatively modify section 23 of the Charter of Rights as this would be tantamount to constitutional amendment. In regard to Quebec, "s.73 of *Bill 101* directly alters the effect of s.23 of the *Charter* for Quebec, without following the procedure laid down for amending the Constitution."[20] For these reasons, section 73 could not be considered a reasonable limitation on section 23 of the Charter as "such limits cannot be exceptions to the rights and freedoms guaranteed by the *Charter* nor amount to amendments of the *Charter*."[21]

The first section 23 ruling by the Supreme Court of Canada suggests that the Trudeau government's intentions were realized – section 73 was invalidated, and the Quebec National Assembly was cautioned that it could not amend Bill 101 to conflict with section 23 of the Charter of Rights. Subsequent amendments to section 73 demonstrate the instability of judicial review as *Protestant School Boards* represents the high-water mark of judicial activism involving Bill 101. In subsequent amendments, the Quebec National Assembly did exactly what the Court ruled it could not do – through ordinary statute, it remade the classification, redefined the classes, and effectively amended section 23 of the Charter of Rights.

Charter of the French Language 1993

Although *Protestant School Boards* was a judicial victory for Quebec's anglophone community, it did not fundamentally transform the policy context in Quebec. Nor did it result in an overall increase in Quebec's English-language education system; demographic changes and interprovincial migration forced the opposite. In the period between 1981 and 2006, the anglophone community declined from 13.3 per cent to 7.8 per cent of the Quebec population, whereas the allophone community increased from 8 per cent to 12.1 per cent. Indeed, since the introduction of language legislation (Bills 63, 22, and 101) in the period 1971–2006, there has been a negative net migration of 284,000 anglophones from Quebec and, since *Protestant School Boards*, a net outflow of 83,900 anglophones. Thus, the Supreme Court's decision does not interfere with the policy objective of preserving the French language by limiting choice in educational instruction as it benefits only anglophones, who are members of a declining linguistic community in Quebec.

New immigrants to Canada, or members of Quebec's allophone community, would benefit from *Protestant School Boards* only if the following conditions existed: first, before their children reached school age, they became Canadian citizens and, second, they had "received their primary school instruction in Canada in English."[22] In truth, few allophones likely benefited from *Protestant School Boards* as their education was probably attained before immigrating to Canada. As a result, their children would be ineligible for minority-language instruction under section 23 of the Charter of Rights as well as section 73 of Bill 101. Subsequent amendments to section 73 of the Charter of the French Language were designed to ensure that the growing allophone community, without exception, was streamlined into the French-language system: the *major part requirement* introduced in 1993 and the prohibition on unsubsidized private schools in 2002.

To qualify for English public instruction in Quebec, citizens educated in Canada must apply, on behalf of their children, for a "certificate of eligibility" to the minister of education, recreation and sports under section 75 of the Charter of the French Language. Once notified of the decision, the applicant can appeal the decision within sixty days to the Administrative Tribunal of Quebec.[23]

Bill 86, the Charter of the French Language 1993, is Quebec's response to *Protestant School Boards*, and it was introduced by the Liberal government of Robert Bourassa. The 1993 amendment to section 73 did incorporate language directly from section 23 of the Charter of Rights, and it does comply with *Protestant School Boards*. For instance, the rights-bearer was amended from "a child whose father or mother received his or her elementary instruction in English, in Quebec" (under section 73(a) of the Charter of the French Language 1977) to "a child whose father or mother is a Canadian citizen and received elementary instruction in English in Canada" under section 73.1 of the Charter of the French Language 1993.

The amendments to section 73 in Bill 86 could be classified as legislative compliance if the National Assembly had simply implemented the

Court's decision and amended this provision to conform to section 23 of the Charter of Rights.[24] However, Bill 86 introduced qualifications to language of instruction that effectively amended section 23 of the Charter of Rights and Freedoms as it relates to the allophone community.

> 73. The following children, at the request of one of their parents, *may receive* instruction in English;
>
> (1) a child whose father or mother is a Canadian citizen and received elementary instruction in English in Canada, *provided that the instruction constitutes the major part of the elementary instruction he or she received in Canada.*[25]

The relevant modifications to section 73 are in italics and are the following. In *Protestant School Boards*, the Court was clear that Canadian citizens *have* access to English instruction in Quebec, whereas Bill 86 only provided only for the possibility of minority-language instruction by including the phrase *may receive*. Further, Bill 86 introduced the major part requirement to evaluate whether Canadian citizens qualified for English instruction in Quebec. Given that *Protestant School Boards* guaranteed the rights of Canadian citizens to minority-language education, the major part requirement was clearly directed against Quebec's growing allophone community. Thus, the constitutional standard was changed from "received or receiving" in section 23 of the Charter to the statutory requirement that the "major part" of a Canadian citizen's education must be in English for parents to allow their children or sibling access to minority-language instruction.

The criteria for assessing the major part requirement were created by ministerial directive, and the Administrative Tribunal of Quebec adopted this interpretation when it heard appeals under section 75 of the Charter of the French Language. The major part requirement was purely quantitative and focused exclusively on the number of months an individual had attended either elementary or secondary school. Indeed, a quantitative approach was established by ministerial directive, as "The Minister will determine eligibility <u>solely</u> on the basis of the number of months spent in each language. Other factors, including the availability of linguistic programs and the presence of learning disabilities or other difficulties, which are developed below, are not considered."[26] This approach to the major part requirement was the central constitutional issue in the *Solski* decision, which is discussed below.

Charter of the French Language 2002

Under Bill 104, the Parti Québécois government of Bernard Landry introduced a new condition governing access to English instruction as it pertained to the allophone community. In 2002, section 73 was amended to prohibit the use of unsubsidized private schools to satisfy the major part requirement introduced in 1993. "Instruction received in English in Quebec in a private educational institution not accredited for the purposes of subsidies by the child for whom the request is made, or by a brother or sister of the child, shall be disregarded."[27]

The chapter by Stéphanie Chouinard in this volume also suggests that this change was motivated by Quebec's growing concern about *écoles passerelles*, unsubsidized private schools, or "bridging schools," used by the allophone community for a short period of time to satisfy the eligibility criteria under section 73 of Bill 101. The Landry government viewed bridging schools as a loophole that allowed allophones, who would not normally qualify for English instruction, to qualify through temporary attendance at private institutions. Under this practice, once one child was briefly educated in English at a private institution, allophone parents would apply for a certificate of eligibility for all their children, arguing that the major part requirement had been met under section 73.2. According to the ATQ, more than 2,100 students attended bridging schools in the 2001–02 academic year without having certificates of eligibility, and this figure increased to 4,000 students in the 2007–08 academic year.[28]

Solski (Tutor of) v. Quebec (Attorney General) [2005]

Twenty-one years passed between *Protestant School Boards* and *Solski*, when the Supreme Court of Canada reviewed the constitutionality of the major part requirement introduced in 1993. Similar to *Protestant School Boards*, the decision was in the name of "The Court."

Unlike the 1984 decision, however, the Court delivered a nuanced decision that upheld the constitutionality of the major part requirement, while determining that the purely quantitative approach established by ministerial directive was unconstitutional. Despite the appearance of a restrained decision, the Court declared Quebec's approach to the major part requirement unconstitutional. Further, the Court outlined a qualitative approach to establishing the constitutionality of the major part requirement. However, as an implementer-dependent institution, the

Court was beholden to the Quebec National Assembly as it required Quebec to comply with the *Solski* framework by amending section 73.1 of the Charter of the French Language.

The Court ruled that a purely quantitative approach violated the purpose of section 23 as only a significant part, and not the majority, of a child's education needed to be in English to qualify for minority-language education in Quebec.[29] While recognizing that provinces retained the discretion to determine eligibility for minority-language education, the criteria had to be consistent with the intention of section 23. In the Supreme Court's view, a qualitative approach to the major part requirement would ensure the constitutionality of section 73(2) of Bill 101 and had to consider the following: how much time a child spent in either language in an educational setting, the stage of education when the language of instruction was chosen, the availability of minority-language education instruction, and finally, whether the child experienced any disabilities or difficulties.[30] In effect, the Court disregarded the ministerial directive on the major part requirement and included the very criteria that had been previously ruled ineligible by ministerial directive.

While the Supreme Court of Canada cautioned against a quantitative approach to section 73 of Bill 101, it did establish the requirement that parents demonstrate a commitment to the educational pathway. "It cannot be enough, in light of the objectives of s.23, for a child to be registered for a few weeks or a few months in a given program to conclude that he or she qualifies for admission, with his or her siblings, in the minority language programs of Quebec."[31] Thus, the Court would not accept "artificial educational pathways" to circumvent Bill 101 – a judicial position that would become significant when Quebec fashioned its response, in the guise of Bill 115, to address both *Solski* and *Nguyen* as the Charter of the French Language 2010.

Nguyen v. Quebec (Education, Recreation and Sports) [2009]

A total of 131 families, denied certificates of eligibility by the ATQ after their children had attended unsubsidized private schools, launched this case.[32] They challenged the prohibition introduced by Bill 104 as a violation of section 23 of the Charter. In a unanimous decision by Justice Lebel, the Supreme Court supported the constitutional challenge against Bill 104.[33] According to the Court, the Charter did not specify the institutional setting necessary to qualify for section 23, and, thus, Bill 104 was unconstitutional.[34]

In light of the small number of students registered in bridging schools, the Court considered the complete prohibition on these institutions as an unreasonable limit. In the view of the Court, the policy instrument lacked proportionality as it was "overly drastic" and "the legislature could have adopted different solutions that would involve a more limited impairment of the guaranteed rights and could more readily be reconciled with the concrete contextual approach recommended in *Solski*."[35] However, the Court was sensitive to the particular challenge that certain bridging schools posed to Bill 101 and the potential return to freedom of choice that their unregulated use posed to the Charter of the French Language. "When schools are established primarily to bring about the transfer of ineligible students to the publicly funded English-language system, and the instruction they give in fact serves that end, it cannot be said that the resulting educational pathway is genuine."[36] Therefore, the Supreme Court suggested that a case-by-case evaluation of bridging schools was necessary. This would determine whether a private institution was legitimate and whether the family demonstrated a genuine commitment to anglophone institutions for the purposes of assessing their application for a certificate of eligibility.

Two remedies were ordered in *Nguyen*: one involving the constitutionality of Bill 104 and a second pertaining to the certificates of eligibility denied to the 131 families by the ATQ. The blanket prohibition on bridging schools in section 73.1 of the Charter of the French Language was declared unconstitutional, and the decision was suspended for one year. The Court did not grant the certificates of eligibility, despite the invalidation of Bill 104's complete prohibition on bridging schools. Instead, with one exception, it ordered the files returned to the Ministry of Education for re-evaluation based on the qualitative approach to the major part requirement established in *Solski* and the genuine commitment principle to the educational pathway established in *Nguyen*.

Charter of the French Language 2010

Bill 115 amended two acts in response to the invalidation of the ministerial directive on the major part requirement in *Solski* and the total prohibition on unsubsidized private schools in *Nguyen* – the Charter of the French Language 2010 and the Act Respecting Private Education 2010. Section 73.1 of the Charter of the French Language was amended to allow the establishment, through regulation, of an analytical framework for assessing the major part requirement to comply with the *Solski* decision. "The analytical framework may, among other things, establish rules, assessment criteria, a weighting system, a cut-off or passing score and interpretive principles."[37] Although the Court declared the general prohibition on unsubsidized private schools unconstitutional in *Nguyen*, it recognized that Quebec had a legitimate concern with educational institutions established to circumvent Bill 101 and section 73. Bill 115 added section 78.2 to the Charter of the French Language to prevent the establishment of these bridging schools.[38]

The total prohibition on "fictitious educational pathways," as the Court referred to these bridging schools in *Nguyen*, was advanced by several amendments to the Act Respecting Private Education. Under section 12.2, "The Minister may refuse to issue a permit if, in the Minister's opinion, doing so could allow the circumvention of section 72 of the Charter of the French language or of other provisions governing eligibility for instruction in English."[39] Further, the minister has the discretion under section 12.2 to prevent circumventions by subjecting "a permit to any condition the Minister judges necessary."[40] As such, Bill 115 commits the National Assembly to a case-by-case evaluation that will prohibit only educational institutions set up with the clear purpose of circumventing sections 72 and 73 of the Charter of the French Language.

Ascertaining the Major Part Requirement

It would be reasonable to conclude that the Quebec National Assembly complied with the *Solski* and *Nguyen* decisions as Bill 115 accepted the main constitutional principles advanced by the Court. A review of the criteria and weighting used to evaluate the major part requirement, however, suggests a contrary interpretation – the National Assembly circumvented the Court and its rulings in *Solski* and *Nguyen*. This occurred through a regulatory framework that is heavily weighted in favour of residency at historic and elite anglophone institutions such as Lower Canada College, Selwyn House, St. George's, or Miss Edgar's and Miss Cramp's.[41] Perhaps most important, the Ministry of Education, through regulation, determines the criteria for categorizing schools established for the purpose of circumventing the Charter of the French Language and those that demonstrate their relationship to the anglophone community. The National Assembly and its designates, therefore, engaged in legislative non-compliance, as the regulatory response to the *Solski* and *Nguyen* once again illustrates the conditions under which an implementer-dependent institution such as the Supreme Court of Canada may not be a powerful policy actor, particularly when an issue is a provincial responsibility.

There are two documents associated with Bill 115 that justify its characterization as non-compliance: (1) Regulation respecting the criteria and weighting used to consider instruction in English received in a private educational institution not accredited for the purposes of subsidies[42] and (2) Catégories des établissements privés non subventionnés (EPNS).[43] To be eligible to *simply apply* for a certificate of eligibility, the regulation establishes a passing score of 15. This score is calculated on a weighted assessment that involves three considerations, or divisions: Division 1, Schooling; Division 2, Consistent, true commitment; and Division 3, Specific situation and overall education.

Under Division 1, greater weight is given for attendance at institutions with a higher percentage of instruction in English, a student body with a specified percentage of certificates of eligibility, and a specified percentage of students that attend elementary and secondary studies at the same institution. Private schools are categorized as type A, B, and C, and points are assigned based on the number of years in attendance as well as the linguistic character of the institution and the student body. For instance, at type A schools, 60 per cent of the student body has a certificate of eligibility or a special authorization to attend English instruction, 70 per cent or more of the students progress to elementary instruction at the institution, and at least 70 per cent of the hours of instruction are in English. Type B schools (B1 to B3) are English-instruction schools, but they fall below the thresholds for type A schools, and type C schools (C1 to C3) are designated as bilingual schools, where less than 60 per cent of the students have a certificate of eligibility.

Under the weighted system, attendance at a type A school for a minimum of three years' residency earns fifteen points, whereas a B1 school (41 to 59 per cent of the students have certificates of eligibility) earns thirteen points after a residency of four years, a B2 institution (26 to 40 per cent of certificates) is awarded sixteen points after seven years, and a B3 school (25 per cent of certificates or less) requires a residency of seven years to be awarded thirteen points. Type C institutions require a minimum of seven years of residency to be awarded eleven points. Somewhat consistent with *Solski*, the regulation provides a maximum of five points if a student attended an institution with a "special mission or purpose," provided "most of whose enrolments are students requiring special services because of a physical or mental handicap, behavioural problems, social maladjustments, learning difficulties or other similar problems."[44] Whereas *Solski* required the major part requirement to consider unique challenges faced by a child, the regulation combines this with an evaluation of whether the institution is structured to provide such services.

Under Division 2, a family is evaluated based on whether it has a consistent, true commitment to the anglophone community, which is an assessment of the educational pathway of each individual child. For instance, if a child attended a French-language institution before attending a private English institution, the weighted score is penalized three points for each year of attendance. Further, if a sibling attended a French-language institution, the weighted score of the child attending a private English institution is penalized on a graduated scale to reflect the number of siblings receiving French instruction.

The implications of Divisions 1 and 2 are the following for the allophone community: the surest path to fifteen points is through attendance at a type A institution for each school-age child. This strongly suggests that the post-*Solski* approach to the major part requirement is still largely quantitative as Divisions 1 and 2, with the exception of attendance at an institution with a special mission or purpose, allocates points based exclusively on years of residency.

The main difference between Bill 115 and the regulation respecting the criteria and weighting can be summarized as the following: Bill 115 complies with *Solski*, and the regulations do not. In *Solski*, the Court cautioned, "The strict mathematical approach lacks flexibility and may even exclude a child from education vital to maintaining his or her connection with the minority community in culture. ... In short, the strict approach mandated by the Minister of Education fails to deal fairly with any person who must be qualified under a purposive interpretation of section 23(2) of the Charter."[45] Further, the Court concluded that the stage at which English education was accessed was irrelevant as a child who spent the first three years in French education would not quality under section 73 of Bill 101, despite having a "sufficient link to the minority language community."[46]

While the Court supported the prohibition against bridging schools that functioned as fictitious educational pathways to circumvent section 73, the regulation effectively creates an extremely difficult, if not impossible, route to section 73. Bridging schools are prohibited, and few English private institutions are viable routes for achieving a weighted score of 15. As the regulation outlines in section 5, a weighted score of

15 provides simply the *ability* to submit a request for a certificate of eligibility. Forty-seven approved institutions appear in EPNS for the 2015–16 academic year, and only five are type A.[47] With one exception, they are located in Westmount or Notre Dame de Grâce, Montreal. Given that these neighbourhoods have the highest concentrations of anglophones in the province, this strongly suggests that they may not be accessible for allophones. Nevertheless, the cost of attending is a clear barrier to achieving a weighted score of 15 as the average tuition is $21,000 per year. At a minimum, it costs approximately $63,000 during a three-year residency at a subsidized *private* institution to achieve a weighted score of 15. However, this weighted score allows a family to only *apply* to the Ministry of Education for a certificate of eligibility, which may or may not be granted, subject to the consideration of further criteria.

Even if a family achieves a weighted score under Division 1 and 2 of fifteen points, section 4 of Division 3 allows the Ministry of Education to assess the authenticity of the commitment to the educational pathway, whereby the family would be interviewed and assessed a weighted score (−8 to +8).[48] Section 4 is clearly at odds with *Nguyen* as the Court accepted that attendance at a bridging school, set up for the sole purpose of circumventing the Charter of the French Language, did not constitute a genuine educational pathway or an authentic commitment to the anglophone community. However, the regulation approaches the question of bridging schools in two ways: whether the school *as an institution* is deemed to be a bridging school and, more controversial, whether the attendance at an approved private institution demonstrates a *desire* by the family to create an artificial educational pathway.

The Quebec ombudsperson noted the large scope for interpretation provided by Division 3 during public hearings before the National Assembly's Committee on Culture and Education. The ombudsperson stated, "The very broad weighting of certain criteria in the bill leaves too much scope for interpretation" and referred explicitly to the weighted score (−8 to +8) permitted by the assessment of "specific situation and overall education."[49] The Quebec English School Board Association (QESBA) voiced the same concern during its presentation.[50] Throughout the hearings, the minister of education clearly outlined the purpose of the responses to *Solski* and *Nguyen*. "I won't deny that the objective is to have as few as possible (approved)."[51] Similarly, the QESBA concluded that "as they stand, we repeat, not a single new student is likely to be registered in an English public school as a result."[52]

The reality of Bill 115, despite the invalidation of Bill 104 in *Nguyen* and the ministerial directive in *Solski,* is that few, if any, certificates of eligibility will be issued by the Ministry of Education to allophones. This has been the consistent approach to judicial invalidation of Bill 101: Quebec's National Assembly has introduced complex legislative responses that have simply the appearance of compliance but an actual policy consequence that defies the Supreme Court of Canada and the central premise of *Protestant School Boards.* "In our opinion, a legislature cannot by ordinary statute validly set aside the means chosen by the framers and affect this classification. Still less can it remake the classification and redefine the classes."[53]

Conclusion: *Plus ça change, plus c'est la même chose*

In *The Hollow Hope,* Rosenberg argued that judicial activism might not result in social change, largely because it requires legislative responses that bring a decision to life.[54] In many ways, the issue of language instruction in Quebec demonstrates Rosenberg's thesis as each invalidation of Bill 101 was reversed through subsequent amendment to the Charter of the French Language or the corresponding regulations. To understand the ability of Quebec's National Assembly to engage in legislative non-compliance with section 23 rulings by the Supreme Court of Canada, this chapter adopted Hall's framework of Supreme Courts as implementer-dependent institutions. The policy implications of legislative non-compliance are clear in Quebec as there has been a steady enrolment decline in English public schools since the introduction of Bill 101. Part of the explanation is the demographic transformation of Quebec, as a net outflow of anglophones to other provinces and a net inflow of new francophone immigrants or allophones has transformed the linguistic character of the province. However, this is not a convincing explanation given the important victories by anglophones and allophones that saw the Supreme Court of Canada declare section 73 unconstitutional in *Protestant School Boards, Solski,* and *Nguyen.*

What lessons can we take from the Supreme Court of Canada as an implementer-dependent institution when it delivers an unpopular lateral ruling? The main lesson is that Quebec's standard response to judicial invalidation creates a strong disincentive to challenge the constitutionality of the Charter of the French Language in the future. Judicial review of Bill 101 has not produced consequential policy change despite the invalidation of section 73, the major part requirement, the ministerial directive, and the total prohibition on unsubsidized private schools. Indeed, this finding is consistent with Stéphanie Chouinard's broader analysis of the limited implementation of section 23 victories across Canada. This conclusion began with the Québécois expression *plus ça change, plus c'est la même chose* ("the more it changes, the more it's the same thing"). Unfortunately, regarding the invalidation of the Charter of the French Language, that is the ultimate lesson of Quebec's response.

NOTES

1 Guy Laforest, *Trudeau and the End of a Canadian Dream* (Montreal and Kingston: McGill-Queen's University Press, 1995), 125–6.
2 *Attorney General (Quebec) v. Protestant School Boards,* [1984] 2 S.C.R. 66 at 79.
3 Michael Behiels, *Canada's Francophone Minority Communities: Constitutional Renewal and the Winning of School Governance* (Montreal and Kingston: McGill-Queen's University Press, 2004), 80–1.
4 Mark Tushnet, *Weak Courts, Strong Rights: Judicial Review and Social Welfare Rights in Comparative Constitutional Law* (Princeton, NJ: Princeton University Press, 2008), 36–7.
5 Matthew E.K. Hall, *The Nature of Supreme Court Power* (New York: Cambridge University Press, 2011), 14.
6 Ibid., 15.
7 Ibid., 16.
8 Ibid., 18.
9 Ibid.
10 Kenneth McRoberts, *Quebec: Social Change and Political Crisis*, 3rd ed. (New York: Oxford University Press, 1993), 276–9.
11 An Act to promote the French language in Québec, S.Q. 1969, c. 9.
12 Official Language Act, S.Q. 1974, c. 6 (chap. V).
13 Ibid. (chap. V, s. 44).
14 William D. Coleman, "From Bill 22 to Bill 101: The Politics of Language under the Parti Québécois," *Canadian Journal of Political Science* 14, no. 3 (1981): 466–72.
15 Charter of the French Language, R.S.Q. 1977, s. 73.
16 F. L. Morton, "The Effect of the Charter of Rights on Canadian Federalism," *Publius: The Journal of Federalism* 25, no. 3 (1995): 180–2.
17 Leslie Pal, *Interests of State: The Politics of Language, Multiculturalism, and Feminism in Canada* (Montreal and Kingston: McGill-Queen's University Press, 1993), 132.

18 *Attorney General (Quebec) v. Protestant School Boards*, [1984] 2 S.C.R. 66 at 84.
19 Ibid. at 86.
20 Ibid.
21 Ibid. at 88.
22 S. 23(1)(b) of the Canadian Charter of Rights and Freedoms.
23 S. 83.1 of the Charter of the French Language.
24 S. 23 of the Charter does not fully apply to Quebec, and it is one example of asymmetrical federalism in the Constitution Act, 1982. In particular, s. 23(1)(a) does not apply to Quebec, and the right to minority-language education rights is attained through s. 23(1)(b).

> 23. (1) Citizens of Canada
> (*a*) whose first language learned and still understood is that of the English or French linguistic minority population of the province in which they reside, or
> (*b*) who have received their primary school instruction in Canada in English or French and reside in a province where the language in which they received that instruction is the language of the English or French linguistic minority population of the province,
> have the right to have their children receive primary and secondary school instruction in that language in that province.

25 Charter of the French Language 1993, s. 73; italics added.
26 *Solski (Tutor of) v. Quebec (Attorney General)*, [2005] 1 S.C.R. 201 at para. 25.
27 Charter of the French Language 2002, s. 73.
28 *Nguyen v. Quebec (Education, Recreation and Sports)*, [2009] 3 S.C.R. 208 at para. 42.
29 *Solski (Tutor of) v. Quebec (Attorney General)*, [2005] 1 S.C.R. 201 at para. 27.
30 Ibid. at para. 25.
31 Ibid. at para. 39.
32 *Nguyen v. Quebec (Education, Recreation and Sports)*, [2009] 3 S.C.R. 208 at para. 13.
33 Ibid. at para. 31.
34 Ibid. at para. 32.
35 Ibid. at para. 42.
36 Ibid. at para. 36.
37 Charter of the French Language 2010, s. 73.1.
38 Ibid., s. 78.2.
39 Act respecting private education, s. 12, R.S.Q. 2010, chap. E-9.1.
40 Ibid.

41 The average tuition at these institutions is approximately $18,000 per year.
42 Regulation respecting the criteria and weighting used to consider instruction in English received in a private educational institution not accredited for the purposes of subsidies (chap. C-11, r. 2.1).
43 Catégories des établissements privés non subventionnés ["Categories of non-subsidized private institutions"]. The original list was issued for the 2010–11 academic year. The list of private schools that can be attended for the purposes of assessing a certificate of eligibility has been modified several times, and the current list for 2015–16 was last modified in 2014–15.
44 Regulation respecting the criteria and weighting used to consider instruction in English received in a private educational institution not accredited for the purposes of subsidies, Division 1, s. 1.2.
45 *Solski (Tutor of) v. Quebec (Attorney General),* [2005] 1 S.C.R. 201 at para. 37.
46 Ibid.
47 The five Type A institutions are Miss Edgar's and Miss Cramp's, St. George's, Selwyn House, Lower Canada College, and Sterling Education.
48 Regulation respecting the criteria and weighting used to consider instruction in English received in a private educational institution not accredited for the purposes of subsidies, s. 4.
49 Bill 103: An Act to amend the Charter of the French Language and other legislative provisions; text of speech by the Quebec ombudsperson before the Committee on Culture and Education, 8 September 2010.
50 QESBA, Brief to the Committee on Culture and Education on Bill 103, 20 October 2010.
51 Don Macpherson, "Bill 103 Is in the Style of Bourassa: Language Law; Charest Government Proposal Reopens English-Education Loophole, but Barely," *Montreal Gazette,* 3 June 2010.
52 QESBA, Brief to the Committee on Culture and Education on Bill 103, 20 October 2010.
53 *Attorney General (Quebec) v. Protestant School Boards,* [1984] 2 S.C.R. 66 at 86.
54 Gerald N. Rosenberg, *The Hollow Hope: Can Courts Bring About Social Change?* 2nd ed. (Chicago: University of Chicago Press, 2008), 8.

13 When Is a Citizen No Longer a Citizen? Analysing Constructions of Citizenship in Canada's Judicial and Legislative Forums

MEGAN GAUCHER

In January 2016, the Supreme Court dismissed Deepan Budlakoti's appeal for citizenship after Citizenship and Immigration Canada (CIC) had ruled him inadmissible. Budlakoti was born in Ottawa to Indian parents working at the Indian high commission; however, according to Canadian law, *jus soli* (citizenship by birth) does not apply to individuals whose parents were in the country as diplomats or representatives of a foreign government. Unknowingly, his parents successfully applied for citizenship, but did not apply for citizenship for their son because he had been born in Canada. After being convicted and sentenced for two criminal offences, Budlakoti was transferred to migrant detention, but he was not recognized as a citizen by India's high commission and was subsequently released with mobility restrictions. Claiming that this was an infringement of his rights under s.7 of the Canadian Charter of Rights and Freedoms, Budlakoti took his case to the Federal Court in 2014, where the Court ruled against him; the Federal Court of Appeal in 2015, where the ruling was upheld; and finally, the Supreme Court in 2016. As a result of that Court dismissing his case, and regardless of being born within Canadian borders, Budlakoti was legally constructed as an illegal non-citizen.

Despite citizenship being a legal matter, the courts have historically been the last line of defence for immigrants whose citizenship is under threat of being revoked or refused. Moreover, once citizenship status is in question, a citizen's or non-citizen's access to Charter protections becomes increasingly restricted. Instead, contemporary citizenship matters are largely taken up by Immigration, Refugees, and Citizenship Canada (IRCC) – more specifically, the Immigration and Refugee Board (IRB) – ultimately shifting authority over citizenship law and policy from the courts to the government in power and bureaucratic departments. This authority was called into question with the passing of multiple citizenship-related bills under the Harper government aimed at further securitizing citizenship, making it more difficult to obtain and easier to lose. While critics have deemed these initiatives unconstitutional, a review of citizenship and non-citizenship Charter decisions shows that legal treatment of citizenship is complex and that the Supreme Court has had a more limited impact than government on Canadian citizenship debates. As a result, Parliament has been given the constitutional space to modify citizenship laws, and a more detailed examination of the substantive characteristics of citizenship remains largely absent from Charter discourse. Indeed, citizenship laws establish the rules of membership, but provide "an unsatisfactory means for resolving a fundamental social and political question: who belongs?"[1]

This chapter examines the role that courts have played in the construction of citizenship/non-citizenship and how the relationship between the Supreme Court and Parliament has contributed to the precariousness of non-citizens living within Canadian borders. In its limited impact on policies implicating the rights of non-citizens, the Supreme Court has contributed to the current system of parliamentary authority in which certain governments – the Harper government, for example – have introduced stricter revocation and refusal measures aimed at further disenfranchising the non-citizen. This will be accomplished in three parts. First, the chapter provides an overview of Canadian judicial treatment of citizenship/non-citizenship, highlighting how citizenship as a legal status has historically been undefined despite its legislative importance. Second, using the Harper government's anti-marriage fraud campaign and the Strengthening Canadian Citizenship Act (Bill C-24) as examples, the chapter examines how this constitutional fuzziness benefited that particular government's citizenship agenda, sparking a larger debate about the parameters of parliamentary autonomy. Finally, the chapter posits some broader questions regarding the role of the courts in deciding a non-citizen's access to Charter protections, addressing the implications that current legal treatment of citizenship presents for citizens, partial citizens, and non-citizens alike.

Brief History of Legal Treatment of Citizenship

Canadian judicial treatment of citizenship/non-citizenship has left both legal and political science scholars unsatisfied.[2] While there have been multiple opportunities for the Supreme Court to situate a non-citizen within a broader framework of Charter rights, the parameters of non-citizenship remain, for the most part, constitutionally fuzzy. As a result, the conceptualization of citizenship/non-citizenship is limited in its "legal or constitutional value."[3] The ambiguousness of citizenship/non-citizenship is largely attributed to three factors. First, structural barriers including, but not limited to, time and financial resources make it difficult for citizens and non-citizens to make Charter claims. Two structural barriers, unique to non-citizens, complicate their ability to have their claims examined: a leave requirement, which obliges non-citizens to seek leave from the Federal Court so that their claim can be judicially reviewed, and a further stipulation that, should the leave requirement be met, a non-citizen claimant needs judicial approval that his or her claim raises a question of general importance.[4] Indeed, one's very capacity to make a Charter claim is further limited by one's citizenship status.

Relatedly, the second factor is the small number of non-citizens' rights claims that the Supreme Court has actually assessed post-Charter. Since the adoption of the Charter in 1982, twenty-four non-citizens' rights claims have been brought before the Supreme Court.[5] Moreover, Dauvergne points out that, within this sample, the majority of cases were not treated as rights claims; instead, the Supreme Court chose to focus more on the context of the claim than the claim itself. While structural barriers exist, the blame cannot be placed solely on the Supreme Court; however, the Court's failure to foster a more substantive narrative of citizenship in these cases has contributed to, and continues to contribute to, the low success rate. The result is that "non-citizens have had little success in making Charter rights claims and even less success in accessing alternative sources of rights protections."[6]

Finally, the Court's inconsistent and complicated treatment of non-citizens' human rights protections, and citizenship more generally, has made it difficult to navigate these types of Charter claims. The Constitution Act, 1867 failed to clearly define citizenship as Canadian nationals were British subjects. The act recognized that the fate of the Canadian nation rested on immigration and, therefore, bestowed authority on Parliament over the admittance and naturalization of immigrants; however, it was unclear whether Parliament had jurisdiction over defining citizenship "through the 'naturalization and aliens' power ... or from its general residual power to legislate for the 'peace, order and good government' of Canada."[7] As a result, the challenge of establishing the parameters of parliamentary power to define what constitutes Canadian citizenship overshadowed more normative discussions of what Canadian citizenship should look like. It was not until the Citizenship Act of 1947 that the legal definition of citizenship was delineated: Canadian citizenship could be obtained through *jus soli, jus sanguinis* (citizenship through descent), or naturalization (when an alien becomes a citizen). This delay in defining Canadian citizenship made the concept a "product of the twentieth century."[8]

After 1947, the assumption was that with Canadian citizenship came a specific set of basic political and legal rights and responsibilities, and these duties and entitlements were determined by the federal and provincial governments. It is worth noting, however, that even if one is a member of the state, access to membership is not universal; rather, access has and continues to be defined along sexist, racist, and colonialist lines.[9] Bound by a commitment to parliamentary supremacy pre-Charter, the courts were limited in their capacity to discuss the more substantive qualities of Canadian citizenship; instead, judicial review focused primarily on questions of federal jurisdiction.[10] For example, in *Union Colliery v. Bryden (1899)*, the Supreme Court evaluated whether the provincial government of British Columbia had the autonomy to prevent the settlement of Chinese immigrants, thereby sparking a series of decisions focused on the constitutional parameters of this very question.[11] The Supreme Court's deference to parliamentary supremacy in citizenship decisions pre-Charter demanded an "exercise of judicial creativity and imagination of conservable magnitude to articulate a conception of citizenship that would embody at the dominion level the authority to define and protect the essential attributes of citizenship, while at the same time respecting the legitimate claims of provincial power;"[12] while the Court recognized the rights of non-citizens in some of these decisions, its authority remained restricted.[13]

The Charter eased reliance on parliamentary supremacy by creating a system in which parliamentary action was held accountable by a framework of human rights and judicial review. With only three rights explicitly reserved for Canadian citizens – the right to vote (s.3), mobility rights (s.6), and minority education rights (s.23) – non-citizens are theoretically entitled to all other rights protections outlined in the Charter. Interestingly, however, institutionally solidified access to rights protection has not necessarily benefited non-citizens in the ways one would think. In fact, Dauvergne argues that while early Supreme Court decisions post-Charter were cognizant of non-citizens' rights – specifically *Singh v. Minister of Employment and Immigration (1985)* and *Andrews v. Law Society of British Columbia (1989)* – more recent jurisprudence highlights a decline in rights protections for non-citizens.[14] Despite Canada's commitment to immigration as part of the national imaginary, non-citizens have, comparatively speaking, less access to human rights protections than in other immigrant-receiving countries.[15]

In *Singh*, Singh claimed that being refused an oral hearing during his determination process infringed his right to "life, liberty and security of the person" (s.7). While the Court unanimously ruled in favour of the claimants and the refugee determination process was subsequently overhauled, Justice Wilson wrote that the s.7 rights protections applied to "every human being who is physically present in Canada," ultimately avoiding any discussion of the connection between non-citizenship and Charter protection.[16] For Wilson, the fact that these nationals were non-citizens seeking entry to Canada was not necessarily linked to the infringement of their s.7 rights; rather, in addition to anyone within Canadian borders being entitled to these specific protections, the absence of an oral hearing infringed the principle of fundamental justice because this part of the process would allow the IRB to identify "serious issues of credibility."[17] Thus, Justice Wilson's focus was the effectiveness of the refugee determination process itself, rather than distinctions of citizenship.

Differing from *Singh*, the Supreme Court established that citizenship was an analogous ground to the characteristics enumerated under s.15's equality rights in *Andrews v. Law Society of British Columbia (1989)*, the first decision dealing with equality rights. Andrews, a permanent resident and British citizen, had been banned from practising law in British Columbia because of his citizenship status, requiring the Supreme Court to assess whether governments could impose benefits or restrictions on the basis of citizenship. Unlike previous decisions involving non-citizens, Justice Wilson addressed the vulnerability of this particular group, stating, "Relative to citizens, non-citizens are a group lacking in political power and as such vulnerable to having their interests overlooked and their rights to equal concern and respect violated."[18] By recognizing the link between non-citizenship and rights, the Court ruled that the ban was a violation of Andrews's rights under s.15. While the significance of this decision for its treatment of citizenship/non-citizenship cannot be overlooked, it is important to remember that *Andrews* was not an immigration case and, therefore, did not address questions of accessibility for those non-citizens seeking entry to Canada.[19] Considering that the majority of rights claims based on citizenship involve non-citizens seeking entry, it was unclear how this decision would extend to those without immigration status.

For Dauvergne, both *Singh* and *Andrews* highlight the beginning of a trend towards human rights overshadowing citizenship rights in Charter decisions involving non-citizens; they framed citizenship as a secondary factor rather than recognize it as a "rights marker" in and of itself.[20] Thus, citizenship was "eliminated as a prerequisite for asserting a claim to most Charter rights" and was "rendered a highly suspect legislative classification."[21] Moreover, these decisions made no reference to a broader context of international human rights, situating rights claims based on citizenship solely within a Charter framework. As a result, non-citizen claimants are "required to make their arguments first and foremost in Charter terms and only secondarily in international human rights terms."[22]

This is evident in a series of non-citizens' rights claims following *Singh* and *Andrews*, with the Court ruling that the following were constitutionally sound: deportation on the basis of criminality in *Chiarelli v. Canada (1992)* and *Medovarski v. Canada (2005)*, the detainment of refugees requiring a "secondary" immigration examination in *Dehghani v. Canada (1993)*, the enacting of ministerial authority in immigration decisions in *Suresh v. Canada (2002)*, and the long-term detention of non-citizens awaiting deportation in *Charkaoui v. Canada (2007)*.[23] While international law has taken up more substantive questions of citizenship rights for both citizens and non-citizens, Canadian jurisprudence post-Charter has failed to create a "space" for international law, despite the fact that courts in countries with similar systems of judicial review have relied quite heavily on this framework for evaluating rights claims involving non-citizens – "Aside from the Refugee Convention cases, the Supreme Court of Canada has not made a single ruling in the Charter era that directly applies an international human rights norm to a non-citizen in Canada."[24]

Another trend present in these decisions has been the Court's focus on particular contexts to justify deferring questions of citizenship/non-citizenship to Parliament. In *Chiarelli v. Canada (1992)*, the Supreme Court ruled that the deportation of a permanent resident who had been convicted of a serious offence was constitutionally sound, explaining that because immigration law dictated that "non-citizens do not have an unqualified right to enter or remain in the country," Parliament had the authority to develop an immigration program that delineated the parameters of entry for non-citizens.[25] Similarly, while the Court ruled in *Suresh v. Canada (2002)* that, generally speaking, the government was unable to deport individuals who were at risk of being tortured in their home country, ministerial authority to base deportation decisions on whether the individual in question is a safety risk to Canada remains within Parliament's constitutional domain. The fact that these decisions were situated in the context of immigration allowed the Court to defer defining the boundaries of non-citizenship to Parliament, resulting in the creation of a "constitutionalized space for discretionary decision making rather than a hard, rights-based response."[26]

Interestingly, more recent decisions highlight a conflation of immigration issues with a narrative of national security.[27] The Court's framing of a non-citizen as a potential security threat in *Suresh v. Canada (2002)* continued in *Charkaoui v. Canada (2007)*; in these cases, the Supreme Court examined the constitutionality of long-term detention of non-citizens issued with a security certificate as outlined in the Immigration and Refugee Protection Act (IRPA).[28] The Court ruled that while the provisions in question were unconstitutional, the detention itself was constitutionally sound as detention was used to protect Canadians from potential foreign security threats. In response, the government was obligated to alter the IRPA provisions; however, "what remains in Canadian law is a procedure whereby non-citizens can be detained for an indeterminate amount of time on the basis of evidence that they can never see."[29] The emergence of security discourse in judicial evaluation of cases involving non-citizens frames them as potential security threats, ultimately allowing the government to continue defining the parameters of detainment and deportation in the name of national security and making it difficult for non-citizens to challenge these processes.

Despite its vital role in (re)producing the Canadian nation, how citizenship has been taken up in Canadian jurisprudence leaves much to be desired. In addition to hearing a small number of Charter cases involving non-citizens, the Supreme Court has opted to avoid discussing the more substantive qualities of citizenship/non-citizenship, often deferring these questions to Parliament. This has typically been accomplished in two ways. First, judicial treatment post-Charter has involved situating the non-citizen within the framework of Charter rights, with minimal acknowledgment of international human rights. While international law has addressed the legal status of non-citizens in greater detail, the Court's reliance on Charter rights highlights what Dauvergne labels a mentality of "Charter hubris," which assumes that the Charter provides non-citizens with all the human rights protections they could possibly need.[30] Second, the Court has used a narrative of immigration and security as justification for deferring questions of access involving non-citizens to the government of the day. By framing non-citizens as a potential security threat, the Court has endorsed a process that solidifies a space for ministerial authority. As a result, Canadian jurisprudence involving non-citizens' rights claims suggests that while "the Charter embodies a rich vision of the relationship between the individual and the state, that vision is not linked to the status of citizenship."[31] Indeed, judicial treatment of citizenship/non-citizenship highlights the analytical shortcomings of formal citizenship as an indicator of rights.

Changes to Immigration and Citizenship Policy under the Harper Government

This narrative of immigration and security adopted by the Supreme Court was in line with the Harper government's reframing of Canada's immigration and refugee program. While changes to the program under Harper reflected a long-standing commitment to neo-liberal values of privatization and self-sufficiency, "their political need to respond to the ideological concerns of their social-conservative base led them to impose a number of extreme sanctions on various categories of 'offenses.'"[32] Compounding this agenda of moral regulation was a post-9/11 security discourse identifying immigration and citizenship as "key sites at which threats to the state must be addressed."[33] As a result, more restrictive changes to Canada's immigration and refugee program were justified as measures to protect Canadians from foreign threat.[34] The securitization of migration, therefore, constructed certain migrants as safe and others as dangerous, establishing a clear precedent that "legal entitlement to citizenship cannot interfere with the state's absolute right to protect itself"[35] – a narrative similar to that used by the Supreme Court in non-citizens' rights claims.

What constituted a threat for the Harper government, however, was quite broad; in addition to deporting, or refusing access to, serious criminals and potential terrorists, it used this language of security to target "'phony' refugees, 'queue jumpers,' 'part-time Canadians,' and other perceived malfeasance that required additional punitive measures."[36] A perceived security threat, therefore, went beyond safety risks to Canadian citizens to include those individuals suspected of undermining the integrity of the immigration system itself. Moreover, changes to the immigration and refugee program under the Harper government increased the vulnerability of those non-citizens already living within Canadian borders by allowing "only those that are permissible until such time as they too are deemed to be threatening to the nation."[37] Thus, the government's discourse of immigration and security not only marked certain individuals as external threats but also stripped non-citizens living in Canada of belonging despite having previously granted them access.

The relationship between the Harper government and the Supreme Court was undoubtedly complex.[38] In addition to cancelling funding for the Court Challenges Program and the Law Commission of Canada in 2006, making it increasingly difficult for potential claimants to overcome the financial cost of bringing a claim to the Supreme Court, the Conservatives bemoaned the Charter as a threat to parliamentary supremacy because it permitted the Court to "use its provisions to override Parliament and generally act like a third legislature whose commands are not subject to review."[39] In fact, this so-called contentious relationship between the Harper government and the Supreme Court became part of the mainstream political narrative after the Supreme Court ruled that Marc Nadon, the government's nominee for Supreme Court Justice, was ineligible for the position and after the government's unsuccessful Senate reference decision in 2014. Lawrence Martin labelled the Court "the Official Opposition in Ottawa," and Vanessa Naughton characterized the relationship as consisting of "flare-ups between the Harper government and the top court … that have put a wrench in the Conservative government's plans."[40]

For Manfredi, this assessment is overly simplistic as an analysis of this relationship measured solely by Charter "wins" and "losses" ignores two important factors.[41] First, governments are typically not involved in constitutional litigation voluntarily; apart from reference cases and decisions involving questions of federal jurisdiction, governments do not make Charter claims.[42] Second, more often than not, governments are obligated to defend legislation established by a predecessor government – eight of eleven Charter litigation losses during the Harper government's tenure focused on legislation enacted before they took power.[43] It is important to make a distinction between the Court's judgments that were contrary to the Harper government's ideological values and those that were an actual refutation of their policy agenda.

In addition to the Harper government's complicated relationship with the Supreme Court, it is worth noting that while in power, it appointed over 600 judges to provincial superior courts, appeal courts, the Federal Court, and the Tax Court.[44] This is significant for two reasons. Unlike the Supreme Court, these lower-level courts are instrumental in executing a government's law-and-order policy agenda. Moreover, the Federal Court was given a prominent role in immigration and refugee issues in 1970;[45] decisions made by the IRB are now subject to judicial review through the IRB's own appeal process, established in 2012, and, if applicable, the Federal Court. Thus, appointed judges are able to implement the government's "tough on crime" mandate as it pertains to immigrants and refugees. As a result, while the number of non-citizens' rights claims brought before the Supreme Court is arguably minimal, resulting in questions of citizenship being unsatisfactorily addressed, lower-level courts have dealt with a much greater number of questions of citizenship, resulting in a "covert culture war over who gets to define Canadian values, Parliament or the courts, and what political party puts the most indelible imprint on the nation's character."[46]

Marriage Fraud Crackdown

In 2011, CIC launched its anti-marriage fraud campaign, aimed at preventing and punishing those immigrants who engaged in a "marriage of convenience."[47] At the time of the launch, sponsored spouses and partners were automatically entitled to permanent residency status, and their sponsor was financially responsible for their loved one for three years. For the Harper government, this made sponsors (i.e., Canadian citizens) vulnerable to abuse and exploitation at the hands of their foreign (i.e., non-citizen) spouses or partners. Claiming an increase in reported cases of marriage fraud, then minister of citizenship, immigration, and multiculturalism Jason Kenney announced a "crackdown" on marriage fraud, targeting those immigrants suspected of undermining the integrity of Canada's immigration system by using marriage to make a fraudulent claim for citizenship.

The passing of the Immigration Appeal Board Act in 1967 gave non-citizens facing deportation the right to an appeal and granted the Immigration Appeals Division (IAD) the authority to consider "humanitarian and compassionate arguments" if an appellant was facing deportation.[48] Taking issue at the time with the resulting shift in power from individual ministers to an administrative tribunal, Progressive Conservative MP Richard Bell contended that decisions involving the residency status of immigrants should continue to be taken up by elected officials rather than an unelected bureaucracy.[49] The Immigration Act (1976) replaced the Immigration Appeal Board Act; however, the IAD's discretionary jurisdiction involving deportation cases remained intact.

Post-Charter, the courts have continued to debate and ultimately reinforce the discretionary jurisdiction of the IAD; cases include *Chieu v. Canada (2002)* and *Wang v. Canada (2005)*. In *Wang*, the Federal Court supported the IAD's claim that, in misrepresentation cases, IAD discretion was permissible when the need arose to "protect the health and safety of Canadians, to maintain the security of Canadian society, and maintain the integrity of the immigration system."[50] Moreover, the Court adopted the IAD's framework for assessing misrepresentation by relying on five factors: seriousness of misrepresentation, remorsefulness of appellant, length of time spent in Canada and degree of settlement/integration, familial impact, and degree of hardship caused by removal.[51] The discretionary jurisdiction of the IAD has therefore played an important role in court treatment of misrepresentation decisions as the theoretical shift in power from elected officials to an unelected administrative body has solidified the IAD's authority to render decisions with minimal judicial interference so long as these conditions are met.

Between 2012 and 2016, the IAD and the Federal Court collectively reviewed 677 published appeal decisions involving couples whose conjugal relationship was ruled one of convenience and who were subsequently denied sponsorship.[52] The majority of these decisions were reviewed solely by the IAD, and fifty of the 677 published decisions were reviewed by both the IAD and the Federal Court. It is important to note that this does not represent the total number of refused applications; the IRB is legally obligated to publish decisions with no appeal only when a decision raises "unusual fact situations or new approaches to issues."[53] Out of the fifty published decisions reviewed by the Federal Court, it dismissed thirty-five (70 per cent) applications for judicial review, concluding that the IAD's rulings were justifiably within its discretionary parameters. In those decisions in which the Court approved the claimant's application for appeal, its focus was generally on whether an administrative error had taken place rather than the details of the application itself. As a result, like earlier discussions regarding the Supreme Court, these decisions involved no substantive discussion of citizenship/non-citizenship.

Initiated by the Harper government and then carried out both by the IAD and by the Federal Court, the crackdown on marriage fraud demonstrates that using "genuine" conjugality as an access point for citizenship allowed the government to define the parameters of permissibility for those non-citizens seeking permanent entry. Moreover, it highlights the secondary role the courts play in defining the discretionary powers of the IAD as the majority of appeals do not make it past the initial appeal process. Contrary to Bell's original concern that enhanced discretionary jurisdiction for the IAD would result in less authority for elected officials, the marriage fraud campaign demonstrates that the "political arm of government" continues to play a role in shaping citizenship priorities and assessment protocol for the IAD.[54]

Strengthening the Canadian Citizenship Act

While academic and non-academic commentary on citizenship refusal and revocation policies passed under the Harper government suggests that such action is a more recent, conservative consequence of 9/11, legal scholars point out that revocation powers are a long-standing resource of the federal government and that their implementation was not unique to that particular government.[55] What distinguishes the Harper government's adoption of these measures from governments past is twofold. First, justification for denaturalization has been extended to include acts of fraud or misrepresentation, a situation that frames an immigration queue-jumper as being as dangerous as a suspected terrorist. Second, these policies have invoked parliamentary debate regarding the role of the courts and who has final say when one's citizenship is hanging in the balance.

Passed in 2014 under the Harper government, the Strengthening Canadian Citizenship Act (Bill C-24) aimed to "send a clear message to those who attempt to take advantage of our generous system" by making sure that those who commit citizenship fraud "face the full force of the law."[56] In addition to making citizenship increasingly restrictive by altering residency and intent-to-reside requirements, the act established harsher penalties for those immigrants and refugees guilty of misrepresentation, thereby permitting CIC to either refuse or revoke citizenship, if the suspicion of fraud existed, without public knowledge or court approval.[57] Moreover, the act legislated ministerial jurisdiction over the majority of revocation decisions, granting the minister of citizenship and immigration authority over cases involving residence fraud, concealing past criminal offences, and identity fraud.[58] Under this new model, a decision can be reviewed with leave by the Federal Court, the Federal Court of Appeal, and the Supreme Court of Canada, but only if it addresses a "serious question of general importance," as determined by the Federal Court.[59] Without leave, a potential citizen or naturalized citizen is denied access to legal resources that Canadian-born citizens enjoy. Indeed, while the act aims to protect Canadian citizenship, it ironically makes it less secure.[60]

Similar objectives were used to justify the Conservatives' passing, in 2015, of the Zero Tolerance for Barbaric Cultural Practices Act, which permits immigration officers to either deport non-citizens suspected of engaging in "barbaric" cultural practices (e.g., child, forced, or polygamous marriage) without a Criminal Code conviction, or finding of misrepresentation, or refuse citizenship altogether.[61] The result is what Aiken refers to as a "two-tiered system of justice," which deprives partial citizens and non-citizens of any type of legal agency and fails to deal with potential "fallout from this expanded scope of inadmissibility."[62]

While not all critics took issue with Canada's ability to deport non-citizens who had been found guilty of breaking the law, they did call attention to the process of ministerial autonomy enshrined in both acts. When debating the constitutional merit of Bill C-24, former New Democratic Party (NDP) MP Lysane Blanchette-Lamothe commented, "We must especially ask ourselves whether someone suspected of fraud should have the right to a fair trial. I believe the answer is yes. If the individual is formally charged, I agree with being able to revoke citizenship, but not as part of a discretionary power."[63] Former NDP MP Jamie Nicholls echoed these sentiments, challenging the need to replace the pre-existing legal process with this new system of bureaucratic autonomy. "We have laws touching on treason and terrorism. Our justice system is robust enough to deal with these acts. ... Does the minister not trust our justice system enough?"[64] Differential treatment between citizens and non-citizens was also addressed by Green Party MP Elizabeth May, who argued that Bill C-24 "runs contrary to the Charter of Rights and Freedoms in treating classes of Canadian citizens differently from each other."[65]

The Harper government defended the legislation both in terms of its streamlined process – arguing that bureaucratic efficiency reflected its zero-tolerance position on citizenship fraud – and its own responsibility to modernize Canadian citizenship laws when necessary. As explained by then minister of citizenship and immigration Chris Alexander,

> The Constitution is not sufficient to provide for the rule of law in our country. We have a Constitution, yes. We have a Charter of Rights and Freedoms. They are important, but we need laws, like the law on citizenship, and we need revisions and modernizations of those laws to tell us what the rules are to make sure that our country is well governed in every sphere. That is why we sit in the House of Commons.[66]

For Alexander, citizenship was not created by the Charter or the Supreme Court; rather, it predates these institutions, and, therefore, it is the role of the government to modify the rules of Canadian citizenship through legislation. For critics of the legislation, while laws should be both created and modernized through the democratic process, one's continued membership in the Canadian state should not be subject to the political whims of the government of the day. In this light, citizenship revocation measures outlined in the act are unconstitutional.[67]

Conclusion

In his comments on the act, NDP MP Robert Aubin stated, "Citizenship is a matter of law and must be kept out of the hands of politicians as much as possible. … The minister is no substitute for justice."[68] Aubin is not wrong – citizenship is technically a legal status defined by rules of "acquiring, retaining and transmitting" membership.[69] Despite the fact that citizenship is a legal matter, however, its more substantive characteristics have been for the most part unaddressed in Canadian jurisprudence. Questions of citizenship/non-citizenship have typically been deferred to Parliament pre- and post-Charter, ultimately limiting the role of the courts as the protector of a non-citizen's Charter rights. Moreover, when the courts do take up citizenship cases, judicial review typically happens in lower-level courts, where justices are appointed by the government in power using a more partisan appointment process than is the case with the Supreme Court. Thus, while Aubin's claim that one's citizenship status should not be subject to political leanings is valid, the legal treatment of Canadian citizenship has established a precedent of parliamentary authority.

The purpose of this chapter is not to debate whether these legislative measures are constitutional; however, one could argue that while their implications are problematic, the Harper government was operating within a constitutional space established before it came to power. Legal rules that define what constitutes a citizen are "intrinsically limited in their capacity to identify, judge and reward 'good' members or punish 'bad' members," so these decisions are left to immigration gatekeepers (e.g., IRCC, IRB, individual ministers, etc.).[70] The Harper government therefore took advantage of citizenship's conceptual blurriness in Canadian jurisprudence, pushing the constitutional barriers to develop policy that redefined who belongs.

Aubin also ignores the reality that, in addition to its legal importance, citizenship reflects intense political and social attachments that go beyond one's legal status within Canadian borders. State capacity to control physical borders has become increasingly challenging, and, as a result, certain governments have resorted to narratives of foreignness to incite moral panic around the threat of illegals. While technically void of actual legal content, the contemporary use of the term *illegal* extends beyond an immigrant's relationship with the law to include an assessment of worthiness.[71] In fact, as Dauvergne contends, "'Illegal' is now established as an identity of its own, homogenizing and obscuring the functioning of the law and replicating layers of disadvantage and exclusion."[72] The legal language of illegality in the context of citizenship/non-citizenship, therefore, has political and social implications for immigrants and refugees because being marked as "illegal" determines whether and to what degree they belong and, relatedly, what claims on the state they are entitled to make. Moreover, the Canadian state's treatment of illegality permeates other policy areas besides immigration and citizenship.

In rendering the affective aspects of citizenship invisible, both the courts and Parliament have failed to effectively address the implications of, and modifications to, the legal definition of citizenship present for citizens and non-citizens alike. The Harper government's anti-marriage fraud campaign and Strengthening Canadian Citizenship Act aimed to protect a particular vision of Canadian citizenship, using a language of moral responsibility to justify revocation and refusal measures that targeted certain immigrants. What is at stake, therefore, is not simply the execution of long-standing citizenship rules; it is also the use of these rules to develop policy that (re)produces political and social narratives of belonging that were consistent with the Conservative Party's policy mandate. As a result, the law's limited capacity to account for the more substantive aspects of citizenship makes the legal processes of "justice," as Kaplan argues, an "unsatisfactory tool" for dictating who belongs and, consequently, who does not.[73]

The current legal treatment of questions of citizenship/non-citizenship, therefore, raises several unsettled constitutional questions. First, are non-citizens entitled to constitutional protections? While they are theoretically entitled to almost all Charter protections, access is limited. Their capacity to fully realize these protections is, therefore, unclear, and their position in our legal system warrants further attention. Second, how can international non-citizens' rights be better incorporated into Canadian jurisprudence? This review of citizenship/non-citizenship decisions highlights the fact that justices have historically taken an either/or approach – either relying completely on Charter language and completely ignoring the language of human rights or vice versa. Deconstructing the more substantive aspects of citizenship to fully comprehend the Canadian state's responsibility to protect non-citizens requires incorporating both types of legal language. Third, what would a more substantive legal definition of citizenship/non-citizenship look like? A judicial review of questions of citizenship/non-citizenship should account for political and social attachments to membership in addition to legal status, recognizing that there is much at stake when one is suddenly stripped of one's right to belong.

Finally, should the courts have a more prominent role in matters of Canadian citizenship? While the Federal Court reviews IRB appeals, establishing their presence in current citizenship debates, the Supreme Court's role is quite limited due to the small number of citizenship/non-citizenship decisions reviewed post-Charter and a trend to deferring questions of citizenship to Parliament. With policy initiatives like the anti-marriage fraud campaign and the Strengthening Canadian Citizenship Act challenging constitutional boundaries, evaluating the non-citizen's position in Canadian jurisprudence is an important debate for the Supreme Court to take up. This is not to suggest that Parliament should be stripped of its ability to alter citizenship policy; however, the current system of parliamentary authority needs to be questioned.

NOTES

1 William Kaplan, "Who Belongs? Changing Concepts of Citizenship and Nationality," in *Belonging: The Meaning and Future of Canadian Citizenship*, ed. William Kaplan (Montreal and Kingston: McGill-Queen's University Press, 1993), 247.

2 Robert J. Sharpe, "Citizenship, the Constitution Act, 1867, and the Charter," in *Belonging: The Meaning and Future of Canadian Citizenship*, ed. William Kaplan (Montreal and Kingston: McGill-Queen's University Press, 1993), 221–44; Catherine Dauvergne, "How the Charter Has Failed Non-citizens in Canada: Reviewing Thirty Years of Supreme Court of Canada Jurisprudence," *McGill Law Journal* 58, no. 3 (2013): 663–728; Audrey Macklin, "Citizenship Revocation, the Privilege to Have Rights and the Production of the Alien," *Queen's Law Journal* 40, no. 1 (2014): 1–54.
3 Sharpe, "Citizenship, the Constitution Act, 1867, and the Charter," 221.
4 Dauvergne, "How the Charter Has Failed Non-citizens in Canada."
5 Ibid., 678.
6 Ibid., 668.
7 Sharpe, "Citizenship, the Constitution Act, 1867, and the Charter," 223.
8 Ibid., 222.
9 Sunera Thobani, *Exalted Subjects: Studies in the Making of Race and Nation in Canada* (Toronto: University of Toronto Press, 2007).
10 Sharpe, "Citizenship, the Constitution Act, 1867, and the Charter," 234.
11 *Union Colliery Company of British Columbia Limited and Others v. John Bryden* [1899] UKPC 58, [1899] AC 580.
12 Sharpe, "Citizenship, the Constitution Act, 1867, and the Charter," 230.
13 Ibid.; Sarah Buhler, "Babies as Bargaining Chips? In Defence of Birthright Citizenship in Canada," *Journal of Law and Social Policy* 17 (2002): 87–114; Lois Harder, "In Canada of All Places: National Belonging and the Lost Canadians," *Citizenship Studies* 14, no. 2 (2010): 203–20; Dauvergne, "How the Charter Has Failed Non-citizens in Canada."
14 *Singh v. Canada (Minister of Employment and Immigration)*, [1985] 1 S.C.R. 177; *Andrews v. Law Society of British Columbia*, [1989] 1 S.C.R. 143.
15 Dauvergne, "How the Charter Has Failed Non-citizens in Canada."
16 *Singh, supra* note 7 at 202, Wilson J.
17 Ibid. at 213–14.
18 *Andrews, supra* note 27 at 152, Wilson J.
19 Dauvergne, "How the Charter Has Failed Non-citizens in Canada."
20 Ibid., 674.
21 Sharpe, "Citizenship, the Constitution Act, 1867, and the Charter," 236.
22 Dauvergne, "How the Charter Has Failed Non-citizens in Canada," 675.
23 *Chiarelli v. Canada (Minister of Employment and Immigration)*, [1992] 1 S.C.R. 711, 90 DLR (4th) 289; *Medovarski v. Canada (Minister of Citizenship and Immigration)*, 2005 SCC 51, [2005] S.C.R. 5389; *Dehghani v. Canada (Minister of Employment and Immigration)*, [1993] 1 S.C.R. 1053, 101 DLR (4th) 654; *Suresh v. Canada (Minister of Citizenship and Immigration)*, 2002 SCC 1, [2002]

1 S.C.R. 3; *Charkaoui v. Canada (Citizenship and Immigration)*, 2007 SCC 9, [2007] 1 S.C.R. 350. Anna Pratt defines "criminality" as a fluid category used by the Canadian state at different moments in time to "exclude or deport 'dangerous foreigners' for various combinations of moral, racial, economic, and ideological reasons"; see *Securing Borders: Detention and Deportation in Canada* (Vancouver: UBC Press, 2005), 109.

24 Dauvergne ("How the Charter Has Failed Non-citizens in Canada") contends that only in *Mugesera v. Canada (Minister of Citizenship and Immigration)* 2005 SCC 40, [2005] 2 S.C.R. 100, in which the Court held up a deportation order for a Rwandan politician for his role in the 1994 genocide, did international law clearly influence the outcome (679, 724).

25 *Chiarelli, supra* note 56 at 733.

26 Dauvergne, "How the Charter Has Failed Non-citizens in Canada," 722.

27 Pratt, *Securing Borders*; Dauvergne, "How the Charter Has Failed Non-citizens in Canada."

28 A security certificate permits CIC to detain and/or deport non-citizens if they are suspected of criminal activity or perceived to be a security threat. In *Charkaoui*, the Court addressed whether this process was an infringement of Charkaoui's s.7, 9, and 10 Charter rights.

29 Dauvergne, "How the Charter Has Failed Non-citizens in Canada," 699.

30 Ibid., 726.

31 Sharpe, "Citizenship, the Constitution Act, 1867, and the Charter," 241.

32 Brooke Jeffrey, *Dismantling Canada: Stephen Harper's New Conservative Agenda* (Montreal and Kingston: McGill-Queen's University Press, 2015), 226.

33 Harder, "In Canada of All Places," 204.

34 Ratna Omidvar, "The Harper Influence on Immigration," in *The Harper Factor: Assessing a Prime Minister's Legacy*, ed. Jennifer Ditchburn and Graham Fox (Montreal and Kingston: McGill-Queen's University Press, 2016), 179–95.

35 Mark Salter, "Citizenship, Borders, and Mobility: Managing the Population of Canada and the World," in *Canada in the World: Internationalism in Canadian Foreign Policy*, ed. Heather A. Smith and Claire Turenne Sjolander (Toronto: Oxford University Press, 2013), 151.

36 Jeffrey, *Dismantling Canada*, 225.

37 Rita Dhamoon, "Security Warning: Multiculturalism Alert!," in *The Ashgate Research Companion to Multiculturalism*, ed. Duncan Ivison (London: Ashgate, 2010), 261.

38 Emmett Macfarlane, "Conservative with the Constitution?," in *The Blueprint: Conservative Parties and Their Impact on Canadian Politics*, ed. J.P. Lewis and Joanna Everitt (Toronto: University of Toronto Press, 2017), 221–41; Tasha Kheiriddin, "Law and Order in the Harper Years," in *The Harper*

Factor: Assessing a Prime Minister's Policy Legacy, ed. Jennifer Ditchburn and Graham Fox (Montreal and Kingston: McGill-Queen's University Press, 2016), 196–219.

39 John Ibbitson, *Stephen Harper* (Toronto: McClelland and Stewart, 2015), 382.

40 Lawrence Martin, "The Supreme Court Is Harper's Real Opposition," *Globe and Mail*, 1 July 2014, http://www.theglobeandmail.com/opinion/the-supreme-court-is-harpers-realopposition/article19395285/; Vanessa Naughton, "Harper vs the Supreme Court of Canada," *Global News*, 12 May 2014, http://globalnews.ca/news/1325937/harper-vs-the-supreme-court-of-canada/.

41 Christopher Manfredi, "Conservatives, the Supreme Court, and the Constitution: Judicial-Government Relations, 2006–15," *Osgoode Hall Law Journal* 52, no. 3 (2015), http://digitalcommons.osgoode.yorku.ca/cgi/viewcontent.cgi?article=1164&context=olsrps.

42 During the Conservatives' tenure, three reference cases were brought to the Supreme Court: *Reference re Securities Act* 2011 SCC 66, [2011] 3 S.C.R. 837; *Reference re Supreme Court Act*, ss.5 and 6, 2014 SCC 21, [2014] 1 S.C.R. 433; and *Reference re Senate Reform* 2014 SCC 32.

43 Manfredi, "Conservatives, the Supreme Court, and the Constitution," 3.

44 Sean Fine, "Stephen Harper's Courts: How the Judiciary Has Been Remade," *Globe and Mail*, 30 December 2015, http://www.theglobeandmail.com/news/politics/stephen-harpers-courts-how-the-judiciary-has-been-remade/article25661306/.

45 Peter McCormick, *The End of the Charter Revolution: Looking Back from the New Normal* (Toronto: University of Toronto Press, 2015), 16.

46 Fine, "Stephen Harper's Courts," 2015.

47 CIC defines a *marriage of convenience* as a marriage or common-law relationship that is not genuine and was entered into primarily for the purpose of acquiring any status or privilege under the Immigration and Refugee Protection Act.

48 Ninette Kelley and Michael Trebilcock, *The Making of the Mosaic: A History of Canadian Immigration Policy* (Toronto: University of Toronto Press, 2000), 368–9.

49 Ibid., 268–9. Even under the Immigration Appeal Board Act, the minister of manpower and immigration had authority to override IAD decisions when the security of Canadian citizens was at stake (s.21). This authority remains in the current Immigration and Refugee Protection Act (s.81).

50 *Cai v. Canada (Citizenship and Immigration)*, 2016 FC 748, *supra* note 5.

51 *Wang v. Canada (Minister of Citizenship and Immigration)*, 2005 FC 1059, *supra* note 11.

52 Published decisions were obtained from the CanLii database (www.canlii.org) using the search term *marriage of convenience*. The majority of these decisions had been reviewed by the IAD as the Federal Court of Canada reviews only those decisions that are (1) being appealed for a second time or (2) raise a series of questions in need of further exploration.

53 Sean Rehaag, "Patrolling the Borders of Sexual Orientation: Bisexual Refugee Claims in Canada," *McGill Law Journal* 53 (2008): 70; Nicholas Hersh, "Challenges to Assessing Same-Sex Relationships under Refugee Law in Canada," *McGill Law Journal* 60, no. 3 (2015): 537.

54 Kelley and Trebilcock, *The Making of the Mosaic*, 368–9.

55 Christopher G. Anderson, "A Long-Standing Canadian Tradition: Citizenship Revocation and Second-Class Citizenship under the Liberals, 1993–2006," *Journal of Canadian Studies* 42, no. 3 (2008): 80–105; Christopher G. Anderson, *Canadian Liberalism and the Politics of Border Control: 1867–1967* (Vancouver: UBC Press, 2013); Audrey Macklin and Francois Crépeau, "Multiple Citizenship, Identity, and Entitlement in Canada" (Montreal: Institute for Research in Public Policy, 2010). While the federal government has always been legally permitted to revoke citizenship, this was not a frequent occurrence. Between 1967 and 2011, only sixty individuals had their citizenship revoked; meanwhile, between 2011 and 2012, the Harper government was responsible for 19 revocations, 3,139 investigations, the flagging of 5,000 permanent residents, and 2,500 recent arrivals being "closely monitored"; see Jeffrey, *Dismantling Canada*, 229. The Trudeau government has announced plans to revisit the act and "make it impossible for the government to take away someone's citizenship"; see Katharine Starr, "Changes Coming Soon to Citizenship Act, John McCallum Says," *CBC News*, 18 February 2016, http://www.cbc.ca/news/politics/mccallum-immigrants-citizenship-act-language-requirement-1.3453658.

56 Costas Menegakis, House of Commons, Debates, 41st Parl., 2nd Sess., vol. 147, no. 053, 27 February 2014. On 19 June 2017, An Act to amend the Citizenship Act (Bill C-6) – introduced by the Trudeau government – was passed by the Senate. The bill reverses many citizenship policies enacted under the Conservatives, including certain revocation measures, residency requirements, and the parameters of ministerial authority.

57 Cases involving war crimes, crimes against humanity, and other security-related issues are to be reviewed by the Federal Court; however, the minister of public safety is able to request a revocation order from the Court while the decision is being reviewed; see Citizenship Act Changes – 2014, https://www.canada.ca/en/immigration-refugees-citizenship/services/canadian-citizenship/improvements/act-changes-2014.html.

58 Ibid.
59 Ibid.
60 Macklin, "Citizenship Revocation, the Privilege to Have Rights and the Production of the Alien."
61 For more on the Zero Tolerance for Barbaric Cultural Practices Act, see Megan Gaucher, "Monogamous Canadian Citizenship, Constructing Foreignness, and the Limits of Harm Discourse," *Canadian Journal of Political Science* 49, no. 3 (2016): 519–38.
62 Sharryn Aiken, House of Commons, Standing Committee on Citizenship and Immigration, Evidence (no. 47, 7 May 2015, 2–3), 41st Parl., 2nd Sess. Rhacel Salazar Parreñas, "Partial Citizenship and the Ideology of Women's Domesticity in State Policies on Foreign Domestic Workers," in *Care and Migration*, ed. Ursula Apitzsch and Marianne Schmidbau (Opladen, Germany: Verlag Barbara Budrich, 1) defines *partial citizens* as legal migrants that are unable to access full juridical rights (e.g., foreign domestic workers).
63 Lysane Blanchette-Lamothe, House of Commons, Debates, 41st Parl., 2nd Sess., vol. 147, no. 053, 27 February 2014.
64 Jamie Nicholls, House of Commons, Debates, 41st Parl., 2nd Sess., vol. 147, no. 092, 29 May 2014.
65 Elizabeth May, House of Commons, Debates, 41st Parl., 2nd Sess., vol. 147, no. 091, 28 May 2014.
66 Chris Alexander, House of Commons, Debates, 41st Parl., 2nd Sess., vol. 147, no. 092, 29 May 2014.
67 Eve Peclet, House of Commons, Debates, 41st Parl., 2nd Sess., vol. 147, no. 091, 28 May 2014; Macklin, "Citizenship Revocation, the Privilege to Have Rights and the Production of the Alien."
68 Robert Aubin, House of Commons, Debates, 41st Parl., 2nd Sess., vol. 147, no. 091, 28 May 2014.
69 Macklin and Crépeau, "Multiple Citizenship, Identity, and Entitlement in Canada," 1.
70 Ibid.
71 The term *illegal* is technically not a legal status unto itself as there is no single, working, legal definition outlining what constitutes an "illegal." Rather, this term has historically been used to describe an immigrant's relationship with the law; see Catherine Dauvergne, *Making People Illegal: What Globalization Means for Migration and Law* (Cambridge: Cambridge University Press, 2008).
72 Ibid., 19.
73 Kaplan, "Who Belongs?," 261.

14 Taking the Harper Government's Refugee Policy to Court

CHRISTOPHER G. ANDERSON AND DAGMAR SOENNECKEN[1]

There is no question that significant changes occurred in Canadian refugee policy under the Conservative government of Stephen Harper during its nearly ten years in power. Indeed, observers note that virtually no aspect was left untouched.[2] The effects of many of these alterations are still unfolding, and while the subsequent Liberal government of Justin Trudeau committed itself to reversing or modifying some of them, many will likely be preserved.[3]

In this chapter, we focus on changes that occurred to Canada's *inland* refugee policy, with two larger goals in mind.[4] First, we aim to demystify the role of the courts in shaping refugee policy in Canada. The literature often attributes a heightened negative (i.e., overly rights-expansive) impact to the courts – largely as a result of the 1985 *Singh* decision, the first Charter case handed down by the Supreme Court of Canada (SCC) that dealt with refugee claims[5] – without providing much empirical evidence[6] or focuses on important points of legal interpretation without more fully engaging their policy implications.[7] Studies that investigate the role of the courts in this policy area on a more empirical basis, in contrast, remain too few.[8]

Second, we seek to contribute to a growing body of work that reflects on the contentious relationship between the Harper government and the courts, which perhaps reached its nadir in the public dispute over Marc Nadon's failed appointment to the SCC.[9] Such conflict was also notably seen in a 2011 speech in which then immigration minister Jason Kenney accused Federal Court of Canada (FC) judges of undermining the government's rights-restrictive approach to refugees.[10]

To shed light on the relationship between the courts and Canadian inland refugee policy, we open with a review of the rights-restrictive heft and tenor of policy changes – and their surrounding discourse – by the Harper government between 2006 and 2015. Next, we discuss the relationship between the courts and public policy, beginning with some remarks on the challenges of studying the impact of the former on the latter. We suggest that shifting the focus to how and why refugee claimants and their supporters mobilized the law in opposition to the Harper government's restrictive agenda is necessary to grasp the nature and impact of judicial involvement. This is then illustrated by examining the mobilization that occurred through and beyond the courts in response to the government's 2012 cuts to the Interim Federal Health Program (IFHP) for refugees.

Our research shows that while the role of the courts in overseeing Canadian refugee policy is generally quite limited, significant mobilization on behalf of refugees occurred in response to the Harper government's particularly rights-restrictive approach. Indeed, notwithstanding an inherently unfriendly legal opportunity structure (LOS), litigation and "rights talk" played an important part in the broader political advocacy work of refugee organizations (ROs), in tandem with other strategies such as public awareness campaigns, coalition-building, and lobbying for policy change. Importantly, there was the 2011 founding of the litigation-savvy Canadian Association of Refugee Lawyers (CARL), which – together with the Canadian Council for Refugees (CCR) – took a lead legal-mobilization role in the refugee advocacy community. As well, there was involvement by new constituencies, especially within the medical profession, which created Canadian Doctors for Refugee Care (CDRC) in response to the IFHP cuts. To understand the relationship between the courts and policy, then, it is necessary to appreciate the broader policy and political contours within which court rulings emerge and the specific contexts that prompt court involvement in the first instance.

The Restrictionist Turn under Harper, 2006–15

During its time in power, the Harper government made it harder for asylum seekers to seek and find protection in Canada. It did not simply adopt a more restrictive approach, however, but also sought to shift the Canadian refugee status determination (RSD) regime away from a rights-based and towards a rights-restrictive and more selective foundation. Many "rights-based principles that underlay the pre-existing regime [were] replaced by other justifications that pay significantly less attention to the interests and experiences of particular claimants," reflecting a privileging of the belief that "the reason to protect is based on *an aspect of the public interest* rather than an individual right."[11] The government thereby increased its discretionary power over refugees as an asylum seeker was "reconfigured as primarily a migrant whom the government may have reason to select" rather than an individual empowered to make rights-based claims against the state.[12]

As they transformed the RSD regime, the Conservatives constrained traditional avenues of communication and influence within the refugee policy community. Although this was in many ways consistent with previous trends, the Harper government was particularly direct in its rejection of groups and individuals who did not share its ideological beliefs and practices.[13] At the same time, it more tightly circumscribed the actions and influence of public servants in favour of policies developed in the Prime Minister's Office.[14] In contrast, although refugee policy had long been dominated by the bureaucracy, there nonetheless had previously been substantial routine interaction (and at times influence) on the part of ROs through such mechanisms as parliamentary committees and regular meetings with, and access to, officials.[15] As the traditional political (and policy) environment was constricted, however, and as the Conservatives consolidated and expanded their rights-restrictive approach, the impetus for ROs to seek extra-parliamentary influence in cases such as the IFHP – especially through the judiciary – increased.

The Harper government expanded and consolidated its rights-restrictive approach in both policy discourse and practice with few political checks, especially during its final, majority-government mandate. Although the balance between refugee protection and border control has long varied over time, Canada had – since the creation of the Immigration and Refugee Board (IRB) in 1989 – adopted a broadly rights-based approach to RSD.[16] For example, a recent comparative study portrays Canada's "Cadillac" model as embodying "a commitment to a system of administrative justice based on a centralized, resource-rich professional judgment."[17] The Conservatives, for their part, sought to redirect the Cadillac along a more rights-restrictive and discretionary road through a range of discursive and policy acts.

This approach was centred on the premise that the Canadian regime was too generous and encouraged those who did not require protection to claim asylum in hopes of obtaining undeserved economic, political, and/or social benefits in Canada or even to threaten its national security.

For example, in introducing legislation in 2010 to increase restrictions on access to and fairness within Canadian RSD, Kenney argued,

> Our generosity is too often abused by false asylum claimants who come here and do not need our protection. They're misusing the asylum system to jump the immigration queue rather than waiting their turn like everyone else. ... They try to enter the country through the back door and they take advantage of our asylum system to avoid waiting in line like everyone should for their application to be processed.[18]

This premise and discourse were used consistently and extensively by the Conservatives to justify a three-pronged, rights-restrictive approach.

First, the government made it more difficult for asylum seekers to travel to and enter Canada. A prominent practice of such interdiction involved imposing visa requirements alongside more rigorous and multilayered document and transit inspections. For example, visitor visa requirements were imposed to prevent Roma and Mexican asylum seekers from travelling to Canada to make refugee claims.[19] New data-sharing arrangements with countries and air carriers were introduced to facilitate tracking and excluding potential asylum seekers before, or removing them after, arrival.[20] The government also reduced the number of exemptions under the restrictive Canada-U.S. Safe Third Country Agreement, and it pursued more vigorous enforcement policies at and beyond the Canadian border, including helping other states intercept sea vessels carrying asylum seekers.[21] These and other measures prevented asylum seekers from being able to make rights-based claims against the state (insofar as they could not reach Canada) and increased the state's discretionary power.

Second, the government made it harder for individuals to pursue asylum claims in Canada after their arrival, both in terms of their access to the RSD system and the fairness with which they were treated within it. Most notably, the Balanced Refugee Reform Act and the Protecting Canada's Immigration System Act "increased the difficulties for all claimants who [were] attempting to navigate the channels that led to the determination of their status, with some being singled out to face additional burdens."[22] Such changes, among other measures, decreased the chances of claimants receiving a fair hearing as new limits were placed on processing and appeal timelines, while decision making was shifted from independent appointees to public servants. A qualified exception involved the creation of the Refugee Appeal Division (RAD), which instituted an appeal of a negative determination of a refugee claim on its merits; this is discussed in more detail in the next section.

Of particular relevance to this chapter is the differentiation created among claimants according to their country of origin and method of arrival, which negatively affected prospects in RSD and appeal rights, for example. The lack of arm's-length authority in designating countries as "safe," as seen under new Designated Country of Origin (DCO) provisions, meant that political interests and pressures could take precedence over an individual's right to seek and find refuge.[23] It is worth noting that when these provisions were first introduced by the Conservative minority government in 2010, a number of limits on ministerial discretion were included; these were removed when new legislation was passed in 2012 under a Conservative majority. At that time, the government also created a Designated Foreign National (DFN) category, targeting "irregular" arrivals of migrants "in groups of two or more in a way that prevents the timely examination of their identity and admissibility" or that appears to involve human smuggling.[24]

The third prong made it harder for asylum seekers to remain in Canada, especially but not only after an initial denial of their claim. Thus, for those from DCOs, removals could be undertaken even if an individual applied for judicial review, and greater restrictions were placed on their ability to apply for a Pre-Removal Risk Assessment (PRRA). Alongside an increased use of detentions and deportations,[25] the Conservatives restricted work permits for those from DCOs and proposed changes through their 2014 omnibus budget bill to allow provinces to deny social assistance to refugee claimants. In addition, greater efforts were made to remove protected status (so-called cessations) from refugees who had "re-availed themselves of the protection of their home country," even those who had received Canadian permanent resident status.[26]

Given the constrained political environment the Harper government created, and the rights-restrictive approach it pursued, the courts provided a logical avenue along which to counter Conservative policies towards asylum seekers. The history of the LOS in this area, however, suggests that groups would have met with limited courtroom success.

Courts, Mobilization, and Policy Outcomes

Although courts are part of the policymaking cycle, analysts have found it challenging to pin down theoretically and empirically the impact of their presence more generally, and their decisions more specifically, on policy outcomes.

Traditional "top-down" impact studies are limited in their conceptualization of the consequences of judicial decisions and assessment of litigation and policy reform efforts as constituting a "success" or "failure." First, most try to draw a linear, causal connection between a decision and its aftermath. As McCann put it, this approach is like a bowling ball rolling down an alley: the greater the number of "pins" that fall following a decision, the greater the impact. If few or none fall, then the "bowl" is judged less effective.[27] Often, the "impact" bar is set quite high – for example, Rosenberg's well-known analysis of US civil rights litigation anticipated that to be deemed to have had an impact, judicial decisions would have to have no less than "nation-wide" effects and produce "significant" social change.[28] Moreover, because of its tendency to equate impact with change, this approach at best discounts but often ignores other responses, ranging from compliance to defiance, that are difficult to conceptualize using the "bowling alley" analogy.[29]

Second, most Canadian research has concentrated on studying instances of *successful* litigation by groups, predominantly by analysing the aftermath of SCC cases involving social movement organizations that resulted in policy change.[30] Cases in which groups did not pursue their goals through the courts, in contrast, are much less frequently studied.[31] Third, many such studies concentrate on tracing the reverberations of a few "big," atypical cases,[32] thereby limiting their generalizability. Finally, a narrow definition of "success" is often attributed to the groups examined, leaving the varied goals that they may have had underexplored or ignored.[33]

In response, a growing interdisciplinary and international literature has emerged. Legal mobilization scholarship understands litigation as only one of a number of political strategies, such as protest and lobbying, employed by societal actors to effect change.[34] This perspective decentres law and the courts and places them back into the policymaking cycle, challenging scholars to understand the effects of courts more broadly than is typical for most litigation-centric analyses. As Galanter famously observed, courts (and the law they apply) can endow subjects with bargaining norms, symbols, and procedures that "radiate" outwards beyond litigation.

> The effects of a court ... cannot be equated with the dispositions in the cases that come before it. There are a host of other effects that flow from

> the activity of a court. ... The patterns of general effects that we attribute to the courts depend on the endowments that actors extract from the messages radiating from the courts.[35]

Research has identified three main factors that structure the degree of mobilization: access to the courts, sufficient "resources" (broadly defined) for effective legal advocacy, and the availability of "legal stock" (existing laws conferring legal rights, legal precedent, and so forth). Generally speaking, more closed and conservative structures deter, while more open and liberal structures encourage, legal mobilization.[36] While any given LOS tends to be relatively stable, each is "shaped by [group] strategies in turn."[37] Thus, some scholars have studied the interaction between structure- and agent-level variables, ranging from group perceptions and internal culture to resources and inter-group dynamics. Others have explored reasons why some groups do not resort to litigation or do so despite a seemingly unfavourable LOS.[38]

The following section highlights factors that structure legal mobilization for asylum seekers and their advocates in Canada. It shows that they managed – despite a fairly "closed" LOS – to forge significant opportunities for themselves during the Harper years.

Refugees in the Courts under Harper: "Contained" Justice?

Canada's refugee policy is governed by both domestic and international legal norms. The definition of a refugee, as established under the 1951 Geneva Convention and 1967 Protocol (to which Canada acceded in 1969), was incorporated into Canadian immigration law in the early 1970s, while the 2002 Immigration and Refugee Protection Act (IRPA) contains a clause that explicitly acknowledges Canada's international human rights commitments. IRPA also grants protection to those who cannot return to their country of origin due to a fear of torture, explicitly referencing the Convention against Torture.[39]

Despite this seemingly strong foundation of legal stock, international human rights norms are mostly irrelevant as a source of rights-claiming because adjudicators largely rely on domestic legal norms in their decision making. Moreover, the administration of Canada's domestic legal norms concerning refugees is controlled almost exclusively by the IRB (Canada's largest administrative tribunal), which makes most final decisions concerning refugees.[40] This high level of "administrative insulation"[41] is no accident. Access to the judiciary for rejected refugee claimants and their supporters is limited in multiple ways, a fact that illustrates how procedural norms structuring access to the courts can "contain" the potential for substantive rights mobilization.[42]

First, before the 2012 creation of the RAD, it was not possible to have a negative decision by the IRB reviewed on its merits. Although the RAD now provides this option and the success rate for rejected claimants is higher than it was previously before the FC,[43] research has already identified a number of systemic restrictive features.[44] Second, the FC can review IRB decisions only from a procedural justice perspective. Compared to a "full-fledged" appeal, judicial review limits court oversight to errors in law and is generally a deferential exercise designed to respect the special expertise of bureaucratic decision makers. Moreover, claimants must obtain "leave" (i.e., permission) from the FC to have their case heard, something that was denied more than 80 per cent of the time during 2003–10.[45] Studies also demonstrate that despite the high stakes involved in refugee determination (stemming from the well-founded fear of persecution under consideration), being granted leave is very much a matter of chance; it depends on the judge involved, the presence or absence of counsel, and access to legal aid.[46]

During the Harper years, between 582 (2008) and 926 (2015) refugee cases were granted leave before the FC each year; this constitutes a low of 13 and a high of 40 per cent of refugee cases granted leave between 2008 and 2015. The most prominent ROs with a dedicated history of involvement in litigation, the CCR and CARL, participated in thirty-two[47] and seven[48] cases as an intervener or public interest party, respectively.

Third, access to the Federal Court of Appeal (FCA) is – unique to immigration and refugee law – restricted. It requires the same FC judge who ruled on a given case to certify (upon request of counsel) that it raises "a serious question of general importance" that necessitates resolution through an appeal to the FCA.[49] While the FCA heard an average of 562 refugee cases a year during the Harper period, only about 300 questions *in total* have been certified to proceed to the FCA since the IRPA came into force in 2001;[50] this further underscores the limits placed on access to the judiciary. During the Harper period, CARL participated in only one case, and the CCR in eight cases, before the FCA.

Two additional cases were to be heard by the FCA but were withdrawn by the new Trudeau government. In each case, key rights restrictions implemented under Harper were involved, and the Conservatives had lost before the FC. In *Y.Z. v. Canada* 2015 FC 892, the FC ruled unconstitutional the denial of appeal rights (to the RAD) for refugee claimants from DCOs that had been implemented in 2012. CARL was granted public interest standing in this case. The FC judge refused, however, to consider the unconstitutionality of the DCO regime as a whole. In *Canadian Doctors for Refugee Health Care v. Canada (AG)* 2014 FC 651, which we discuss in more detail shortly, an FC judge ruled the 2012 IFHP cuts unconstitutional.

Of the cases heard by the FCA, the one case supported by CARL (the decision was released in February 2016) involved the Harper policy of foreclosing most appeal avenues to individuals from DCOs – more specifically, the thirty-six-month "bar" on accessing PRRA. Although the FC and FCA rejected this legal challenge, litigation on this matter continues.[51] Meanwhile, in *Bermudez v. Canada*, the FCA affirmed the lawfulness of a 2012 Harper government policy change regarding cessations, mentioned earlier. It has not been reversed to date, although public hearings on reforming Canada's refugee law, including cessations, were held during the summer of 2016.[52]

Given that a leave to appeal barrier also governs access to the SCC, it is perhaps not surprising that the Court hears refugee (and immigration) cases infrequently. During the Harper years, the overall leave-grant rate did not deviate much from its historical average, ranging from 12 per cent (or fifty-five cases) in 2006 to 8 per cent (or forty cases) in 2015.[53] Of the 569 cases heard by the SCC during this entire period, only fourteen involved non-citizens (roughly 2.5 per cent), which is in line with previous years.[54] The CCR, often together with other ROs like CARL, intervened in *all* these cases.

Of the fourteen, *B010 v. Canada* and *R. v. Appuloappa* were brought before the courts in 2015 following legislative changes in response to the arrival of mostly Tamil asylum seekers aboard the *Ocean Lady* and the *Sun Sea* in 2009 and 2010, respectively. These arrivals had led the Harper government to toughen IRPA's human-smuggling provisions, chiefly by codifying the DFN category for "irregular arrivals" into law in 2012, as discussed previously.[55] Although both cases can be considered rights-defensive "wins"[56] since the SCC sided with the argument (supported by the interveners) that the legislation was overbroad, both cases actually turned on pre-Harper, anti-smuggling, IRPA provisions. In fact, thus far, most of the 2012 human-smuggling amendments remain in place (including the controversial DFN category).

All but two of the remaining ten SCC cases involved scenarios relating to non-citizens and security, broadly defined.[57] None challenged legislative changes originally introduced by the Harper government, although one, the 2014 *Canada v. Harkat* case, upheld the Harper government's legislative response to the SCC striking down the pre-Harper security certificate regime in the 2007 *Charkaoui v. Canada* case.[58] In another case (*Agraira v. Canada*), involving an argument over the grounds on which the public safety minister could set aside decisions of inadmissibility, the government (after having won before the FCA) incorporated narrower inadmissibility grounds (which removed humanitarian and compassionate factors from consideration) in its 2013 Faster Removal of Foreign Criminals Act, despite the fact that it could have still lost the argument before the SCC (which later sided with the government).[59]

Finally, one last SCC case is worth noting here since it illustrates the "dialogue" between the SCC and the Harper government in the broader arena of immigration, even though it did not involve a refugee claimant.[60] In *R. v. Pham*, the SCC allowed the reduction of a sentence of a "foreign criminal" to two years less a day to facilitate access to an appeal of his removal order. That same year, the Harper government moved the appeal "cut-off" from two years of imprisonment to six months as part of its Faster Removal of Foreign Criminals Act.

In her extensive analysis of SCC cases concerning non-citizens, Dauvergne concludes that the Canadian Charter of Rights and Freedoms has "failed to deliver on its promises for human rights protection" for non-citizens (for more on the Charter and non-citizens, see Gaucher, this volume).[61] Earlier observers of the Court's jurisprudence in the mid-1990s similarly argued that rights-expansive decisions like *Singh v. Canada* were followed by a "swing" towards more rights-restrictive ones.[62] This brief analysis of the Harper government's refugee policy in the courts confirms this overall trend. Most of the government's rights-restrictive policy innovations are still in place or have not been subject to extensive litigation. The so-called wins (rights restrictions struck down) have been few and far between.

Yet despite this track record and a highly constrained LOS, there was significant mobilization inside and outside the courts on behalf of refugees during the Harper years. As we will now see, law "mattered"[63] in the broader political struggle of ROs as rights talk and litigation were employed in tandem with other strategies. We now turn to a closer examination of the context surrounding one such case – *Canadian Doctors for Refugee Health Care* – to illustrate this point.

Fighting the Restrictionist Turn inside and outside the Courts: The Cuts to the IFHP

With its origins at the end of the Second World War, the IFHP had become – by the mid-1990s – "a temporary health insurance program available to refugees, protected persons, and refugee claimants in Canada," with "coverage … similar to the level of coverage that provincial and territorial governments provide[d] for people receiving social assistance, including coverage for prescription drugs, dental, and vision care."[64] In April 2012, the Conservatives announced the removal for rejected refugee claimants and those from DCOs of all benefits except emergency coverage, and cut supplemental coverage for all others. Eventually, an estimated 86 per cent of individuals previously covered under the IFHP (including asylum seekers) could be denied access to preventive and even – for some – emergency care.[65]

In justifying its actions, the government claimed that the cuts would save money, prevent refugees from accessing "gold-plated" benefits above those available to "ordinary Canadians," protect public health and safety, and deter abuse by "bogus refugees."[66] Although the cuts prompted widespread opposition on rights-based, ethical, and practical grounds, the government remained intransigent despite mounting evidence that its policy goals were not being met and that the health of some refugees and asylum seekers was being undermined.

The political environment for those opposed to the cuts was constrained from the outset as there were no consultations with the provinces, the medical profession, social welfare organizations, or ROs before the announcement. Rick Dykstra (Jason Kenney's parliamentary secretary) maintained that since the policy "was part of the economic action plan, budget 2012, and was under budget secrecy," stakeholders could not be consulted and that the government possessed sufficient internal medical expertise to develop an appropriate health policy for refugees on its own.[67] A subsequent analysis, however, found that "the exclusion of refugee advocates and the public health sector from this process was both deliberate and systematic."[68] Indeed, repeated efforts on the part of national medical stakeholders, such as the Canadian Medical Association, to sit down with the government on this issue were rebuffed.[69]

This likely stemmed from the fact that the medical profession was unequivocal in its opposition to the cuts. Apart from labelling them unethical, unfair, and inhumane, it anticipated that the overall costs associated with refugee health would grow as preventable and treatable health problems persisted and worsened, putting the health of refugees and the broader Canadian public at risk.[70] The cuts were, moreover, held to be discriminatory in distinguishing health care access by factors such as country of origin.

In response, the government portrayed the criticisms as being unfounded and ideological, labelling critics in the medical profession "left-wing militants" who were "ideologically motivated" and belonged to "hard-core pressure groups."[71] The government accused opponents of not understanding the policy,[72] being unrepresentative of "the entire medical profession in Canada,"[73] and making claims that were "unsubstantiated" or "factually incorrect," in which they purposefully altered facts.[74] Government representatives even attacked individual doctors by disclosing their donations to non-Conservative political parties and interactions with non-Conservative politicians.[75]

The constrained political environment also arose with the government's reluctance to engage with criticism on a factual basis, frequently responding instead with its negative discourse concerning refugees. For example, when questioned in the House of Commons about the possible "cost in long-term health care expenditure," Kenney replied, "I will say what is unfair and unethical: a health program that gave better benefits to smuggled false asylum claimants than to Canadian seniors who have been paying their taxes their whole lives."[76] The juxtaposition of "bogus" refugees with "hard-working, taxpaying Canadian citizens" was repeatedly offered by Conservatives in support of the cuts.[77] When challenged to listen to the concerns of medical professionals, the government often responded that it chose instead to listen to average Canadians. When opposition MPs persisted, then immigration minister Chris Alexander (who succeeded Kenney in 2013) accused critics of proposing "that anyone who comes to Canada – and 10 million people come a year – should receive provincial health care."[78] As evidence of the policy's negative effects on refugees and asylum seekers mounted, Alexander alleged that opponents were enacting a "vindictive campaign against honesty."[79]

This combative approach continued in the Standing Committee on Citizenship and Immigration. When Liberal MP Kevin Lamoureux introduced a motion on 26 September 2012 to study the effects of the cuts on refugees and asylum seekers, it was voted down by a united bloc of six Conservative MPs. When Lamoureux invited a witness to address the cuts, government MPs introduced obstructive points of order, a tactic used again when opposition committee members questioned Kenney on the IFHP. Ultimately, the IFHP cuts received no sustained scrutiny by the standing committee, and no critic was invited to discuss them. As a result, this traditional avenue of state-societal interaction and debate was essentially foreclosed.[80]

The constrained political environment also arose in the government's decision to sideline evidence-based policymaking. The IFHP decision – which Sheridan and Shankardass label a social policy failure – was taken despite "a lack of an evidentiary basis for major government claims in defense of the" decision and in the face of contrary evidence generated and shared internally.[81] When the government received internal advice that challenged its claims, such voices were marginalized.[82]

For their part, opponents pursued various political strategies before and after turning to the courts. Notably, there was a significant mobilization and expansion of societal actors. Apart from traditional voices such as ROs, human rights organizations, and religious leaders, a wide range of medical professionals and professional associations began to address this issue. Indeed, more than twenty national and provincial medical associations became directly engaged in opposing the government's policy,[83] joined by numerous hospitals, medical centres, clinics, and social welfare organizations, among others. Alongside collecting signatures on petitions, writing to and meeting with MPs and the media, using the Internet and social media to raise awareness, occupying Conservative MPs' offices, and interrupting government photo ops, opponents instituted a National Day of Action for Refugee Health, held in June each year from 2012 to 2015 in some twenty cities across Canada. Medical professionals also created networks through which to mobilize and share information, both within the profession and with ROs.[84]

In response to the cuts, medical professionals collected and analysed data from front-line health workers and institutions, publishing and releasing results to the broader public. For example, a 2013 Wellesley Institute study documented how "the new system creates confusion, lessens access to health care services among vulnerable populations, leads to inconsistency in care across Canada, and results in poorer health and avoidable illness for refugees and refugee claimants."[85] Other studies highlighted the negative effects on refugee children[86] and reported the decreased willingness of many practices and clinics to administer to those covered under the new IFHP rules given the confusion and uncertainty surrounding coverage.[87] Although the cuts had negatively affected "a very significant number of people in very dramatic fashion," CARL President Lorne Waldman observed, it was "quite clear that the government [was] not willing to change its mind."[88]

In the context of the rights-restrictive nature of the cuts, and the tightly constrained political environment, three individuals who had been denied medical assistance under the new IFHP rules, alongside CDRC and CARL, argued in their FC submissions in late February 2013 that the policy violated the rights of refugees under the Charter.[89] In particular, they claimed that the cuts:[90]

- threatened the rights to life and security of the person in section 7 of the Charter;
- amounted to cruel and unusual treatment, contrary to section 12 of the Charter;
- discriminated against refugees from certain countries, and discriminated against people based on their immigration status, contrary to section 15 of the Charter; and
- were inconsistent with Canada's international law obligations.

Arguments were heard in December 2013 and January 2014, and the Honourable Madam Justice Anne L. Mactavish handed down her ruling on 4 July 2014.

Although the section 7 argument was denied, Mactavish accepted the section 12 challenge, finding that the government had "intentionally set out to make the lives of these disadvantaged individuals even more difficult than they already are in an effort to force those who have sought the protection of this country to leave Canada more quickly, and to deter others from coming here."[91] She emphasized that the cuts "potentially jeopardize the health, the safety and indeed the very lives, of ... innocent and vulnerable children in a manner that shocks the conscience and outrages our standards of decency."[92] Moreover, she "found as a fact that the 2012 changes to the IFHP are causing illness, disability, and death."[93] As for section 15, Mactavish ruled that the restraints on DCO claimants put "their lives at risk and perpetuates the stereotypical view that they are cheats and queue-jumpers, that their refugee claims are 'bogus,' and that they have come to Canada to abuse the generosity of Canadians."[94] For these and other reasons, she concluded that "the profoundly deleterious effects of the 2012 changes to the IFHP greatly outweigh the salutary goals of the Governor in Council in making these changes," especially as "it has not been established that the changes will in fact contribute in a material way to the realization of *any* of these goals."[95]

Although the Harper government immediately appealed the case to the FCA and only reluctantly moved to reverse the cuts after losing a stay on the FC decision in advance of the appeal, quite soon after the 2015 election, the Trudeau government signalled its intention not to pursue the appeal. By 1 April 2016, coverage was reinstated, with an anticipated expansion of the program one year later.

Conclusions

The IFHP case provides an opportunity to explore the intersection of refugee policy and the courts in Canada at close hand. First, and in keeping with one of the two framing objectives of this chapter, it helps to clarify the Harper government's contentious relationship with the courts during its years in office. As we have seen, the Conservatives worked to weaken the rights-based foundations of Canadian inland refugee policy, which had supported the RSD regime since the 1980s. Moreover, they constrained the traditional political environment, shutting out alternative points of view and marginalizing evidence-based policymaking. Their actions thus strongly encouraged opponents to seek rights-based and judicial avenues of influence. In short, the government adopted an approach that increased the chances of its policies being challenged and even overturned through judicial venues, even as it sought to undermine the legitimacy of such judicial intervention through its political discourse (particularly evidenced by Kenney's public criticisms of the courts, noted at the outset).

Second, the IFHP case assists in demystifying the role of the courts in shaping refugee policy in Canada. At first glance, the success of this case (alongside other cases, such as *Y.Z.*) seems to confirm the rights-expansionist effects of the courts in this policy area, a claim that is commonly made in the literature on both Canadian refugee policy and the Charter. However, a major contribution of this chapter lies in situating such cases within the broader contexts of (a) the constrained LOS that defines Canadian inland refugee policy generally *and* (b) the especially constrained political environment that existed during the Harper years. Only when this is done can the political import of these examples be evaluated and understood more fully. In the IFHP case, the potential for a court ruling that would go against the government was increased by the rights-restrictive nature of the changes and the inadequate evidentiary basis offered to support them as well as the effective legal mobilization fostered by the government's actions and discourse. Additional contextual factors – such as the newly elected Trudeau government's decision not to pursue the FCA appeal and the willingness of the judge who heard the case to accept many of the rights-based arguments made by the litigants – were also critical to the eventual policy outcome.

Finally, the significant growth of legal mobilization in the refugee-advocacy community during the Harper years – especially with respect to legal stock and "resources," broadly understood – merits further exploration. For instance, can these advocates transform the remaining structural constraints that limit their access to the courts under the Trudeau government? What are the costs of directing so much of their efforts to litigation? To what extent will the existence of the RAD change the "contained" role of the courts in this policy area? Overall, more holistic research on the impact of the courts (which transcends the traditional litigation-centric analysis) is needed to understand better the effects of courts in shaping public policy.

NOTES

1 We would like to thank Pierre-André Thériault as well as the anonymous reviewers for their suggestions and comments.
2 Naomi Alboim and Karen Cohl, "Shaping the Future" (Toronto: Maytree Foundation, October 2012).
3 Stephen Meurrens, "Immigration after the Conservative Transformation," *Policy Options*, 9 September 2015, http://policyoptions.irpp.org/magazines/september-2015/election-2015/immigration-after-the-conservative-transformation/.
4 Inland refugee policy refers to the government's response to asylum seekers (or refugee claimants) who are already in the country and who claim to possess a well-founded fear of persecution if returned beyond Canada's borders.
5 *Singh v. Canada (Minister of Employment and Immigration)*, [1985] S.C.R. 177.
6 This argument made an early appearance in the Charter politics literature, as seen in Rainer Knopff and F.L. Morton, *Charter Politics* (Scarborough, ON: Nelson Canada, 1992) and Christopher P. Manfredi, *Judicial Power and the Charter: Canada and the Paradox of Liberal Constitutionalism* (Toronto: Oxford University Press, 2001). It also appears in works on Canadian immigration

and refugee policy, such as Valerie Knowles, *Strangers at Our Gates* (Toronto: Dundurn Press, 1997) and Martin Collacott, "Reforming the Canadian Refugee Determination System," *Refuge* 27, no. 1 (2010): 110–18. At a political level, it is a position commonly advanced by Conservative parliamentarians. For an interpretation of *Singh* that situates it within the policy and political context of the times, see Christopher G. Anderson, "Restricting Rights, Losing Control: The Politics of Control over Asylum Seekers in Liberal-Democratic States – Lessons from the Canadian Case, 1950–1989," *Canadian Journal of Political Science* 43, no. 4 (2010): 937–59.

7 E.g., Donald Galloway, "Rights and the Re-identified Refugee," in *Refugee Protection and the Role of Law: Conflicting Identities*, ed. Susan Kneebone, Dallal Stevens, and Loretta Baldassar (London: Routledge, 2014), 36–55; Audrey Macklin, "Disappearing Refugees," *Columbia Human Rights Law Review* 36 (2005): 365–426.

8 E.g., Catherine Dauvergne, "How the Charter Has Failed Non-citizens in Canada," *McGill Law Journal* 58, no. 3 (2013): 663–728; Rebecca Hamlin, *Let Me Be a Refugee* (Oxford: Oxford University Press, 2014); Dagmar Soennecken, "Extending Hospitality," *Studies in Law, Politics and Society* 60 (2013): 85–109.

9 Christopher Manfredi, "Conservatives, the Supreme Court of Canada, and the Constitution," *Osgoode Hall Law Journal* 52, no. 3 (2015): 951–84.

10 Jason Kenney, speaking notes, University of Western Ontario, 11 February 2011, http://www.cic.gc.ca/english/department/media/speeches/2011/2011-02-11.asp.

11 Galloway, "Rights and the Re-identified Refugee," 44, 50; emphasis in original.

12 Ibid., 38.

13 Miriam Smith, *A Civil Society?* (Peterborough: Broadview Press, 2005); Lawrence Martin, *Harperland* (Toronto: Viking Canada, 2010); Paul Wells, *The Longer I'm Prime Minister* (Toronto: Vintage, 2014).

14 Evert A. Lindquist and Chris Eichbaum, "Remaking Government in Canada: Dares, Resilience, and Civility in Westminster Systems," *Governance* 29, no. 4 (2016): 553–71.

15 Gerald E. Dirks, *Controversy and Complexity* (Montreal and Kingston: McGill-Queen's University Press, 1995); Alan B. Simmons and Kieran Keohane, "Canadian Immigration Policy: State Strategies and the Quest for Legitimacy," *Canadian Review of Sociology and Anthropology* 29, no. 4 (1992): 421–52.

16 Christopher G. Anderson, *Canadian Liberalism and the Politics of Border Control: 1867–1967* (Vancouver: UBC Press, 2013).

17 Hamlin, *Let Me Be a Refugee*, 100.

18 Jason Kenney, speaking notes, 30 March 2010, http://www.cic.gc.ca/english/department/media/speeches/2010/2010-03-30.asp. On the deep roots of this political discourse, see Anderson, *Canadian Liberalism and the Politics of Border Control*; on its extensive use by the Harper government, see Alex Neve and Tiisetso Russell, "Hysteria and Discrimination," *University of New Brunswick Law Journal* 62, no. 9 (2011): 37–45.

19 Cynthia Levine-Rasky, Julianna Beaudoin, and Paul St Clair, "The Exclusion of Roma Claimants in Canadian Refugee Policy," *Patterns of Prejudice* 48, no. 1 (2014): 67–93; Paloma E. Villegas, "Assembling a Visa Requirement against the Mexican 'Wave,'" *Ethnic and Racial Studies* 36, no. 12 (2013): 2200–19. The previous Liberal government had imposed visa restrictions on the Czech Republic and Hungary to interdict Roma refugee claimants. While the Conservatives removed these restrictions soon after gaining power, they reimposed them on the Czech Republic in 2009 and then lifted them again in 2013. As Levine-Rasky, Beaudoin, and St Clair relate, both the Liberals and the Conservatives pursued a number of other mechanisms to limit access to and fairness within the Canadian RSD with respect to Roma refugees.

20 Christopher G. Anderson, "Out of Sight, Out of Mind: Electronic Travel Authorization and the Interdiction of Asylum Seekers at the Canada-U.S. Security Perimeter," *American Review of Canadian Studies* 47, no. 4 (2017): 385–407. With less controversy, the government imposed visitor visa requirements on Botswana, Namibia, St Lucia, St Vincent, and Swaziland in 2012.

21 François Crépeau and Idil Atak, "The Securitization of Asylum and Human Rights in Canada and the European Union," in *Contemporary Issues in Refugee Law*, ed. Savinder Juss and Colin Harvey (Cheltenham, UK: Edward Elgar Publishing, 2013), 227–57.

22 Galloway, "Rights and the Re-identified Refugee," 37.

23 Dagmar Soennecken, "Shifting Back and Up," *Comparative Migration Studies* 2, no. 1 (2014): 102–22.

24 See Alboim and Cohl, "Shaping the Future," 38. Such claimants are subject to mandatory detention and a five-year prohibition on obtaining permanent residence after a positive refugee determination, s. 20.1 and 55 (3.1) IRPA.

25 Carrie Dawson, "Refugee Hotels," *University of Toronto Quarterly* 83, no. 4 (2014): 826–46.

26 Andrea Woo, "'Draconian' Changes to Refugee Act Put Those with Protected Status on Edge," *Globe and Mail*, 7 May 2014.

27 Michael McCann, "Causal versus Constitutive Explanations (or, On the Difficulty of Being So Positive …)," *Law and Social Inquiry* 21 (1996): 459.
28 Gerald N. Rosenberg, *The Hollow Hope* (Chicago: University of Chicago Press, 1991), 4.
29 Mary Volcansek, *Judicial Politics in Europe* (New York: Peter Lang, 1986), 8; Charles A. Johnson and Bradley C. Canon, *Judicial Policies: Implementation and Impact* (Washington, DC: Congressional Quarterly Press, 1984).
30 Lori Hausegger, Matthew Hennigar, and Troy Riddell, *Canadian Courts: Law, Politics, and Process* (Don Mills, ON: Oxford University Press, 2009), 366.
31 Dagmar Soennecken, "The Growing Influence of the Courts over the Fate of Refugees," *Review of European and Russian Affairs* 4, no. 2 (2008): 55–88; Lisa Vanhala, "Legal Opportunity Structures and the Paradox of Legal Mobilization by Environmental Movements in the UK," *Law and Society Review* 46, no. 3 (2012): 523–56.
32 Volcansek, *Judicial Politics in Europe*, 9.
33 Miriam Smith, "Ghosts of the Judicial Committee of the Privy Council," *Canadian Journal of Political Science* 35, no. 1 (2002): 1–29.
34 Chris Hilson, "New Social Movements," *Journal of European Public Policy* 9 (2002): 238–55; Ellen Ann Andersen, *Out of the Closets and into the Courts* (Ann Arbor: University of Michigan Press, 2005).
35 Marc Galanter, "The Radiating Effects of Courts," in *Empirical Theories of Courts*, ed. Keith D. Boyum and Lynn Mather (New York: Longman, 1983), 123–4, at 123 and 127.
36 Rhonda Evans Case and Terri E. Givens, "Re-engineering Legal Opportunity Structures in the European Union?," *Journal of Common Market Studies* 48 (2010): 221.
37 Andersen, *Out of the Closets and into the Courts*, 9; see also Lisa Vanhala, "Legal Opportunity Structures."
38 Karen Alter and Jeannette Vargas, "Explaining Variation in the Use of European Litigation Strategies," *Comparative Political Studies* 33 (2000): 452–82; Lisa Vanhala, "Disability Rights Activists in the Supreme Court of Canada," *Canadian Journal of Political Science* 42, no. 4 (2009): 981–1002; Soennecken, "The Growing Influence of the Courts over the Fate of Refugees."
39 S. 96 and 97 IRPA.
40 Gerald P. Heckman, "Securing Procedural Safeguards for Asylum Seekers in Canada," *International Journal of Refugee Law* 15, no. 2 (2003): 212–53; Catherine Dauvergne, "International Human Rights in Canadian Immigration Law," *Indiana Journal of Global Legal Studies* 19, no. 1 (2012): 305–26.
41 Hamlin, *Let Me Be a Refugee*, 90.

42 Lisa Conant, *Justice Contained* (Ithaca, NY: Cornell University Press, 2002).
43 The RAD success rate for rejected refugee claimants was 26.4% in 2013–14 – much higher than before the FC under the pre-2012 system, when the average was 7.8% in 2005–10; see Sean Rehaag, "Judicial Review of Refugee Determinations," *Queen's Law Journal* 38, no. 1 (2012): 1–58. The scope of the RAD's powers was subject to litigation in *Canada (CIC) v. Huruglica* 2016 FCA 93. The Conservatives also limited access to the RAD, rendering it unavailable to DCOs, DFNs, claims deemed "manifestly unfounded" or "with no credible basis," and claimants falling under an exception of the Safe Third Country Agreement.
44 Sean Rehaag and Angus Grant, "Unappealing," *University of British Columbia Law Review* 49 (2016): 203–74.
45 Dauvergne, "International Human Rights in Canadian Immigration Law."
46 Ian Greene and Paul Shaffer, "Leave to Appeal and Leave to Commence Judicial Review in Canada's Refugee Determination System," *International Journal of Refugee Law* 4 (1992): 71–83; Jon B. Gould, Colleen Sheppard, and Johannes Wheeldon, "A Refugee from Justice," *Law and Policy* 32 (2010): 454–86; Rehaag, "Judicial Review of Refugee Determinations."
47 Dagmar Soennecken, "The Growth of Judicial Power over the Fate of Refugees" (PhD diss., University of Toronto, 2008).
48 The calculation of granting rate in percentage terms may be somewhat inaccurate due to the court's backlog. Unless otherwise noted, all data in this section are available from the authors on request.
49 IRPA 2001, s. 74 (4) (d).
50 Hamlin, *Let Me Be a Refugee*, 94.
51 *Savuntharasa v. Canada (Public Safety and Emergency Preparedness)* 2016 FCA 51 at 22; Canadian Association of Refugee Lawyers, "Brief: Reform Proposals for Canada's Inland Refugee Determination System and Other Aspects of the Immigration System," July 2016, http://www.carl-acaadr.ca/sites/default/files/CARL%20brief%20FINAL_July2016.pdf.
52 *Bermudez v. Canada (CIC)* 2016 FCA 131, http://ccrweb.ca/en/release-cessation-reform-urgent-following-bermudez-court-decision; http://www.carl-acaadr.ca/sites/default/files/CARL%20%20Cessation%20Briefing%20Note%20for%20Minister%20McCallum%2019%2004.pdf.
53 See Supreme Court statistics; 2015 rate not final.
54 Soennecken, "The Growth of Judicial Power over the Fate of Refugees."
55 CIC, "Backgrounder – Overview: Ending the Abuse of Canada's Immigration System by Human Smugglers," http://www.cic.gc.ca/english/department/media/backgrounders/2012/2012-02-16d.asp?_ga=1.74316048.349030836.1486237210.

56 F.L. Morton and Avril Allen, "Feminists and the Courts: Measuring Success in Interest Group Litigation in Canada," *Canadian Journal of Political Science* 34 (2001): 55–84.

57 *Kanthasamy v. Canada* 2015 SCC 58 involved a rejected seventeen-year-old refugee claimant who was subsequently denied the right to remain in Canada on humanitarian and compassionate grounds. Although many lawyers consider the case to have far-reaching effects yet to be seen, it did not test any Harper government policy changes. *Ezokola v. Canada* 2013 SCC 4, *Febeles v. Canada* 2014 SCC 68, and *Nemet v. Canada* 2010 SCC 56 involved refugee claimants and war crimes or serious crimes, but none involved policy changes made by the Harper government.

58 *Canada (Citizenship and Immigration) v. Harkat* 2014 SCC 37; *Charkaoui v. Canada (Citizenship and Immigration)* 2007 SCC 9.

59 *Agraira v. Canada (Public Safety and Emergency Preparedness)* 2013 SCC 36.

60 *R. v. Pham* 2013 SCC 15.

61 Dauvergne, "How the Charter Has Failed Non-citizens in Canada," 666.

62 F. Pearl Èliadis, "The Swing from *Singh*," *Immigration Law Reporter* 26 (1994): 130–47.

63 Michael McCann, *Rights at Work: Pay Equity Reform and the Politics of Legal Mobilization* (Chicago: University of Chicago Press, 1994).

64 Steven Barnes, "The Real Costs of Cutting the Interim Federal Health Program" (Wellesley Institute, 2013), 4, http://www.wellesleyinstitute.com/wp-content/uploads/2013/10/Actual-Health-Impacts-of-IFHP.pdf.

65 Ruby Dhand and Robert Diab, "Canada's Refugee Health Law and Policy from a Comparative, Constitutional, and Human Rights Perspective," *Canadian Journal of Comparative and Contemporary Law* 1, no. 1 (2015): 351–406.

66 Paul Sheridan and Ketan Shankardass, "The 2012 Cuts to Refugee Health Coverage in Canada," *Canadian Journal of Political Science* 48, no. 4 (2016): 905–31.

67 Rick Dykstra, House of Commons, Debates, 41st Parl., 1st Sess., vol. 146, no. 177, 6 November 2012.

68 Sheridan and Shankardass, "The 2012 Cuts to Refugee Health Coverage in Canada," 907.

69 E.g., eight national medical associations "three times requested a meeting with Kenney to discuss the cuts. He has not officially responded for over a year except to indicate that he did not have time to fit such a meeting into his schedule"; see Meb Rashid and Philip Berger, "Let's End the Nasty Fight on Refugee Health Care," *Toronto Star*, 5 July 2013.

70 Sonal Marwah, "Refugee Health Care Cuts in Canada" (Wellesley Institute, 2014), http://www.wellesleyinstitute.com/wp-content/uploads/2014/02/Refugee-Health-Care-Cuts-In-Canada-.pdf.
71 Laura Eggertson, "Health Care Organizations Wait to Talk to Citizenship Minister about Cuts to Refugee Benefits," *Canadian Medical Association Journal* 185, no. 7 (2013): E279–80.
72 Gloria Galloway, "Nobel Laureate Joins Toronto Rabbi Group in Condemning Refugee Health Cuts," *Globe and Mail*, 7 July 2012.
73 Tobi Cohen, "Protesters in Lab Coats Pose New Challenges," *Montreal Gazette*, 21 July 2012.
74 Louisa Taylor, "Refugee Health Cuts Cause Chaos, Doctors Say," *Ottawa Citizen*, 28 September 2012.
75 Tobi Cohen, "Refugee Health Ignites Political War," *Ottawa Citizen*, 4 February 2014.
76 Jason Kenney, House of Commons, Debates, 41st Parl., 1st Sess., vol. 146, no. 120, 9 May 2012.
77 Christopher Olsen, Rowan El-Bialy, Mark McKelvie, Peggy Rauman, and Fern Brunger, "'Other' Troubles: Deconstructing Perceptions and Changing Responses to Refugees in Canada," *Journal of Immigrant and Minority Health* 18, no. 1 (2014): 58–66.
78 Chris Alexander, House of Commons, Debates, 41st Parl., 2nd Sess., vol. 147, no. 087, 15 May 2014.
79 Chris Alexander, House of Commons, Debates, 41st Parl., 2nd Sess., vol. 147, no. 165, 29 January 2015.
80 As well, the cuts were scarcely broached in the Senate.
81 Sheridan and Shankardass, "The 2012 Cuts to Refugee Health Coverage in Canada," 923.
82 Stephanie Levitz, "Bureaucrats Forced into Last-Minute Pitch to Save Some Refugee Health Benefits," *Canadian Press*, 7 January 2013.
83 An incomplete list of organizations includes the Canadian Association of Optometrists, Canadian Association of Social Workers, Canadian Dental Association, Canadian Medical Association, Canadian Nurses Association, Canadian Pharmacists Association, Canadian Association of Midwives, Canadian Psychiatric Association, College of Family Physicians of Canada, Royal College of Physicians and Surgeons of Canada, Canadian Paediatric Society, Canadian Association of Social Workers, Canadian Association of Community Health Centres, Community Health Nurses of Canada, Association of Medical Microbiology and Infectious Diseases Canada, and Canadian Federation of Medical Students as well as numerous provincial associations and the newly formed CDRC.

84 There was also significant mobilization against the cuts on the part of the provinces, primarily but not only on the grounds that the changes would increase costs at the provincial level.

85 Barnes, "The Real Costs of Cutting the Interim Federal Health Program," 1.

86 Andrea Evans, Alexander Caudarella, Savithiri Ratnapalan, and Kevin Chan, "The Cost and Impact of the Interim Federal Health Program Cuts on Child Refugees in Canada," *PLoS ONE* 9, no. 5 (2014).

87 Taylor, "Refugee Health Cuts Cause Chaos, Doctors Say."

88 Michael Woods, "Doctors, Lawyers to Challenge Conservative Refugee Health-Care Cuts," *Postmedia News*, 24 February 2013.

89 An earlier, unsuccessful court case had been filed in 2012 by the Anglican Synod of the Diocese of Rupert's Land and Hospitality House Refugee Ministry of Winnipeg on the grounds of breach of contract as the government would no longer – under the IFHP changes – be providing medical coverage for refugees whom it had already cleared for private sponsorship resettlement.

90 Canadian Association of Refugee Lawyers, "Doctors and Lawyers Challenge Federal Health Cuts to Refugees," press release, 25 February 2013, http://www.carl-acaadr.ca/our-work/issues/IFHP.

91 *Canadian Doctors for Refugee Health Care*, 7–8.

92 Ibid.

93 Ibid.

94 Ibid.

95 Ibid., 256; emphasis in original.

15 *Carter* Conflicts: The Supreme Court of Canada's Impact on Medical Assistance in Dying Policy

ELENI NICOLAIDES AND MATTHEW HENNIGAR

The 2015 ruling of the Supreme Court of Canada (SCC) in *Carter v. Canada*[1] struck down the ban on assisted suicide, sparking a remarkable contest in Parliament – including the House, Senate, and their committees – over the proper legislative response. While the heart of the debate focused on the eligibility criteria for medical assistance in dying (henceforth MAID), this disagreement was often articulated as two issues: whether Parliament needed to defer to the SCC's interpretation in *Carter* of what the Canadian Charter of Rights and Freedoms' section 7 rights to life, liberty, and security of the person required and what constituted a "reasonable limit" on those rights under section 1. Those in favour of wider access to MAID, in line with the *Carter* ruling, advocated strict adherence to the ruling and a preference for judicial supremacy in constitutional interpretation. The Liberal majority government, backed by opponents of MAID, preferred more restrictive access, and it launched what was arguably the most sustained challenge to date by a Canadian government to the SCC's interpretive monopoly. Rather than favouring judicial supremacy, it insisted that both courts and Parliament could legitimately engage in constitutional interpretation – the central tenet of what is known as the *coordinate construction* approach.[2] Yet this position was misleadingly described by some key policymakers as "dialogue";[3] others used that term to advocate for the use of the notwithstanding clause, while accepting the Court's interpretive supremacy.

Thus, a key impact of the *Carter* ruling was that it shaped the rhetorical framework of Parliament's subsequent policymaking exercise, which – without the Court's decision or the threat of future judicial review – might otherwise have been articulated simply in terms of whether competing policy proposals were feasible, beneficial, or detrimental to the public or consistent with some ethical or moral standard. Instead, much of the debate over C-14 concerned whether the law did, or needed to, comply with the SCC's *Carter* ruling. In this sense, *Carter* and its legislative sequel in Bill C-14: An Act to amend the Criminal Code and to make related amendments to other Acts (medical assistance in dying[4]) are a good example of how politics in Canada have been judicialized[5] since the adoption of the Charter in 1982. Moreover, our analysis of *Carter*'s policy impact is aligned with McCann's "bottom-up," or "dispute-centred," approach to assessing the impact of judicial rulings, which, as Riddell phrases it, "seeks to analyze how legal claims and judicial decisions are interpreted, utilized, and/or circumvented by differently situated actors (interest group leaders and litigators, government officials, judges) within legal, social, and political communities and institutions."[6] Judicial decisions are thus "constitutive in nature and provide frameworks for interpretation and action."[7]

In this paper, we map the impact of the *Carter* decision on the subsequent policymaking process of Bill C-14 by focusing on how competing parliamentary factions and their interest group allies characterized the proper parliamentary-judicial relationship to promote their policy preferences on MAID. To do so, we employ an interpretive approach using qualitative analysis of publicly accessible archival data: speeches by politicians and interest groups in the media, parliamentary debates and committee proceedings, committee reports, and official government backgrounders released online and to the press. The results reveal that *Carter*'s chief impact was not to establish Canada's MAID policy, but to shape the terms of the debate and to spark a surprising parliamentary conflict among MPs, senators, legal experts, interest groups, and, ultimately, the public about Parliament's proper role in constitutional interpretation.

Theories of the Judicial-Legislative Relationship regarding Constitutional Interpretation

Few topics in the courts and politics literature, if any, have received more attention than the relationship between the judicial and legislative branches. The Constitution Act, 1982 fundamentally altered that relationship by establishing constitutional supremacy (section 52) and explicitly empowering judges to review and remedy government action on the basis of Charter rights (section 24). But the constitution does *not* specify how to resolve ambiguities in the meaning of its own text – for example, whether "freedom of association" (section 2(d)) includes the right to strike or to collective bargaining. It is widely accepted that interpretation of often-vague constitutional provisions is necessary. But who should have the authority to do it?

Judicial supremacy is "unquestionably the orthodox position of legal scholars" in Canada – not to mention prominent jurists – despite being a relatively recent notion.[8] The argument for judicial supremacy over constitutional interpretation is ultimately rooted in the observation that parliamentary democracy in Canada is not simply majority rule but also a system of government in which the majority is limited by the constitution, including a set of diverse, legally binding rights and freedoms.[9] Authors such as former chief justice Beverley McLachlin of the SCC hold that there is an inherent conflict of interest if legislatures can define the rules that are supposed to bind them, and so there must be a separation of roles between Parliament and the courts. According to her view, the former debates, drafts, and passes laws as a "political activity," while the latter interprets laws as a "legal activity."[10] More boldly, this view sees judges as the "guardians" of the constitution against the tyranny of the majority,[11] the excessive power of the political executive in Canada,[12] and/or politicians' failure to address controversial issues.[13]

In contrast, there is a long tradition of critics who see "rule by judges" as the tyranny of an unelected minority or what Bickel termed the counter-majoritarian difficulty.[14] Defenders of judicial supremacy point to the explicit empowerment of the judiciary, by democratic consent of the Charter's drafters, in section 24,[15] but that argument relates only to judicial activism, not interpretive supremacy. The coordinate construction model rejects the notion that *any* single branch of the state should have a monopoly over constitutional interpretation. Rather, this approach holds that every branch has a continuous responsibility to abide by the constitution when it acts, and doing so necessitates interpretation of the constitution by each branch. Part of the justification is a normative appeal to democratic self-government, but another part is simply pragmatic: as Hiebert observes, only a small fraction of legislation will ever be subject to judicial review and then, usually, after the fact (references, or advisory opinions, on draft bills being the exception).[16]

While government lawyers and some legislators certainly look to judicial rulings on related issues for guidance when drafting laws,[17] unless Parliament explicitly re-enacts a law struck down by the courts (exceptionally rare) or refers it to the Court for an advisory opinion, the new law is, by definition, one that has not been judicially reviewed. The consequence, Hiebert concludes, is that to ensure that all laws respect the constitution, proactive engagement in constitutional review and interpretation by Parliament are essential – or what Slattery refers to as the "first-order" duty of all branches "to assess the reasonableness of their own anticipated acts in light of fundamental rights and to act accordingly."[18] The coordinate construction approach has its roots in US constitutional theory and the separation of powers doctrine, and it can be traced back to Madison's work in *The Federalist Papers*.[19] It is thus viewed by some as foreign to the Canadian parliamentary system,[20] but Knopff and Morton, Slattery, and Baker mount compelling arguments to the contrary.[21]

The well-known *dialogue theory* lies somewhere between judicial interpretive supremacy and coordinate construction.[22] First articulated in Canada by Peter Hogg and Allison Bushell, the concept of *dialogue* has taken on a variety of different and often incompatible meanings,[23] but its chief proponents contend that legislatures can almost always respond to judicial rulings that invalidate laws on constitutional grounds in such a way as to reverse, modify, or avoid the ruling in practical policy terms.[24] Dialogue theory was thus intended to rebut concerns about the counter-majoritarian difficulty raised by Charter-based judicial review. The theory was heavily criticized on empirical, theoretical, and normative grounds,[25] but the key criticism for purposes here is that dialogue theorists held that policy responses cannot legitimately challenge judicial interpretations of the constitution.[26] Rather, legislatures could respond by more clearly explaining – for example, through expanded legislative preambles – why their infringements of (judicially defined) rights were "reasonable" under the Charter's section 1 limitations clause, or the various internal limits on some rights,[27] or by using the section 33 notwithstanding clause. Judges have interpretive supremacy, according to this view, while legislatures help determine "the appropriate balance between rights (*as judicially understood*) or between judicially defined rights and other, non-rights considerations."[28]

As Baker notes, this is the key distinction between dialogue theory and coordinate construction as the latter "contemplates inter-institutional 'dialogues' *about*, not merely *within*, judicially defined limits."[29] Several critics objected to the narrow scope of *dialogue* as envisioned by proponents like Hogg et al. and Roach, and they argued that "genuine dialogue" requires more robust exchanges about constitutional meaning as well as a "creative element" to legislative responses.[30] However, those critics are better understood as advocating for coordinate construction.[31]

In the analysis that follows, it is important to note that while the conceptions of the judicial-legislative relationship in constitutional interpretation shape the debate about MAID policy post-*Carter*, parliamentarians and interest groups do not always explicitly associate themselves with these labels. This is especially true of those advocating coordinate construction, which is perhaps not unexpected given its "unorthodox" position in Canadian constitutional thought. Moreover, we do not assume that actors were sincere rather than strategic in their support for judicial or parliamentary interpretive authority; in particular, those advocating judicial supremacy here may take a very different position if the Court opposed their policy preference elsewhere. The SCC enjoys strong institutional legitimacy, and it is not unusual that some political actors will attempt to employ that as a resource for their own ends – especially institutions (such as the Senate) that possess less legitimacy.

Carter v. Canada (2015)

On 6 February 2015, the SCC ruled unanimously in *Carter v. Canada* that the Criminal Code prohibitions on assisted suicide in sections 14 and 241(b) were unconstitutional under section 7 of the Charter, which guarantees, "Everyone has the right to life, liberty, and security of the person and the right not to be deprived thereof except in accordance with the principles of fundamental justice."[32] The *Carter* decision effectively reversed the SCC's 1993 *Rodriguez v. B.C.* precedent, which had upheld these sections from a section 7 challenge despite the fact that neither the applicable Criminal Code provisions nor the text of section 7 had changed in the intervening twenty-two years. This fact emphasizes that it is the Court's interpretation of the constitution, rather than the constitution itself, that influenced the subsequent policymaking process for Bill C-14. The SCC declared the prohibition invalid, but suspended its declaration for one year to give Parliament time to adopt new legislation complying with the Charter. (For discussion of how the suspended declaration reduced judicial influence on Bill C-14, see Snow and Puddister, this volume.) In addition to the five plaintiffs – a doctor, the British Columbia Civil Liberties Association (BCCLA), an individual seeking assisted suicide, and two family members who were present during a physician-assisted death – the case attracted twenty-six third party interveners, including Dying with Dignity, the Canadian Medical Association (CMA), many religious organizations, and two provincial attorneys general.

The Court agreed with the plaintiffs that the ban on assisted suicide infringed all three of section 7's rights: "life" because the ban could force some individuals to end their own lives earlier than they wished, while still physically able to do so; "liberty" because the law prevented individuals from making medical decisions deeply entwined with their dignity, autonomy, and bodily integrity; and "security of the person" because the prohibition forced some individuals to "endure intolerable suffering."[33] The SCC ruled that these infringements were not consistent with the "principles of fundamental justice" in section 7 because the blanket prohibition was overbroad: specifically, that while the ban's objective – to protect the vulnerable from being pressured to end their lives – was legitimate, it could not justify preventing individuals who were *not* vulnerable from receiving MAID. Notably, the Court rejected the attorney general of Canada's argument that the prohibition's objective was the "preservation of life" (in addition to the protection of vulnerable people)[34] – an argument that had helped the five-judge majority uphold the law in *Rodriguez* – for being too imprecise. Under the section 1 "reasonable limits" test, the prohibition similarly failed for restricting rights more than necessary to achieve the law's objective. The Court based this conclusion, in large part, on the evidence from other countries that had legalized MAID since *Rodriguez*, which showed convincingly that legalization had not created a "slippery slope" towards ethically dubious assisted deaths.

In striking down sections 14 and 241(b), the Court urged Parliament and the provincial legislatures to respond, and it outlined the parameters for MAID eligibility based on what the justices argued the Charter required. Specifically, the SCC stated that a prohibition would be unconstitutional insofar as it prohibited "physician-assisted death for a competent adult person who (1) clearly consents to the termination of life and (2) has a grievous and irremediable medical condition (including an illness, disease or disability) that causes enduring suffering that is intolerable to the individual in the circumstances of his or her condition."[35] The Court further specified that "irremediable" did not "require the patient to undertake treatments that are not acceptable to the individual."[36] To protect the vulnerable, the SCC urged lawmakers to adopt "properly designed and administered safeguards," as were found elsewhere in the world,[37] and also pointed to existing medical practices for ensuring informed consent and decision-making capacity.[38] Finally, the Court warned that the Charter rights of patients and physicians (in particular, freedom of religion and conscience) would need to be reconciled.[39]

Overview of Bill C-14 Policy Process

The Conservative government was slow to respond to *Carter*, naming an external panel – two-thirds of whose members had been government witnesses in *Carter* and were known critics of MAID – only five months after the ruling to explore legislative options. After the election in October 2015, the new Liberal government retained the panel to conduct consultations, but removed its mandate to provide legislative options.[40] The government also petitioned the SCC on 3 December 2015 to extend its suspended remedy for another six months; the Court voted 5–4 in favour of a four-month extension, until 6 June 2016.[41]

In the meantime, the House and Senate formed the Special Joint Committee (SJC) on Physician-Assisted Dying. It heard from a wide range of advocacy groups and legal scholars, including Peter Hogg, and released its report on 25 February 2016.[42] The SJC's proposed eligibility criteria respected those articulated in *Carter*,[43] but also recommended access for both mature minors and individuals with mental illness who otherwise met those eligibility criteria. Further, the SJC suggested that advance requests for MAID should be available for individuals diagnosed with competence-eroding conditions.[44] (For public reaction, see Snow and Puddister, this volume.)

Justice Minister Jody Wilson-Raybould tabled Bill C-14 in the House of Commons on 14 April 2016, but did not adopt the SJC's recommendations.[45] Subsection 241.2(1) sets out the MAID eligibility criteria, which require that an individual must be eligible for Canadian public health services, be a minimum of eighteen years old, have a grievous and irremediable medical condition, have given a voluntary request, and have provided informed consent about MAID. While these criteria use much of the same language as the *Carter* ruling, paragraphs 241.2(2) (a), (b), and (d) consider an individual to have a grievous and irremediable medical condition only if they have a "serious and incurable illness, disease or disability"; are in an "advanced state of irreversible decline in capability"; and if their "natural death has become reasonably foreseeable" – the last a phrase left undefined. These restrictions differ starkly from the *Carter* ruling and the SJC's report. In its preamble, the bill committed to further study the issues of MAID access for mature minors, those with mental illness as their only medical condition, and those seeking advance requests. The justice minister subsequently issued a legislative backgrounder defending the bill.[46]

The House Standing Committee on Justice and Human Rights began its review of Bill C-14 on 2 May 2016. Given the Liberal majority on the committee, its final report rejected the substantive amendments to the bill proposed by opposition members, instead making primarily technical amendments.[47] After Bill-14 was accepted at report stage, Bill C-14 passed at third reading in the House of Commons on 31 May, with a vote of 186–137.[48] While Bill C-14 made its way through Parliament, two lower court rulings were delivered on eligibility for MAID: the Court of Appeal of Alberta in *Canada (Attorney General) v. E.F.* on 17 May[49] and Justice Perell of the Ontario Superior Court of Justice in *I.J. v. Canada (Attorney General)* on 24 May.[50] Both concluded that *Carter* was clear that "grievous and irremediable" did not mean "terminal," casting doubt on Bill C-14's constitutionality.

This mounting doubt informed the scrutiny of the bill in the Senate, which questioned the justice minister as a Committee of the Whole on 6 June 2016. On 8 June, the Senate voted 41–30 to adopt Senator Joyal's amendment to remove the restrictive definition of a "grievous and irremediable medical condition" contained in subsection 241.2(2), thus restoring the criteria from *Carter*.[51] On 13 June, Minister Wilson-Raybould replied with an addendum to the legislative backgrounder, defending the restrictions,[52] but on 15 June, the Senate voted 64–12 to adopt the amended bill at third reading.[53] The next day, the Liberal government replied with a motion in the House on which Senate amendments it would accept, most notably rejecting Senator Joyal's amendment to restore *Carter*'s eligibility criteria;[54] the motion passed 190–108.[55] The following day, the Senate backed down, voting 44–28 to accept the House's revised bill and to "not insist" on the Senate's rejected amendments.[56] Senator Joyal moved to force the House to suspend the paragraph containing the reasonable foreseeability requirement until the SCC had pronounced on its Charter compliance through a reference, but this was rejected 42–28.[57] With its restrictive eligibility criteria intact, the bill received royal assent on 17 June.

Carter's Impact on Bill C-14 Policy Process

This section maps the impact of *Carter* on Bill C-14's policy process by demonstrating how competing parliamentary factions and their interest group allies characterized the proper parliamentary-judicial relationship to promote their policy preferences on MAID. The focus is on how these factions' proposed eligibility criteria compare to those in *Carter*.

Judicial Supremacists

Those who supported wider access to MAID, in line with the SCC ruling, advocated strict adherence to *Carter* and judicial supremacy in constitutional interpretation. The SJC was a primary proponent of judicial supremacy, copying its proposed eligibility criteria from *Carter*, while adding that those with mental illness, mature minors, and those seeking advance requests should have access. Key champions of this view were its co-chairs, Conservative Senator Kelvin Ogilvie and Liberal MP Rob Oliphant, as well as New Democratic Party (NDP) MP Murray Rankin and Independent Liberal Senator Serge Joyal.

Liberal MP Rob Oliphant voiced his concerns about the terms "incurable" and "foreseeable death" found in subsection 241.2(2).[58] Following the rejection of the amendments to subsection 241.2(2) in the House committee, Oliphant announced that he would not support Bill C-14 given his belief that it was neither Charter- nor *Carter*-compliant.[59] Two other Liberal MPs – Nathaniel Erskine-Smith and Parliamentary Secretary David Lametti – joined Oliphant in opposing the bill at third reading due to concerns about the constitutionality of its restrictive eligibility criteria.[60] After the justice minister moved to reject Senator Joyal's amendment, Oliphant relented and supported her motion, while Erskine-Smith and Lametti opposed it.[61]

As the NDP's justice critic, Murray Rankin was also a key proponent of strict adherence to *Carter*. Rankin criticized the reasonable foreseeability requirement, insisting that Parliament must comply with both the Charter and *Carter*,[62] and he stated that it was unclear whether Kay Carter would have been eligible under C-14.[63] In committee, he unsuccessfully attempted to delete subsection 241.2(2),[64] and at report stage, he unsuccessfully moved to have the bill sent back to committee to ensure that the eligibility criteria complied with *Carter*.[65] After the justice minister motioned to reject Senator Joyal's amendment to delete subsection 241.2(2), Rankin unsuccessfully moved to instead accept the amendment.[66] Rankin's position on Bill C-14 was indicative of the sentiment among NDP MPs: all who were present at third reading voted against Bill C-14.[67] Similarly, Green Party and Bloc Québécois MPs unsuccessfully proposed amendments to align eligibility requirements with *Carter* and voted against C-14 at third reading.

A combination of forty-one Conservative, Independent Liberal, and Independent senators also favoured strict adherence to *Carter* when they voted for Senator Joyal's amendment to remove subsection 241.2(2) from the bill on 8 June.[68] Conservative Senator Kelvin Ogilvie challenged the reasonable foreseeability requirement, pointing out that the arguments in favour of such restrictions had been turned down in both *Carter* and *Canada v. E.F.*[69] Independent Liberal Senator Serge Joyal – a noted constitutional expert – argued that Bill C-14 was not Charter-compliant. He explained that the reasonable foreseeability requirement excluded a "whole class of people" based on perceived vulnerability, rather than creating an appropriate system of safeguards to protect the vulnerable.[70] Despite support from senators of all affiliations for adherence to *Carter*, the Senate ultimately conceded after the House rejected Joyal's amendment.

Various interest group allies also advocated for strict adherence to *Carter*'s eligibility criteria. Both the BCCLA and Dying with Dignity – the first a plaintiff in *Carter*, the second an intervener in favour of legalizing MAID in the case – opposed Bill C-14. They challenged the bill's constitutionality, and, in briefs submitted to the House committee, both recommended amendments to subsection 241.2(2) to restore the *Carter* criteria.[71] Indeed, all the organizations that intervened in favour of legalizing MAID in *Carter* and offered reactions to the bill shared the opinion that the bill must comply with the ruling.

Finally, many legal experts argued that the bill's eligibility criteria were unconstitutional because they did not comply with the SCC's ruling in *Carter*. They included representatives from the Barreau du Québec,[72] the Canadian Bar Association,[73] and Joseph Arvay, lead counsel in *Carter*. In support of his position, Arvay referenced an exchange between Justice Karakatsanis and federal government lawyer Rob Frater during *Carter II*, in which Karakatsanis had explicitly stated that the SCC rejected that an individual needed to be terminally ill to receive MAID in *Carter*, arguing that Parliament could not remove the rights given by the Court using a section 1 justification.[74] Peter Hogg, perhaps Canada's foremost constitutional scholar and advocate of the dialogue theory, similarly emphasized the SCC's statement in *Carter* that the legislation must follow the ruling's constitutional parameters. He explained that the bill should have addressed any gaps the *Carter* decision left, such as procedural safeguards, but that the SCC prohibited the use of section 1 to restrict the constitutional parameters.[75] Hogg recommended that a solution would be to take out the restrictive definition found in subsection 241.2(2). In short, Arvay and Hogg noted that it was inappropriate for Parliament to engage in dialogue with the courts over MAID eligibility using a section 1 justification, and they asserted that Parliament needed to heed the Court's interpretation of what the Charter required.

Coordinate Constructionists

Rather than allowing judicial supremacy, the Liberal government invoked the tenets of coordinate construction to advance its preference for more restrictive access. It defended subsection 241.2(2) by asserting that Parliament could legitimately engage in constitutional interpretation. The bill's preamble laid the groundwork by offering legislative objectives, including the need for robust safeguards, to avoid negative views of the "quality of life of persons who are elderly, ill or disabled"; to protect the vulnerable from being influenced into seeking MAID; and to acknowledge the negative effects of suicide on communities.[76] It further identified that these legislative objectives justified limiting MAID to competent adults who met the reasonable foreseeability requirement and struck "the most appropriate balance" between competing rights.[77]

At second reading, the justice minister argued that Gloria Taylor and Kay Carter would have been eligible under subsection 241.2(2). She then contended that Bill C-14's eligibility criteria complied with *Carter*, but that Parliament's legislative response was "never as simple as simply cutting and pasting the words from a court's judgment into a new law."[78] Rather, she indicated that there were always diverse legal opinions about how Parliament should respond to a Court ruling and that Parliament had "not only to respect the court's decision, but also to listen to diverse voices and decide what the public interest demands."[79]

At report stage, the justice minister contended, "The key takeaway is that *nobody has a monopoly on interpreting the charter*," reiterating that Parliament was responsible for passing a law that complied with the Charter.[80] As further indictments of the bill's constitutionality continued to come in from experts and lower courts, the minister reneged on her earlier reassurance that the bill complied with *Carter*, stating on 31 May that the law must "comply with the charter, but that *does not require replicating the Carter decision*."[81] She later expressed her opinion that the bill was "a *justifiable* response to the Carter decision."[82] She also explicitly referenced the dialogue metaphor, elaborating, "Just as Parliament must respect the court's ruling, so too must the court respect Parliament's determination of how to craft a statutory scheme in response to the court's judgment."[83] Indeed, she went so far as to predict that the courts would defer to this scheme.[84]

While the justice minister invoked dialogue theory to justify Bill C-14, what she more accurately advocated was coordinate construction. Contrary to her assertions, Bill C-14 does not simply use section 1 to rebalance competing rights and other interests, but attempts to restrict judicially articulated rights using arguments that the Court had already explicitly rejected in *Carter*: specifically, that protecting "the vulnerable" can justify blanket prohibitions for competent, suffering adults who voluntarily seek MAID. The Court made it clear that a system of safeguards that assessed individual requests was necessary in its view. As such, C-14 represents a challenge to judicial interpretive supremacy. This is also evident in the minister's argument that the courts did not have a "monopoly" over constitutional interpretation. The fact that the minister never explicitly identified her position with coordinate construction is not particularly surprising given its "unorthodox" position in Canadian constitutional thought, and her rhetorical use of the dialogue metaphor was most likely an attempt to garner greater legitimacy by employing a more recognized doctrine.

Despite the descriptive inaccuracy of the justice minister's appeal to dialogue theory, she continued to invoke the metaphor when she appeared before the Senate.[85] The Senate rejected this framing and her justification for C-14, and it passed Senator Joyal's amendment to restore *Carter*'s eligibility criteria. The minister subsequently released an addendum to the legislative backgrounder, replicating her justification from 31 May by emphasizing that "the question is not whether the Bill 'complies with *Carter*' but rather, whether it complies with the *Charter*," and repeating her argument that the courts did "not hold a monopoly" on rights protection.[86] She also reiterated her endorsement of institutional dialogue and referenced an example of successful parliamentary non-compliance with the SCC (in the *O'Connor-Mills* sequence[87]) as precedent. Like the minister, Professor Tom McMorrow used the *O'Connor-Mills* sequence as an example of the Court deferring to Parliament through dialogue to defend the bill.[88] Unlike *Carter* and Bill C-14, however, *O'Connor* was a divided (6–3) ruling, and the legislative reply complied with the minority opinion. Moreover, leading dialogue theorists Hogg and Roach reject the idea that the reply to *O'Connor* is an example of dialogue, and they criticize the Court for accepting Parliament's non-compliance in *Mills*.

The justice minister was thus the main proponent of coordinate construction, albeit cloaked in the language of dialogue. Aside from four Liberal MPs, all other Liberals present at third reading voted in favour of Bill C-14.[89] In doing so, they fell – implicitly or explicitly – in line with the justice minister's justification. While fourteen Conservative MPs voted in favour of Bill C-14 at third reading,[90] the available reasons for their votes showed little support for coordinate construction.[91] The Liberal government also had few interest group allies on Bill C-14. Indeed, the CMA seemed to be the only organization that supported the bill and certainly was among those that had intervened in *Carter*. While the CMA recommended the passage of Bill C-14 without any amendments,[92] it did not explicitly associate itself with a certain view of the proper parliamentary-judicial relationship.

Dialogue Theorists

Other legal experts defended C-14 by invoking the tenets of dialogue theory, as described above, rather than coordinate construction. Gerald D. Chipeur argued that Parliament "always has the final say" in this "dialogue with the courts," and that it was "likely that that court will respect your response in this dialogue."[93] Professor Dianne Pothier contended that subsection 241.2(2) of the bill was constitutional, given that it was consistent with section 7 or was otherwise reasonable under section 1. She held that to exclude that subsection would invite a Charter challenge to defend the rights of the vulnerable and that the only certain way to ensure that the bill was "Charter-proof" was to use the notwithstanding clause.[94]

Some parliamentarians opposed the bill as too permissive, suggesting the use of dialogic instruments such as the section 33 notwithstanding clause. A minority of Conservative MPs – including Michelle Rempel,[95] Todd Doherty,[96] Cathay Wagantall,[97] Bob Zimmer,[98] Brad Trost,[99] Candice Bergen,[100] Kelly Block,[101] James Bezan,[102] Bev Shipley,[103] and Harold Albrecht[104] – suggested using the notwithstanding clause as an option. Among the interest groups that had intervened in *Carter* to maintain the prohibition, the Catholic Civil Rights League appears to have been the only group, in its committee brief, to recommend using the notwithstanding clause.[105] The Association for Reformed Political Action also recommended that "Parliament can enact a complete prohibition on assisted suicide … by explicitly stating in a new law that the purpose of the prohibition is broader" than the original objective, but it implicitly relied on section 1 by arguing that Parliament could do so without using section 33.[106] For those interest groups with available responses, all that intervened in support of the prohibition in

Carter opposed Bill C-14 as too permissive. While remaining opposed to MAID, most groups realized that the *Carter* decision required the legalization of MAID, with several approving that the government had denied the SJC's recommendations or had restricted eligibility. Most also turned their attention to advocating for safeguards through the Vulnerable Persons Standard.[107]

Discussion and Conclusions

The impact of *Carter* was not, ultimately, to dictate MAID policy in Canada as the Liberal government unexpectedly – given Justin Trudeau's 2015 campaign pledge to respect the ruling – insisted on stricter eligibility requirements. Rather, the case shaped the discourse around MAID by policymakers by putting the issue of whether and how to comply with the Court's ruling – and thus the respective roles of the courts and Parliament in constitutional interpretation – at the centre of the debate. It is likely that the apparent adoption of coordinate constructionism by a sitting majority government – a Trudeau Liberal one, no less – was a consequence unanticipated by the Court's justices.

The longer-term impact of *Carter* remains to be seen. Further judicial involvement is virtually guaranteed as the BCCLA is, as of this writing, recruiting participants for a constitutional challenge to Bill C-14, and an eventual appeal to the SCC seems quite likely. These cases will help address (but possibly not resolve) the constitutional questions left unsettled by the events following *Carter* – in particular, does Parliament's clearer emphasis on deterring suicide and "protecting the vulnerable" justify stricter eligibility requirements, in the context of section 7's principles of fundamental justice and/or section 1's reasonable limits, by making the legislative means used to achieve those objectives less "overbroad"?

Finally, the response to *Carter* may hold important lessons for political decision makers seeking to resist judicial activism as it represents an unprecedented degree of not just policy non-compliance, but also rejection of judicial supremacy over constitutional interpretation. It was already clear that non-compliance was possible, from the experience in *Mills* as well as the responses to *Daviault* (rescinding the "drunkenness defence" for assault) and *Feeney* (restoring the rules regarding warrantless entry of homes by police).[108] But those were criminal process cases, in which Parliament responded to judicial changes to common law rules, not invalidations of legislation.[109] Moreover, those cases involved divided courts, and Parliament's responses complied with the views of the dissenting judges.

In contrast, *Carter* was decided unanimously, and the legislative response directly rejects the Court's interpretation of what the rights set out in section 7 require regarding MAID eligibility. Nor is the response to *Carter* analogous to that after *Morales*, when Parliament replied with a "textual retort," citing in the legislation the plain language of the constitution to challenge a novel judicial interpretation of that language.[110] With judicial challenges to C-14 looming, time will tell whether Parliament is able to assert a truly meaningful role for itself in constitutional interpretation. As Baker observes, inter-branch struggles over the power to interpret the constitution never truly end, and they are shaped at any given time by which side the public takes.[111] Between the public's strong demand for MAID and its considerable support for judicial interpretive authority, even popular governments asserting coordinate construction face an uphill battle.

NOTES

1 2015 SCC 5.

2 See Dennis Baker, *Not Quite Supreme: The Courts and Coordinate Constitutional Interpretation* (Montreal and Kingston: McGill-Queen's University Press, 2010).

3 See Peter W. Hogg and Allison A. Bushell, "The Charter Dialogue between Courts and Legislatures (or Perhaps the Charter of Rights Isn't Such a Bad Thing After All)," *Osgoode Hall Law Journal* 35 (1997): 75–124.

4 S.C. 2016, c. 3. For ease and space reasons, we will refer to this law as "Bill C-14" throughout.

5 C. Neal Tate and Torbjörn Vallinder, eds., *The Global Expansion of Judicial Power* (New York: New York University Press, 1995).

6 Troy Q. Riddell, "The Impact of Legal Mobilization and Judicial Decisions: The Case of Official Minority-Language Education Policy in Canada for Francophones outside Quebec," *Law and Society Review* 38, no. 3 (2004): 586. See also Michael McCann, "Reform Litigation on Trial," *Law and Social Inquiry* 17 (1992): 715–43; Michael McCann, *Rights at Work: Pay Equity Reform and the Politics of Legal Mobilization* (Chicago: University of Chicago Press, 1994); and Michael McCann, "Causal versus Constitutive Explanations (or, On the Difficulty of Being So Positive …)," *Law and Social Inquiry* 21, no. 2 (1996), 457–82.

7 Riddell, "The Impact of Legal Mobilization and Judicial Decisions," 586.
8 Baker, *Not Quite Supreme*, 5.
9 Beverley McLachlin, "The Judiciary's Distinctive Role in Our Constitutional Democracy," *Policy Options* 24, no. 8 (2003): 5.
10 Ibid., 7.
11 Beverley McLachlin, "Courts, Legislatures, and Executives in the Post-Charter Era," in *Judicial Power and Canadian Democracy*, ed. Paul Howe and Peter H. Russell (Montreal and Kingston: McGill-Queen's University Press, 2001), 68.
12 Ian Greene, Carl Baar, Peter McCormick, George Szablowski, and Martin Thomas, *Final Appeal: Decision-Making in Canadian Courts of Appeal* (Toronto: Lorimer, 1998); Lorne Sossin, "The Ambivalence of Executive Power in Canada," in *The Executive and Public Law: Power and Accountability in Comparative Perspective*, ed. Paul Craig and Adam Tomkins (Oxford: Oxford University Press, 2006), 52–88.
13 Chief Justice Antonio Lamer, quoted in Janice Tibbetts, "Politicians Duck Divisive Issues, Chief Justice Says," *National Post*, 12 July 1999, A1. For a fuller review of the arguments typically made in support of judicial interpretive supremacy, see Grant A. Huscroft, "'Thank God We're Here': Judicial Exclusivity in Charter Interpretation and Its Consequences," *Supreme Court Law Review* 25, no. 2D (2004): 241–67.
14 Alexander Bickel, *The Least Dangerous Branch: The Supreme Court at the Bar of Politics* (New York: Bobbs-Merrill, 1962).
15 E.g., Chief Justice Brian Dickson, quoted in Robert Sharpe and Kent Roach, *Brian Dickson: A Judge's Journey* (Toronto: University of Toronto Press, 2003), 380; Lorraine Eisenstat Weinrib, "The Activist Constitution," in *Judicial Power and Canadian Democracy*, ed. Paul Howe and Peter H. Russell (Montreal and Kingston: McGill-Queen's University Press, 2001), 80–6; Bertha Wilson, "We Didn't Volunteer," in *Judicial Power and Canadian Democracy*, ed. Paul Howe and Peter H. Russell (Montreal and Kingston: McGill-Queen's University Press, 2001), 73–9.
16 Janet L. Hiebert, *Charter Conflicts: What Is Parliament's Role?* (Montreal and Kingston: McGill-Queen's University Press, 2002), x.
17 Matthew A. Hennigar, "Expanding the 'Dialogue' Debate: Canadian Federal Government Responses to Lower Court Charter Decisions," *Canadian Journal of Political Science* 37, no. 1 (2004): 16–17.
18 Hiebert, *Charter Conflicts*; Brian Slattery, "A Theory of the Charter," *Osgoode Hall Law Journal* 25, no. 4 (1987): 707. Grant Huscroft makes a similar argument in "Constitutionalism from the Top Down," *Osgoode Hall Law Journal* 45, no. 1 (2007): 101.

19 Alexander Hamilton, James Madison, and John Jay, *The Federalist Papers* (1787–88), ed. Clinton Rossiter (New York: Penguin Books), nos. 47, 48, and 51. For a more contemporary articulation of US coordinate constructionism, see Mark Tushnet, *Taking the Constitution Away from the Courts* (Princeton, NJ: Princeton University Press, 1999).
20 E.g., Kent Roach, *The Supreme Court on Trial: Judicial Activism or Democratic Dialogue* (Toronto: Irwin Law, 2001).
21 Rainer Knopff and F.L. Morton, *Charter Politics* (Scarborough: Nelson Canada, 1992) characterizes the judicial supremacy approach as "oracular legalism"; Slattery, "A Theory of the Charter"; Baker, *Not Quite Supreme.*
22 Baker, *Not Quite Supreme*; Emmett Macfarlane, "Conceptual Precision and Parliamentary Systems of Rights: Disambiguating 'Dialogue,'" *Review of Constitutional Studies* 17, no. 2 (2012): 73–100.
23 Macfarlane, "Conceptual Precision and Parliamentary Systems of Rights."
24 Hogg and Bushell, "The Charter Dialogue between Courts and Legislatures."
25 Christopher P. Manfredi and James B. Kelly, "Six Degrees of Dialogue: A Response to Hogg and Bushell," *Osgoode Hall Law Journal* 37, no. 3 (1999): 513–27; F.L. Morton, "Dialogue or Monologue?," in *Judicial Power and Canadian Democracy*, ed. Paul Howe and Peter H. Russell (Montreal and Kingston: McGill-Queen's University Press, 2001): 111–17; Matthew A. Hennigar, "Expanding the 'Dialogue' Debate: Canadian Federal Government Responses to Lower Court Charter Decisions," *Canadian Journal of Political Science* 37, no. 1 (2004): 3–21; Christopher P. Manfredi, "The Day the Dialogue Died: A Comment on *Sauvé v. Canada*," *Osgoode Hall Law Journal* 45, no. 1 (2007): 105–23; Grant Huscroft, "Rationalizing Judicial Power: The Mischief of Dialogue Theory," in *Contested Constitutionalism: Reflections on the Canadian Charter of Rights and Freedoms*, ed. James B. Kelly and Christopher P. Manfredi (Vancouver: UBC Press, 2009); Emmett Macfarlane, "Dialogue or Compliance? Measuring Legislatures' Policy Responses to Court Rulings on Rights," *International Political Science Review* 34, no. 1 (January 2013): 39–56.
26 Roach, *The Supreme Court on Trial*, 249–50; Peter W. Hogg, Allison Bushell Thornton, and Wade K. Wright, "Charter Dialogue Revisited – Or 'Much Ado about Metaphors,'" *Osgoode Hall Law Journal* 45, no. 1 (2007): 31.
27 E.g., as detailed below, section 7 permits limitations on its rights to life, liberty, and security of the person if those limits are consistent with "the principles of fundamental justice." Internal limits can be found in many Charter rights, including section 15's equality rights ("Every individual is equal before and under the law and has the right to the equal protection and equal benefit of the law *without discrimination*"), section 8's right

against "*unreasonable* search and seizure," and section 9's "right not to be *arbitrarily* detained or imprisoned"; emphasis added.

28 Baker, *Not Quite Supreme*, 6; emphasis in original.
29 Ibid.; emphasis in original.
30 Hennigar, "Expanding the 'Dialogue' Debate," 8.
31 Ibid.; Roach, *The Supreme Court on Trial*, 239–46.
32 Section 14 says that no person may consent to death being inflicted on them, and section 241(b) says that everyone who aids or abets a person in committing suicide commits an indictable offence.
33 2015 SCC 5, at 9.
34 Factum of the Attorney General of Canada, Respondent, *Carter v. Canada*, Court File No. 35591, 4 July 2014, para. 4.
35 *Carter v. Canada* SCC 2015, para. 4.
36 Ibid., para. 127.
37 Ibid., para. 105.
38 Ibid., para. 27.
39 Ibid., para. 132.
40 Government of Canada, "Letter from Minister Wilson-Raybould and Minister Philpott to the External Panel on Options for a Legislative Response to *Carter v. Canada*," 14 November 2015, accessed 14 December 2015, http://news.gc.ca/web/article-en.do?nid=1020779.
41 *Carter v. Canada (Attorney General)* 2016 SCC 4 ["*Carter II*"].
42 House of Commons, Special Joint Committee on Physician-Assisted Dying, *Medical Assistance in Dying: A Patient-Centred Approach* (Ottawa: Speaker of the House of Commons, 2016).
43 Ibid., 3.
44 Ibid., 14–24.
45 Bill C-14: An Act to amend the Criminal Code and to make related amendments to other Acts (medical assistance in dying), 1st Reading, 14 April 2016, 42nd Parliament, 1st Session, http://www.parl.gc.ca/content/hoc/Bills/421/Government/C-14/C-14_1/C-14_1.PDF.
46 Government of Canada, *Legislative Background: Medical Assistance in Dying (Bill C-14)*, 2016, accessed 12 July 2016, http://www.justice.gc.ca/eng/rp-pr/other-autre/ad-am/ad-am.pdf.
47 House of Commons, Standing Committee on Justice and Human Rights, 42nd Parl., 1st Sess., Second Report: Bill C-14, An Act to amend the Criminal Code and to make related amendments to other Acts (medical assistance in dying), 2016, accessed 19 July 2016, http://www.parl.gc.ca/HousePublications/Publication.aspx?Language=e&Mode=1&Parl=42&Ses=1&DocId=8255777.

48 House of Commons, Vote Details: Vote No. 102, 42nd Parl., 1st Sess., Sitting no. 74, 16 June 2016, accessed 25 July 2016, http://www.parl.gc.ca/HouseChamberBusiness/ChamberVoteDetail.aspx?Language=E&Mode=1&Parl=42&Ses=1&FltrParl=42&FltrSes=1&Vote=102.
49 Court of Appeal of Alberta, *Canada (Attorney General) v. E.F.* 2016, ABCA 155.
50 Ontario Superior Court of Justice, *I.J. v. Canada (Attorney General)* 2016, ONSC 3380.
51 Senate, Debates of the Senate, 42nd Parl., 1st Sess., no. 45, 8 June 2016, accessed 24 July 2016, http://www.parl.gc.ca/Content/Sen/Chamber/421/Debates/pdf/045db_2016-06-08-e.pdf.
52 Government of Canada, "Legislative Background: Medical Assistance in Dying (Bill C-14) – Addendum," 15 July 2016, accessed 24 July 2016, http://www.justice.gc.ca/eng/rp-pr/other-autre/addend/index.html.
53 Senate, Debates of the Senate, 42nd Parl., 1st Sess., no. 50, 15 June 2016, accessed 24 July 2016, http://www.parl.gc.ca/Content/Sen/Chamber/421/Debates/pdf/050db_2016-06-15-e.pdf.
54 House of Commons, Debates, 42nd Parl., 1st Sess., vol. 148, no. 074, 16 June 2016, accessed 25 July 2016, http://www.parl.gc.ca/HousePublications/Publication.aspx?Language=E&Mode=1&Parl=42&Ses=1&DocId=8377402.
55 House of Commons, Vote Details: Vote No. 103, 42nd Parl., 1st Sess., Sitting no. 74, 16 June 2016, accessed 25 July 2016, http://www.parl.gc.ca/HouseChamberBusiness/ChamberVoteDetail.aspx?Language=E&Mode=1&Parl=42&Ses=1&FltrParl=42&FltrSes=1&Vote=103.
56 Senate, Debates of the Senate, 42nd Parl., 1st Sess., no. 52, 17 June 2016, accessed 25 July 2016, http://www.parl.gc.ca/Content/Sen/Chamber/421/Debates/pdf/052db_2016-06-17-e.pdf.
57 Ibid.
58 House of Commons, Debates, 42nd Parl., 1st Sess., vol. 148, no. 046, 2 May 2016, accessed 14 July 2016, http://www.parl.gc.ca/HousePublications/Publication.aspx?Language=E&Mode=1&Parl=42&Ses=1&DocId=8225684.
59 Joan Bryden, "Rob Oliphant, Liberal MP Who Co-chaired Assisted Dying Committee, Won't Support Bill," *Canadian Press*, 11 May 2016, accessed 19 July 2016, http://www.huffingtonpost.ca/2016/05/11/senators-told-they-re-last-hope-for-suffering-canadians-who-aren-t-near-death_n_9915392.html.
60 Cherise Seucharan, "Bill C-14: Some Liberal MPs Worry Assisted Dying Bill Isn't Constitutional," *Huffington Post*, 1 June 2016, accessed 21 July 2016, http://www.huffingtonpost.ca/2016/06/01/bill-c-14-liberals-assisted-dying-unconstitutional_n_10246820.html.

61 House of Commons, Vote Details: Vote No. 103.

62 House of Commons, Debates, 42nd Parl., 1st Sess., vol. 148, no. 045, 22 April 2016, accessed 14 July 2016, http://www.parl.gc.ca/HousePublications/Publication.aspx?Language=E&Mode=1&Parl=42&Ses=1&DocId=8218810.

63 House of Commons, Standing Committee on Justice and Human Rights, Evidence (Issue no. 010, 2 May 2016), 42nd Parl., 1st Sess., accessed 18 July 2016, http://www.parl.gc.ca/HousePublications/Publication.aspx?Language=e&Mode=1&Parl=42&Ses=1&DocId=8225950.

64 House of Commons, Standing Committee on Justice and Human Rights, Evidence (Issue no. 015, 9 May 2016), 42nd Parl., 1st Sess., accessed 18 July 2016, http://www.parl.gc.ca/HousePublications/Publication.aspx?Language=e&Mode=1&Parl=42&Ses=1&DocId=8251838.

65 House of Commons, Debates, 42nd Parl., 1st Sess., vol. 148, no. 057, 17 May 2016, accessed 19 July 2016, http://www.parl.gc.ca/HousePublications/Publication.aspx?Language=E&Mode=1&Parl=42&Ses=1&DocId=8284973.

66 House of Commons, Debates, 16 June 2016.

67 House of Commons, Vote Details: Vote No. 76, 42nd Parl., 1st Sess., Sitting no. 62, 31 May 2016, accessed 21 July 2016, http://www.parl.gc.ca/HouseChamberBusiness/ChamberVoteDetail.aspx?Language=E&Mode=1&Parl=42&Ses=1&FltrParl=42&FltrSes=1&Vote=76.

68 Senate, Debates of the Senate, 8 June 2016.

69 Senate, Debates of the Senate, 42nd Parl., 1st Sess., no. 41, 1 June 2016, accessed 22 July 2016, http://www.parl.gc.ca/Content/Sen/Chamber/421/Debates/pdf/041db_2016-06-01-e.pdf.

70 Ibid.

71 British Columbia Civil Liberties Association, "This Bill Does Not Respect the *Carter* Decision and Must Be Amended," 5 May 2016, accessed 15 September 2016, http://www.parl.gc.ca/Content/HOC/Committee/421/JUST/Brief/BR8279666/br-external/BritishColumbiaCivilLibertiesAssociation-e.pdf; Dying with Dignity Canada, "Dying with Dignity Canada's Submission to the House Standing Committee on Justice and Human Rights – Brief on Bill C-14," 2 May 2016, accessed 11 July 2016, http://www.parl.gc.ca/Content/HOC/Committee/421/JUST/Brief/BR8300568/br-external/DyingWithDignityCanada-e.pdf.

72 House of Commons, Standing Committee on Justice and Human Rights, 2 May 2016.

73 Canadian Bar Association, "Re: Bill C-14 – Medical Assistance in Dying," 4 May 2016, accessed 20 July 2016, http://www.parl.gc.ca/

content/sen/committee/421/LCJC/Briefs/LCJC_May10,2016_SubmissionCdnBarAssc_e.pdf.

74 House of Commons, Standing Committee on Justice and Human Rights, Evidence (Issue no. 014, 5 May 2016), 42nd Parl., 1st Sess., accessed 20 July 2016, http://www.parl.gc.ca/HousePublications/Publication.aspx?Language=e&Mode=1&Parl=42&Ses=1&DocId=8243908.

75 Senate, Standing Committee on Legal and Constitutional Affairs, Minutes of Proceedings (6 June 2016), 42nd Parl., 1st Sess., accessed 24 July 2016, http://www.parl.gc.ca/Content/SEN/Committee/421/lcjc/52666-e.htm?Language=E&Parl=42&Ses=1&comm_id=11.

76 Bill C-14.

77 Ibid.

78 House of Commons, Debates, 22 April 2016.

79 Ibid.

80 House of Commons, Debates, 42nd Parl., 1st Sess., vol. 148, no. 055, 13 May 2016, accessed 19 July 2016, http://www.parl.gc.ca/HousePublications/Publication.aspx?Language=E&Mode=1&Parl=42&Ses=1&DocId=8263399; emphasis added.

81 House of Commons, Debates, 42nd Parl., 1st Sess., vol. 148, no. 062, 31 May 2016, accessed 19 July 2016, http://www.parl.gc.ca/HousePublications/Publication.aspx?Language=E&Mode=1&Parl=42&Ses=1&DocId=8310832; emphasis added.

82 Ibid.; emphasis added.

83 Ibid.

84 Ibid.

85 Senate, Debates of the Senate, 1 June 2016.

86 Government of Canada, "Legislative Background – Addendum."

87 *R. v. O'Connor* (1995), 4 SCR 411; *R. v. Mills* (1999), 3 SCR 668. The cases concerned the rules for disclosure of third party evidence (including the complainant's medical and therapeutic records) to the accused in sexual assault cases.

88 Senate, Standing Committee on Legal and Constitutional Affairs, 6 June 2016.

89 Liberal MPs Erskine-Smith, Lametti, and Oliphant voted against Bill C-14 because it was too restrictive, while Liberal MP Robert-Falcon Ouellette voted against it because it permitted MAID; House of Commons, Vote Details: Vote No. 76.

90 Ibid.

91 Common reasons included fear of a legal vacuum or the use of *Carter*'s more permissive eligibility criteria if Bill C-14 did not pass, personal experiences with grievous medical conditions, and constituents' support for the bill.

92 House of Commons, Standing Committee on Justice and Human Rights, Evidence (Issue no. 013, 4 May 2016), 42nd Parl., 1st Sess., accessed 15 September 2016, http://www.parl.gc.ca/HousePublications/Publication.aspx?Language=e&Mode=1&Parl=42&Ses=1&DocId=8237876.

93 Senate, Standing Committee on Legal and Constitutional Affairs, 6 June 2016.

94 House of Commons, Standing Committee on Justice and Human Rights, 4 May 2016. In her statement, Professor Pothier referenced paragraphs 241.1(2)(b) and (d), but she was actually referring to these paragraphs in subsection 241.2(2).

95 House of Commons, Debates, 2 May 2016.

96 Ibid.

97 House of Commons, Debates, 42nd Parl., 1st Sess., vol. 148, no. 047, 3 May 2016, accessed 18 July 2016, http://www.parl.gc.ca/HousePublications/Publication.aspx?Language=E&Mode=1&Parl=42&Ses=1&DocId=8230111.

98 Ibid.

99 Ibid.

100 Ibid.

101 House of Commons, Debates, 31 May 2016.

102 Ibid.

103 House of Commons, Debates, 42nd Parl., 1st Sess., vol. 148, no. 068, 8 June 2016, accessed 15 September 2016, http://www.parl.gc.ca/HousePublications/Publication.aspx?Language=E&Mode=1&Parl=42&Ses=1&DocId=8343299.

104 House of Commons, Debates, 16 June 2016.

105 Catholic Civil Rights League, "The Standing Committee on Justice and Human Rights," press release, 2 May 2016, accessed 11 July 2016, http://www.parl.gc.ca/Content/HOC/Committee/421/JUST/Brief/BR8300467/br-external/CatholicCivilRightsLeague-Updated-e.pdf.

106 Association for Reformed Political Action Canada, "Re: Bill C-14," 29 April 2016, accessed 11 July 2016, http://www.parl.gc.ca/Content/HOC/Committee/421/JUST/Brief/BR8235576/br-external/AssociationForReformedPoliticalAction-e.pdf.

107 Vulnerable Persons Standard, "Introducing the Vulnerable Persons Standard," 2016, accessed 11 July 2016, http://www.vps-npv.ca/readthestandard.

108 *R. v. Daviault* (1994), 3 SCR 63; *R. v. Feeney* (1997), 2 SCR 13. For more information on these cases, see Hiebert, *Charter Conflicts*, and James B. Kelly and Matthew A. Hennigar, "The Canadian Charter of Rights

and the Minister of Justice: Weak-Form Review within a Constitutional Charter of Rights," *International Journal of Constitutional Law* 10, no. 1 (2012): 35–68.

109 Some have argued that the Conservative government's legislative reply to *Bedford* on prostitution was also an example of non-compliance, but this is not as clear as the reply to *Carter*. After *Bedford*, Parliament adopted a new regulatory approach by criminalizing the *buying* of sex and prosecuting pimps and johns. Some argue that this sidestepped the Court's core concern in *Bedford* of making sex workers safer, but the new law exempts sex workers from prosecution and adopts the Court's legalization of brothels and security staff for sex workers.

110 *R. v. Morales* (1992), 3 SCR 711. The Court narrowly accepted that response in *R. v. Hall* (2002), 3 SCR 309, while refusing to explicitly endorse the tenets of coordinate construction; see Baker, *Not Quite Supreme*, 29–38.

111 Baker, *Not Quite Supreme*, 150–2.

16 Canadian Abortion Policy and the Limitations of Litigation

RACHAEL JOHNSTONE

This chapter explores the evolution of abortion policy in Canada from the *R. v. Morgentaler* (1988) decision to the present. Focusing on the interpretation of the Canadian Charter of Rights and Freedoms by judges in this and related cases, I evaluate the role of the courts and politicians in producing the abortion policies currently in place across the country. In so doing, I aim to show that the courts were instrumental in striking down Canada's abortion law and subsequently informing the parameters of provincial policies. However, the nature of reforms made possible by litigation thus far has been limited, and it has also potentially helped provincial governments avoid their rights obligations. To date, judges have largely kept their rulings concerning abortion within a negative rights reading of the Charter, and governments have used the reality of legal intervention in provincial abortion regulations to avoid engaging with the rights dimensions of their policies outside court. In a few cases, when governments have amended their regulations on abortion without pressure from the courts, these changes were clearly made in anticipation of judicial intervention.

The result has been a kind of limbo for abortion rights. Although abortion is often acknowledged as a rights issue, neither the courts nor governments have made any definitive declaration regarding its significance to women's Charter rights. The provinces maintain jurisdiction over abortion so long as it is a health procedure, and even when their regulation of the procedure lacks grounding as a health issue, they seem reticent to see abortion reclassified in a way that would remove this power. Thus, while politicians may talk about abortion as a rights issue, and acknowledge their Charter obligations, they continue to regulate it as a matter of health policy. As a result, unsettled constitutional issues at the heart of this issue remain. Chief among them is whether abortion will be recognized as an equality right by the Supreme Court or the federal government. To date, the unwillingness of most governments to engage openly with their Charter obligations, as they relate to abortion, suggests that such recognition is unlikely.

To advance these claims, I consider a number of landmark court cases, including *R. v. Morgentaler* (1988), *Tremblay v. Daigle* (1989), *and R. v. Morgentaler* (1993), alongside the most notable policy responses from the provinces. Only through careful consideration of the interactions between the courts and governments in these cases do the origins of provincial policy become clear. For instance, the failure of the Mulroney government to institute a new abortion law in the wake of the 1988 *Morgentaler* decision came, no doubt, as a surprise to the Court. In the policy vacuum that followed, provincial governments took steps to develop their own policies to regulate abortion, keeping to justifications related to health to solidify their jurisdiction, but many of these were subsequently challenged in court cases.

The Court's clear expectation that the federal government would enact a new law to replace the impugned law, and the reality that the case in question turned on the constitutionality of a federal statute, meant that it did not offer any clear policy prescriptions for the provinces. Although subsequent decisions helped clarify the constitutional obligations of the provinces, these cases were themselves fraught. Many provincial governments adopted strategies of avoidance concerning litigation, either drawing out cases or amending their policies so that the substance of rights claims could not be heard. The result is a patchwork of policies across Canada that has persisted for nearly three decades.

These policies were not guided by the Court, which did not anticipate the need for provincial policy guidance. Attempts to create policies on abortion were further hampered by the uniqueness of the decriminalization of abortion in Canada in the global context, coupled with the absence, at least initially, of any jurisprudence on the regulation of the procedure. Most provinces responded by restricting access, ostensibly, where justifications were offered, with the goal of protecting women's health or safeguarding access to health care more generally.[1] The reality of these policies, however, is that they relied on assumptions of the moral impermissibility of abortion, and, following a series of provincial court cases, they were slowly struck down, although typically on jurisdictional grounds. Today, in spite of these challenges, variance in access continues to reflect the values that specific provinces hold, albeit subject to certain strictures of the courts.

The Morgentaler Decision (1988)

Although it was not Henry Morgentaler's first challenge to Canada's abortion law, or even his first appearance in the Supreme Court, the landmark decision in *R. v. Morgentaler* (1988) was by far the most significant for its reach and impact. The ruling resulted in major policy changes concerning the regulation of abortion access in Canada, in conjunction with the federal government's response to the case. The 1988 *Morgentaler* case concerned the constitutionality of section 251 of the Criminal Code, which allowed for legal abortions only when the procedure had first been approved by a therapeutic abortion committee. Morgentaler successfully challenged the law on the grounds that it violated women's Charter rights to life, liberty, and security of the person, but the Mulroney government's struggle to implement a new law greatly amplified the significance of the case's implications.

The case began in Ontario following a 1983 raid on the abortion clinic of Drs Henry Morgentaler, Leslie Smoling, and Robert Scott, which was operating illegally in Toronto. Although they were acquitted when the jury refused to convict them, the Ontario attorney general appealed the verdict. The Court of Appeal ordered a retrial, and the physicians in the case would eventually appeal the decision all the way to the Supreme Court, where they challenged the constitutionality of Canada's abortion law on the grounds that it violated women's section 7 Charter rights to life, liberty, and security of the person.

The ruling was split 5–2 in favour of overturning section 251 of the Criminal Code on the grounds that it violated women's section 7 rights.[2] Chief Justice Brian Dickson and Justice Antonio Lamer famously wrote that "forcing a woman, by threat of criminal sanction, to carry a foetus to term unless she meets certain criteria unrelated to her own priorities and aspirations, is a profound interference with a woman's body and thus a violation of security of the person."[3] It was Justice Bertha Wilson's ruling, however, that made the most definitive statement regarding this violation, calling the decision to have an abortion

> one that will have profound psychological, economic and social consequences for the pregnant woman. The circumstances giving rise to it can be complex and varied and there may be, and usually are, powerful

> considerations militating in opposite directions. It is a decision that deeply reflects the way the woman thinks about herself and her relationship to others and to society at large. It is not just a medical decision; it is a profound social and ethical one as well. Her response to it will be the response of the whole person.[4]

Conspicuously the only woman on the Court, Wilson's ruling came the closest to suggesting the existence of a right to abortion access. Even so, her ruling allowed for the state to potentially limit women's access to abortion, which the Mulroney government promptly attempted to do.

Despite having a comfortable majority in the House, Brian Mulroney's Progressive Conservative government faced significant obstacles in its attempt to create a new law. The caucus was divided on the issue, with the pro-choice supporters concerned about creating new restrictions on the procedure and the anti-abortion supporters vying to tighten restrictions on abortion beyond those created by section 251. Attempts to reach a compromise in the caucus failed as a new case, one that would test the boundaries of *Morgentaler*, made its way to the Supreme Court.

In the aftermath of the *Morgentaler* decision, several men attempted to stop their pregnant partners from accessing legal abortion services.[5] One of these cases progressed all the way to the Supreme Court, in which the Court was asked to consider whether a fetus had a right to life. In *Tremblay v. Daigle* (1989), Jean-Guy Tremblay took out an injunction against his ex-girlfriend, Chantal Daigle, to prevent her from having an abortion. Both parties were residents of Quebec, and the case turned on Tremblay's contention that "under Quebec law a foetus has a right to life and a potential father has a right of veto over a woman's decision to have an abortion."[6] Before reaching the Supreme Court, Tremblay had already been successful in the Quebec lower and appeal courts, which had held that "a foetus is a 'human being' under the Quebec *Charter of Human Rights and Freedoms* and therefore enjoys a 'right to life' under s. 1."[7]

By the time the case reached the Supreme Court, Daigle had already travelled to the United States to terminate her pregnancy, but the Court opted to rule on the case anyway, to "resolve the important legal issue raised so that the situation of women in the position in which Ms. Daigle found herself could be clarified."[8] In the end, the Court overturned the lower court rulings, noting that the Quebec Charter did not "display any clear intention on the part of its framers to consider the status of a foetus."[9] The decision found that the fetus had no legal status in Canada, although, much like the *Morgentaler* decision that preceded it, it left room for the government to create fetal-rights protections if it so chose.[10]

Feeling increased pressure to regulate abortion in the wake of the Court's most recent decision, the Mulroney government attempted to pass a new bill. Bill C-43, which would recriminalize abortion, with exceptions to protect physicians if they found that a woman's health was at risk, was presented to the House in November 1989.[11] Unsurprisingly, the bill failed to please the various factions within the party. Nonetheless, the government narrowly succeeded in pushing the bill through the House, but was met with new opposition in the Senate.

Feeling significant pressure from physicians, many of whom were already refusing to provide abortion services to protest the threat of criminal sanction should Bill C-43 be passed, senators began to question the impact of the bill. When it came to a vote in January 1991, the Senate was still divided and produced a stalemate with a vote of 43–43.[12] A tie vote in the Senate constitutes a loss, making Bill C-43 "the first government bill that the Senate had defeated in thirty years."[13]

In the aftermath of this failed vote, the Mulroney government did not attempt to resurrect the bill, and neither have any subsequent governments. Little political will exists to draft legislation addressing a subject that is so divisive.[14] In the absence of a new law, abortion was classified as a health care issue, and primary responsibility for the provision of abortion services fell to the provinces. However, the Supreme Court, in dealing explicitly with an impugned section of the Criminal Code – a federal statute – and anticipating that the federal government would successfully usher in new legislation, did not make any policy prescriptions relating to the regulation of abortion as a health issue. Without this guidance, the provinces took a variety of approaches to the regulation of abortion access, with some effectively attempting to recriminalize the procedure by creating substantive barriers to access.

Although the patchwork of abortion services available in Canada today differs significantly from the spectrum of access available in the immediate aftermath of the *Morgentaler* decision, with access across the provinces considerably improved, variance in access persists. The changes to access that have occurred since 1988 have overwhelmingly been the result of litigation or threats of litigation. In the following section, I detail some of the most significant cases and the policy responses to them.

I discuss five cases as they unfolded in Nova Scotia, New Brunswick, Prince Edward Island, Quebec, and Manitoba. Although the government responses in each case vary, from commitments by the legislature to recognize women's rights to abortion access in Quebec to the shift from impossible restrictions to nearly impossible-to-negotiate barriers in Prince Edward Island, each of these cases has resulted in changes to abortion access in its respective province. Although, for some, these cases demonstrate the continued utility of litigation as a means of improving access across Canada, I believe they also provide a cautionary tale about the limitations of litigation.

Access in the Provinces

Nova Scotia

One of the most significant cases concerning the regulation of abortion to follow the *Morgentaler* decision has its roots in Nova Scotia. In 1989, the government of Nova Scotia prohibited the performance of abortion anywhere except in approved hospital facilities through its Medical Services Act.[15] This amendment to the act was not limited to abortion services; indeed, its stated purpose was the prohibition of certain privatized services "in order to maintain a single high-quality health-care delivery system."[16] That said, the timing of the amendment suggested that the motivation for its implementation was a desire to restrict access to the procedure using the provinces' new authority over access.

It is perhaps not surprising, then, that shortly after opening an abortion clinic in Halifax, Morgentaler was charged for violating the act, and the Nova Scotia attorney general secured an injunction to prevent him from performing more procedures at his clinic.[17] In response, Morgentaler challenged the constitutionality of the charges laid against him and was acquitted on the grounds that "the legislation was *ultra vires* the province because it was in pith and substance criminal law."[18] The case was appealed to the Supreme Court, which in 1993 upheld the lower court's verdict, calling the amendment an "indivisible attempt by the province to legislate in the area of criminal law."[19] However, the Court chose to limit its ruling to concerns relating to federalism and the distribution of powers, and it did not pronounce on Morgentaler's argument that the Nova Scotia law violated women's sections 7 (life, liberty, and security of the person) and 15 (equality) Charter rights.

In this case, the province fought Morgentaler on its regulation all the way to the Supreme Court, only removing the regulation after it was found unconstitutional. However, even after this move, the province did not address the claims Morgentaler had raised about the regulation's violation of women's Charter rights, and the larger conversation about the relationship between abortion and women's rights that Morgentaler was attempting to start was effectively stifled.[20] Even so, attempts to prevent doctors from performing clinic abortions was a tactic adopted by other provinces in the wake of the 1993 ruling.

New Brunswick

In 1994, Morgentaler opened an abortion clinic in Fredericton, but it had barely opened its doors before the New Brunswick government shut it down. The government cited the clinic's violation of the provincial Medical Act, which stipulated that "physicians could be found guilty of professional misconduct if they were involved in performing an abortion elsewhere than in a hospital approved by the Minister of Health."[21] Notably, an amendment to the Medical Act, which would have penalized a physician for performing an abortion outside a hospital, had been enacted when abortion was still regulated under the Criminal Code, and, importantly for Morgentaler, had been created with the express goal of preventing him from establishing a clinic. The court found the amendment unconstitutional on the grounds that it had been designed to "prohibit the establishment of free-standing abortion clinics and, particularly, the establishment of such a clinic by Dr. Morgentaler" rather than to safeguard women's health.[22] The amendment was removed, and the Morgentaler clinic was able to reopen, but the battle for access in the province was by no means at an end.

Although one problematic regulation was off the books, Morgentaler's victory did not address the regulations still in place in the province's Medical Services Payment Act, and neither did it seem to spark any debate on the government's restrictions in New Brunswick's legislature. Indeed, Regulation 84-20 of the Medical Services Payment Act continued to limit payment for abortion services to procedures performed in a registered hospital by an obstetrician or gynaecologist, but only after two physicians had deemed, in writing, that a procedure was medically necessary. These regulations remained firmly in place after Morgentaler's 1994 legal victory, but would bring him back to court less than a decade later.

In July 2003, Morgentaler sued the New Brunswick government, challenging the funding restrictions laid out in Regulation 84-20. Specifically, he argued that the regulation was unconstitutional for its violation of sections 7 and 15 of the Charter and its contravention of the Canada Health Act.[23] Like his previous challenge in Nova Scotia, this case was structured around claims to Charter rights, an area that the government seemed anxious to avoid.

It is important at this point to mention that many judges have also been somewhat reluctant to recognize Charter rights claims if they take on a positive character, and for good reason. Emmett Macfarlane explains that "basic principles of accountability and legitimacy suggest that decision-makers like justices are properly reluctant to impose major spending commitments on governments," something that a recognition of abortion, as necessary for women's equality, would certainly entail.[24] After all, judges are appointed, and they lack the democratic legitimacy to pronounce on how tax dollars should be allocated. Although a positive rights pronouncement is by no means out of the question,[25] litigation is unlikely to result in the kind of substantive changes necessary for women to achieve recognition of a positive right to abortion care, particularly given the widespread need for services and the costs associated with creating and preserving access.

Unfortunately, the substance of Morgentaler's claims was heard neither in court nor by the legislature. In 2004, a coalition of anti-abortion groups joined forces to apply for intervener status in the case, but this was subsequently denied. The groups appealed the decision in 2005, but were once again unsuccessful.[26] In 2007, the government challenged Morgentaler's standing to bring the case forward. Although Morgentaler acknowledged that, in Justice Garnett's words, "there are persons who are more directly affected by the legislation than he," he argued that "these persons for a variety of reasons are unlikely or unable to challenge it."[27] For these reasons, Morgentaler applied for, and was granted, public interest standing to bring the case forward. As with the activist groups mentioned earlier, the government appealed the decision to grant Morgentaler standing in 2009, but it was upheld.[28] Following half a decade of delays, Morgentaler stopped pursing the case, likely due to his deteriorating health. A few short years later, in May 2013, Morgentaler passed away at the age of ninety from a heart attack, and the case was later officially dropped.[29]

Despite the government's boasts leading up to Morgentaler's filing that its policies were constitutional and that it would willingly defend them "as far as the Supreme Court of Canada,"[30] it went to great lengths to avoid engaging with Morgentaler's claims. Interestingly, although Regulation 84-20 is still in effect in the province, it was eventually amended in 2014 by the province's newly elected Liberal government under Brian Gallant. Although the hospital requirement is still in effect, as of 1 January 2016, the procedure no longer requires approval from two physicians, and it does not need to be performed by a specialist. These changes were brought about in response to a concerted campaign to repeal the restrictions on abortion access by a local activist group, Reproductive Justice New Brunswick. This change was one of very few in the country since 1988 that came about because of activism rather than threats of legal action. Although this fact is, itself, worth celebrating, the change did not abolish Regulation 84-20 and did not substantively engage with issues of women's rights in the legislature or the courts.

In a statement following the regulation change, Gallant acknowledged that, "as a province, we have a responsibility to respect women's rights and our legal obligations by providing this procedure in a safe environment like any other insured service under Medicare."[31] However, this justification did not address the reason for limiting funding to the only abortion clinic in the province, where a majority of the abortions in the province had been performed in the years leading up to the regulatory change, and neither did the change necessitate a discussion of abortion rights in the legislature.

Prince Edward Island

In *Morgentaler v. Prince Edward Island (Minister of Health and Social Services)* (1995), Morgentaler challenged the constitutionality of the province's restrictive abortion policy. At the time, before a woman could gain access to an abortion in the province, she first had to have her request approved by a medical advisory committee of five physicians, and then she could have the procedure performed at a hospital.[32] Morgentaler won his case, but the ruling was promptly overturned in a split decision on appeal. The appeal decision turned on the authority of the government to create policies regulating the funding of medical procedures on the Island. Interestingly, as Morgentaler began the process of appealing this ruling, the government amended its policies to avoid further appeals. Under the new policy, women in the province could be referred to the Queen Elizabeth II (QEII) hospital in Halifax to access abortion care, but only in very select circumstances. To qualify, "women needed a PEI physician to provide a referral to a physician at the QEII hospital. They also needed to be less than fifteen weeks pregnant, have had an ultrasound, and not have had a previous referral for an abortion."[33] This policy change continued to keep the performance of abortions off the Island for many years to come.

It was only in 2016 that a relatively new activist group, Abortion Access Now PEI, announced its intention to challenge the government's latest policy in court. It cited a lack of government engagement with the issue of abortion access as motivating the action, noting, "It is clear to us that nothing short of a court order will prompt the government to comply with its obligations to PEI residents under the Charter of Rights and Freedoms."[34] In a surprise move, in response to the announcement, Premier Wade MacLauchlan acknowledged that "the province likely wouldn't have been able to successfully defend itself against that suit" as "a provincial abortion rights policy – like the one P.E.I. has – is contrary to the Canadian Charter of Rights and Freedoms."[35] Instead of fighting the case, the premier moved to create a new reproductive health centre in the province that would supply abortion services. This admission, and change in policy, has brought abortion services to the Island for the first time in over thirty years, but it still falls short of any acknowledgment of the right to abortion. Although the premier accepted the problems with the existing policies from a rights perspective, this acknowledgment was not followed by recognition of what access must look like for women's rights to be respected or even what Charter rights he thought were being violated.

Quebec

Quebec's response to the *Morgentaler* decision was markedly different than that of other provinces since the procedure had been de facto legalized in 1976 following a series of provincial court cases. Indeed, abortion care was already available in provincial hospitals and some community health centres, and some coverage was also available in clinics and the Centre de santé des femmes de Montréal (CSFM), although it and the clinics charged non-refundable fees "ranging from $40 to $350."[36] These fees resulted from a funding arrangement between the Quebec Department of Health and the Federation of General Practitioners of Quebec, by which "fees of doctors practising in private clinics were reduced by 75% after they performed a certain number of abortions."[37] Without these fees, these clinics would likely have had to close. Moreover, a significant proportion of women in the province accessed services from these offices, likely because of the significant wait times for care in hospitals.[38] In response to growing concerns about the cost of abortion care, the Association pour l'accès à l'avortement filed a class action lawsuit against the government, asking it to "reimburse women who had paid for an abortion from 1999 to 2005."[39]

The province lost the case and was required to reimburse women who had accessed care at either a clinic or the CSFM within that nine-year span. This repayment would amount to $13 million, although most of the women who had used these services did not collect their reimbursements.[40] The government did not appeal the ruling and took steps to ensure that a similar case would not be raised again. The Ministry of Health and Social Services worked to grow "the public system's capacity to meet the demand for abortion," while the Montreal Health and Social Services Agency "had been mandated to negotiate an agreement with medical clinics and with the CSFM so that they could offer their abortion services for free."[41] As a result of these efforts, women in Quebec have had access to free abortion care since 2008 – in hospitals, health centres, and clinics.[42] Quebec was also the first province to agree to fund a new abortion pill in Canada under its provincial drug plan[43] and the only province to call out the federal government, under Stephen Harper, for its anti-abortion policies. Specifically, in response to the federal government's decision not to fund abortion as part of its maternal health initiative for developing countries, the Quebec government put forward a motion that read,

> THAT the National Assembly reaffirms the rights of women to freedom of choice and to free and accessible abortion services and asks the federal Government and the Prime Minister of Canada to put an end to the ambiguity that persists in relation to this question; and that the National Assembly reaffirms the fact of supporting the rights of women to an abortion must in no way be adduced by the federal Government as a reason to cut subsidies to women's groups.[44]

Manitoba

Doe et al. v. The Government of Manitoba (2004) is another standout case, but this time due to the decision itself rather than the governmental response to it. The case was brought forward by two women, known to the Supreme Court as Jane Doe 1 and Jane Doe 2, who were challenging a provincial regulation that excluded abortion care provided in clinics from its list of insured services. Both women had paid out of pocket to obtain an abortion at the Morgentaler Clinic after being informed that they would face significant delays if they wished to have the procedure at their local Winnipeg hospital.[45] Both women feared the "severe emotional stress and increased physical risk" of delaying the procedure, and they chose to pay to have it done at the clinic, which was exempt from public funding by virtue of regulations in the Health Services Insurance Act.[46] In their case, they claimed that these regulations were in violation of the Charter, and the judge agreed. Justice Oliphant's ruling clearly stated that the relevant sections of the act

> are of no force and effect insofar as they pertain to therapeutic abortions because they are in violation of the rights and freedoms as guaranteed by sections 2(a), 7 and 15 of the Charter and do not constitute a reasonable and demonstrably justified limit on those rights and freedoms within the meaning of s. 1 of the Charter.[47]

This case was subsequently set aside on appeal as not "an appropriate case for summary judgment."[48]

Even though the case was set aside on appeal, it set an important precedent as the only ruling concerning abortion in a provincial or federal court to recognize restrictions on abortion access as violating women's Charter rights to equality. Indeed, Justice Oliphant called the government's policies "a gross violation of the rights guaranteed to both Jane Doe 1 and Jane Doe 2 by the Charter."[49] Even though this case did not progress to the Supreme Court, or force any policy change, the government of Manitoba began to fund clinic abortions before the 2004 ruling came down. On 1 July 2004, "the Winnipeg Regional Health Authority began to pay for abortions at Jane's Clinic, formerly the Morgentaler clinic,"[50] before the provincial government formally amended the regulation in November 2005.[51] In so doing, however, the government was clear that "it was under no legal obligation to do so."[52]

This sentiment seems to have become the norm in provincial politics since *Morgentaler* because the provinces have taken the approach that interpreting the Charter, and taking seriously the spirit of the rights it outlines, is better left to the courts. Moreover, absent any kind of legal intervention, it is generally assumed that provincial policies are constitutional. This attitude towards the Charter has left women who have struggled to access abortion care, advocacy groups, and physicians to fight for access to a service necessary for women's equality.

The Limitations of Litigation

The above cases were some of the most influential in shaping abortion access in Canada. Cumulatively, they demonstrate that the courts played a key role in the development of abortion policy across Canada, even when they did not influence policy directly. In most instances, cases were brought forward that challenged existing provincial regulations, and the relevant regulations were struck down or amended. In a few more recent cases, governments acted pre-emptively to alter problematic regulations in anticipation of drawn-out legal battles. Since litigation has been a successful catalyst for amendments to government regulations limiting access to abortion care, it is still widely seen as the best (if not the only successful) means by which to push for positive change to the regulation of abortion. Despite the successes of this approach, however, it has significant problems.

First, after the 1988 *Morgentaler* decision normalized litigation as a pathway to change, it also normalized government inaction on abortion regulation. In the wake of the decision, questions concerning rights have been increasingly seen as the domain of the courts rather than legislatures, which generally amend only those regulations and laws that have failed to stand up to legal scrutiny. Provincial governments seem reticent to engage in substantive debates about whether their regulations would stand up to Charter scrutiny, waiting instead to see whether these regulations will be challenged, if these debates are had at all. (For more on legislative scrutiny, see Janet Hiebert, this volume.) Indeed, recognition of the rights implications of abortion access risks undermining provincial jurisdiction over the procedure as a matter of health.

Second, this tendency to rely on legal pressure to alter regulations produces far more limited changes than active legislative debate might bring about. Although politicians have the democratic legitimacy to amend law and policy in substantial ways, judges are constrained by law and the scope of the questions that are put to them. Moreover, judges in Canada have been wary of interpreting Charter rights in a positive way, preferring to limit themselves to negative rights interpretations.[53] This approach is of particular concern for abortion rights activists as the recognition of abortion as being necessary to women's equality would need to mandate some kind of state action. In the decades since the *Morgentaler* decision, we have yet to see a Supreme Court case openly address the Charter rights allegations made against various provincial governments: the respective cases in New Brunswick, Prince Edward Island, Quebec, and Manitoba were not appealed as far as the Supreme Court. Only *R. v. Morgentaler* (1993), originating in Nova Scotia, made it to the Supreme Court in this period, and the Court declined to hear Charter rights claims in this case, focusing instead on the division of federal and provincial powers.

In recent years, the two provinces that seemed most likely to experience litigation on abortion policies that would escalate to the Supreme Court were New Brunswick and Prince Edward Island. Although both have recently either been involved in, or threatened with, legal action, their governments chose to act outside the legal system, amending their regulations to better fit the spirit of the Charter. This strategy of avoiding legal battles has helped to safeguard provincial dominion over access and stifle rights debates in court, a situation that might have mandated action. Despite the changes in policy that did occur, inequalities persist in access to abortion in Canada, and a case concerning violations of women's equality rights rooted in unequal access to abortion care seems less and less likely to enter the Supreme Court any time soon.

Even when litigation puts pressure on governments to amend restrictions on access, it is normally not enough to require a substantive engagement with the Charter, in which governments attempt to clarify their rights obligations pertaining to abortion. Likewise, governments are unlikely to take on the potentially divisive issue themselves when rights are increasingly seen as a matter for the courts. In the absence of a major change to this relationship, it seems unlikely that abortion will be recognized as an equality right by the provinces in the foreseeable future.

In spite of these shortcomings, there is no question that access to abortion in Canada has dramatically improved since 1988. Where once most provinces had regulations in place to block access to services in a variety of ways, often by attempting to prevent doctors from performing abortions or removing public funds from the procedure, now few regulations formally limiting access exist. Unfortunately, the removal of offending regulations is not tantamount to progressive policy formation. With a few minor exceptions (e.g., "bubble zones" around abortion clinics in Ontario), there continues to be a notable lack of defined abortion policy in the Canadian provinces. Access to services has been subsumed under access to health care, and the specific challenges posed by the often-stigmatized procedure have not been addressed.

As of 2016, abortion is considered a medically necessary service in every province, which means that it should be covered by provincial insurance schemes, but restrictions on access persist (e.g., policies like New Brunswick's Regulation 84-20, which restricts abortion to hospital settings). Quebec has come the closest of all the provinces to laying the foundation for a provincial policy by framing abortion as a right in its legislature, but other provinces have not followed suit. Reluctance to create a clear abortion policy results in no small part from the way Canadian abortion policy has been successfully changed following the *Morgentaler* decision.

The trajectory that legal and regulatory changes to abortion access have taken in Canada have acted to mitigate any significant policy developments. Although governments have reacted to legal mandates, or threats thereto, these responses have largely worked to bandage existing concerns rather than engage with the substantive rights questions that underlie them in the creation of policy. This tendency to react rather than consider, debate, and produce new policies has stagnated abortion policy in Canada.

The 2015 election of the federal Liberal Party, under Justin Trudeau, who made headlines after winning the Liberal leadership for his pronouncement that all future Liberal Party candidates would be expected to vote in a way consistent with a pro-choice position, has given some renewed hope that the issue of abortion access may be tackled head on in federal politics.[54] However, to date, this engagement has not yet occurred. Despite reassurances that abortion is a fundamental right for women,[55] and assurances that the Liberal Party is "the party of the Charter," the government has thus far kept its investigations of abortion strictly within the realm of health care.[56] Although positive changes have occurred, such as the government lifting a ban on the use of foreign aid money to fund international abortion care,[57] it is not yet clear what its approach to issues of abortion access will be. If abortion is treated only as a health care issue, access to which is not protected by the Charter, its implications as a fundamental right will continue to go unaddressed.

Without a legal declaration that abortion constitutes an equality right, which the Court may well believe is beyond its purview to make, it is left to the federal government to pronounce on this issue. Although the Trudeau government seems much more willing than its predecessors to discuss abortion and recognize access to the procedure as a Charter right, it has thus far refrained from making any explicit declaration that abortion is an equality right, relying instead on addressing access as a matter of health care. Unfortunately, despite rhetorical acknowledgment to the contrary, designating abortion as a matter of health care leaves the standing of the procedure as a fundamental right in abeyance, failing to alter the status quo in any meaningful way. Without formal protections, abortion will continue to be precariously regulated, subject to a range of arbitrary influences that fail to match the significance of the interests such recognitions are meant to protect. Although major changes to abortion regulation have been made possible through litigation, only a formal recognition of abortion as a fundamental right, necessary for women's equality, can hope to put this right on solid ground.

NOTES

1 The obvious exception is Prince Edward Island, where, in the wake of the 1988 *Morgentaler* decision, the legislature condemned abortion when it passed Resolution 17, which asserts that "life begins at conception, and any policy that permits abortion is unacceptable"; see *CBC News*, "P.E.I. Abortion Policy Needs Clarity, Says Group," 28 January 2013, http://www.cbc.ca/news/canada/prince-edward-island/p-e-i-abortion-policy-needs-clarity-says-group-1.1413174.
2 Although the 5–2 split appears straightforward, the justices ruling in favour of striking down s. 251 of the Criminal Code wrote three separate decisions. For more on the nuances of their perspectives, see Rachael Johnstone and Emmett Macfarlane, "Public Policy, Rights, and Abortion Access in Canada," *International Journal of Canadian Studies* 51 (2015): 97–120.
3 *R. v. Morgentaler*, [1988] 1 S.C.R. 30, p. 32.
4 Ibid., p. 171.
5 *Tremblay v. Daigle* (1989) became the most well known of these cases, but attempts were also made by men in Ontario (*Murphy v. Dodd*, [1989]) and Manitoba (*Diamond v. Hirsch*, [1989] M.C.Q.B.) (unreported).
6 Donna Greschner, "Abortion and Democracy for Women: A Critique of *Tremblay v. Daigle*," *McGill Law Journal* 35, no. 3 (1990): 656.
7 *Tremblay v. Daigle*, [1989] 2 S.C.R. 530, p. 531 [Tremblay].
8 Ibid., p. 571.
9 Ibid., p. 555.
10 Although the outcome of *Tremblay v. Daigle* (1989) was a victory for the pro-choice movement, the lower court rulings suggest that the outcome

of this case was by no means certain. Indeed, the nature of the case before the Court concerning fetal rights could have been very different if it had occurred even a few months later. When *Tremblay v. Daigle* (1989) was being heard, another case concerning fetal rights was making its way through the Supreme Court. The case, initiated by Joe Borowski, a former MPP and MP for the Saskatchewan New Democratic Party, set out to challenge the 1969 law (which had been struck down in *Morgentaler* before Borowski reached the Supreme Court) on the grounds that it violated fetal rights, which he thought should be recognized by the state. Borowski had already appeared before the Supreme Court in his quest to secure standing to bring his case forward (because he was, after all, neither a woman nor an abortion provider). The Court ruled, however, 5–2, that he could proceed as the most interested parties would be unlikely to bring forward a case that would undermine the protections from criminal sanctions that the existing law gave them; see Frederick L. Morton, *Morgentaler v. Borowski: Abortion, the Charter, and the Courts* (Toronto: McClelland and Stewart, 1992), 102. When Borowski finally reached the Court, the outcome of *Tremblay v. Daigle* (1989) had rendered his case moot; see Morton, *Morgentaler v. Borowski.*

11 Janine Brodie, "Choice and No Choice in the House," in *The Politics of Abortion*, ed. Janine Brodie, Shelley Gavigan, and Jane Jenson (Toronto: Oxford University Press, 1992), 97.

12 Ibid., p. 115.

13 Ibid.

14 Quebec, National Assembly of Quebec, 19 May 2010. For a more in-depth explanation of the political climate surrounding abortion in Canada, both federally and in the provinces, see Rachael Johnstone, *After Morgentaler: The Politics of Abortion in Canada* (Vancouver: UBC Press, 2017).

15 *R. v. Morgentaler,* [1993] 3 S.C.R. 463, p. 463 [Morgentaler 1993].

16 Ibid., p. 470.

17 *Nova Scotia (Attorney General) v. Morgentaler*, [1989] N.S.S.C. 5201.

18 *Morgentaler 1993,* p. 464.

19 Ibid., p. 481.

20 Indeed, although abortion access could now be provided in clinics, the Halifax Morgentaler clinic is no longer in operation, having closed its doors in 2003.

21 Library of Parliament, Parliamentary Information and Research Service, "Abortion: Constitutional and Legal Developments," by Mollie Dunsmuir, *Current Issue Review* 89-10E (Ottawa: Supply and Services Canada, 1998).

22 *Morgentaler v. New Brunswick*, [1994] N.B.Q.B. No. 302, para. 44.

23 *Morgentaler v. New Brunswick*, [2009] N.B.C.A. No. 26, paras. 1 and 14.
24 Emmett Macfarlane, "The Dilemma of Positive Rights: Access to Health Care and the *Canadian Charter of Rights and Freedoms*," *Journal of Canadian Studies* 48, no. 3 (2014): 59.
25 As Macfarlane stresses, there are a number of sections of the Charter that outline rights that are explicitly positive in nature, and many legal scholars have noted the appeal of interpreting other Charter rights in a positive way, especially s. 15 (equality rights) and s. 7 (the right to life, liberty, and security of the person); see ibid., 51. Indeed, a number of s. 15 cases have already been interpreted along these lines; see ibid., 53.
26 Although they attempted to appeal the decision again, the Supreme Court declined to hear their final appeal.
27 *Morgentaler v. The Province of New Brunswick*, [2008] N.B.Q.B. No. 258, para. 19.
28 *Morgentaler v. New Brunswick*, [2009] N.B.C.A. No. 26.
29 Kevin van Paassen, "Morgentaler's Lawsuit over New Brunswick Abortion Funding Dropped," *Globe and Mail*, 15 April 2014, http://www.theglobeandmail.com/life/health-and-fitness/health/morgentalers-lawsuit-over-new-brunswick-abortion-funding dropped/article18007959/.
30 Quoted in Donalee Moulton, "New Brunswick Assailed over 'Sexist' Abortion Laws," *Canadian Medical Association Journal* 169, no. 7 (2003): 700.
31 *CBC News*, "New Brunswick Abortion Restriction Lifted by Premier Brian Gallant," 26 November 2014, http://www.cbc.ca/news/canada/new-brunswick/new-brunswick-abortion-restriction-lifted-by-premier-brian-gallant-1.2850474.
32 This barrier was, in fact, insurmountable since no hospitals were performing abortion services on the Island at the time.
33 Lori Brown, J. Shoshanna Ehrlich, and Colleen MacQuarrie, "Subverting the Constitution: Anti-abortion Policies and Activism in the United States and Canada," in *Abortion: History, Politics, and Reproductive Justice after Morgentaler*, ed. Shannon Stettner, Kristin Burnett, and Travis Hay (Vancouver: UBC Press, 2017) at 254.
34 Abortion Rights Network, "Abortion Access Now PEI Challenges PEI's Abortion Policy," *Abortion Rights Network*, 1 July 2016, accessed 1 September 2016, http://www.abortionrightspei.com/content/page/front_news/article/43.
35 Sara Fraser and Jesara Sinclair, "Abortion Services Coming to P.E.I., Province Announces," *CBC News*, 31 March 2016, http://www.cbc.ca/news/canada/prince-edward-island/pei-abortion-reproductive-rights-1.3514334.

36 CFC and FQPN, *Focus on Abortion Services in Quebec* (Ottawa: Canadians for Choice / Montreal: Fédération du Québec pour le planning des naissances, 2010), 32.

37 Canada, Library of Parliament, Parliamentary Information and Research Service, "Abortion in Canada: Twenty Years after *R. v. Morgentaler*," by Karine Richer, PRB 08-22E, 24 September 2008, http://www.lop.parl.gc.ca/content/lop/researchpublications/prb0822-e.htm#5association.

38 According to the Council on the Status of Women, "one in four women had to pay to receive abortion services throughout the province of Quebec"; CFC and FQPN, *Focus on Abortion Services in Quebec*, 32.

39 Ibid.

40 Ibid.

41 Ibid., 34.

42 Ibid.

43 Kelly Grant, "Most Provincial Drug Plans Won't Cover Abortion Pills in Canada," *CBC News*, 26 September 2016, http://www.theglobeandmail.com/news/national/most-provincial-drug-plans-wont-cover-abortion-pills-in-canada/article32047302/.

44 Quebec, National Assembly of Quebec, 19 May 2010.

45 Jane Doe 1 was told she would need to wait between six and eight weeks for an appointment, while Jane Doe 2 was told she would need to wait between four and six weeks for her first appointment, but would then require two subsequent appointments; see *Doe et al. v. The Government of Manitoba*, [2004] M.B.Q.B. 285, para. 8, 11.

46 Ibid., para. 12

47 Ibid., para. 90.

48 *Jane Doe et al. v. Manitoba*, [2005] M.B.C.A. 109, para. 9.

49 *Doe et al. v. The Government of Manitoba*, [2004] M.B.Q.B. 285, para. 88.

50 *CBC News*, "Manitoba to Pay for Abortions at Clinic," 8 July 2004, http://www.cbc.ca/news/canada/manitoba-to-pay-for-abortions-at-clinic-1.470206.

51 Joanna Erdman, "In the Back Alleys of Health Care: Abortion, Equality and Community in Canada," *Emory Law Journal* 56 (2007): 1098.

52 Ibid.

53 Emmett Macfarlane, "The Dilemma of Positive Rights: Access to Health Care and the *Canadian Charter of Rights and Freedoms*," *Journal of Canadian Studies* 48, no. 3 (2014): 59.

54 Susana Mas, "Anti-abortion Candidates Need Not Apply in 2015, Justin Trudeau Says," *CBC News*, 7 May 2014, http://www.cbc.ca/news/

politics/anti-abortion-candidates-need-not-apply-in-2015-justin-trudeau-says-1.2634877; Daniel LeBlanc, "Trudeau Now Says All Liberal MPs Must Vote Pro-choice," *Globe and Mail*, 18 June 2014, http://www.theglobeandmail.com/news/politics/trudeau-says-all-liberals-mp-will-have-to-vote-pro-choice/article19218815/.

55 Justin Trudeau, Twitter post, 31 March 2016, https://twitter.com/justintrudeau/status/715600442328268800.

56 Michelle Zilio, "Trudeau Defends Abortion Position after Graphic Flyers Target Liberal Leader," *CTV News*, 13 May 2015, http://www.ctvnews.ca/politics/trudeau-defends-abortion-position-after-graphic-flyers-target-liberal-leader-1.2371906.

57 David Akin, "Trudeau OKs Canadian Dollars for Foreign Abortion Services," *Toronto Sun*, 10 May 2015, http://www.torontosun.com/2016/05/10/trudeau-oks-canadian-dollars-for-foreign-abortion-services.

17 Contrasting Visions of Indigenous Rights, Recognition, and Territory: Assessing Crown Policy in the Context of Reconciliation and Historic Obligations

MICHAEL MCCROSSAN

In the areas of Canadian politics and law, Indigenous peoples have regularly sought recognition of their status as distinct nations with inherent rights to governance and territorial responsibilities. While increased Indigenous mobilization over the course of the past fifty years has resulted in successful reversals of explicit governmental efforts aimed at assimilation[1] as well as constitutional recognition of Aboriginal and treaty rights,[2] the extent to which such recognition has served to fundamentally alter the colonial relations of power undergirding the state remains open to consideration. One consistent perspective advanced and expressed by Indigenous peoples, particularly as governmental actors have engaged in forms of "mega constitutional politics,"[3] is that, as distinct nations with inherent legal orders and jurisdictional responsibilities, they have rights to be consulted about governmental actions and policies that could affect their interests.[4]

Although, at times, governments have displayed a willingness to engage with and consult Indigenous peoples on matters of governance,[5] Indigenous scholars have argued that such efforts fall far short of any form of meaningful dialogue that respects Indigenous cultural traditions and legal systems.[6] Indeed, Indigenous legal and political scholars have argued that governmental policies surrounding the recognition of rights and "reconciliation" continue to function as assimilatory mechanisms by ultimately "hinder[ing] Aboriginal choice in the development of their lands and resources, rather than enhancing it."[7] While Canadian courts in the late 1990s often expressed a clear preference for "negotiations" to occur between Indigenous peoples and the state in "good faith,"[8] the underlying interpretations and reasoning of Canadian judges continued to sustain and support the sovereign authority of the Canadian state over the rights of Indigenous peoples.[9]

However, one judicial doctrine that has gained increased prominence and attention over the course of the last decade is *the duty to consult*. In the early stages of its development, some suggested that the doctrine possessed great potential to act as a "functional mechanism that promise[d] to move the relationship between the government and Aboriginal peoples forward" and ultimately "reconfigure Aboriginal-state relations in Canada."[10] While the courts have created a number of interpretive tests and doctrines surrounding the rights "recognized and affirmed" in section 35(1) of the Constitution Act, 1982, due to spatial constraints, I intend to limit my discussion primarily to issues surrounding reconciliation and "honourable" duties of the Crown in an effort to assess the extent to which the actions and policies of Canadian governments have been reconfigured in a manner that fundamentally disturbs prior colonial legacies and relations of power.

This chapter will argue that non-Indigenous renderings and developmental visions concerning the land – as well as the proper role of government in relation to Indigenous rights – have served to simultaneously define the policy field and undermine Indigenous legal orders and territorial responsibilities. This chapter will begin by outlining theories of Indigenous policy and settler-colonial geographic frameworks. It will then move towards a brief examination of the jurisprudential development of reconciliation and the duty to consult before turning its attention to the manner in which governmental policy has both responded and remained relatively fixed in the wake of these developments over the last decade.

Persisting Paradigms and Settler-Colonial Mentalities

In the fields of Indigenous politics and law, it has often been asserted that there is a well-entrenched colonial mentality, or paradigm, embedded in both governmental policies and legal decisions concerning Indigenous peoples. For instance, Kiera Ladner and Michael Orsini have argued that federal policy in relation to Indigenous peoples is governed by a predominant "policy paradigm," which views Indigenous peoples as *objects* of bureaucratic management and control rather than as nations with the capacity to govern themselves according to their own legal and political traditions.[11] Building upon the work of Peter Hall, who described policy paradigms as structured visions of the world replete with "an overarching set of ideas that specify how the problems facing them (policy makers) are to be perceived, which goals might be attained through policy and what sorts of techniques can be used to achieve these goals,"[12] Ladner and Orsini located a long-standing colonial policy paradigm revolving around the ideas of "civilization" and "assimilation." In this regard, Ladner and Orsini argued that federal policy concerning issues of Indigenous governance ultimately continued to follow a colonial trajectory predicated upon eliminating inherent Indigenous rights and assimilating Indigenous peoples into Canadian governmental structures.[13] In Ladner and Orsini's estimation, a number of conceptual constraints, including the likely fear that recognition of Indigenous nationhood and legal orders could result in the dismantling of both an established bureaucratic regime and Canadian "territorial integrity" itself, have served to preclude such recognition from the space of political possibilities.[14]

Although Ladner and Orsini do not engage with or elaborate upon the issue of territory, it is worthwhile to consider how the issue of territory might function within the colonial legacies observed by the authors. Theorists such as Patrick Wolfe have noted that in settler-colonial contexts, the issue of controlling and extracting resources from the land – particularly land governed by pre-existing Indigenous legal and political regimes – is central to the ongoing development of settler-colonial societies. In Wolfe's estimation, the "logic," or need to *eliminate* Indigenous peoples and dispossess them of their territories, has been fuelled by an "insatiable dynamic whereby settler colonialism always needs more land. … The whole range of primary sectors can motivate the project. In addition to agriculture, therefore, we should think in terms of forestry, fishing, pastoralism and mining. …"[15]

Likewise, Glen Coulthard has noted that, "as a structure of domination predicated on dispossession, [colonialism] is not 'a thing,' but rather the sum effect of the diversity of interlocking oppressive social relations that constitute it."[16] According to Coulthard, to truly grasp the ongoing and persisting effects of colonial dispossession, it is essential to engage an assortment of "sites and relations of power that inform our settler-colonial present."[17] In other words, it may not be enough to ruminate upon ill-defined threats to bureaucratic structures or a desire to preserve the state's territorial integrity as it is the underlying ideas and logic at the core of settler-colonial societies that need to be situated within a broader institutional matrix and territorial assemblage of power relations.

As Peter Hall perceptively noted, "the argument that 'policy legacies' determine the course of subsequent policy raises questions about why some legacies are more influential than others."[18] In Hall's assessment, "the policymaking process can be structured by a particular set of ideas, just as it can be structured by a set of institutions. The two often reinforce each other. ..."[19] Indeed, political geographers have long recognized that the law reinforces and produces – through the institution of the courts – particular ideas and understandings of territory that function to undermine alternative or conflicting territorial claims. According to Matthew Sparke, the law often reinforces homogenizing depictions of "abstract space,"[20] which serve to subvert Indigenous traditions and alternative relationships to land through the "abstraction of [a] single territorial collectivity constituting the state."[21]

In the case of settler-colonial contexts structured by ongoing forms of Indigenous dispossession, these understandings – and judicial productions – of a unified territory belonging to the state can be particularly damaging to the rights of Indigenous peoples. As Gordon Christie has noted, "contemporary jurisprudence not only borrows from colonial justifications developed and maintained during Canada's overtly colonial period, but actually sanctions, affirms and strengthens this colonial conceptual framework."[22] In fact, according to Christie, it is particular ideas about land – and relating to land – that continue to structure the field of Aboriginal policy. In this regard, he argues that "non-Aboriginal visions of land use" continue to remain embedded within both Canadian jurisprudence and Crown policy – or visions in which land and resources tend to be valued primarily as objects to be exploited and "properly used for wealth-creation."[23] This predominantly non-Aboriginal vision of the land stands in sharp contrast to the non-dominating and non-exploitative understanding of land as deriving from a "*system of reciprocal relations and obligations*"[24] between both human and non-human beings that is regularly articulated by Indigenous peoples and scholars.[25]

Given that many of the contemporary cases that have led to the formation of the duty to consult involved situations where governments granted rights to third parties to develop and extract resources within traditional Indigenous territories, to what extent has this doctrine fundamentally altered the colonial framework observed by legal and political scholars? I intend to draw together the territorial insights from settler-colonial theorists and political geographers to show how particular representations and understandings of territory have served to continue to dispossess Indigenous peoples of their rights "recognized and affirmed" under section 35(1) of the Constitution Act, 1982.[26] While the Supreme Court of Canada (SCC) has constructed notions of reconciliation and binding obligations on governments in relation to Indigenous peoples, these doctrines need to be situated within a larger field of territorial relations of power. Therefore, I will engage in a close textual reading of SCC decisions surrounding reconciliation and the duty to consult as well as governmental policies and legislative responses constructed in the aftermath of this legal context. I intend to show not only the manner in which particular understandings and representations of territory have been produced through legal discourse but also how similar understandings shape governmental policy and ultimately undermine the jurisdictional rights and interests of Indigenous peoples.

Contrasting Political and Legal Visions of Rights and Duties

When considering the policy impact of the entrenchment of Aboriginal and treaty rights, it is clear that a fundamental tension exists at the core of judicial interpretations of the text of section 35. While members of the judiciary may be struggling to ensure that the Crown fulfil historic obligations to Indigenous peoples, their decisions have also simultaneously undermined Indigenous jurisdictions and responsibilities through particular representations and understandings of territory. For instance, as it is commonly known, the word *existing* was initially added to the proposed section dealing with Aboriginal and treaty rights at the prodding of Albertan Premier Peter Lougheed in an effort to circumscribe and limit the rights available to Indigenous peoples.[27] Indeed, this was precisely the position advocated by federal and provincial Crown counsels[28] when they appeared before the SCC during its first opportunity to consider the meaning of the constitutional guarantees pertaining to Aboriginal rights under section 35(1) in the *Sparrow*[29] case.

However, this attempt to define Aboriginal rights out of existence, and thus undercut the interpretive authority of the judiciary, did not go unchallenged. In fact, the Dickson Court indicated that federal and provincial governments could no longer presume unbridled authority over Aboriginal rights.[30] According to the SCC, a number of "fundamental effects" resulted from the constitutional entrenchment of Aboriginal and treaty rights, including the establishment of "a solid constitutional base upon which subsequent negotiations [could] take place" between Indigenous peoples and the Crown.[31] In effect, *Sparrow* offered a vision of reconciliation in which "federal power must be reconciled with federal duty"[32] and Crown fiduciary obligations towards Indigenous peoples. According to the SCC, section 35(1) acted as a fundamental limitation on the power of the federal government such that it was now legally required to justify "any government regulation that infringes upon or denies aboriginal rights."[33] It is in this context that the SCC highlighted the need to also consider whether the government had "consulted" with Indigenous peoples about its legislative measures.[34] In this respect, the *Sparrow* decision planted the jurisprudential seeds for not only imposing a "high standard of honourable dealing"[35] on governments in their legislative and policy interactions with Indigenous peoples but also reconceptualizing the relationship between Crown assertions of authority and the rights of Indigenous peoples.

Subsequent decisions by the SCC, however, built upon these notions of Crown honour and necessary consultations, while simultaneously retranslating reconciliation into a form of territorial subordination. For instance, in *Van der Peet*,[36] Chief Justice Lamer also noted that "the honour of the Crown is at stake" when considering the relationship between the Canadian government and Aboriginal peoples.[37] In fact, Lamer noted that the honour of the Crown was central to understanding the purpose and scope of section 35.[38] However, when describing the purpose underpinning the constitutional guarantee of Aboriginal and treaty rights, Lamer moved away from *Sparrow*'s vision of moderating the powers of the federal government and instead proclaimed that the section was designed to ensure that "the aboriginal rights recognized and affirmed by s. 35(1) must be directed towards the reconciliation of the pre-existence of aboriginal societies with the sovereignty of the Crown."[39]

While this conception of reconciliation has been called a doctrine "plucked from thin air,"[40] it is important to recognize that this development occurred at the very moment that Indigenous parties were arguing for forms of territorial control grounded in the historic occupancy of land under their own legal orders.[41] In fact, Lamer's decision proceeded to further contain the territorial claims of Indigenous peoples by noting that the "recognition and affirmation" of Aboriginal rights was directed towards "the reconciliation of pre-existing aboriginal claims to the territory that now constitutes Canada, with the assertion of British sovereignty over that territory."[42] In effect, this representation of reconciliation demonstrates a clear moment in which the present territorial space of "Canada" is both presented as an established fact and asserted in the face of conflicting territorial claims.[43] This judicial production of territory and form of spatial reconciliation ultimately serves to undercut Indigenous legal orders, alternative territorial understandings, and ongoing forms of resistance to initial "British" assertions by representing the present territorial boundaries of Canada as the prism through which Indigenous claims will be measured and ultimately absorbed.

It is this homogenizing depiction of "Canadian" territory in response to ongoing Indigenous claims that continues to be produced in judicial decisions concerning Indigenous rights and the types of permissible Crown infringements upon those rights. For instance, in the SCC's germinal *Delgamuukw*[44] decision concerning the content of Aboriginal title under section 35(1), Chief Justice Lamer's first reference to "reconciliation" in the judgment noted that Aboriginal rights "are aimed at the reconciliation of the prior occupation of North America by distinctive aboriginal societies with the assertion of Crown sovereignty over Canadian territory."[45] Within this framework, there is never any doubt that Indigenous claims will be determined and subsumed within the territorial boundaries perceived as *belonging* to Canada.

Regardless of how the boundaries of Canada were established – or what alternative territorial relationships might have been eclipsed in the course of that establishment – the fact that Indigenous peoples currently exist within Canadian territory is enough to presume governmental authority and the power to justifiably infringe Indigenous rights in the name of benefiting the entire Canadian "community" (and its additional Indigenous components).[46] With this framework of territorial belonging and control now in place, the types of justifiable infringements upon Aboriginal title lands – including "agriculture, forestry, mining" and even foreign "settlement" itself[47] – look remarkably similar to the developmental project and *insatiable* desire to settle Indigenous lands that Wolfe suggested was at the core of settler-colonial societies.[48] In effect, it is naturalized understandings about the territory belonging to Canada and its developmental potential that serve to preclude and undermine the strength of Indigenous legal orders and territorial jurisdictions.

The development of subsequent doctrines such as the duty to consult need to be understood in this context. Although the SCC has built upon *Sparrow*'s invocation of consultation and Crown obligations in such cases as *Delgamuukw*, *Haida Nation*,[49] and *Taku River*,[50] the power and jurisdictional authority of governments to infringe Indigenous lands – if necessary – is not seriously disputed in the texts of the decisions.

For instance, the SCC has determined that the Crown has a legal duty to consult and accommodate Indigenous peoples "when the Crown has knowledge, real or constructive, of the potential existence of the Aboriginal right or title and contemplates conduct that might adversely affect it."[51] This recognition of respecting potential or unproved interests appears promising, particularly as "[t]he Crown, acting honourably, cannot cavalierly run roughshod over Aboriginal interests where claims affecting these interests are being seriously pursued in the process of treaty negotiation and proof."[52] And yet, in cases where Indigenous rights or title claims are not yet "established," or where they are determined by the Crown to be "weak," "the only duty on the Crown may be to give notice, disclose information, and discuss any issues raised in response to the notice."[53] Under this judicial framework, the continuing power of the Crown to develop lands governed by Indigenous laws, but situated within "Canadian" territorial space, is not seriously questioned.

In fact, in 2010, the SCC issued a judgment in the case of *Rio Tinto Alcan*[54] that potentially further destabilizes the protective capabilities of the Crown's obligations in relation to Aboriginal peoples. One of the issues to be determined in the case revolved around at what time the duty to consult could be triggered. According to the SCC, the duty to consult should be considered as arising in the context of situations where Aboriginal rights "may be adversely impacted by the *current* government conduct or decision in question. Prior and continuing breaches, including prior failures to consult, will only trigger a duty to consult if the present decision has the potential of causing a novel adverse impact on a present claim or existing right."[55] In other words, historical and ongoing infringements stemming from development projects could be justified as long as they did not contribute to "novel" or additionally adverse effects on current Aboriginal rights or claims. When considered in the context of a persisting policy or settler-colonial legacy, this privileging of the economic interests of the state and third party developers lends considerable weight to the legal trajectory observed by Gordon Christie more than a decade ago.

> [T]he Crown is imagined as working within and through nothing but its vision, with the duty to consult operating to potentially modify the activities that fall under this vision. … In seeking to trigger the duty to consult, an Aboriginal nation is acknowledging its lack of alternative recourse, and seeking to bring to bear this inadequate, assimilative tool upon problems

> generated by the larger colonial context within which its members have lived for many generations. … The duty to consult enters the scene in a broad sense to do no more than potentially shift the exploitation into a slightly different form. …[56]

While the SCC's initial jurisprudence may have seemingly indicated that the visions of federal and provincial actors would need to be fundamentally rethought in the context of entrenching Aboriginal and treaty rights in 1982, the ability of Indigenous peoples to challenge ongoing infringements or incursions upon their rights and title lands appears to remain fundamentally limited when those infringements relate to broader developmental ideas surrounding how the lands and resources within Canada's territorial boundaries should be properly managed and used.

Jurisdictional Authority and Policy Exclusions

Now that the SCC has clearly delineated a legal duty of consultation that is grounded in the "core precept" of the "honour of the Crown,"[57] to what extent have governments fundamentally altered their relationships with Indigenous peoples and/or approaches concerning Indigenous rights? When considering governmental policy over the past decade in the context of reconciliation and Crown obligations towards Indigenous peoples, it is clear that similar settler-colonial visions concerning the developmental potential of land and the proper role of government have served to simultaneously define the field and undermine the strength and effectiveness of the constitutional entrenchment of Aboriginal and treaty rights.

For instance, in the wake of judicial decisions concerning the duty to consult, in June 2006, the Conservative government appointed Wendy Grant-John as ministerial representative to assist and advise Indian and Northern Affairs Canada (INAC), the Assembly of First Nations (AFN), and the Native Women's Association of Canada (NWAC) in developing "a viable legislative solution" for addressing the issue of "matrimonial real property."[58] Indeed, the need to develop a matrimonial property regime on reserves had long been recognized as a human rights concern as the federal government's jurisdictional authority over reserve lands denied First Nations women the ability to access provincial and territorial laws governing the division of property upon marriage or relationship breakdowns.[59]

As part of Grant-John's mandate to help provide a solution in this area, her activities included "facilitat[ing] consultation sessions … between INAC, AFN & NWAC on a monthly basis and provid[ing] advice to the parties."[60] The government's consultation process ran for four months, between September 2006 and January 2007. However, while "INAC consulted officials from all the provincial and territorial governments, with the exception of Nunavut,"[61] it was left to the national Aboriginal organizations to "ensur[e] that the voices of women were heard" and to "conduc[t] dialogue sessions with representatives of First Nation communities."[62] Not only did Aboriginal organizations criticize the short time frame and lack of respect for Indigenous jurisdictions,[63] but some First Nations leaders also criticized the government's approach to the consultation itself.[64] Perhaps even more telling, the government's own ministerial representative expressed significant reservations regarding the government's approach to consultation.

As noted by Grant-John, "Serious issues about consultation of a legal and policy nature nevertheless arose throughout the consultation and consensus-seeking phase."[65] In fact, Grant-John stated that while the government was initially unclear about whether there was, in fact, a legal duty to consult, it nevertheless did take the position that "there [was] no legal duty to consult in the matter of matrimonial real property on reserves."[66] Given the historical legacy of governmental policy under the Indian Act regime and section 91(24) of the Constitution Act, 1867, it is perhaps not surprising that the government decided that there was no *legal* duty to consult in this area.[67] Governmental policy concerning Indigenous peoples has displayed not only a clear orientation towards the existing territorial and jurisdictional divisions from which it derives its own authority over Indigenous peoples[68] but also a conception of Indigenous peoples as a "target population" whose interests need to be managed and controlled by a legitimate and rational governing power. As Ladner and Orsini have argued, "The policy legacy of colonialism virtually freezes out any possibility of establishing a meaningful two-way dialogue" by conceptually eliminating Indigenous jurisdictions and practices of governance.[69] Indeed, if the federal government truly recognized Indigenous peoples as distinct nations with their own inherent jurisdictions and governing structures, INAC would likely have consulted well beyond the "official" governments recognized within the established Canadian federal-provincial-territorial framework.

Nevertheless, it should be noted that while the government may not have initially followed the duty to consult as defined in cases such as

Haida Nation and *Taku River*, INAC's ministerial representative specifically recommended that consultation policies be developed as quickly as possible.[70] Eight months after Grant-John submitted her report, the government of Canada introduced an "action plan" on consultation, in which it engaged Indigenous communities and sought their views on developing policy in this area.[71] The government released interim guidelines for federal officials in February 2008,[72] which were then updated in March 2011 so as to "reflec[t] evolving case law."[73]

On the one hand, the government's policy guidelines clearly recognize that "legal parameters"[74] structure its policies in relation to Indigenous peoples. The guidelines begin by noting that the decisions of the SCC surrounding the duty to consult provide the context that shapes and guides governmental decisions and approaches to policymaking.[75] Indeed, the document's section outlining the government's guiding principles and directives concerning consultation declares that a "number of landmark [SCC] decisions" affirm the fact that "the Crown has a duty to consult."[76] Thus, the policy guidelines set out a number of consultative principles and approaches that the federal government must follow when contemplating actions that might affect Aboriginal rights[77] as well as the manner in which governmental departments and agencies should plan to address issues surrounding consultation and accommodation.[78] Not only does the policy framework set out four distinct phases[79] that encompass the government's consultation analysis and implementation plans, including early engagement with Indigenous groups, notification of proposed activities, and efforts to accommodate Indigenous concerns, but it also specifically notes that consultation will be "integrated" into environmental assessment procedures and regulatory approval processes.[80]

However, while the document's contextual framework provides for at least nominal recognition of the impact of particular SCC rulings, this does not necessarily mean that previous policy legacies and approaches have come undone. In fact, in 2012, the Harper government seemingly undercut its own policy framework by introducing changes in two omnibus pieces of legislation that make it easier for the federal government to ignore Indigenous rights and jurisdictional responsibilities.[81] For instance, one of the changes to the Navigable Waters Protection Act (in addition to renaming it the Navigation Protection Act[82]) involved eliminating protection for millions[83] of bodies of water that had been previously covered under the act. According to the schedule of "navigable waters" listed in the act, protective mechanisms and enforcement measures apply to only ninety-seven lakes, sixty-two rivers, and three oceans.[84] These changes were made so as to reduce "unnecessary red tape" and make it easier for "important infrastructure to be built on waterways."[85]

However, by eliminating the majority of navigable waterways in Canada from the act's scope of authority, there would be limited governmental oversight in infrastructure projects that might occur along or near those waters. Given that many of the waterways contained within Canada's borders are intricately connected to Indigenous cultural practices and legal traditions,[86] the elimination of governmental oversight could prove particularly damaging to Indigenous peoples. As John Borrows has noted, the removal of protective mechanisms ultimately means that it will be far more difficult to "trigge[r] federal environmental assessments and Crown duties to consult and accommodate Indigenous peoples."[87] In effect, by asserting its jurisdictional authority and privileging the interests of developers over the constitutionally protected rights of Indigenous peoples, the federal government undercut and disregarded not only Indigenous legal traditions, jurisdictional responsibilities, and treaty rights but also its own policies and obligations in regard to Indigenous peoples.

Likewise, the federal government unilaterally made changes to the Fisheries Act[88] that directly affect Indigenous peoples. For instance, one of the primary changes found in the act is the insertion of the following definition of *Aboriginal* in regard to fisheries in Canada:

> *Aboriginal*, in relation to a fishery, means that fish is harvested by an Aboriginal organization or any of its members for the purpose of using the fish as food, for social or ceremonial purposes or for purposes set out in a land claims agreement entered into with the Aboriginal organization.[89]

It should be noted that this delineation explicitly excludes mention of Aboriginal commercial fishing.[90] While *commercial* fisheries are defined in the act as areas where "fish is harvested under the authority of a licence for the purpose of sale, trade or barter," there is no mention of Aboriginal commercial fisheries, where such fishing may occur under historic treaties.[91] These exclusions become particularly problematic when considered alongside the provisions concerning "fisheries protection." According to section 35(1) of the act, "No person shall carry on any work, undertaking or activity that results in serious harm to fish that are part of a commercial, recreational or Aboriginal fishery, or to fish that support such a fishery."[92] However, under the act, *serious harm to fish* is defined as "the death of fish or any permanent alteration to, or destruction of, fish habitat."[93] Previous versions of the act did not incorporate such notions of permanency. In effect, not only is momentary modification or harm to fish permitted, but "permanent alteration" in relation to Aboriginal commercial fisheries could very well proceed as a result of developmental activities as those fisheries are not recognized in the act.

While Indigenous peoples have been successful in asserting rights to "fish for food and social and ceremonial purposes," it is also important to note that, in the traditions of many Indigenous peoples such as the Coast Salish, fish were "not only an important source of food but played an important part in the system of beliefs. ... The salmon were held to be a race of beings. ... Toward the salmon, as toward other creatures, there was an attitude of caution and respect which resulted in effective conservation of the various species."[94] In other words, momentary alteration or harm to fish could have particularly significant effects for the cultural traditions, food practices, and understandings of reciprocal relationships held by many Indigenous peoples. Contrary to its own policy guidelines, the Harper government did not consult with or involve Indigenous peoples in either its decision to impose[95] Aboriginal fisheries definitions or its decision to weaken governmental protections against work or activities that might adversely affect and harm Aboriginal fisheries.[96]

This continual denial of Indigenous legal traditions and privileging of governmental jurisdictions can also be observed in the SCC's *Tsilhqot'in Nation*[97] decision, in which it granted a declaration of Aboriginal title for the first time under section 35(1) of the Constitution Act, 1982. However, in the same decision in which Indigenous *control* over particular territorial boundaries was recognized, the permeability and erosion of those borders by Canadian governments was nevertheless permitted in the name of broader "public interest" concerns and/or necessary settler-colonial "incursions."[98] Barsh and Henderson once described the territorial "logic" underpinning forms of governmental reasoning as "Indians are here, so they must be Canadian – being Canadian, they must be just like other Canadians."[99]

A somewhat similar logic seems to be playing out through the SCC's jurisprudence. While the SCC recognizes the existence of territories subject to Indigenous laws, the territorial boundaries of the "Canadian" nation are simultaneously prioritized and thrust towards Indigenous territorial space. While the SCC does recognize that Aboriginal laws can potentially be used to demonstrate title – particularly Aboriginal laws concerning the defence of territory – the strength of those laws appears to offer little protection when confronted with valid governmental incursions deemed beneficial for "all Canadians."[100] Given that Aboriginal peoples presently exist "within Canada's borders,"[101] the SCC seems to be operating under the presumption that they must ultimately be Canadian and therefore can be subjected to infringements that will benefit the larger community "of which they are part."[102] That is to say that a continuing orientation towards the present territorial and jurisdictional divisions in Canada has led the SCC to sanction ongoing Indigenous dispossession and settlement of "Canadian" territory. As such, there seems to be little doubt in both the legal and the political realms that the territorial and jurisdictional authority of Canadian governments can continue to be enacted in a manner that undercuts and denies Indigenous territorial relationships, jurisdictions, and alternative legal traditions.

Conclusion

John Borrows has recently suggested that "the constitutional rooting of Aboriginal and treaty rights in Canada's constitution has not led to significant legislative recognition and affirmation of those rights."[103] Certainly the manner in which the Conservative government ignored its own constitutional obligations towards Indigenous peoples lends considerable credence to this perspective. Nevertheless, this is not to suggest that the duty to consult holds no potential for restraining Canadian governments. On 23 June 2016, the Federal Court of Appeal (FCA) issued a critical condemnation of the Conservative government's approach to its approval of the Northern Gateway Pipeline project and the manner in which the government had "consulted" with Indigenous peoples. According to the FCA, the federal government had "failed to maintain the honour of the Crown" by ultimately neglecting to engage in "a real and sustained effort to pursue meaningful two-way dialogue."[104] In fact, the FCA noted that the decision at "the highest level of government"[105] to purposefully withhold the Crown's own assessment of the potential impacts on Aboriginal rights stemming from the project "was legally unacceptable … [and] frustrated the sort of genuine dialogue the duty to consult is meant to foster."[106]

In this sense, Canadian courts have made it clear that if governments fail to abide by their legal responsibilities and obligations to Indigenous peoples, the future of their resource development projects could very well be in jeopardy. Indeed, it is here that one can observe a fundamental tension at the core of governmental policies about the duty to consult. Although the SCC's decisions in this area have ostensibly produced policy changes, particularly at the federal level – including recognition of a "whole of government approach," in which each department or agency "must assess the consultation requirements that relate to their respective activities and develop approaches to consultation and accommodation that will allow the Crown as a whole to meet its duty"[107] – the strength of these consultative duties remains paralysed and undermined by ongoing desires to settle and develop Indigenous territories for the benefit of the broader "Canadian" community.

While the current Liberal government under Justin Trudeau has made re-establishing dialogue and forms of reconciliation a priority, it is likely that forms of Indigenous mobilization and litigation challenges will continue to occur unless both legal and political actors fully recognize that Aboriginal rights find their origins not simply in the constitutional text of section 35(1) of the Constitution Act, 1982 but rather within Indigenous legal orders and jurisdictions. For instance, in the summer of 2017, the federal government released ten principles "Respecting the Government of Canada's Relationship with Indigenous Peoples."[108] While the document's first principle invokes recognition of Indigenous "self-determination" as an organizing framework for all its relations with Indigenous peoples, this recognition is simultaneously situated within judicial conceptions of the potential of section 35 and the need to reconcile Indigenous peoples with "the assertion of Crown sovereignty."[109] Indeed, while the "assertion of Crown sovereignty" is continually referenced throughout the document,[110] there is no reference to the continuing existence of forms of Indigenous sovereignty. Instead, the document locates Indigenous peoples within the established and settled boundaries of the lands now *belonging* to Canada: "Canada's constitutional and legal order recognizes the reality that Indigenous peoples' ancestors owned and governed the lands which now constitute Canada prior to the Crown's assertion of sovereignty."[111]

Likewise, while the document begins by noting that "[t]he implementation of the United Nations Declaration on the Rights of Indigenous Peoples (UN Declaration) requires transformative change in the Government's relationship with Indigenous peoples,"[112] its sixth principle states that the government "recognizes that meaningful engagement with Indigenous peoples aims to secure their free, prior, and informed consent... ."[113]

Rather than "obtain"[114] or *require* their free, prior, and informed consent to proposals that may affect their interests, this principle reads as if the government simply aspires to secure Indigenous consent to proposals that will be implemented, whether or not that consent is granted.

Ultimately, for the federal government to truly overcome its persistent "paradigm paralysis," ideas concerning both the "proper" way of using land, as well as taken-for-granted assumptions concerning the jurisdictional and territorial authority of Canadian governments over Indigenous peoples, need to give way to a pluralistic conception of the law that recognizes the jurisdictional rights, responsibilities, and interpretive authority of Indigenous peoples over their lands and resources.

NOTES

1 For a discussion of some of the mobilization efforts of Indigenous peoples against the federal government's assimilatory White Paper of 1969, see Alan Cairns, *Citizens Plus: Aboriginal Peoples and the Canadian State* (Vancouver: UBC Press, 2000), 65–9.

2 See Douglas Sanders, "The Indian Lobby," in *And No One Cheered: Federalism, Democracy, and the Constitution Act*, ed. Keith Banting and Richard Simeon (Agincourt, ON: Methuen Publications, 1983), 301–32.

3 See Peter H. Russell, *Constitutional Odyssey: Can Canadians Become a Sovereign People?* (Toronto: University of Toronto Press, 2004).

4 For a discussion of the significance of the actions of Elijah Harper in the demise of the Meech Lake Accord, see M.E. Turpel and P.A. (Trisha) Monture, "Ode to Elijah: Reflections of Two First Nations Women on the Rekindling of Spirit at the Wake for the Meech Lake Accord," *Queen's Law Journal* 15, no. 2 (1990): 345–59.

5 See Minister Robert Nault's expressed position on the First Nations Governance Act at 1600: http://www.parl.gc.ca/HousePublications/Publication.aspx?Pub=CommitteeMeetingEvidence&Acronym=AANR&Mee=14&Language=E&Mode=1&Parl=37&Ses=2.

6 See John Borrows, "Stewardship and the First Nations Governance Act," *Queen's Law Journal* 29 (2003): 103–32; see also Kiera Ladner and Michael Orsini, "The Persistence of Paradigm Paralysis: The *First Nations Governance Act* as the Continuation of Colonial Policy," in *Canada: The State of the Federation 2003: Reconfiguring Aboriginal-State Relations*, ed. Michael Murphy (Montreal and Kingston: McGill-Queen's University Press, 2003), 185–203.

7 John Borrows, "Domesticating Doctrines: Aboriginal Peoples after the Royal Commission," *McGill Law Journal* 46 (2001): 661; see also Glen Sean Coulthard, *Red Skin, White Masks: Rejecting the Colonial Politics of Recognition* (Minneapolis: University of Minnesota Press, 2014).
8 *Delgamuukw v. British Columbia*, [1997] 3 S.C.R. 1010, para. 186 [*Delgamuukw*].
9 See Patricia Monture-Angus, *Journeying Forward: Dreaming First Nations' Independence* (Halifax: Fernwood, 1999).
10 Richard F. Devlin and Ronalda Murphy, "Reconfiguration through Consultation? A Modest (Judicial) Proposal," in *Canada: The State of the Federation 2003: Reconfiguring Aboriginal-State Relations*, ed. Michael Murphy (Montreal and Kingston: McGill-Queen's University Press, 2003), 269.
11 Ladner and Orsini, *supra* note 6, 200.
12 Quoted in ibid., 195.
13 Ibid., 198.
14 Ibid., 196–7.
15 Patrick Wolfe, "Settler Colonialism and the Elimination of the Native," *Journal of Genocide Research* 8, no. 4 (2006): 395.
16 Coulthard, *supra* note 7, 15.
17 Ibid.
18 Peter A. Hall, "Policy Paradigms, Social Learning, and the State: The Case of Economic Policymaking in Britain," *Comparative Politics* 25, no. 3 (1993): 275.
19 Ibid., 290.
20 Matthew Sparke, "A Map That Roared and an Original Atlas: Canada, Cartography, and the Narration of Nation," *Annals of the Association of American Geographers* 88, no. 3 (1998): 465.
21 Ibid., 468; see also Shiri Pasternak, "Jurisdiction and Settler Colonialism: Where Do Laws Meet?," *Canadian Journal of Law and Society* 29, no. 2 (2014): 154; Michael McCrossan, "Shifting Judicial Conceptions of 'Reconciliation': Geographic Commitments Underpinning Aboriginal Rights Decisions," *Windsor Yearbook of Access to Justice* 31, no. 2 (2013): 173.
22 Gordon Christie, "A Colonial Reading of Recent Jurisprudence: *Sparrow*, *Delgamuukw* and *Haida Nation*," *Windsor Yearbook of Access to Justice* 23, no. 1 (2005): 21.
23 Ibid., 48.
24 Coulthard, *supra* note 7, 13, emphasis in original.
25 See John Borrows, *Canada's Indigenous Constitution* (Toronto: University of Toronto Press, 2010); Kiera L. Ladner, "Governing within an Ecological Context: Creating an AlterNative Understanding of Blackfoot Governance," *Studies in Political Economy* 70, no. 1 (2003): 125–52.

26 S. 35(1) of the Constitution Act, 1982 reads as follows: "The existing aboriginal and treaty rights of the aboriginal peoples of Canada are hereby recognized and affirmed," Constitution Act, 1982, being Schedule B to the Canada Act 1982 (UK), c. 11.
27 See Peter H. Russell, "Patriation and the Law of Unintended Consequences," in *Patriation and Its Consequences: Constitution Making in Canada*, ed. Lois Harder and Steve Patten (Vancouver: UBC Press, 2015), 236.
28 See McCrossan, *supra* note 21, 161–3.
29 *R. v. Sparrow*, [1990] 1 S.C.R. 1075 [*Sparrow*].
30 Ibid., 1110.
31 Ibid., 1105.
32 Ibid., 1109.
33 Ibid.
34 According to the Court, "Within the analysis of justification, there are further questions to be addressed, [including] … whether the aboriginal group in question has been consulted with respect to the conservation measures being implemented"; see ibid., 1119.
35 Ibid., 1109.
36 *R. v. Van der Peet*, [1996] 2 S.C.R. 507 [*Van der Peet*].
37 Ibid., para. 24; see also *Sparrow*, *supra* note 29, 1114.
38 *Van der Peet*, *supra* note 36, para. 24.
39 Ibid., para. 31.
40 Russel Lawrence Barsh and James Youngblood Henderson, "The Supreme Court's *Van Der Peet* Trilogy: Naive Imperialism and Ropes of Sand," *McGill Law Journal* 42, no. 4 (1997): 998.
41 See McCrossan, *supra* note 21, 167.
42 *Van der Peet*, *supra* note 36, para. 36.
43 For further discussion, see McCrossan, *supra* note 21, 173.
44 See *Delgamuukw*, *supra* note 8.
45 Ibid., para. 81.
46 Ibid., para. 165; Gordon Christie has suggested, in fact, that reconciliation is a construction designed to justify judicial rulings by ensuring that "Aboriginal societies exist in the public sphere"; see Gordon Christie, "Judicial Justification of Recent Developments in Aboriginal Law," *Canadian Journal of Law and Society* 17, no. 2 (2002): 65.
47 *Delgamuukw*, *supra* note 8, para. 165.
48 While Lamer does note that "some cases" may require the "full consent" of the Indigenous Nation affected, the examples in this instance are not in relation to the broad developmental aspects noted above, but rather

"particularly when provinces enact hunting and fishing regulations in relation to aboriginal lands"; see ibid., para. 168.

49 *Haida Nation v. British Columbia (Minister of Forests)*, [2004] 3 S.C.R. 511 [*Haida Nation*].

50 *Taku River Tlingit First Nation v. British Columbia (Project Assessment Director)*, [2004] 3 S.C.R. 550 [*Taku River*].

51 See *Haida Nation, supra* note 49, para. 35.

52 Ibid., para. 27.

53 Ibid., para. 43.

54 *Rio Tinto Alcan Inc. v. Carrier Sekani Tribal Council*, [2010] 2 S.C.R. 650 [*Rio Tinto Alcan*].

55 Ibid., para. 49.

56 Christie, *supra* note 22, 45.

57 *Haida Nation, supra* note 49, para. 16.

58 Wendy Grant-John, *Report of the Ministerial Representative: Matrimonial Real Property Issues on Reserves* (Ottawa: Indian and Northern Affairs Canada, 2007), Appendix A.

59 See Mary Ellen Turpel, "Home/Land," *Canadian Journal of Family Law* 10, no. 1 (1992): 39; see also Kiera Ladner, "Gendering Decolonisation, Decolonising Gender," *Australian Indigenous Law Review* 13, no. 1 (2009): 67.

60 Grant-John, *supra* note 58, Appendix A.

61 Ibid., *Appendix B, INAC Consultation Report on Matrimonial Real Property*, 6.

62 However, INAC did consult with Aboriginal organizations not represented by NWAC or the AFN. Ibid., 5.

63 Jeannette Corbiere Lavell, NWAC President, Senate of Canada, *Proceedings of the Standing Senate Committee on Human Rights*, Evidence (Issue no. 3, 31 May 2010), 40th Parl., 3rd Sess., 13; see also Jody Wilson-Raybould, Regional Chief, British Columbia, Assembly of First Nations, Senate of Canada, *Proceedings of the Standing Senate Committee on Human Rights*, Evidence (Issue no. 3, 31 May 2010), 17.

64 See statements by Randall Phillips, Grand Chief, Association of Iroquois and Allied Indians and Chief Louise Hillier (Caldwell First Nation), ibid., 29–33.

65 Grant-John, *supra* note 58, 37.

66 Ibid.

67 However, given the long-established emphasis and desire by the "new right" to establish "private property" regimes on Aboriginal reserves, it could perhaps also be argued that filling this legislative absence would not simply solve a chronic issue that had particularly disadvantaged and discriminated against Aboriginal women on reserves but would also dovetail with particular "ideas" and goals concerning land and property, which

could be further realized through legislation. As Grant-John observed, governmental understandings of the "legislative gap" surrounding matrimonial real property are "rooted in non-Aboriginal notions of individual property ownership and the relationships of property, family and the proper role of law in regulating relationships to land and family relations"; see ibid., 19. For further discussion on this point, see Michael McCrossan, "Enduring Eliminatory Logics, Market Rationalities, and Territorial Desires: Assessing the Harper Government's Legacy concerning Aboriginal Rights," *Review of Constitutional Studies* 21, no. 2 (2016): 193–9.

68 See Radha Jhappan, "The Federal-Provincial Power-Grid and Aboriginal Self-Government," in *New Trends in Canadian Federalism*, ed. François Rocher and Miriam Smith (Peterborough: Broadview Press, 1995), 155–84.

69 Ladner and Orsini, *supra* note 6, 191.

70 Grant-John, *supra* note 58, 76.

71 See Michelle Mann, "Summary of Input from Aboriginal Communities and Organizations on Consultation and Accommodation," 20 June 2011, http://www.aadnc-aandc.gc.ca/eng/1308577845455/1308578030248.

72 Government of Canada, *Aboriginal Consultation and Accommodation: Interim Guidelines for Federal Officials to Fulfill the Legal Duty to Consult*, February 2008.

73 Department of Aboriginal Affairs and Northern Development Canada, *Aboriginal Consultation and Accommodation: Updated Guidelines for Federal Officials to Fulfill the Duty to Consult*, March 2011, 1 [Updated Guidelines].

74 Ibid., 5.

75 Ibid., 6.

76 Ibid., 11.

77 Ibid., 11–15.

78 Ibid., 20–32.

79 Ibid., 36–58.

80 Ibid., 14.

81 See Jobs, Growth and Long-term Prosperity Act, S.C. 2012, c. 19; see also Jobs and Growth Act, 2012, S.C. 2012, c. 31. These pieces of legislation were also motivating factors behind the Indigenous grassroots social movement known as Idle No More. For discussions of the movement, see the Kino-nda-niimi Collective, ed., *The Winter We Danced* (Winnipeg: ARP Books, 2014).

82 Navigation Protection Act, R.S.C., 1985, c. N-22.

83 Dennis Kirchhoff et al., "The Canadian Environmental Assessment Act, 2012 and Associated Policy: Implications for Aboriginal Peoples," *International Indigenous Policy Journal* 4, no. 3 (2013): 7.

84 Navigation Protection Act, *supra* note 82, Schedule Navigable Waters, Part 1 and Part 2.

85 See Dennis Lebel, Minister of Transport, Infrastructure and Communities and the Minister of the Economic Development Agency of Canada, "Government of Canada Introduces Navigation Law Amendments," 18 October 2012, https://www.canada.ca/en/news/archive/2012/10/government-canada-introduces-navigation-law-amendments.html.

86 Douglas C. Harris, *Fish, Law, and Colonialism: The Legal Capture of Salmon in British Columbia* (Toronto: University of Toronto Press, 2001), 19–20.

87 John Borrows, "Legislation and Indigenous Self-Determination in Canada and the United States," in *From Recognition to Reconciliation*, ed. Patrick Macklem and Douglas Sanderson (Toronto: University of Toronto Press, 2016), 504.

88 Fisheries Act (R.S.C., 1985, c. F-14).

89 Ibid., s. 2(1); bolding in original.

90 This movement was recognized by Chief Shining Turtle of the Whitefish River First Nation; see his "Open Letter to My Non-Aboriginal Neighbours," http://www.huffingtonpost.ca/chief-shining-turtle/idle-no-more-movement_b_2551116.html.

91 See *R. v. Marshall*, [1999] 3 S.C.R. 456.

92 Fisheries Act, *supra* note 88, s. 35(1).

93 Ibid., s. 2(2).

94 *Sparrow*, *supra* note 29, 1094–5, quoting a summation of evidence by the British Columbia Court of Appeal.

95 Borrows, *supra* note 87.

96 Fisheries Act, *supra* note 88, s. 35(2). It should be noted that in February 2018, the Liberal government introduced two bills before the House of Commons (Bill C-68 and Bill C-69) that would amend the Fisheries Act and the Navigation Protection Act. However, while proposed changes to the Fisheries Act would substitute "Indigenous" for "Aboriginal" in subsection 2 (1) discussed above, there is no recognition of Indigenous rights to commercial fisheries in its current incarnation. See Bill C-68, "An Act to amend the Fisheries Act and other Acts in consequence," https://www.parl.ca/LegisInfo/BillDetails.aspx?Language=E&billId=9630814.

97 *Tsilhqot'in Nation v. British Columbia*, [2014] 2 S.C.R. 256 [*Tsilhqot'in Nation*].

98 See ibid., paras. 82–8. For further discussion of the Court's decision, see Michael McCrossan and Kiera L. Ladner, "Eliminating Indigenous Jurisdictions: Federalism, the Supreme Court of Canada, and Territorial Rationalities of Power," *Canadian Journal of Political Science* 49, no. 3 (2016): 411–31.

99 Russel Lawrence Barsh and James Youngblood Henderson, "Aboriginal Rights, Treaty Rights, and Human Rights: Indian Tribes and 'Constitutional Renewal,'" *Journal of Canadian Studies* 17, no. 2 (1982): 70.

100 *Tsilhqot'in Nation, supra* note 97, para. 125.
101 Barsh and Henderson, *supra* note 99.
102 See *Tsilhqot'in Nation, supra* note 97, para. 16; see also McCrossan, *supra* note 21, 173–4.
103 Borrows, *supra* note 87, 504–5.
104 *Gitxaala Nation v. Canada*, [2016] FCA 187, para. 279.
105 Ibid., para. 305.
106 Ibid., para. 309.
107 See Updated Guidelines, *supra* note 73, 17.
108 See Minister of Justice and Attorney General of Canada, *Principles Respecting the Government of Canada's Relationship with Indigenous Peoples* (Ottawa: Minister of Justice and Attorney General of Canada, 2018).
109 Ibid., 5.
110 See ibid., 5–7.
111 Ibid., 6. Although the prime minister announced on 14 February 2018 that the government would "develop, in full partnership with first nations, Inuit, and Métis people, a new recognition and implementation of indigenous rights framework," he also potentially limited the rights available to Indigenous peoples by using similar communal logic depicted in the SCC decisions discussed above. "We will also be engaging the provinces and territories, non-indigenous Canadians, people from civil society, industry, and the business community, and the public at large, because all Canadians have a stake in getting this right. … Indigenous Canadians and all Canadians are ready for change, ready for a new relationship based on recognition, rights, respect, co-operation, and partnership." See Right Hon. Justin Trudeau, House of Commons, Debates, 42nd Parl., 1st Sess., No. 264 (14 February 2018), 1555–1600, http://www.ourcommons.ca/DocumentViewer/en/42-1/house/sitting-264/hansard.
112 Minister of Justice and Attorney General of Canada, *Principles Respecting the Government of Canada's Relationship with Indigenous Peoples*, 3.
113 Ibid., 12.
114 Article 19 of the United Nations Declaration on the Rights of Indigenous Peoples reads as follows: "States shall consult and cooperate in good faith with the indigenous peoples concerned through their own representative institutions in order to obtain their free, prior and informed consent before adopting and implementing legislative or administrative measures that may affect them"; see http://www.un.org/esa/socdev/unpfii/documents/DRIPS_en.pdf.

18 After Marriage Equality: Courting Queer and Trans Rights

KYLE KIRKUP

In 2005, the Canadian government passed the Civil Marriage Act. Following two decades of queer[1] advocacy, which had used section 15 of the Canadian Charter of Rights and Freedoms as the primary vehicle for realizing the goal of marriage equality, the new legislation brought same-sex marriage to every province and territory in Canada. In view of the history of marriage equality, members of queer communities have often been described as one of the key beneficiaries of the Charter.[2] They have also been described as a group whose approach to advocacy focuses primarily on courts to advance policy goals. While some scholars and activists have viewed this development in positive terms,[3] others have remained sceptical about the consequences of using the Charter as a de facto policy tool. Hiebert, for example, has argued that courts became sites of queer advocacy in large part because legislatures refused to do the difficult work of wading into complex and often controversial policy issues. Writing just before Parliament recognized same-sex marriage, she presciently noted, "If legislatures are too slow in changing social policy, courts will likely become impatient with legislative indecision and more active in proffering remedies."[4] Morton and Knopff have been less charitable in their readings of the ways queer activists have used courts to achieve policy outcomes: they have suggested that organizations such as Egale Canada, a leading national queer and trans[5] organization,[6] have formed a so-called Court Party – that is, a broadly constituted coalition of groups that "seek to constitutionalize policy preferences that could not be easily achieved through the legislative process."[7]

By contrast, the comparatively newer story of trans legal activism has been one of turning to federal, provincial, and territorial human rights tribunals as a means of redressing discrimination – indeed, trans people did not even make the argument that they constituted an analogous ground under section 15 of the Charter until 2014.[8] Beginning in the 1990s, human rights tribunals across Canada consistently made findings of trans discrimination – on the basis of the enumerated categories of sex, disability, or both – on policy issues ranging from birth certificates[9] to policing.[10] More recently, legislatures have responded by formally adding *gender identity*[11] and *gender expression*[12] to federal, provincial, and territorial human rights codes, while administrative bodies have sought to shape the future directions of both law and policymaking. In comparison with the marriage-equality cases, section 15 has played virtually no role in these policy developments.

This chapter asks why two deeply intertwined rights-seeking groups have pursued such different advocacy strategies. Drawing on political and legal opportunity theories, it argues that while marriage equality was a battle fought primarily using section 15, in large part because activists thought courts would be more amenable to their claims than legislatures, trans rights have unfolded in more complicated, and often less predictable, ways. With comparatively fewer sources of funding for complex constitutional litigation than their queer counterparts, trans people have used the variegated opportunity structures of human rights tribunals to challenge discriminatory policies and practices. As public support for trans rights has grown, activists have also turned to political and administrative actors to advance their policy agendas.

The argument proceeds in three parts. The first part uses political and legal opportunity theories to analyse the queer and trans history of turning to courts and tribunals to effect policy change, along with attendant legislative responses. The second part examines two contemporary trans-rights case studies unfolding in the era after marriage equality: legal challenges to the process of changing sex markers on government-issued identification, such as driver's licences, and human rights complaints alleging discrimination in policing and correctional settings. Ultimately, the third part suggests that while Canada may have recognized same-sex marriage over a decade ago in large part because of section 15 Charter advocacy, the struggle for trans rights promises to play out in courts and tribunals – but also legislatures and administrative bodies – in far more complicated and unpredictable ways for years to come.

A History of Queer and Trans Engagement with Courts and Tribunals in Canada

Queer activists' decision to turn to the courts to realize the goal of marriage equality is perhaps best understood as a story of political and legal opportunities. Political opportunity theory underscores the importance of exogenous factors in shaping how social movements make decisions. Meyer suggests that political opportunity theory helps to account for how groups (1) mobilize, (2) advance certain claims over others, (3) cultivate alliances, (4) employ particular political strategies and tactics, and (5) ultimately affect institutional politics and policy.[13] Building on political opportunity theory, Andersen explains that legal opportunity structure theory examines social movements' "ability to gain access to the formal apparatus of the law with respect to a specific claim, the configuration of power among decision makers with respect to that claim, the nature of the alliance and conflict systems surrounding that claim, and the availability of relevant legal and cultural frames."[14]

Until 1969, when the federal government led by Prime Minister Pierre Elliott Trudeau decriminalized aspects of homosexuality, queer people regularly found themselves in conflict with the criminal law.[15] Similarly, police and other criminal law actors targeted various aspects of trans identity and experience.[16] As they moved away from political strategies focused on pushing back against the criminal law in the 1980s, activist organizations turned to section 15 of the Charter to realize the goal of marriage equality in the courts. Egale Canada, a newly minted rights organization, recognized that it could more readily mobilize courts to achieve public policy outcomes than it could legislatures – while the majority of Canadians now support same-sex marriage, public opinion has historically been far less favourable.[17] The organization also received significant funding from the federal government's Court Challenges Program – a program designed to support equality-seeking groups in advancing constitutional rights claims[18] – to launch a series of section 15 challenges. As McCaskell notes, for the activists at the helm of Egale Canada, "This turn to the courts reflected impatience with the slow rate of political change, and the perception that the Charter opened a window of opportunity."[19]

In examining this history, however, it would be a mistake to overemphasize the role of the Charter. Rather, Rayside notes that activists also developed strategic alliances with local and provincial government actors who seemed amenable to developing human rights protections and benefits for same-sex couples. While legislatures were often slow to react to the claims of queer activists, Rayside's careful analysis of this history cautions against a simple reading of the Charter as the sole locus of policymaking.[20]

Decided in 1993, *Mossop v. Canada*[21] became the first sexual orientation case heard by the Supreme Court of Canada under section 15. In this early precursor to marriage equality, Brian Mossop challenged his employer's decision to refuse to grant him bereavement leave to attend the funeral of his partner's father. He argued that his employer's decision to deny him leave constituted discrimination on the basis of *family status* within the meaning of the Canadian Human Rights Act.[22] When the case was heard, sexual orientation had not yet been added as a prohibited ground of discrimination under the act. Writing for the majority, Chief Justice Lamer dismissed Mossop's appeal, reasoning that the employer's decision to deny Mossop leave was based on sexual orientation discrimination, not family status discrimination. Absent a challenge to the constitutionality of the Canadian Human Rights Act under section 15 of the Charter, Mossop's appeal could not succeed.[23]

Two years later, the Supreme Court heard its next queer rights case: *Egan v. Canada*.[24] In this case, James Egan and John Norris Nesbitt argued that the different-sex definition of *spouse* in section 2 of the Old Age Security Act[25] violated section 15 of the Charter. Because same-sex partners did not meet the definition of *spouse*, they were denied a spousal allowance, which otherwise would have been available to them when Nesbit turned sixty. In a heavily split decision, five judges rejected the couple's claim, while four judges found in favour of the couple.[26] While not the outcome that activists had hoped for, the Court unanimously held that sexual orientation constituted an analogous ground of discrimination under section 15 of the Charter. This decision would prove to be a turning point in the next decade of marriage-equality activism.[27]

The Supreme Court heard the case of *Vriend v. Alberta*[28] in 1998. In this case, Delwin Vriend's employer fired him because of his sexual orientation. Vriend argued that the failure to include sexual orientation as an enumerated category in the Alberta Individual's Rights Protection Act[29] constituted discrimination under section 15 of the Charter. Applying its decision in *Egan*, which had read sexual orientation into the Charter, the majority found that the Alberta act violated section 15 and could not be saved by section 1. In a move that proved controversial at the time, the Court remedied the discrimination by reading sexual orientation into the act.[30] This decision brought queer activists even closer to the altar.

In the last precursor case to federal same-sex marriage legislation in 2005, the Supreme Court was again tasked with weighing in on queer familial-recognition issues in the 1999 decision of *M. v. H.* This case involved two women who had been in a relationship and had lived together for ten years. When their relationship ended, M. brought an application for spousal support against H. under Ontario's Family Law Act.[31] Section 29 of that act defined *spouse* as including unmarried, opposite-sex couples – but not same-sex couples – who had continuously cohabited for three years or longer. M. challenged the constitutionality of this definition of the term *spouse*. The majority of the Court concluded that the definition of *spouse* constituted discrimination on the basis of sexual orientation[32] and could not be saved by section 1.[33] By successfully arguing that the opposite-sex definition of *spouse* for the purposes of common law relationships violated the Charter, queer activists were on the brink of achieving marriage equality.

Armed with a decade's worth of Supreme Court precedents, queer activists returned to their respective superior courts in Ontario,[34] Quebec,[35] and British Columbia.[36] In tandem, they launched constitutional challenges to the opposite-sex definition of *marriage*. In Ontario and Quebec, courts found that prohibiting same-sex couples from marrying constituted discrimination on the basis of sexual orientation under the Supreme Court's section 15 Charter jurisprudence and could not be saved by section 1. Despite this finding, however, the courts suspended their declarations of invalidity for two years to give the governments an opportunity to respond to the potentially far-reaching implications of the rulings. Following the initial Ontario decision in *Halpern* in 2002, the parties appealed. In its landmark decision, the Court of Appeal agreed with the claimants that the opposite-sex definition of marriage constituted discrimination that could not be saved by section 1. However, it refused to suspend its declaration of invalidity,[37] making Ontario the first jurisdiction in North America to recognize marriage equality. Soon after, the British Columbia Court of Appeal issued a nearly identical ruling, bringing same-sex marriage to that province.[38] While the struggle for marriage equality had played out primarily in the courts because of activists' assessment that their claims would be ineffectual in legislatures, the issue now required a response from the federal government.

Rather than appealing the rising tide of Charter rulings in jurisdictions across Canada, Prime Minister Jean Chrétien announced that the federal government would draft the Civil Marriage Act[39] and proceeded to refer the matter directly to the Supreme Court. In *Reference re Same-Sex Marriage*,[40] the Court explained that the federal government had the jurisdiction to enact the Civil Marriage Act, but refused to say whether the proposed legislation complied with the Charter. After a contentious debate in the House of Commons, the Civil Marriage Act passed third reading by a vote of 158–133. Chief Justice Beverley McLachlin, acting in her capacity as deputy of the governor general due to the illness of Governor General Adrienne Clarkson, gave the bill royal assent on 20 July 2005. As this brief history suggests, queer activists made the conscious decision to use section 15 as a de facto policy instrument. Indeed, their tactics proved successful – within the span of three decades, they had moved from the criminalization of their very identities to marriage equality.

In contrast with their queer counterparts, the comparatively newer story of trans rights in Canada has not been a Charter one. Without funding from organizations such as the Court Challenges Program, which the federal government disbanded in 2006, trans activists have turned to federal, provincial, and territorial human rights regimes to advance their policy goals. As Sossin and Hill suggest, "While administrative decisions are subject to the oversight of judicial review, the barriers of cost and complexity mean that for the overwhelming majority of people, an administrative tribunal will be their first and final recourse to protect their social rights."[41] Indeed, trans people did not even argue that they constituted an analogous ground for the purposes of section 15 of the Charter until the 2014 decision of *C.F.*[42] In *C.F.*, the claimant was ultimately successful in their challenge to Alberta's Vital Statistics Act[43] requirement that they undergo surgery to be able to change the sex on their birth certificate. The Alberta Court of Queen's Bench concluded that the issue could be resolved using the enumerated section 15 category of sex, declining to recognize trans people – unlike their queer counterparts – as an analogous ground of discrimination. Writing about the limitations of the case, Koshan argues that it is "unfortunate that Justice Burrows did not take the next step and formally recognize gender identity or status as a transgendered person as an analogous ground for the purposes of section 15 of the Charter."[44]

In the early days of trans legal activism, one of the central questions for human rights tribunals across the country was whether trans discrimination fit within any of the existing categories of discrimination or whether legislative amendments were required. In a 1998 decision, Quebec's Commission des droits de la personne et des droits de la jeunesse concluded that trans discrimination fit within the enumerated category of sex;[45] in other cases, tribunals reasoned that trans discrimination fit within the category of disability.[46] Less frequently, tribunals concluded that trans discrimination was best understood as a combination of the two.[47] In light of the unpredictable application of the grounds analysis in trans-rights cases, the Northwest Territories became the first jurisdiction in Canada to expressly recognize gender identity as a prohibited ground of discrimination when it introduced its new human rights regime in 2002.[48] This decision on the part of the government of the Northwest Territories would foreshadow the complex and, at times, unpredictable interactions among courts, tribunals, legislatures, and administrative bodies in the recognition of trans human rights in Canada. Put differently, the template of the marriage-equality movement – whereby queer activists used section 15 of the Charter as the primary vehicle, and courts as the central locus, of policy change – would not readily graft onto the burgeoning trans-rights movement.

Trans Rights and Activism: Contemporary Case Studies

Having used political and legal opportunity theories to survey the history of queer and trans legal advocacy in Canada, the chapter proceeds to analyse two contemporary case studies taking shape in the aftermath of marriage equality: legal challenges to the process of changing sex markers on government-issued identification, such as driver's licences, and human rights complaints alleging trans discrimination in policing and correctional settings. In contrast with the story of the Charter and marriage equality, these contemporary case studies illustrate the complicated push and pull of trans human rights in courts, tribunals, legislatures, and administrative bodies across Canada.

Sex Markers on Government-Issued Identification

In jurisdictions across Canada, trans people experience widespread barriers when attempting to access government-issued identification that reflects who they are. Federal, provincial, and territorial governments have a long history of imposing surgical requirements on people seeking to change the sex designation on identity documents such as birth certificates, driver's licences, and passports.[49] Activists have sought to challenge the imposition of these requirements using a multifaceted approach – one that conscripts courts, tribunals, legislatures, and administrative bodies in bringing about policy change.

In 2012, Ontario became the first jurisdiction in Canada to remove the surgical requirements imposed on individuals seeking to change the sex designation on their birth certificates. The policy emerged as a direct consequence of the Ontario Human Rights Tribunal decision in *XY v. Ontario*, but it would ultimately have more far-reaching consequences.[50] In this case, the claimant argued that section 36 of the Vital Statistics Act, which required that any person seeking to change the sex marker on their birth certificate produce two medical certificates that independently confirmed that they had undergone "transsexual surgery," constituted sex-based discrimination under the Ontario Human Rights Code. The case preceded the Ontario government's decision, with support from all three parties, to add gender identity and gender expression as protected categories of discrimination under the Human Rights Code later that year.[51] Having made a finding of discrimination, the tribunal gave Ontario 180 days to remove the surgical requirement. In arriving at this conclusion, it relied on a relatively straightforward formal equality analysis – one premised on the government's differential treatment of trans and cisgender people. The tribunal found that the surgical requirement was "based on the stereotypical belief that transgendered persons can only 'be' their gender by having surgery; and that surgery somehow changes them from male to female, or vice versa."[52]

In October 2012, Ontario responded to the decision. The new policy no longer requires individuals seeking to change the sex designation on their birth registration to undergo surgery. Instead, they must now undertake two steps. First, they are required to complete a statutory declaration, indicating that they have assumed or have always had the gender identity that accords with the change in sex designation, that they are living full-time in that gender identity, and that they intend to maintain that gender identity. Second, they must provide a letter from a physician or psychologist who can support the requested change. Following the decision, jurisdictions across Canada have started to remove the imposition of surgical requirements – in Alberta, for example, this change occurred after the first case to argue that trans people constituted an analogous ground under section 15 of the Charter.[53] With the exponential growth in public support for trans rights across

Canada,[54] other jurisdictions including British Columbia, Manitoba, and Nova Scotia have voluntarily amended their respective legislative frameworks.[55]

To further complicate the picture of the burgeoning trans-rights movement in Canada, administrative bodies have emerged, often in unexpected ways, to remedy potentially discriminatory legislation. Policy learning theory understands policymaking as an iterative process – over time, administrative actors acquire knowledge from counterparts grappling with similar issues.[56] For example, after a trans man initiated a human rights complaint to the surgical requirement contained in Yukon's Vital Statistics Act,[57] the territory's Department of Health and Social Services issued him new documents with the appropriate marker, without making legislative amendments. As Sabin explains, this piecemeal approach, which was influenced by changes in other jurisdictions across Canada and growing support for trans rights, "envisions transgender Yukoners appealing directly to the government to ask for an extra-statutory salutation and gender affirming identity documents, neither of which have a clear basis in Yukon's legislation."[58] In comparison with the relatively linear political opportunity story of the Charter, courts, and the marriage-equality movement, challenging the imposition of surgical requirements for government-issued identity documents has been far more complicated; this emerging dynamic reflects the overlapping and often unstable role that courts, tribunals, legislatures, and administrative bodies play in bringing about policy change.

Discrimination in Policing and Correctional Settings

The growing number of cases involving allegations of trans discrimination in policing and correctional settings also underscores the diffuse nature of the trans-rights movement. While the Charter has played a key role in shaping criminal justice policy, trans people have tended to frame their arguments using the language made available to them by human rights law rather than the Canadian constitution.[59]

In a 2015 case, a trans woman named Angela Dawson successfully argued that her experiences with the Vancouver Police Board (VPB) constituted discrimination on the basis of sex. This decision provides a window into the experiences of trans legal subjects who find themselves targeted by the criminal legal system. Known by Vancouver locals for her love of directing traffic while wearing headphones and brightly coloured clothing, Dawson reported that police had failed to "recognize and treat her as a woman" during six separate interactions on the street in Vancouver's Downtown Eastside. This refusal to recognize and treat her as a woman often expressed itself through the use of inappropriate pronouns.[60] During one incident, a constable wrote "F(?)" on the arrest form "because he was not sure how she would be treated in jail." Despite his regular interactions with Dawson, the constable also referred to her by the male name she was given at birth, along with male pronouns.

At the hearing, the constable testified that he used Dawson's birth name and male pronouns because of the information that was listed in PRIME, a police database containing information including a person's name, aliases, and criminal record status. The tribunal explained that "no one told him to do this, but that this was his practice."[61] Dawson argued that these experiences constituted a form of systemic discrimination, suggesting that "in light of the absence of any training or policies on how to deal with trans members of the public in a respectful and non-discriminatory manner, it is not surprising that the attitudes and conduct of VPB members run the gamut from entirely appropriate to offensive."[62]

The British Columbia Human Rights Tribunal agreed, finding that the "interactions between Ms. Dawson and members of the VPB show that there is significant inconsistency in approach of how officers deal with and identify Dawson."[63] Making a finding of discrimination related to two of the six incidents, the tribunal ordered the VPB to refrain from committing similar discriminatory behaviour; to pay Dawson $15,000 as damages for injury to dignity, feelings, and self-respect; and to create trans-inclusive policies and training programs within one year.[64]

Echoing many of the findings of Dawson, Rosalyn Forrester brought an Ontario Human Rights Code complaint against the Peel Police Services Board in 2006, alleging discrimination on the basis of sex. She alleged that, over a series of arrests, the police had questioned, mocked, incarcerated, and inappropriately strip-searched her. While Forrester repeatedly requested that female officers perform these searches, her requests were denied. On two occasions, male officers performed the strip-searches alone – police reasoned that because Forrester had not undergone gender-affirming surgery, she should be treated as a man. On one other occasion, male and female officers performed a "split search": male officers examined Forrester's lower body, while female officers inspected her upper body. The Ontario Human Rights Tribunal agreed that this treatment constituted discrimination, finding that the police should be required to offer trans detainees three options before performing a strip-search – a male officer–only search, a female officer–only search, and a split search, whereby different officers would complete the strip-search based on the area of the body being searched.[65] Following this decision, police services across Canada – although not legally required as a result of the decision – responded by developing and implementing new trans strip-search policies.[66] The introduction of these policies again underscores the complex interplay among courts, tribunals, legislatures, and administrative bodies.

A similar story has taken shape in a series of recent challenges to the treatment of trans people in carceral settings. In 2014, Avery Edison launched a human rights complaint against Ontario's Ministry of Community Safety and Correctional Services, alleging discrimination with respect to services on the basis of disability, gender identity, and gender expression.[67] In early 2014, a month after a trans man named Boyd Kodak had launched a similar complaint, Edison arrived at Toronto Pearson International Airport from London, England. She was carrying a passport issued by the United Kingdom that identified her as a woman. The United Kingdom no longer requires individuals to undergo any form of surgery to change the sex markers on government-issued identity documents.

When Edison arrived at the airport, Canada Border Services Agency officers detained her. Edison eventually learned that the stated reason for the detention was that she had overstayed a student visa in 2013. Despite initially telling Edison that she would be held in an immigration detention centre, officers eventually indicated that she would be placed in administrative segregation in a provincial jail. They assured her, however, that she would be admitted to a women's facility. After being photographed and fingerprinted, Edison told officials that she had not undergone gender-confirming surgery. Following a series of delays, officials advised Edison that they would immediately transport her to Maplehurst Correctional Complex (a men's correctional facility located in Milton, Ontario, and adjacent to the Vanier Centre for Women).

Edison objected to this decision. According to her materials filed with the Ontario Human Rights Tribunal, "The supervisor explained that a 'policy' dictated that Ms. Edison should be detained in a men's facility 'because [she hadn't] had the surgery.'"[68] Despite her legal sex and self-identification as a woman, prison administrators repeatedly referred to Edison as "he," "him," or "sir." As she put it on Twitter as events were unfolding, "Change of plan AGAIN. Will be moved, soon, to Maplehurst correctional facility and assessed by a nurse before placed in male or female cell."[69] Officials also advised her that because of her identity as a trans woman who had not undergone surgery, she would be placed in administrative segregation at Maplehurst. Later that evening, however, officials transferred Edison to Vanier,[70] and, after a hearing, she was ordered to leave Canada.[71]

Following the international attention that the human rights complaints of Kodak and Edison received, the Ministry of Community Safety and Correctional Services created an Admission, Classification and Placement of Transgender Inmates policy and launched it, in January 2015, to much fanfare and media attention. In addition to new trans sensitivity training, the policy replaces the ad hoc, case-by-case process that had previously existed in Ontario's jails. The central policy shift is a significant one: Ontario has become the first jurisdiction in North America to allow trans people to self-identify their gender for admission, classification, and placement purposes – regardless of whether they have undergone gender-confirming surgery. Following Ontario's lead, British Columbia recently updated its policy in all provincial jails, and similar discussions are taking place in jurisdictions across the country.[72] Again, the story of trans discrimination in correctional settings points to the competing and, at times, contradictory interplay among courts, tribunals, legislatures, and administrative bodies in bringing about policy change. While Canada's trans-rights movement continues to gain momentum, section 15 of the Charter has played no meaningful role in these developments.

Conclusion: Future Directions

Using the comparative story of queer and trans rights in Canada as a case study, this chapter has asked why two deeply intertwined rights-seeking groups have pursued such different advocacy strategies. Drawing on political and legal opportunity theories, this chapter has argued that while marriage equality was a battle fought primarily using section 15 of the Charter, in large part because activists thought courts would be more amenable to their claims than legislatures, trans rights have unfolded in more complicated, and often less predictable, ways. In some moments, trans rights have emerged in courts and tribunals. With comparatively fewer sources of funding for complex constitutional litigation than their queer counterparts, trans people have turned to the opportunity structures provided by human rights tribunals to challenge discriminatory policies and practices. As public opinion on trans rights has shifted, trans activists have simultaneously turned to political and administrative actors to advance their policy goals. In comparison with their queer counterparts, who are often described as some of the key beneficiaries of the so-called Charter Revolution,[73] trans-rights activism promises to play out in invariably complex and unpredictable ways for years to come.

NOTES

1 I use the term *queer* an as "an umbrella term for nonconforming genders and various sexualities, ones that d[o] not easily submit to categorization"; see Sara Ahmed, "Interview with Judith Butler," *Sexualities* 19, no. 4 (2016): 482 at 490.

2 Canadian Charter of Rights and Freedoms, Part 1 of the Constitution Act, 1982, being Schedule B to the Canada Act 1982 (UK), 1982, c. 11.

3 See, e.g., Donald G. Casswell, *Lesbians, Gay Men and Canadian Law* (Toronto: Emond Montgomery Publications, 1996); Kathleen A. Lahey, *Are We "Persons" Yet? Law and Sexuality in Canada* (Toronto: University of Toronto Press, 1999); Bruce MacDougall, *Queer Judgments: Homosexuality, Expression and the Courts in Canada* (Toronto: University of Toronto Press, 2000).

4 Janet L. Hiebert, *Charter Conflicts: What Is Parliament's Role?* (Montreal and Kingston: McGill-Queen's University Press, 2002), at 199.

5 I use *trans* as a term that "suggests many forms of crossing gender boundaries, whether in terms of behaviour, self-representation or identity, or in terms of how such crossings are experienced and understood"; see Krista Scott-Dixon, *Trans/Forming Feminisms: Trans Feminist Voices Speak Out* (Toronto: Sumach Press, 2006), 11 at 12–13.

6 Egale Canada was formerly known as Equality for Gays and Lesbians Everywhere.

7 Ted Morton and Rainer Knopff, *The Charter Revolution and the Court Party* (Peterborough: Broadview Press, 2002), at 25.

8 *C.F. v. Alberta (Vital Statistics)*, 2014 ABQB 237 [*C.F.*].

9 *XY v. Ontario (Government and Consumer Services)*, 2012 HRTO 726 [*XY*].

10 *Forrester v. Peel (Regional Municipality) Police Services Board et al.*, 2006 HRTO 13 [*Forrester*].

11 I use the term *gender identity* to refer to "each person's internal and individual experience of gender. It is their sense of being a woman, a man,

both, neither, or anywhere along the gender spectrum. A person's gender identity may be the same as or different from their birth-assigned sex. Gender identity is fundamentally different from a person's sexual orientation"; see Ontario Human Rights Commission, *Policy on Preventing Discrimination Because of Gender Identity and Gender Expression* (Toronto: Ontario Human Rights Commission, 2014) [Ontario Human Rights Commission, *Policy on Preventing Discrimination Because of Gender Identity and Gender Expression*].

12 I define the term *gender expression* as "how a person publicly presents their gender. This can include behaviour and outward appearance such as dress, hair, make-up, body language, and voice. A person's chosen name and pronoun are also common ways of expressing gender"; see Ontario Human Rights Commission, *Policy on Preventing Discrimination Because of Gender Identity and Gender Expression*, ibid.

13 David S. Meyer, "Protest and Political Opportunities," *American Review of Sociology* 30 (2004): 125 at 126. See also David S. Meyer and Suzanne Staggenborg, "Movements, Countermovements, and the Structure of Political Opportunity," *American Journal of Sociology* 101, no. 6 (1996): 1628.

14 Ellen Ann Andersen, *Out of the Closets and into the Courts: Legal Opportunity Structure and Gay Rights Litigation* (Ann Arbor: University of Michigan Press, 2004), at 204. See also Chris Hilson, "New Social Movements: The Role of Legal Opportunity," *Journal of European Public Policy* 9, no. 2 (2002): 238; Lisa Vanhala, *Making Rights a Reality? Disability Rights Activists and Legal Mobilization* (Cambridge: Cambridge University Press, 2011).

15 For further discussion, see, e.g., David Kimmel and Daniel J. Robinson, "Sex, Crime, Pathology: Homosexuality and Criminal Code Reform in Canada, 1949–1969," *Canadian Journal of Law and Society* 16 (2001): 147; Gary Kinsman, *The Regulation of Desire: Sexuality in Canada* (Montreal: Black Rose Books, 1986).

16 Viviane Namaste, *Sex Change/Social Change: Reflections on Identity, Institutions, and Imperialism*, 2nd ed. (Toronto: Women's Press, 2011).

17 Ashley Csanady, "Canadians Still Support Same-Sex Marriage Ten Years in, but Even More of Us Are Coming Around: Poll," *National Post*, 2 July 2015, http://nationalpost.com/news/canada/canadians-still-support-same-sex-marriage-ten-years-in-but-even-more-of-us-are-coming-around-poll.

18 See, e.g., Jennifer Klinck and Kyle Kirkup, "Courting Controversy: Substantive Equality and the New Court Challenges Program," *Slaw.ca*, 25 April 2016, http://www.slaw.ca/2016/04/25/courting-controversy-substantive-equality-and-the-new-court-challenges-program/.

19 Tim McCaskell, *Queer Progress: From Homophobia to Homonationalism* (Toronto: Between the Lines Press, 2016), at 253. For further discussion of

these early queer familial-recognition cases and others, see, e.g., Robert Wintemute, "Sexual Orientation Discrimination as Sex Discrimination: Same-Sex Couples and the Charter in Mossop, Egan and Layland," *McGill Law Journal* 39 (1993–94): 429; Brenda Cossman, "Same Sex Couples and the Politics of Family Status," in *Women and Public Policy in Canada*, ed. Janine Brodie (Toronto: Harcourt Brace, 1995).

20 David Rayside, *Queer Inclusions, Continental Divisions: Public Recognition of Sexual Diversity in Canada and the United States* (Toronto: University of Toronto Press, 2008), at 92–125.

21 *Mossop v. Canada*, [1993] 1 SCR 554 [*Mossop*].

22 RSC 1985, c. H-6.

23 *Mossop*, *supra* at 554–600. For further discussion of *Mossop* and its relationship to the policy goal of marriage equality, see, e.g., Brenda Cossman, "Lesbians, Gay Men, and the Charter," *Osgoode Hall Law Journal* 40 (2002): 223.

24 *Egan v. Canada*, [1995] 2 SCR 513 [*Egan*].

25 RSC, 1985, c. O-9.

26 *Egan*, *supra* at 526–40.

27 Cossman, *supra*.

28 [1998] 1 SCR 493 [*Vriend*].

29 RSA 1980, c. I-2.

30 *Vriend*, *supra* at paras. 1–181.

31 RSO 1990, c. F 3.

32 *M. v. H.*, *supra* at 57.

33 Ibid. at 87.

34 *Halpern v. Canada (Attorney General)* (2002), 95 CRR (2d) 1.

35 *Hendricks v. Quebec*, [2002] R.J.Q. 2506.

36 *Barbeau v. British Columbia*, 2003 BCCA 251.

37 *Halpern v. Canada (Attorney General)*, [2003] O.J. No. 2268.

38 *Barbeau v. British Columbia (Attorney General)*, 2003 BCCA 251.

39 Civil Marriage Act, *supra*.

40 2004 SCC 79, [2004] 3 SCR 698.

41 Lorne Sossin and Andrea Hill, "Social Rights and Administrative Justice," in *Advancing Social Rights in Canada*, ed. Martha Jackman and Bruce Porter (Toronto: Irwin Law, 2014), at 1.

42 *C.F.*, *supra*.

43 RSA 2000, c. V-4.

44 Jennifer Koshan, "A Vital Judgment: Upholding Transgendered Rights in Alberta," *ABlawg.ca*, 7 May 2014, https://ablawg.ca/2014/05/07/4349/.

45 *Quebec (Commission des droits de la personne et des droits de la jeunesse) c. Maison des jeunes A-Ma-Baie Inc.* (1998), 33 CHRR D/263, 1998 Carswell Que 2602 (TDPQ).
46 See, e.g., *Hogan v. Ontario (Health and Long-Term Care)*, 2006 HRTO 32, 58 CHRR D/317.
47 See, e.g., *Kavanagh v. Canada (Attorney General)*, [2001] CHRD no 21 (QL) (CHRT).
48 SNWT 2002, c. 18 s. 5(1). For further discussion, see Jena McGill and Kyle Kirkup, "Locating the Trans Legal Subject in Canadian Law: *XY v. Ontario*," *Windsor Review of Legal and Social Issues* 33 (2013): 96 at 108.
49 McGill and Kirkup, ibid.
50 *XY*, *supra*.
51 RSO 1990, c. H 19.
52 *XY*, *supra* at para. 212.
53 *C.F.*, *supra*.
54 Ryan Maloney, "Liberals' Transgender Rights Bill Backed by Majority of Canadians: Angus Reid Institute Poll," *Huffington Post*, 7 September 2016, http://www.huffingtonpost.ca/2016/09/07/liberals-transgender-rights-bill-angus-reid-institute_n_11892032.html.
55 Jerald Sabin, "Why Is Yukon Lagging Behind on Transgender Rights?," *Policy Options*, 22 September 2015, http://policyoptions.irpp.org/2015/09/22/why-is-yukon-lagging-behind-on-transgender-rights/.
56 See, e.g., Max Visser and Kim Van Der Togt, "Learning in Public Sector Organizations: A Theory of Action Approach," *Public Organization Review* 16, no. 2 (2016): 235; Frank Fisher, *Reframing Public Policy: Discursive Politics and Deliberate Practices* (Oxford: Oxford University Press, 2003).
57 RSY 2002, c. 225.
58 Sabin, *supra*.
59 For further discussion, see, e.g., Jamie Cameron, *Charter's Impact on the Criminal Justice System* (Toronto: Carswell, 1996); Jamie Cameron and James Stribopoulos, eds., *The Charter and Criminal Justice: Twenty-Five Years Later* (Markham: LexisNexis, 2008).
60 *Dawson v. Vancouver Police Board (No. 2)*, 2015 BCHRT 54 at para. 47 [*Dawson*].
61 Ibid. at para. 183.
62 Ibid.
63 Ibid. at para. 243.
64 Ibid. at paras. 272–3.
65 Forrester, *supra*.
66 Kyle Kirkup, *Best Practices in Policing and LGBTQ Communities in Ontario* (Toronto: Ontario Association of Chiefs of Police, 2013), http://www.oacp.on.ca/.

67 Ontario Human Rights Code, s. 1, *supra*.
68 Avery Edison, Factum, Ontario Human Rights Commission, 2 July 2014 at 3.
69 Avery Edison, Twitter post (@aedison), 11 February 2014, 1:18 a.m. For further discussion on the experiences of Avery Edison, see, e.g., "What Canada's Legal System Can Do to Respect Transgender People," *Globe and Mail*, 28 February 2014, https://www.theglobeandmail.com/video/video-what-canadas-legal-system-can-do-to-respect-transgender-people/article33021999/.
70 Avery Edison, Factum, *supra* at 5.
71 Ibid.
72 Kyle Kirkup, "How Ontario's Prisons Pioneered Sensitivity to Transgender Inmates," *TVO*, 26 January 2016, https://tvo.org/article/current-affairs/shared-values/how-ontarios-prisons-pioneered-sensitivity-to-transgender-inmates.
73 Morton and Knopff, *supra*.

Conclusion: Policy Influence and Its Limits – Assessing the Power of Courts and the Constitution

EMMETT MACFARLANE

As Canada celebrates 150 years since Confederation and the thirty-fifth anniversary of the entrenchment of the Charter of Rights and Freedoms and Aboriginal and treaty rights, few question the policy relevance of the courts or the constitution. Scholars have examined and debated the role of the Judicial Committee of the Privy Council and the Supreme Court in shaping Canadian federalism,[1] and they have acknowledged the Charter's relevance in advancing equality rights for gays and lesbians, and the rights of the criminally accused.[2]

Yet the extent and *nature* of the courts' influence on public policy remains an understudied topic in the Canadian context. The contributions in this volume shed light on the range and depth of the courts' impact on a diverse set of policy issues across a range of institutional contexts. It is perhaps not surprising that the degree of policy change attributable to the courts or specific constitutional provisions varies widely depending on a host of factors, including the political preferences of the government of the day, public opinion, the willingness and ability of front-line state actors to implement judicial decisions, intervening variables like federalism, and even the exceptional nature of specific policy areas.

The preceding chapters not only identify the nature of judicial impact – including invalidating existing policies, prescribing substantive policy changes or policy processes, affirming existing policies, and indirectly conditioning policy change – but also explore the limits of the courts' role. Limits on judicial policymaking include judicial deference to elected policymakers, institutional pushback from governments or legislatures in the face of adverse judicial decisions, institutional aspects like federalism that mitigate change, and poor or weak policy implementation of judicial decisions. This volume also sheds light on policy change relating to, or influenced by, a number of specific constitutional provisions, including Aboriginal and treaty rights, the division of powers, and a host of provisions under the Charter, including the limitation clause of section 1 and the notwithstanding clause.

In this concluding chapter, I explore these modes of, and limits on, judicial policy change by offering a loose typology. I then briefly discuss potential areas of further exploration and study.

Judicial Policy Impact

Invalidation

Judicial decisions that effectively nullify existing policies reflect the most obvious method by which courts induce policy change. The judicial power to veto public policies has existed in some form since Confederation. Judicial review of division of powers cases, for example, can result in policies being found *ultra vires* the authority of the enacting level of government. In the modern context, judicial invalidation can occur with respect to not only which order of government has the authority to implement a policy but also whether that policy contravenes rights under the Charter. This is a notable enhancement of judicial power in that it evolved from the ability to decide "who can do what" to determining "what can be done." Judicial invalidation of existing criminal laws surrounding assisted suicide and abortion, and finding unconstitutional the Harper government's cuts to the Interim Federal Health Program (IFHP) for refugees, are among the examples examined in this volume.

In chapter 3, Zanoni notes that the "striking down" remedy can result in large-scale punctuations of the policy environment. This is particularly evident in the case of abortion policy following the Supreme Court's 1988 decision in *Morgentaler*.[3] As Johnstone explores in chapter 16, the invalidation of the criminal law provisions and resulting federal policy vacuum marked a permanent shift in both policy delivery and interest group mobilization around the issue. Similarly, both chapter 2 by Snow and Puddister and chapter 15 by Nicolaides and Hennigar engage in analysis that reflects the fundamental shift that occurred following the Court's decision in *Carter v. Canada*:[4] the policy environment became focused on what constitutional limitations or regulations could be imposed on medical aid in dying, but the former policy status quo in the form of a prohibition was permanently disrupted.

By contrast, other decisions to invalidate policies do not punctuate a policy equilibrium as much as restore one. The Federal Court's decision blocking cuts to the IFHP represents a relatively straightforward policy veto by the courts, even as Anderson and Soennecken's analysis in chapter 14 notes the exceptional nature of this case and the emergence of new legal mobilization as it relates more broadly to refugee policy.

Courts can also have an impact by effectively vetoing *proposed* policies. This occurs in the context of advisory opinions, as Glover Berger explores in chapter 6. The Senate reform reference[5] is illustrative in that it signalled an end to the federal Conservative government's attempts to pass legislation establishing consultative elections and term limits for senators.

Prescription

Courts also prescribe policy. This can happen in two distinct ways. First, judicial decisions might dictate specific policy prescriptions. Often this occurs in the context of judges setting out guidelines or thresholds for constitutionally permissible action. The Supreme Court's decision in *Carter* is an example of this as the Court determined that the prohibitions on physician-assisted death were "void insofar as they prohibit physician-assisted death for a competent adult person who (1) clearly consents to the termination of life; and (2) has a grievous and irremediable medical condition (including an illness, disease or disability) that causes enduring suffering that is intolerable to the individual in the circumstances of his or her condition. 'Irremediable,' it should be added, does not require the patient to undertake treatments that are not acceptable to the individual."[6] Notably, such prescriptions result in policy change only if legislatures and government actors adhere to them. As examined below, Parliament's legislative response to the *Carter* decision does not. However, there is systematic evidence to suggest that when courts do provide such guidelines, legislatures tend to follow them.[7]

Judicial decisions enforcing positive obligations on government, such as those relating to the Charter's minority-language education rights under section 23, are also effectively prescriptive by the very nature of the provisions.[8] A decision that a provincial government is obligated to provide minority-language services requires obvious policy action. In the context of section 23, judicial policy prescription took a considerably pronounced turn when, in the 2003 case *Doucet-Boudreau*,[9] the Supreme

Court upheld a trial judge's extensive remedy, including establishing deadlines by which certain facilities and programs should be provided. As Chouinard describes in chapter 11, the judge remained seized of the case, setting up a series of follow-up meetings to ensure reasonable advancement on implementation of the decision. Chouinard correctly notes that *Doucet-Boudreau* thus establishes an important precedent for judicial involvement in prescribing policies and even control over their implementation.

A more direct form of policy prescription occurs when courts employ the remedy of *reading in* to effectively rewrite constitutionally offensive legislation. A notable example of this was the Supreme Court's decision in *Vriend v. Alberta*, in which the Court found that Alberta's decision not to include sexual orientation as a prohibited ground in its human rights legislation was contrary to the Charter and, employing the remedy, effectively added it rather than declare the entire policy invalid.[10]

A second form of judicial prescription occurs when courts dictate or influence the policy process. The Supreme Court's impact on federalism and intergovernmental relations, as described by Schertzer in chapter 5, is an important example of this. By encouraging collaboration and negotiation over unilateral action in the context of intergovernmental conflict, Schertzer suggests that the *Secession Reference*[11] established the normative foundations of collaborative federalism as the Court detailed the purpose of federalism as a pillar of Canada's constitutional order and emphasized its deliberative nature. Schertzer describes several cases in which the Court mitigates unilateral action on the part of one order of government in favour of urging collaboration, such as in relation to the federal government's desire to establish a national securities regulator.[12] He notes that the Court has also minimized the use of the inter-jurisdictional immunity doctrine, which was applied in the past as a way of protecting a "basic, minimum and unassailable"[13] core of each order of government's jurisdiction under the division of powers.

In other contexts, the Court interprets constitutional provisions in a way that changes the process for enacting policies. Recent jurisprudence pertaining to the amending formula is one example of how this works.[14] As Glover Berger explains in chapter 6, the Supreme Court's decision in the *Supreme Court Act Reference* determined that changes to the eligibility criteria for Supreme Court justices falls under the unanimity procedure of the amending formula, which refers to any changes to the *composition* of the Court. This means that unanimous agreement of the provinces is required for changes to the act's eligibility provisions, something that arguably has unintended consequences; for example, following the Court's logic, Parliament alone is not permitted to amend the act to require mandatory bilingualism for appointees to the Court.

Finally, few judicial doctrines have had as great an impact on the policy process as the duty to consult embedded in the Supreme Court's Aboriginal and treaty rights jurisprudence. Across government, in both federal and provincial departments and agencies, public authorities are required to assess requirements for, and develop approaches to, consulting and accommodating on policies implicating the section 35 rights of Indigenous peoples. In chapter 17, McCrossan provides a compelling argument that however pervasive the impact the duty to consult has on government policy processes, its substantive impact on the fundamental relationship between Indigenous peoples and the Crown remains impoverished by a colonial mindset regarding land ownership and use. As discussed further below, sweeping changes to the policy process may not be sufficient to result in meaningful changes to policy outcomes.

Affirmation

Judicial decisions do not always directly induce policy change; instead, they may affirm existing policies in ways that strengthen an established policy status quo or condition an existing policy environment. Adopting the lens of punctuated equilibrium in chapter 3 of this volume, Zanoni suggests that this might occur when a contested policy issue venue-shifts to the judiciary and the courts uphold a particular policy, thereby strengthening the existing equilibrium.

Affirming policies is not limited to contexts in which the constitution *dictates* or constrains particular policy options. In some cases, the courts will uphold policies, and thus, the legislature is free to enact new amendments or repeal an existing policy. Policies regulating third parties in the context of elections is an example of this dynamic. In chapter 10, Crandall and Lawlor explore the ways in which the Supreme Court decision in *Harper v. Canada*[15] effectively entrenched an egalitarian model of election regulation in Canada by upholding fairly restrictive third party spending limits. Notably, Crandall and Lawlor contend that the Court's earlier election law decision in *Libman*[16] influenced the federal government's design of, and justification for, the policy on spending limits. The *Harper* decision's potentially symbolic effect in strengthening the egalitarian model is particularly notable – in part, because the Conservative government under Prime Minister Stephen Harper maintained the policy status quo once in power and despite the fact that the case bears Harper's own name as he had been the head of the interest group that brought the constitutional challenge.

Indirect Impact

Courts indirectly influence policy change when political decision makers alter their behaviour in anticipation of judicial action. There is evidence that the threat of legal challenge can spur policy change. The recent decision by the government of Prince Edward Island to finally offer abortion services on the island is an example of this. As Johnstone notes in chapter 16, PEI Premier Wade MacLauchlan publicly stated, when announcing the change, that the province was likely to lose a recently launched Charter challenge. (It is worth noting that it is not clear that the premier's presumption was accurate. The litigation could have been viewed as demanding a positive right to abortion access, something that the extant jurisprudence does not necessarily support. It is perhaps just as likely that the provincial government did not want to deal with the divisiveness of a prolonged legal battle.)

In another context, executive review of policies and legislation for rights compatibility in the Canadian context has been portrayed as risk-averse as "politicians are reluctant to make decisions that risk their being branded as insensitive to rights."[17] A direct form of this influence occurs when governments wish to respond to judicial invalidation of legislation but believe themselves constrained by recently established precedent. The federal government's response to the invalidation of its legislation imposing restrictions on tobacco advertising, for example, has been described as "timid."[18] This timidity was thought to apply in a more indirect way to the "Charter vetting" of legislation by the executive generally, not just when governments were responding to judicial decisions. However, as Hiebert describes in chapter 4, new information about the scrutiny process suggests that this is not the case (see more on this below).

Limits on Judicial Influence

Deference

Judicial deference to governmental or legislative objectives is the most fundamental *self-imposed* limit on the policy impact of courts or specific constitutional provisions. Puddister's analysis in chapter 9 illustrates that, for much of the Charter period, the Supreme Court has emphasized deference to Parliament's decisions about the range of penalties imposed on those found guilty of criminal offences and that courts should be reluctant to interfere with those choices. Only recently has the Court adopted a less deferential approach to assessing sentencing policy decisions under section 12's right against cruel and unusual punishment.

Similarly, in chapter 13, Gaucher notes that the Court has largely deferred questions of citizenship/non-citizenship to Parliament. Deference can thus occur not only when courts interpret particular constitutional provisions narrowly, as was previously the case with respect to section 12 of the Charter, but also when they avoid elaborating on substantive definitional issues, as Gaucher describes in relation to the categories of citizenship and non-citizenship. Moreover, Gaucher argues that the Court compounded this dynamic by framing issues of non-citizenship and immigration as matters implicating security, leaving pronounced space for deference to ministerial authority in that policy environment.

And in chapter 17, McCrossan elaborates on a fundamental refusal of courts to pay heed to Indigenous renderings and developmental visions of land. By privileging non-Indigenous or colonial conceptions of the law, the courts effectively undermine the duty to consult concept. Although McCrossan does not explain this overall approach as one of simple judicial deference, the space that the Court has ultimately granted the Crown to pursue its particular vision for land use, and the overall Indigenous-Crown relationship, might be portrayed as being deferential in this sense.

Institutional Pushback

The most important external limit imposed on judicial policymaking stems from the actions of other political actors. When governments or legislatures wish to vigorously defend their policy objectives, they sometimes have the capacity to respond to unfavourable judicial decisions. This is the starting premise of the famed *dialogue* metaphor, although the utility of that concept has been weakened by significant empirical and conceptual contestation.[19]

The most obvious method by which a legislature can preserve a policy status quo in the face of judicial policy impact is the use of the notwithstanding clause in section 33 of the Charter. Although the clause applies only to laws implicating sections 2 and 7 through 15 of the Charter, and it must be renewed every five years, it effectively immunizes legislation from the effects of judicial review. However, as Albert explores in chapter 7, the notwithstanding clause is arguably close to becoming a constitutional dead letter. One of the principal reasons for this is the perception that section 33 "overrides" the Charter itself, as opposed to signalling disagreement with judicial interpretations of rights. This perception has contributed to an environment in which the clause is regarded as a political third rail, so while it remains a legal option for governments to preserve policies in the face of judicial influence, it is unlikely to see much use.

Legislatures can successfully mitigate judicial policy impact by amending impugned laws or bringing in new policies that depart from the courts' policy prescriptions. The recent federal legislation to regulate medical aid in dying is a prime example of this, as explored by both Snow and Puddister in chapter 2 and Nicolaides and Hennigar in chapter 15. As described above, in the *Carter* decision, the Court outlined a clear threshold of access for medical aid in dying. Parliament's response legislation flouts that threshold by limiting the scope of access to individuals whose deaths are reasonably foreseeable. As Nicolaides and Hennigar describe, the federal government asserted Parliament's own capacity to interpret the Charter's requirements, even as that interpretation fundamentally differed from the policy prescription outlined by the Court. While the *Carter* decision still generated considerable policy change, Parliament was able to constrain the effects of the decision. It remains to be seen whether this will be temporary as the new legislation is already facing a constitutional challenge.[20]

Another area in which legislatures have been successful in mitigating the impact of judicial policymaking is minority-language education. As Chouinard notes in chapter 11, the impact of section 23 of the Charter and the Supreme Court's jurisprudence has been substantial, but legislatures have enjoyed significant flexibility to adapt. Chouinard argues persuasively that the litigation model, while successful for many claimants on a case-by-case basis, has failed to result in systemic implementation of the basic rules set out by courts requiring services where numbers warrant. This is evidenced by the continued deluge of litigation facing many provinces across Canada. Chouinard also notes that implementation in the context of positive rights like section 23 can be severely slowed by government foot-dragging. Kelly's analysis in chapter 12 on section 23's impact on Quebec arrives at a similar conclusion. He explores the extent to which section 23 produced policy change, but finds that such change was often short-lived and mitigated by Quebec's National Assembly reasserting its autonomy over language and education policy. Drawing on Hall's work in the US context, which describes courts as "implementer-dependent institutions,"[21] Kelly's conclusion strongly suggests that future litigation in Quebec over the Charter of the French Language will prove futile.

Federalism can serve as an important factor in enabling legislatures to mitigate the policy impact of courts. As noted above, Johnstone explores in chapter 16 how the *Morgentaler* decision produced profound change in the policy environment surrounding abortion, particularly given that Parliament was unable to pass any new criminal law to regulate access. Johnstone describes how many provinces enacted legislation following the Court's ruling in an attempt to limit access to services. Some of these new provincial policies were subsequently challenged and overturned,[22] but provincial action (and inaction) has generated marked disparities in access across the country, despite a commonly held narrative that the 1988 Supreme Court decision resulted in "abortion on demand."[23]

Finally, in chapter 4, Hiebert presents a new analysis of executive scrutiny of policies and legislation for Charter compatibility. Her examination reveals that judicial norms about Charter compatibility do not hold the indirect influence that was previously thought as governments do not seem to equate their political interests with avoiding judicial censure. Instead, the strong executive, party discipline, and little attention to constitutional issues by a relatively weak Parliament come together to permit determined governments to pursue their policy and political objectives.

Weak Implementation or Mobilization

Governments and legislatures are not the only actors that can constrain the implementation of judicial policy prescriptions. Given the volume of Charter jurisprudence that relates to the criminal justice process, front-line state actors like the police are crucial to ensuring that judicial decisions influence behaviour on the ground. As Riddell and Baker's study of police implementation of Charter decisions in chapter 8 reveals, there is some evidence that low levels of standardization, asymmetrical communication, and lack of ongoing training limit the degree to which the police are kept up to date on the latest Charter decisions. Riddell and Baker note that front-line officers are briefed on the most important cases and that there is a generally strong commitment to professionalism, which limits the extent and magnitude of potential Charter violations. Nonetheless, systemic procedures are not in place to ensure widespread and consistent dissemination of the latest rules of conduct under the Charter, a situation that suggests weaker implementation than is possible.

Interest group mobilization and litigation activity in particular policy areas might also be weaker than expected. In some cases, this is the result of little judicial oversight over a policy area, as Anderson and Soennecken describe in chapter 14 in relation to refugee policy. While the courts were influential in effectively vetoing policies under the Harper government, the authors suggest that this was the result of exceptional mobilization in response to particularly egregious policies.

In other contexts, a lack of Charter mobilization reflects a complex mixture of factors. As Kirkup describes in chapter 18, the trans-rights movement has combated discrimination in human rights tribunals and commissions rather than pursuing section 15 equality rights claims in the courts. At the same time, legislatures and administrative bodies – taking cues from human rights decisions and public opinion – have amended human rights laws by adding protections based on gender identity and gender expression. Kirkup suggests that the future of trans rights may continue to play out in unpredictable ways in the foreseeable future, but the lack of mobilization around section 15 marks a fascinating departure from the preceding years of queer advocacy, particularly in relation to equality rights for same-sex couples.

A Brief Summary of Court Impact

Based on the various methods of, and limits on, judicial policy change described above, what is the overall picture of the impact that courts and the constitution have had on the policies discussed in this book? Table 19.1 provides a general summary.

As table 19.1 makes clear, there is a considerable variance in the magnitude of policy change, its nature, and whether the courts' policy impact is mitigated by the behaviour of other actors. Although the plethora of issues explored by the contributors to this volume is neither comprehensive nor necessarily representative, the diversity of policy issues analysed and affected by judicial decision making reinforces the

Table 19.1 Magnitude of Court Policy Impact, Nature of Change, Mitigation

Policy issue/area	Magnitude	Nature of change	Mitigation of impact
Abortion policy	Major	Disruption of policy status quo	Federalism: resistance by some provinces
Assisted dying policy	Major	Disruption of policy status quo; prescription	New federal legislation narrowed prescribed rules of access
Citizenship policy	Weak	N/A	Deference to Parliament
Duty to consult (process)	Significant	Prescription	Uneven/poor implementation
Duty to consult (Indigenous conceptions of law)	Weak/no change	N/A	Deference to Crown
Election regulation	Significant	Affirmation (egalitarian model)	N/A
Equality rights of trans persons	Weak	N/A	Lack of Charter mobilization
Intergovernmental relations/ federalism	Significant	Veto (in cases of unilateral action – e.g., national securities regulator); prescription (encouraging collaboration)	N/A
Mandatory minimum sentences	Significant	Veto	Recent decisions follow long period of deference to Parliament
Police powers	Significant	Disrupting policy status quo; prescription (laying out rules for police conduct)	Mixed implementation of Charter decisions
Prostitution	Moderate/weak	Veto	Policy effectively re-established by new legislation
Refugee health cuts	Significant	Veto	N/A
Refugee policy (general)	Weak	N/A	Little judicial oversight, in part due to lack of mobilization
Senate reform proposal (term limits, consultative elections)	Major	Veto	N/A

importance of courts as policy actors. The courts have had a significant impact on a range of issues, including police conduct, social and health policies, criminal justice policy, the rights of Indigenous peoples, election regulation, and institutional reform. Where courts have had less impact, it is generally the result of a lack of mobilization over the policy area, deference to elected decision makers, or factors that mitigate the impact of their decisions, such as further legislative action to re-establish policy objectives or poor implementation.

What effect might this general overview have on normative debates about the role of courts or judicial activism that preoccupied the scholarly literature in decades past? Although systemic studies have suggested that the courts often have the "final say" in policies that come up against constitutional challenge,[24] the in-depth analyses of policy change conducted here allow for an assessment of the context and mechanisms that provide for, or limit, judicial power. Ultimately, whether the judicial role in affecting these policies is appropriate or desirable is a normative question that scholars will continue to debate. The empirical assessment of policy change, the inter-institutional interactions involved, and the various stages of the policy process implicated by judicial decision making allow for a more exacting evaluation and will hopefully inspire further, and more informed, engagement on these important questions and debates.

Studying Policy Change and Courts

As public law scholarship in Canada continues to evolve from largely descriptive and normative work to increasingly rigorous empirical study,[25] one of the most significant and uncharted areas of pursuit remains integrating the insights of the broader public policy literature with scholarship on courts and the constitution. The preceding sections outline a loose typology of the forms of judicial policy influence and the limits of judicially inspired policy change. Based as it is on the contributions to this volume, this typology is not comprehensive. Nonetheless, it reflects the diverse set of factors and considerations examined by the authors.

More work is necessary to elaborate on the various factors and mechanisms that drive, condition, or constrain policy change by courts. Do's clarion call in chapter 1 for more explicit attention to approaches or theories of policy change in relation to courts is especially fitting for this reason. Much of the judicial politics literature draws implicitly on the variety of interest-driven, institutional, or ideational analyses she describes.

One example of how these approaches might prove useful is explaining when judicial deference arises and examining the degree to which it reflects a self-imposed limitation on judicial policy change. Accounting for when and how deference occurs has proved challenging for scholars of courts. A traditional legal view might posit that judicial deference, like its debatable counterpart, "activism," is simply a by-product of the courts' work in interpreting and applying the constitution. In this sense, deference is simply a label that assumes motivations on the part of the courts where none may exist.

By contrast, the political science literature on judicial behaviour accounts for the political nature of constitutional interpretation. Behavioural studies that assume that judges' ideology is a principal factor in decision making[26] might suggest that deference occurs when the policy issue at stake in a case aligns with the preferences of the justices. This falls neatly into the interest-driven approach Do describes in chapter 1. However, other studies of judicial decision making adopt a neo-institutional and ideational approach that may help to explain when deference arises. Scholars examining judicial decision making through the lens of institutional-role norms[27] assert that judges pay heed to conceptions of their role and the role of their institution, meaning that deference may be called for depending on a myriad of factors and as dictated by considerations like the Court's relationship with the other branches of government. For example, judges may be wary of outcomes that dictate significant government spending. The behavioural and role-normative explanations may not be incompatible: when judicial consensus over role norms breaks down, it opens up a window for the ideological preferences of judges to have more influence.[28] As Do argues, further research might assist the judicial behaviour scholarship to further situate courts in relation to other policy actors and the varied mechanisms that contribute to particular outcomes.

Some of the contributions to this volume serve as excellent baselines for future research in this vein. Snow and Puddister's adaptation of the multiple streams approach to the case of medical aid in dying policy in chapter 2 not only inserts courts as actors providing "policy solutions" under a popular theory of policy change but also helps to explain the mechanisms behind policy change instigated by a recent and highly visible case. Beyond that, Snow and Puddister's analysis also poses challenges for the theory, particularly as it relates to identifying and accounting for the *politics stream*, which requires the existence of a political opportunity to proceed and responsiveness from decision makers. Thus, while the authors demonstrate that a formal theory like the multiple streams approach has utility for analysing courts as actors within the policy process, they also highlight potential challenges or problems with the theory itself, particularly in relation to which stream judicial decisions might implicate in the theory.

Similarly, Zanoni's examination of punctuated equilibrium in chapter 3 offers an analysis of the ways in which judicial remedies might be incorporated into that framework. Many elements of Zanoni's analysis resemble the loose typology of impact that I describe above. This suggests some promise for the underlying premise that punctuated equilibrium theory can incorporate courts as important actors in the policy process: the more cases that fit the various ways that courts' influence operates, the more likely it can contribute to future comprehensive or large-*N* studies of court impact in addition to case studies of specific policy issues.

Future studies of policy change in the area of public law will, I hope, take up the challenge of applying theories of the policy process to other cases or engage in systematic, large-*N* studies that seek to measure policy change by courts. One advantage of large-*N* cases is that they hold greater potential for allowing scholars to identify which factors tend to produce different types of policy change across different issue areas. Scholars might begin to make more broadly generalizable conclusions about the role and impact of courts in the policy process. Systematic studies will also be fruitful for making comparisons – across provinces, across courts, across various policy issues, and across different components of the constitution.

Comprehensive studies of court impact will face particular challenges. To briefly examine one example, in addition to deriving measures for the magnitude and nature of a judicial decision's impact on a particular policy, comprehensive studies will need to examine questions like issue salience. Where the case studies in this volume explore a set of diverse, important policy issues, not all policies – nor all instances of policy change – are as relevant or fundamental to society, government, or various interests and actors as some other policies may be. Measuring the importance of issues at stake in judicial decisions is an inherently difficult task.[29] In Canadian studies, salient cases are usually identified by the type of case (whether a constitutional issue is raised, for example), meaning that all Charter cases are considered salient.[30]

Obviously, this is not a particularly helpful indicator when trying to distinguish among policies implicated by the Charter. Another indicator of issue salience may include whether (or even how many) third party interveners took part in a case.[31] Scholars should be careful when using this indicator to examine early Charter cases given that the Court's policy on allowing interveners grew considerably more liberal after the first few years of the Charter.

One common indicator of salience in legal circles is how often the Court itself cites a particular case as precedent.[32] While this may be an excellent indicator of a case's *legal* importance, it may be a less useful reflection of a case's *policy* significance. Perhaps the best example of this distinction is represented by the 1986 *Oakes* case,[33] in which the Court struck down a provision of the Narcotics Control Act that created a reverse onus with regard to the possession of controlled substances (requiring an individual to prove that unlawful possession was not for the purposes of trafficking). While *Oakes* is widely cited, it is almost universally for the test that the Court created for determining the reasonableness of a rights limitation rather than the substantive issue involved in the case.

A more reliable indicator of policy significance may be the amount of news media attention that a case receives.[34] Caution is warranted here, too, given that the media may sensationalize particular issues. However, news coverage tends to give prominent focus to cases that have societal implications relative to those that may be important only for their technical or legal detail. Finally, one recent study applied as a proxy for salience the presence of a policy issue in a governing party's campaign platform.[35] This measure arguably helps to identify the importance of a policy issue to the government of the day.

In-depth, qualitative case studies of the sort in this volume will remain fundamental for continuing to explore institutional processes and contexts, and issues at various stages of the policy process (from agenda setting to implementation) and to draw inferences about causal mechanisms. This book has sought to shed light on these issues, and particularly, to begin to deliberate more explicitly about courts as drivers of policy change. The contributions confirm that courts in Canada have become increasingly important policy actors and that the magnitude and nature of their impact on an array of policy issues are, not surprisingly but nonetheless importantly, contingent on the actions and motivations of the institutions traditionally considered by the literature to be vital to the policy process. Until courts are recognized as regular players in that scholarship, our understanding of the nature of policy change and the policy process remains incomplete.

NOTES

1 Alan C. Cairns, "The Judicial Committee and Its Critics," *Canadian Journal of Political Science* 4, no. 3 (1971): 301–45; Robert Schertzer, *The Judicial Role in a Diverse Federation: Lessons from the Supreme Court of Canada* (Toronto: University of Toronto Press, 2016).
2 See, e.g., discussion on these topics by Janet Hiebert, *Charter Conflicts: What Is Parliament's Role?* (Montreal and Kingston: McGill-Queen's University Press, 2002); F.L. Morton and Rainer Knopff, *The Charter Revolution and the Court Party* (Peterborough, ON: Broadview Press, 2000).
3 *R. v. Morgentaler*, [1988] 1 S.C.R. 30.
4 *Carter v. Canada (Attorney General)*, 2015 SCC 5, [2015] 1 S.C.R. 331.
5 *Reference re Senate Reform*, 2014 SCC 32.
6 *Carter* at para. 127.
7 Emmett Macfarlane, "Dialogue or Compliance? Measuring Legislatures' Policy Responses to Court Rulings on Rights," *International Political Science Review* 34 (2013): 39–56, prepublished 13 April 2012, doi: 10.1177/0192512111432565.
8 For more on positive rights and the particular nature of their impact on the policy process, see Emmett Macfarlane, "The Dilemma of Positive Rights: Access to Health Care and the *Canadian Charter of Rights and Freedoms*," *Journal of Canadian Studies* 48, no. 3 (2014): 49–78.
9 *Doucet-Boudreau v. Nova Scotia (Minister of Education)*, [2003] 3 S.C.R. 3.
10 *Vriend v. Alberta*, [1998] 1 S.C.R. 493.
11 *Reference re Secession of Quebec*, [1998] 2 S.C.R. 217.
12 *Reference re* Securities Act, 2011 SCC 66, [2011] 3 S.C.R. 837.
13 *Canadian Western Bank v. Alberta*, 2007 SCC 22, [2007] 2 S.C.R. 3 at para. 33.
14 *Reference re Senate Reform; Reference re Supreme Court Act, ss. 5 and 6*, 2014 SCC 21, [2014] 1 S.C.R. 433. For more on the impact of the amending formula, see Emmett Macfarlane, ed. *Constitutional Amendment in Canada* (Toronto: University of Toronto Press, 2016).
15 *Harper v. Canada (Attorney General)*, [2004] 1 S.C.R. 827, 2004 SCC 33.
16 *Libman v. Quebec (Attorney General)*, [1997] 3 S.C.R. 569.
17 Janet L. Hiebert, "Parliamentary Bills of Rights: An Alternative Model?" *Modern Law Review* 69, no. 1 (2006): 7–28, at 20.
18 Ibid., 19.

19 Macfarlane, "Dialogue or Compliance?"; Emmett Macfarlane, "Conceptual Precision and Parliamentary Systems of Rights: Disambiguating 'Dialogue,'" *Review of Constitutional Studies* 17, no. 2 (2012): 73–100.
20 Mike Leanela, "Assisted-Dying Legislation Faces New Legal Challenge," *CBC News*, 27 June 2016, http://www.cbc.ca/news/canada/british-columbia/bccla-assisted-dying-legislation-1.3654220.
21 Matthew E.K. Hall, *The Nature of Supreme Court Power* (New York: Cambridge University Press, 2011), 15.
22 See, e.g., *R. v. Morgentaler*, [1993] 3 S.C.R. 463.
23 For further analysis of the policy environment surrounding abortion, see Rachael Johnstone and Emmett Macfarlane, "Public Policy, Rights, and Abortion Access in Canada," *International Journal of Canadian Studies* 51 (2015): 97–120.
24 Macfarlane, "Dialogue or Compliance?"
25 Dave Snow and Mark S. Harding, "From Normative Debates to Comparative Methodology: The Three Waves of Post-Charter Supreme Court Scholarship in Canada," *American Review of Canadian Studies* 45, no. 4 (2015): 451–66.
26 C.L. Ostberg and Matthew Wetstein, *Attitudinal Decision Making in the Supreme Court of Canada* (Vancouver: UBC Press, 2007).
27 Emmett Macfarlane, *Governing from the Bench: The Supreme Court of Canada and the Judicial Role* (Vancouver: UBC Press, 2013).
28 Ibid.
29 Saul Brenner, "Measuring the Importance of Supreme Court Decisions," *Law Library Journal* 90, no. 2 (1998): 183–92.
30 Lori Hausegger and Stacia Haynie, "Judicial Decisionmaking and the Use of Panels in the Canadian Supreme Court and the South African Appellate Division," *Law and Society Review* 37, no. 3 (2007): 635–57; Matthew A. Hennigar, "Why Does the Federal Government Appeal to the Supreme Court of Canada in Charter of Rights Cases? A Strategic Explanation," *Law and Society Review* 41, no. 1 (2007): 225–50.
31 Hennigar, "Why Does the Federal Government Appeal to the Supreme Court of Canada in Charter of Rights Cases?," 235.
32 Brenner, "Measuring the Importance of Supreme Court Decisions."
33 *R. v. Oakes*, [1986] 1 S.C.R. 103.
34 Emmett Macfarlane, "Terms of Entitlement: Is There a Distinctly Canadian 'Rights Talk'?" *Canadian Journal of Political Science* 41, no. 2 (2008): 303–28.
35 Emmett Macfarlane, "'You Can't Always Get What You Want': Regime Politics, the Supreme Court of Canada, and the Harper Government," *Canadian Journal of Political Science* 51, no. 1 (2018): 1–21, prepublished on FirstView, doi:10.1017/S0008423917000981.

Selected Bibliography

Albert, Richard. "Constitutional Amendment by Constitutional Desuetude." *American Journal of Comparative Law* 62, no. 3 (2014): 641–4.

Alfred, Taiaiake. *Peace, Power, Righteousness: An Indigenous Manifesto*. Oxford: Oxford University Press, 2009.

Alter, Karen, and Jeannette Vargas. "Explaining Variation in the Use of European Litigation Strategies." *Comparative Political Studies* 33 (2000): 452–82.

Andersen, Ellen Ann. *Out of the Closets and into the Courts*. Ann Arbor: University of Michigan Press, 2005.

Anderson, Christopher G. *Canadian Liberalism and the Politics of Border Control: 1867–1967*. Vancouver: UBC Press, 2013.

– "A Long-Standing Canadian Tradition: Citizenship Revocation and Second-Class Citizenship under the Liberals, 1993–2006." *Journal of Canadian Studies* 42, no. 3 (2008): 80–105.

Arthurs, Harry W., and Brent Arnold. "Does the Charter Matter?" *Review of Constitutional Studies* 11, no. 1 (2005): 37–117.

Atkinson, Michael. "Policy, Politics and Political Science." *Canadian Journal of Political Science* 46, no. 4 (2013): 751–72.

Attaran, Amir. "Unanimity on Death with Dignity – Legalizing Physician-Assisted Dying in Canada." *New England Journal of Medicine* 372, no. 22 (2015): 2080–2.

Baier, Gerald. *Courts and Federalism: Judicial Doctrine in the United States, Australia and Canada*. Vancouver: UBC Press, 2006.

– "The Courts, the Constitution, and Dispute Resolution." In *Canadian Federalism: Performance, Effectiveness, and Legitimacy*. 3rd ed., edited by Herman Bakvis and Grace Skogstad, 79–95. Don Mills, ON: Oxford University Press, 2012.

Baker, Dennis. *Not Quite Supreme: The Courts and Coordinate Constitutional Interpretation*. Montreal and Kingston: McGill-Queen's University Press, 2010.

Baker, Dennis, and Mark D. Jarvis. "The End of Informal Constitutional Change in Canada?" In *Constitutional Amendment in Canada*, edited by Emmett Macfarlane, 185–207. Toronto: University of Toronto Press, 2016.

Bakvis, Herman, and Grace Skogstad. "Conclusion: Taking Stock of Canadian Federalism." In *Canadian Federalism: Performance, Effectiveness, and Legitimacy*. 3rd ed., edited by Herman Bakvis and Grace Skogstad, 340. Don Mills, ON: Oxford University Press, 2012.

Banfield, Andrew C., and Rainer Knopff. "'It's the Charter, Stupid!' The Charter and the Courts in Federal Partisan Politics." *Supreme Court Law Review* (2d) 45 (2009): 37–57.

Barclay, Scott, and Thomas Birkland. "Law, Policymaking, and the Policy Process: Closing the Gaps." *Policy Studies Journal* 26, no. 2 (1998): 227–43.

Barnes, Jeb. "Bringing the Courts Back In: Interbranch Perspectives on the Role of Courts in American Politics and Policy Making." *Annual Review of Political Science* 10 (2007): 25–43.

Barsh, Russel Lawrence, and James Youngblood Henderson. "Aboriginal Rights, Treaty Rights, and Human Rights: Indian Tribes and 'Constitutional Renewal.'" *Journal of Canadian Studies* 17, no. 2 (1982): 55–81.

– "The Supreme Court's *Van der Peet* Trilogy: Naive Imperialism and Ropes of Sand." *McGill Law Journal* 42, no. 4 (1997): 993–1009.

Bateman, Thomas M.J., Janet L. Hiebert, Rainer Knopff, and Peter H. Russell. *The Court and the Charter: Leading Cases*. Toronto: Emond Montgomery, 2008.

Baumgartner, Frank R., Bryan D. Jones, and Peter B. Mortensen. "Punctuated-Equilibrium Theory: Explaining Stability and Change in Public Policymaking." In *Theories of the Policy Process*. 3rd ed., edited by Paul A. Sabatier and Christopher M. Weible, 59–104. Boulder, CO: Westview Press, 2014.

Beaudoin, Gérald A. "La Loi 22: À propos du désaveu, du référé et de l'appel à l'Exécutif fédéral." *Revue générale de droit* 5, no. 2 (1974): 385–6.

Behiels, Michael D. *Canada's Francophone Minority Communities: Constitutional Renewal and the Winning of School Governance*. Montreal and Kingston: McGill-Queen's University Press, 2004.

Bennett, Andrew, and Colin Elman. "Complex Causal Relations and Case Study Methods: The Example of Path Dependence." *Political Analysis* 14, no. 3 (2006): 250–67.

Berger, Benjamin L. "A More Lasting Comfort? The Politics of Minimum Sentences, the Rule of Law, and *R. v. Ferguson*." *Supreme Court Law Review* (2d) 47 (2009): 1–25.

Bickel, Alexander. *The Least Dangerous Branch: The Supreme Court at the Bar of Politics*. New York: Bobbs-Merrill, 1962.
Bickerton, James. "Deconstructing the New Federalism." *Canadian Political Science Review* 4, no. 2–3 (2010): 56–72.
Blankenau, Joe. "The Fate of National Health Insurance in Canada and the United States: A Multiple Streams Explanation." *Policy Studies Journal* 29, no. 1 (2001): 38–55.
Blidook, Kelly. *Constituency Influence in Parliament: Countering the Centre*. Vancouver: UBC Press, 2012.
Bogart, W.A. *Courts and Country: The Limits of Litigation and the Social and Political Life of Canada*. Oxford: Oxford University Press, 1994.
Borrows, John. *Canada's Indigenous Constitution*. Toronto: University of Toronto Press, 2010.
– "Domesticating Doctrines: Aboriginal Peoples after the Royal Commission." *McGill Law Journal* 46 (2001): 615–61.
– "Legislation and Indigenous Self-Determination in Canada and the United States." In *From Recognition to Reconciliation*, edited by Patrick Macklem and Douglas Sanderson, 474–505. Toronto: University of Toronto Press, 2016.
– "Stewardship and the First Nations Governance Act." *Queen's Law Journal* 29 (2003): 103–32.
Bossé, Daius, François Larocque, and Mark C. Power. "Constitutional Litigation, the Adversarial System and Some of Its Adverse Effects." *Review of Constitutional Studies* 17, no. 2 (2012): 1–40.
Brenner, Saul. "Measuring the Importance of Supreme Court Decisions." *Law Library Journal* 90, no. 2 (1998): 183–92.
Brodie, Janine. "Choice and No Choice in the House." In *The Politics of Abortion*, edited by Janine Brodie, Shelley Gavigan, and Jane Jenson, 57–116. Toronto: Oxford University Press, 1992.
Brouillet, Eugénie. *La négation de la nation: L'identité culturelle québécoise et le fédéralisme canadien*. Sillery, QC: Éditions du Septentrion, 2005.
Brown, Lori, J. Shoshanna Ehrlich, and Colleen MacQuarrie. "Subverting the Constitution: Anti-abortion Policies and Activism in the United States and Canada." In *Abortion: History, Politics, and Reproductive Justice after Morgentaler*, edited by Shannon Stettner, Kristin Burnett, and Travis Hay, 239–61. Vancouver: UBC Press, 2018.
Burningham, Sarah. "A Comment on the Court's Decision to Suspend the Declaration of Invalidity in *Carter v. Canada*." *Saskatchewan Law Review* 78, no. 2 (2015): 201–7.
Bynum, Timothy S., Donna Murasky, Dennis Rogan, and Craig D. Uchida. "Acting in Good Faith: The Effects of *United States v. Leon* on the Police and Courts." *Arizona Law Review* 30 (1988): 467–95.

Bzdera, André. "Comparative Analysis of Federal High Courts: A Political Theory of Judicial Review." *Canadian Journal of Political Science* 26, no. 1 (1993): 3–29.

Cairney, Paul. *Understanding Public Policy: Theories and Issues*. New York: Palgrave Macmillan, 2012.

– "Using Devolution to Set the Agenda? Venue Shift and the Smoking Ban in Scotland." *British Journal of Politics and International Relations* 9, no. 1 (2007): 73–89.

Cairns, Alan C. *Citizens Plus: Aboriginal Peoples and the Canadian State*. Vancouver: UBC Press, 2000.

– "The Judicial Committee and Its Critics." *Canadian Journal of Political Science* 4, no. 3 (1971): 301–45.

Cameron, David, and Richard Simeon. "Intergovernmental Relations in Canada: The Emergence of Collaborative Federalism." *Publius* 32, no. 2 (2002): 49–72.

Cameron, Jamie. "Fault and Punishment under Sections 7 and 12 of the *Charter*." *Supreme Court Law Review* (2d) 40 (2008): 553–92.

Campbell, John. "Ideas, Politics and Public Policy." *Annual Review of Sociology* 28 (2002): 22–5.

Canon, Bradley C. "Testing the Effectiveness of Civil Liberties Policies at the State and Federal Levels." *American Politics Quarterly* 5 (1977): 57–82.

Canon, Bradley C., and Charles A. Johnson. *Judicial Policies: Implementation and Impact*. 2nd ed. Washington, DC: CQ Press, 1999.

Capano, Giliberto. "Understanding Policy Change as an Epistemological and Theoretical Problem." *Journal of Comparative Policy Analysis* 11, no. 1 (2009): 7–31.

Capoccia, Giovanni, and Daniel Keleman. "The Study of Critical Junctures: Theory, Narrative and Counterfactuals in Historical Institutionalism." *World Politics* 59, no. 3 (2007): 341–69.

Cardinal, Linda. "La judiciarisation de la politique, les droits des minorités et le nationalisme canadien. "*Forum constitutionnel* 13, no. 3 (2005): 60–4.

– "Le pouvoir exécutif et la judiciarisation de la politique au Canada: Une étude du Programme de contestation judiciaire." *Politique et sociétés* 19, no. 2–3 (2000): 43–64.

Cardinal, Linda, and Selma Sonntag. *State Traditions and Language Regimes*. Montreal and Kingston: McGill-Queen's University Press, 2015.

Carter, Mark. "*Carter v. Canada*: Societal Interests under Sections 7 and 1." *Saskatchewan Law Review* 78, no. 2 (2015): 209–16.

Case, Rhonda Evans, and Terri E. Givens. "Re-engineering Legal Opportunity Structures in the European Union?" *Journal of Common Market Studies* 48, no. 2 (2010): 221–41.

Casper, Jonathan D. "The Supreme Court and National Policy Making." *American Political Science Review* 70, no. 1 (1976): 50–63.

Casswell, Donald G. *Lesbians, Gay Men and Canadian Law*. Toronto: Emond Montgomery Publications, 1996.

Caylor, Lincoln, and Gannon G. Beaulne. "Parliamentary Restrictions on Judicial Discretion in Sentencing: A Defence of Mandatory Minimum Sentences." Research paper, Macdonald-Laurier Institute, Ottawa, May 2014.

Choudhry, Sujit, and Claire E. Hunter. "Measuring Judicial Activism on the Supreme Court of Canada: A Comment on *Newfoundland (Treasury Board) v. NAPE*." *McGill Law Journal* 48 (2003): 525–62.

Christie, Gordon. "A Colonial Reading of Recent Jurisprudence: *Sparrow, Delgamuukw* and *Haida Nation*." *Windsor Yearbook of Access to Justice* 23, no. 1 (2005): 17–53.

– "Judicial Justification of Recent Developments in Aboriginal Law." *Canadian Journal of Law and Society* 17, no. 2 (2002): 41–71.

Cossman, Brenda. "Lesbians, Gay Men, and the Charter." *Osgoode Hall Law Journal* 40, no. 3/4 (2002): 223–49.

– "Same Sex Couples and the Politics of Family Status." In *Women and Public Policy in Canada*, edited by Janine Brodie, 232–44. Toronto: Harcourt Brace, 1995.

Coulthard, Glen Sean. *Red Skin, White Masks: Rejecting the Colonial Politics of Recognition*. Minneapolis: University of Minnesota Press, 2014.

Crandall, Erin, and Andrea Lawlor. "Third Party Election Spending in Canada and the United Kingdom: A Comparative Analysis." *Election Law Journal: Rules, Politics, and Policy* 13, no. 4 (2014): 476–92.

Dahl, Robert A. "Decision-Making in a Democracy: The Supreme Court as a National Policy-Maker." *Journal of Public Law* 6 (1957): 279–95.

Daly, Paul. "Supreme Court's Place in the Constitutional Order: Contrasting Recent Experiences in Canada and the United Kingdom." *Queen's Law Journal* 41, no. 1 (2015): 1–40.

Dauvergne, Catherine. "How the Charter Has Failed Non-citizens in Canada: Reviewing Thirty Years of Supreme Court of Canada Jurisprudence." *McGill Law Journal* 58, no. 3 (2013): 663–728.

– "International Human Rights in Canadian Immigration Law." *Indiana Journal of Global Legal Studies* 19, no. 1 (2012): 305–26.

Dawood, Yasmin. "Democracy, Power, and the Supreme Court: Campaign Finance Reform in Comparative Context." *International Journal of Constitutional Law* 4, no. 2 (2006): 269–93.

Dawson, Carrie. "Refugee Hotels." *University of Toronto Quarterly* 83, no. 4 (2014): 826–46.

Dawson, Mary. "The Impact of the Charter on the Public Policy Process and the Department of Justice." *Osgoode Hall Law Journal* 30, no. 3 (1992): 595–603.

Devonshire, Reginald A. "The Effects of Supreme Court Charter-Based Decisions on Policing: More Beneficial Than Detrimental?" *Crim. R. (4th)* 31 (1994): 82–99.

Dhamoon, Rita. "Security Warning: Multiculturalism Alert!" In *The Ashgate Research Companion to Multiculturalism*, edited by Duncan Ivison, 255–75. London: Ashgate, 2010.

Dick, Caroline. *The Perils of Identity: Group Rights and the Politics of Intragroup Difference*. Vancouver: UBC Press, 2011.

Dodek, Adam M. "Chief Justice Lamer and Policy Design at the Supreme Court of Canada." In *The Sacred Fire: The Legacy of Antonio Lamer*, edited by Adam Dodek and Daniel Jutras. Markham, ON: LexisNexis, 2009.

Doob, Anthony N., and Carla Cesaroni. "The Political Attractiveness of Mandatory Minimum Sentences." *Osgoode Hall Law Journal* 39, no. 2/3 (2001): 287–304.

Doob, Anthony N., and Cheryl M. Webster. "Weathering the Storm? Testing Long-Standing Canadian Sentencing Policy in the Twenty-First Century." *Crime and Justice* 45, no. 1 (2016): 359–418.

Downie, Jocelyn. *Dying Justice: A Case for Decriminalizing Euthanasia and Assisted Suicide in Canada*. Toronto: University of Toronto Press, 2004.

Dunn, Christopher. "Harper without Jeers, Trudeau without Cheers: Assessing 10 Years of Intergovernmental Relations." *IRPP Insight* 8 (2016).

Eisenberg, Avigail. *Reasons of Identity: A Normative Guide to the Political and Legal Assessment of Identity Claims*. Oxford: Oxford University Press, 2009.

Elliot, Robin. "References, Structural Argumentation and the Organizing Principles of Canada's Constitution." *Canadian Bar Review* 80 (2001): 67–142.

Ely, John Hart. *Democracy and Distrust: A Theory of Judicial Review*. Cambridge, MA: Harvard University Press, 1980.

Engeli, Isabelle, and Christine Rothmayr Allison. "Conceptual and Methodological Challenges in Comparative Public Policy." In *Comparative Policy Studies: Conceptual and Methodological Challenges*, edited by Isabelle Engeli and Christine Rothmayr Allison, 1–13. London: Palgrave Macmillan, 2015.

Epp, Charles. *The Rights Revolution*. Chicago: University of Chicago Press, 1998.

Erdman, Joanna. "In the Back Alleys of Health Care: Abortion, Equality and Community in Canada." *Emory Law Journal* 56 (2007): 1093–555.

Feeley, Malcolm M., and Edward L. Rubin. *Judicial Policy Making and the Modern State: How the Courts Reformed America's Prisons*. Cambridge: Cambridge University Press, 1998.

Fisher, Frank. *Reframing Public Policy: Discursive Politics and Deliberate Practices*. Oxford: Oxford University Press, 2003.

Flanagan, Thomas. "Canada's Three Constitutions: Protecting, Overturning, and Reversing the Status Quo." In *The Myth of the Sacred: The Charter, the Courts, and the Politics of the Constitution in Canada*, edited by Patrick James, Donald E. Abelson, and Michael Lusztig, 125–46. Montreal and Kingston: McGill-Queen's University Press, 2002.

Fleischmann, Aldys, Cody Maccaroll, and Nancy van Styvendale. *Narratives of Citizenship: Indigenous and Diasporic Peoples Unsettle the Nation-State*. Edmonton: University of Alberta Press, 2011.

Flemming, Roy. *Tournament of Appeals: Granting Judicial Review in Canada*. Vancouver: University of British Columbia Press, 2004.

Flemming, Roy, and B. Dan Wood. "The Public and the Supreme Court: Individual Justice Responsiveness to American Policy Moods." *American Journal of Political Science* 4, no. 2 (1997): 468–98.

Flynn, Greg, and Tanya Kuzman. "Meaningful Participation? The Judicialization of Electoral Reform in Canada Post-*Figueroa v. Canada*." *Canadian Political Science Review* 7, no. 1 (2013): 37–46.

Foucher, Pierre. "Les gardiens de la paix: La Cour suprême du Canada et le contentieux des droits linguistiques; Montée en puissance des juges, pourquoi?" In *La montée en puissance des juges: Ses manifestations, sa contestation*, edited by Mary Jane Mossman and Ghislain Otis, 129–60. Montréal: Éditions Thémis, 2000.

Galanter, Marc. "The Radiating Effects of Courts." In *Empirical Theories of Courts*, edited by Keith D. Boyum and Lynn Mather, 117–42. New York: Longman, 1983.

Galloway, Donald. "Rights and the Re-identified Refugee." In *Refugee Protection and the Role of Law: Conflicting Identities*, edited by Susan Kneebone, Dallal Stevens, and Loretta Baldassar, 36–55. London: Routledge, 2014.

Gardbaum, Stephen. "The New Commonwealth Model of Constitutionalism." *American Journal of Comparative Law* 49, no. 4 (2001): 707–60.

Gaucher, Megan. "Monogamous Canadian Citizenship, Constructing Foreignness, and the Limits of Harm Discourse." *Canadian Journal of Political Science* 49, no. 3 (2016): 519–38.

Goldsworthy, Jeffrey. "Judicial Review, Legislative Override, and Democracy." *Wake Forest Law Review* 38, no. 2 (2003): 451–67.

– *Parliamentary Sovereignty: Contemporary Debates*. Cambridge: Cambridge University Press, 2010.

Gould, Jon B., and Stephen D. Mastrofski. "Suspect Searches: Assessing Police Behaviour under the US Constitution." *Criminology and Public Policy* 3 (2004): 316–62.

Greene, Ian, Carl Baar, Peter McCormick, George Szablowski, and Martin Thomas. *Final Appeal: Decision-Making in Canadian Courts of Appeal*. Toronto: Lorimer, 1998.

Greene, Ian, and Paul Shaffer. "Leave to Appeal and Leave to Commence Judicial Review in Canada's Refugee Determination System." *International Journal of Refugee Law* 4 (1992): 71–83.

Green-Pedersen, Christoffer. *The Conflict of Conflicts: Euthanasia in Denmark, Belgium, and the Netherlands*. Aarhus, Denmark: Aarhus University.

Green-Pederson, Christoffer, and John Wilkerson. "How Agenda Attributes Shape Politics." *Journal of European Public Policy* 13: 1039–52.

Greschner, Donna. "Abortion and Democracy for Women: A Critique of *Tremblay v. Daigle*." *McGill Law Journal* 35, no. 3 (1990): 633–69.

– "The Supreme Court, Federalism, and Metaphors of Moderation." *Canadian Bar Review* 79, no. 2 (2000): 47–76.

Hacker, Jacob, Paul Pierson, and Kathleen Thelen. "Drift and Conversion: Hidden Faces of Institutional Change." In *Advances in Comparative-Historical Analysis*, edited by James Mahoney and Kathleen Thelen, 181–8. New York: Cambridge University Press, 2015.

Halberstam, Daniel. "Comparative Federalism and the Role of the Judiciary." In *The Oxford Handbook of Law and Politics*, edited by Keith Whittington, R. Daniel Kelemen, and Gregory Caldeira, 142–64. Oxford: Oxford University Press, 2008.

Hall, Matthew E.K. *The Nature of Supreme Court Power*. New York: Cambridge University Press, 2011.

Hall, Peter A. "Policy Paradigms, Social Learning, and the State: The Case of Economic Policymaking in Britain." *Comparative Politics* 25, no. 3 (1993): 275–96.

Hall, Peter A., and Rosemary C.R. Taylor. "Political Science and the Three New Institutionalisms." *Political Studies* 44, no. 5 (1996): 936–57.

Harder, Lois. "In Canada of All Places: National Belonging and the Lost Canadians." *Citizenship Studies* 14, no. 2 (2010): 203–20.

Harris, Douglas C. *Fish, Law, and Colonialism: The Legal Capture of Salmon in British Columbia*. Toronto: University of Toronto Press, 2001.

Hausegger, Lori, Matthew Hennigar, and Troy Riddell. *Canadian Courts: Law, Politics, and Process*. Oxford: Oxford University Press, 2015.

Hayday, Matthew. *Bilingual Today, United Tomorrow: Official Languages in Education and Canadian Federalism*. Montreal and Kingston: McGill-Queen's University Press, 2005.

Heard, Andrew. *Canadian Constitutional Conventions: The Marriage of Law and Politics*. Toronto: Oxford University Press, 1991.

Heckman, Gerald P. "Securing Procedural Safeguards for Asylum Seekers in Canada." *International Journal of Refugee Law* 15, no. 2 (2003): 212–53.

Hennigar, Matthew A. "Expanding the 'Dialogue' Debate: Canadian Federal Government Responses to Lower Court Charter Decisions." *Canadian Journal of Political Science* 37, no. 1 (2004): 3–21.

– "Why Does the Federal Government Appeal to the Supreme Court of Canada in Charter of Rights Cases? A Strategic Explanation." *Law and Society Review* 41, no. 1 (2007): 225–50.

Henschen, Beth M., and Edward L. Sidlow. "The Supreme Court and the Congressional Agenda-Setting Process." *Journal of Law and Politics* 5, no. 4 (1988): 685–724.

Hersh, Nicholas. "Challenges to Assessing Same-Sex Relationships under Refugee Law in Canada." *McGill Law Journal* 60, no. 3 (2015): 527–71.

Hiebert, Janet L. *Charter Conflicts: What Is Parliament's Role?* Montreal and Kingston: McGill-Queen's University Press, 2002.

– "Money and Elections: Can Citizens Participate on Fair Terms amidst Unrestricted Spending?" *Canadian Journal of Political* Science 31, no. 1 (1998): 91–111.

– "Parliamentary Bills of Rights: An Alternative Model?" *Modern Law Review* 69, no. 1 (2006): 7–28.

Hiebert, Janet L., and James B. Kelly. *Parliamentary Bills of Rights: The Experiences of New Zealand and the United Kingdom.* Cambridge: Cambridge University Press, 2015.

Hilson, Chris. "New Social Movements." *Journal of European Public Policy* 9 (2002): 238–55.

Hirschl, Ran. *Towards Juristocracy: The Origins and Consequences of the New Constitutionalism.* Cambridge, MA: Harvard University Press, 2004.

Hogg, Peter W. "Is the Supreme Court of Canada Biased in Constitutional Cases?" *Canadian Bar Review* 57, no. 4 (1979): 721–39.

Hogg, Peter W., and Allison A. Bushell. "The *Charter* Dialogue between Courts and Legislatures (or Perhaps the *Charter of Rights* Isn't Such a Bad Thing After All)." *Osgoode Hall Law Journal* 35, no. 1 (1997): 75–124.

Howlett, Michael. "Beyond Legalism? Policy Ideas, Implementation Styles and Emulation-Based Convergence in Canadian and U.S. Environmental Policy." *Journal of Public Policy* 20, no. 3 (2000): 305–29.

– "Predictable and Unpredictable Policy Windows: Institutional and Exogenous Correlates of Canadian Federal Agenda-Setting." *Canadian Journal of Political Science* 31, no. 3 (1998): 495–524.

Huffman, James L., and MardiLyn Saathoff. "Advisory Opinions and Canadian Constitutional Development: The Supreme Court's Reference Jurisdiction." *Minnesota Law Review* 74, no. 6 (1990): 1251–336.

Huscroft, Grant. "Constitutionalism from the Top Down." *Osgoode Hall Law Journal* 45, no. 1 (2007): 99–104.

– "Rationalizing Judicial Power: The Mischief of Dialogue Theory." In *Contested Constitutionalism: Reflections on the Canadian Charter of Rights and Freedoms*, edited by James B. Kelly and Christopher P. Manfredi, 50–65. Vancouver: UBC Press, 2009.

– "'Thank God We're Here': Judicial Exclusivity in Charter Interpretation and Its Consequences." *Supreme Court Law Review* (2d) 25 (2004): 241–67.

Ibbitson, John. *Stephen Harper*. Toronto: McClelland and Stewart, 2015.

Jacobs, Alan, and R. Kent Weaver. "When Policies Undo Themselves: Self-Undermining Feedback as a Source of Policy Change." *Governance* 28, no. 4 (2014): 441–57.

Jansen, Harold J., and Lisa Young. "Cartels, Syndicates, and Coalitions: Canada's Political Parties after the 2004 Reforms." In *Money, Politics, and Democracy: Canada's Party Finance Reforms*, edited by Lisa Young and Harold J. Jansen, 82–103. Vancouver: UBC Press, 2011.

Jenson, Jane, and Susan D. Phillips. "Regime Shift: New Citizenship Practices in Canada." *International Journal of Canadian Studies* 14 (1996): 111–36.

Jervis, Robert. *System Effects: Complexity in Political and Social Life*. Princeton, NJ: Princeton University Press, 1997.

Johnstone, Rachael, and Emmett Macfarlane. "Public Policy, Rights, and Abortion Access in Canada." *International Journal of Canadian Studies* 51 (2015): 97–120.

Kagan, Robert A. "Adversarial Legalism and American Government." *Journal of Policy Analysis and Management* 10, no. 3 (1991): 369–406.

Kahana, Tsvi. "Legalism, Anxiety and Legislative Constitutionalism." *Queen's Law Journal* 31, no. 2 (2006): 536–55.

Katz, Richard S., and Peter Mair. "Changing Models of Party Organization and Party Democracy: The Emergence of the Cartel Party." *Party Politics* 1, no. 1 (1995): 5–28.

Kelemen, R. Daniel. *Eurolegalism: The Transformation of Law and Regulation in the European Union*. Cambridge, MA: Harvard University Press, 2011.

Kelley, Ninette, and Michael Trebilcock. *The Making of the Mosaic: A History of Canadian Immigration Policy*. Toronto: University of Toronto Press, 2000.

Kelly, James B. *Governing with the Charter: Legislative and Judicial Activism and Framers' Intent*. Vancouver: UBC Press, 2005.

Kelly, James B., and Matthew A. Hennigar. "The Canadian Charter of Rights and the Minister of Justice: Weak-Form Review within a Constitutional Charter of Rights." *International Journal of Constitutional Law* 10, no. 1 (2012): 35–68.

Kelly, James B., and Michael Murphy. "Shaping the Constitutional Dialogue on Federalism: Canada's Supreme Court as Meta-political Actor." *Publius* 35, no. 2 (2005): 217–43.

Kingdon, John W. *Agendas, Alternatives, and Public Policies*. 2nd ed. New York: Addison Wesley Longman, 1995.

Kirchhoff, Dennis et al. "The Canadian Environmental Assessment Act, 2012 and Associated Policy: Implications for Aboriginal Peoples." *International Indigenous Policy Journal* 4, no. 3 (2013): 1–14.

Kuo, Ming-Sung. "Discovering Sovereignty in Dialogue: Is Judicial Dialogue the Answer to Constitutional Conflict in the Pluralist Legal Landscape?" *Canadian Journal of Law and Jurisprudence* 26, no. 2 (2013): 341–9.

Ladner, Kiera. "Gendering Decolonisation, Decolonising Gender." *Australian Indigenous Law Review* 13, no. 1 (2009): 62–77.

– "Governing within an Ecological Context: Creating an AlterNative Understanding of Blackfoot Governance." *Studies in Political Economy* 70 (2003): 125–52.

Ladner, Kiera, and Michael Orsini. "The Persistence of Paradigm Paralysis: The *First Nations Governance Act* as the Continuation of Colonial Policy." In *Canada: The State of the Federation 2003*, edited by Michael Murphy, 185–203. Montreal and Kingston: McGill-Queen's University Press, 2003.

Laforest, Guy. *Trudeau and the End of a Canadian Dream*. Montreal and Kingston: McGill-Queen's University Press, 1995.

Lahey, Kathleen A. *Are We "Persons" Yet? Law and Sexuality in Canada*. Toronto: University of Toronto Press, 1999.

Lasswell, Harold. "The Emerging Conception of the Policy Sciences." *Policy Sciences* 1, no. 1 (1970): 3–14.

Lawlor, Andrea, and Erin Crandall. "Third Parties in the 2015 Federal Election: Partying Like It's 1988?" In *Canadian Election Analysis 2015: Communication, Strategy, and Democracy*, edited by Alex Marland and Thierry Giasson, 52–3. Vancouver: UBC Press, 2015.

Leckey, Robert. *Bills of Rights in the Common Law*. Cambridge: Cambridge University Press, 2016.

Lederman, W.R. "Unity and Diversity in Canadian Federalism: Ideals and Methods of Moderation." *Canadian Bar Review* 53, no. 3 (1975): 597–620.

Lee, Emery G., III. "Policy Windows on the U.S. Courts of Appeals." *Justice System Journal* 24, no. 3 (2003): 301–23.

Lemieux, Scott E., and George Lovell. "Legislative Defaults: Interbranch Power Sharing and Abortion Politics." *Polity* 42, no. 2 (2010): 210–43.

Leo, Richard A. "The Impact of *Miranda* Revisited." *Journal of Criminal Law and Criminology* 86 (1996): 621–92.

Levi, Margaret. "A Model, a Method, and a Map: Rational Choice in Comparative and Historical Analysis." In *Comparative Politics: Rationality, Culture, and Structure*, edited by Mark Lichbach and Alan Zuckerman, 22–6. Cambridge: Cambridge University Press, 1997.

Levitt, Steven D. "Using Repeat Challengers to Estimate the Effect of Campaign Spending on Election Outcomes in the US House." *Journal of Political Economy* 102, no. 4 (1994): 777–98.

Lindquist, Evert A., and Chris Eichbaum. "Remaking Government in Canada: Dares, Resilience, and Civility in Westminster Systems." *Governance* 29, no. 4 (2016): 553–71.

Lusztig, Michael. "Constitutional Paralysis: Why Canadian Constitutional Initiatives Are Doomed to Fail." *Canadian Journal of Political Science* 27, no. 4 (1994): 747–71.

MacDougall, Bruce. *Queer Judgments: Homosexuality, Expression and the Courts in Canada*. Toronto: University of Toronto Press, 2000.

Macfarlane, Emmett. "Conceptual Precision and Parliamentary Systems of Rights: Disambiguating 'Dialogue.'" *Review of Constitutional Studies* 17, no. 2 (2012): 73–100.

– "Conservative with the Constitution? Moderation, Strategy, and Institutional Distrust." In *The Blueprint: Conservative Parties and Their Impact on Canadian Politics*, edited by J.P. Lewis and Joanna Everitt. Toronto: University of Toronto Press, 2017.

– "Dialogue or Compliance? Measuring Legislatures' Policy Responses to Court Rulings on Rights." *International Political Science Review* 34, no. 1 (2013): 39–56.

– "The Dilemma of Positive Rights: Access to Health Care and the Canadian Charter of Rights and Freedoms." *Journal of Canadian Studies* 48, no. 3 (2014): 49–78.

– *Governing from the Bench: The Supreme Court of Canada and the Judicial Role*. Vancouver: UBC Press, 2013.

– "Terms of Entitlement: Is There a Distinctly Canadian 'Rights Talk'?" *Canadian Journal of Political Science* 41, no. 2 (2008): 303–28.

– "Unsteady Architecture: Ambiguity, the *Senate Reference*, and the Future of Constitutional Amendment in Canada." *McGill Law Journal* 60, no. 4 (2015): 883–903.

– "'You Can't Always Get What You Want': Regime Politics, the Supreme Court of Canada, and the Harper Government." *Canadian Journal of Political Science* 51, no. 1 (2018): 1–21, prepublished on FirstView, doi:10.1017/S0008423917000981.

MacKay, A. Wayne. "The Legislature, the Executive and the Courts: The Delicate Balance of Power or Who Is Running This Country Anyway?" *Dalhousie Law Journal* 24, no. 2 (2001): 37–56.

Macklem, Patrick. *Indigenous Difference and the Constitution of Canada*. Toronto: University of Toronto Press, 2001.

Macklin, Audrey. "Citizenship Revocation, the Privilege to Have Rights and the Production of the Alien." *Queen's Law Journal* 40, no. 1 (2014): 1–54.

– "Disappearing Refugees." *Columbia Human Rights Law Review* 36 (2005): 365–426.

Manfredi, Christopher P. "Conservatives, the Supreme Court of Canada, and the Constitution: Judicial-Government Relations, 2006–15." *Osgoode Hall Law Journal* 52, no. 3 (2015): 951–83.

– "The Day the Dialogue Died: A Comment on *Sauvé v. Canada*." *Osgoode Hall Law Journal* 45, no. 1 (2007): 105–23.
– *Feminist Activism in the Supreme Court: Legal Mobilization and the Women's Legal Education and Action Fund*. Vancouver: University of British Columbia Press, 2004.
– *Judicial Power and the Charter: Canada and the Paradox of Liberal Constitutionalism*. 2nd ed. Don Mills, ON: Oxford University Press, 2001.
Manfredi, Christopher P., and James B. Kelley. "Misrepresenting the Supreme Court's Record? A Comment on Choudhry and Hunter, 'Measuring Judicial Activism on the Supreme Court of Canada.'" *McGill Law Journal* 49, no. 3 (2004): 741–64.
– "Six Degrees of Dialogue: A Response to Hogg and Bushell." *Osgoode Hall Law Journal* 37, no. 3 (1999): 513–27.
Manfredi, Christopher P., and Mark E. Rush. "Electoral Jurisprudence in the Canadian and U.S. Supreme Courts: Evolution and Convergence." *McGill Law Journal* 52, no. 3 (2007): 457–93.
March, James G., and Johan P. Olsen. "The New Institutionalism: Organizational Factors in Political Life." *American Political Science Review* 78, no. 3 (1984): 734–49.
Martel, Marcel, and Martin Pâquet. *Langue et politique au Canada et au Québec: Une synthèse historique*. Montreal: Boréal, 2010.
Maveety, Nancy. *The Pioneers of Judicial Behavior*. Ann Arbor: University of Michigan Press, 2006.
McCann, Michael. "Causal versus Constitutive Explanations (or, On the Difficulty of Being So Positive …)." *Law and Social Inquiry* 21, no. 2 (1996): 457–82.
– "Reform Litigation on Trial." *Law and Social Inquiry* 17, no. 4 (1992): 715–43.
– *Rights at Work: Pay Equity Reform and the Politics of Legal Mobilization*. Chicago: University of Chicago Press, 1994.
McCaskell, Tim. *Queer Progress: From Homophobia to Homonationalism*. Toronto: Between the Lines Press, 2016.
McCormick, Peter. *The End of the Charter Revolution: Looking Back from the New Normal*. Toronto: University of Toronto Press, 2015.
McCrossan, Michael. "Shifting Judicial Conceptions of 'Reconciliation': Geographic Commitments Underpinning Aboriginal Rights Decisions." *Windsor Yearbook of Access to Justice* 31, no. 2 (2013): 155–79.
McMurtry, R. Roy. "The Creation of an Entrenched Charter of Rights – A Personal Memoir." *Queen's Law Journal* 31, no. 2 (2006): 456–67.
McRoberts, Kenneth. *Quebec: Social Change and Political Crisis*. 3rd ed. New York: Oxford University Press, 1993.
Meyer, David S., and Suzanne Staggenborg. "Movements, Countermovements, and the Structure of Political Opportunity." *American Journal of Sociology* 101, no. 6 (1996): 1628–60.

Miller, Mark C. *The View of the Courts from the Hill: Interactions between Congress and the Federal Judiciary*. Charlottesville: University of Virginia Press, 2009.

Miller, Mark C., and Jeb Barnes, eds. *Making Policy, Making Law: An Interbranch Perspective*. Washington, DC: Georgetown University Press, 2004.

Monahan, Patrick. "At Doctrine's Twilight: The Structure of Canadian Federalism." *University of Toronto Law Journal* 34, no. 1 (1984): 47–99.

– *Politics and the Constitution: The Charter, Federalism and the Supreme Court of Canada*. Agincourt, ON: Carswell, 1987.

Monture-Angus, Patricia. *Journeying Forward: Dreaming First Nations' Independence*. Halifax: Fernwood, 1999.

Moore, Kathryn. "Police Implementation of Supreme Court of Canada Charter Decisions: An Empirical Study." *Osgood Hall Law Journal* 30 (1992): 547–77.

Morton, F.L. "The Effect of the Charter of Rights on Canadian Federalism." *Publius* 25, no. 3 (1995): 173–88.

Morton, F.L., and Avril Allen. "Feminists and the Courts: Measuring Success in Interest Group Litigation in Canada." *Canadian Journal of Political Science* 34, no. 1 (2001): 55–84.

Morton, F.L., and Rainer Knopff. *The Charter Revolution and the Court Party*. Peterborough, ON: Broadview Press, 2000.

Morton, F.L., Peter H. Russell, and Troy Riddell. "The Canadian Charter of Rights and Freedoms: A Descriptive Analysis of the First Decade, 1982–1992." *National Journal of Constitutional Law* 5 (1995): 1–60.

Morton, F.L., Peter H. Russell, and Michael J. Withey. "The Supreme Court's First One Hundred Charter of Rights Decisions: A Statistical Analysis." *Osgoode Hall Law Journal* 30, no. 1 (1992): 1–56.

Mucciaroni, Gary. "The Garbage Can Model and the Study of Policy Making: A Critique." *Polity* 24 (1992): 459–82.

Namaste, Viviane. *Sex Change/Social Change: Reflections on Identity, Institutions, and Imperialism*. 2nd ed. Toronto: Women's Press, 2011.

Neve, Alex, and Tiisetso Russell. "Hysteria and Discrimination." *University of New Brunswick Law Journal* 62, no. 9 (2011): 37–45.

Newman, Dwight. "Judicial Method and Three Gaps in the Supreme Court of Canada's Assisted Suicide Judgment in *Carter*." *Saskatchewan Law Review* 78, no. 2 (2015): 217–24.

Normand, Martin. "De l'arène politique à l'arène juridique: Les communautés francophones minoritaires au Canada et la *Charte canadienne des droits et libertés*." In *Un nouvel ordre constitutionnel canadien: Du rapatriement de 1982 à nos jours*, edited by François Rocher and Benoît Pelletier, 179–203. Quebec: Presses de l'Université du Québec, 2013.

North, Douglass. "Institutions." *Journal of Economic Perspectives* 5, no. 1 (1991): 97–112.

Olsen, Mancur. *The Logic of Collective Action: Public Goods and the Theory of Groups*. Cambridge, MA: Harvard University Press, 1965.
Orfield, Myron W., Jr. "Deterrence, Perjury, and the Heater Factor: An Exclusionary Rule in the Chicago Criminal Courts." *University of Colorado Law Review* 63 (1992): 63–119.
– "The Exclusionary Rule and Deterrence: An Empirical Study of Chicago Narcotics Officers." *University of Chicago Law Review* 54 (1987): 1016–69.
Paciocco, David. "The Law of Minimum Sentences: Judicial Responses and Responsibility." *Canadian Criminal Law Review* 19, no. 2 (2015): 173–294.
Pal, Leslie. *Interests of State: The Politics of Language, Multiculturalism, and Feminism in Canada*. Montreal and Kingston: McGill-Queen's University Press, 1993.
Palmer, Stephanie. "'The Choice Is Cruel': Assisted Suicide and Charter Rights in Canada." *Cambridge Law Journal* 74, no. 2 (2015): 191–4.
Pasternak, Shiri. "Jurisdiction and Settler Colonialism: Where Do Laws Meet?" *Canadian Journal of Law and Society* 29, no. 2 (2014): 145–61.
Patenaude, Pierre. "The Provincial Court Judges Case and Extended Judicial Control." In *Judicial Power and Canadian Democracy*, edited by Paul Howe and Peter H Russell, 99–105. Montreal and Kingston: McGill-Queen's University Press, 2001.
Peabody, Bruce G. "Congressional Attitudes toward Constitutional Interpretation." In *Congress and the Constitution*, edited by Neal Devins and Keith E. Whittington, 9–63. Durham, NC: Duke University Press, 2005.
Petter, Andrew. *The Politics of the Charter: The Illusive Promise of Constitutional Rights*. Toronto: University of Toronto Press, 77–98.
Pickerill, J. Mitchell. *Constitutional Deliberation in Congress: The Impact of Judicial Review in a Separated System*. Durham, NC: Duke University Press, 2004.
Pierson, Paul. "Increasing Returns, Path Dependence, and Sequence in Political Processes." *American Political Science Review* 94, no. 2 (2000): 251–67.
– "Not Just What, But *When*: Timing and Sequence in Political Processes." *Studies in American Political Development* 14, no. 1 (2000): 72–92.
Pralle, Sarah. "Timing and Sequence in Agenda-Setting and Policy Change: A Comparative Study of Lawn Care Pesticide Politics in Canada and the US." *Journal of European Public Policy* 13, no. 7 (2006): 987–1005.
Radmilovic, Vuk. "Strategic Legitimacy Cultivation at the Supreme Court of Canada: Quebec *Secession Reference* and Beyond." *Canadian Journal of Political Science* 43, no. 4 (2010): 834–69.
Rayside, David. *Queer Inclusions, Continental Divisions: Public Recognition of Sexual Diversity in Canada and the United States*. Toronto: University of Toronto Press, 2008.
Rehaag, Sean. "Judicial Review of Refugee Determinations." *Queen's Law Journal* 38, no. 1 (2012): 1–58.

– "Patrolling the Borders of Sexual Orientation: Bisexual Refugee Claims in Canada." *McGill Law Journal* 53 (2008): 59–102.

Riddell, Troy Q. "The Impact of Legal Mobilization and Judicial Decisions: The Case of Official Minority-Language Education Policy in Canada for Francophones outside Quebec." *Law and Society Review* 38, no. 3 (2014): 583–609.

Roach, Kent. *Constitutional Remedies in Canada*. 2nd ed. Toronto: Thomson Reuters, 2016.

– "Dialogic Judicial Review and Its Critics." *Supreme Court Law Review* (2d) 23 (2004): 49–104.

– "Remedial Consensus and Dialogue under the Charter: General Declarations and Delayed Declarations of Invalidity." *University of British Columbia Law Review* 35 (2002): 271–328.

– "Searching for *Smith*: The Constitutionality of Mandatory Sentences." *Osgoode Hall Law Journal* 39, no. 2/3 (2001): 367–412.

– *The Supreme Court on Trial: Judicial Activism or Democratic Dialogue*. Toronto: Irwin Law, 2001: 156–76.

Robinson, Scott E., and Warren S. Eller. "Testing the Separation of Problems and Solutions in Subnational Policy Systems." *Policy Studies Journal* 38, no. 2 (2010): 199–216.

Rosenberg, Gerald N. *The Hollow Hope: Can Courts Bring About Social Change?* 2nd ed. Chicago: University of Chicago Press, 2008.

– "Knowledge and Desire: Thinking about Courts and Social Change." In *Leveraging the Law: Using the Courts to Achieve Social Change*, edited by David A. Schultz, 251–91. New York: Peter Lang, 1998.

– "Positivism, Interpretivism, and the Study of Law." *Law and Social Inquiry* 21 (1996): 435–55.

Russell, Peter H. "Canadian Constraints on Judicialization from Without." *International Political Science Review* 15 (1994): 165–75.

– *Constitutional Odyssey: Can Canadians Become a Sovereign People?* Toronto: University of Toronto Press, 2004.

– "Constitutional Reform of the Canadian Judiciary." *Alberta Law Review* 7, no. 1 (1969): 103–23.

– "Patriation and the Law of Unintended Consequences." In *Patriation and Its Consequences: Constitution Making in Canada*, edited by Lois Harder and Steve Patten, 229–43. Vancouver: UBC Press, 2015.

Salter, Mark. "Citizenship, Borders, and Mobility: Managing the Population of Canada and the World." In *Canada in the World: Internationalism in Canadian Foreign Policy*, edited by Heather A. Smith and Claire Turenne Sjolander, 146–65. Toronto: Oxford University Press, 2013.

Sanders, Douglas. "The Indian Lobby." In *And No One Cheered: Federalism, Democracy, and the Constitution Act*, edited by Keith Banting and Richard Simeon, 301–32. Agincourt, ON: Methuen Publications, 1983.

Schertzer, Robert. "Intergovernmental Relations in Canada's Immigration System: From Bilateralism towards Multilateral Collaboration." *Canadian Journal of Political Science* 48, no. 2 (2015): 383–412.

– *The Judicial Role in a Diverse Federation: Lessons from the Supreme Court of Canada*. Toronto: University of Toronto Press, 2016.

– "Recognition or Imposition? Federalism, National Minorities and the Supreme Court of Canada." *Nations and Nationalism* 14, no. 1 (2008): 105–26.

Schertzer, Robert, Andrew McDougall, and Grace Skogstad. "Collaboration and Unilateral Action: Recent Intergovernmental Relations in Canada." *IRPP Study* 62, December 2016.

Schmidt, Vivien. "Discursive Institutionalism: The Explanatory Power of Ideas and Discourse." *Annual Review of Political Science* 11, no. 1 (2008): 303–26.

Schneiderman, David, and Kate Sutherland, eds. *Charting the Consequences: The Impact of Charter Rights on Canadian Law and Politics*. Toronto: University of Toronto Press, 1997.

Schultz, David, and Stephen E. Gottlieb. "Legal Functionalism and Social Change: A Reassessment of Rosenberg's *The Hollow Hope*." In *Leveraging the Law: Using the Courts to Achieve Social Change*, edited by David A. Schultz, 169–207. New York: Peter Lang, 1998.

Sheridan, Paul, and Ketan Shankardass. "The 2012 Cuts to Refugee Health Coverage in Canada." *Canadian Journal of Political Science* 48, no. 4 (2016): 905–31.

Simeon, Richard. "Studying Public Policy." *Canadian Journal of Political Science* 9, no. 4 (1976): 548–80.

Simmons, Julie M., and Peter Graefe. "Assessing the Collaboration That Was 'Collaborative Federalism' 1996–2006." *Canadian Political Science Review* 7, no. 1 (2013): 25–36.

Sirota, Léonid. "'Third Parties' and Democracy 2.0." *McGill Law Journal* 60, no. 2 (2015): 253–93.

Skogstad, Grace. "International Trade Policy and the Evolution of Canadian Federalism." In *Canadian Federalism: Performance, Effectiveness, and Legitimacy*. 3rd ed., edited by Herman Bakvis and Grace Skogstad, 203–22. Don Mills, ON: Oxford University Press, 2012.

Skolnick, Jerome. *Justice without Trial: Law Enforcement in Democratic Society*. 3rd ed. New York: Macmillan, 1994.

Slattery, Brian. "A Theory of the Charter." *Osgoode Hall Law Journal* 25, no. 4 (1987): 701–47.

Smith, Jennifer, and Gerald Baier. "Fixed Election Dates, the Continuous Campaign, and Campaign Advertising Restrictions." In *From New Public Management to New Political Governance: Essays in Honour of Peter C. Aucoin*, edited by Herman Bakvis and Mark D. Jarvis, 128–49. Montreal and Kingston: McGill-Queen's University Press, 2012.

Smith, Miriam. "Ghosts of the Judicial Committee of the Privy Council." *Canadian Journal of Political Science* 35, no. 10 (2002): 1–29.

– "The Impact of the Charter: Untangling the Effects of Institutional Change." *International Journal of Canadian Studies* 36 (2007): 17–40.

– "Social Movements and Judicial Empowerment: Courts, Public Policy, and Lesbian and Gay Organizing in Canada." *Politics and Society* 33, no. 2 (2005): 327–53.

Snow, Dave, and Mark S. Harding. "From Normative Debates to Comparative Methodology: The Three Waves of Post-Charter Supreme Court Scholarship in Canada." *American Review of Canadian Studies* 45, no. 4 (2015): 451–66.

Snow, Dave, and Benjamin Moffitt. "Straddling the Divide: Mainstream Populism and Conservatism in Howard's Australia and Harper's Canada." *Commonwealth and Comparative Politics* 50, no. 3 (2012): 271–92.

Soennecken, Dagmar. "Extending Hospitality." *Studies in Law, Politics and Society* 60 (2013): 85–109.

– "The Growing Influence of the Courts over the Fate of Refugees." *Review of European and Russian Affairs* 4, no. 2 (2008): 55–88.

– "The Growth of Judicial Power over the Fate of Refugees." PhD diss., University of Toronto, 2008.

– "Shifting Back and Up." *Comparative Migration Studies* 2, no. 1 (2014): 102–22.

Sossin, Lorne. "The Ambivalence of Executive Power in Canada." In *The Executive and Public Law: Power and Accountability in Comparative Perspective*, edited by Paul Craig and Adam Tomkins, 52–88. Oxford: Oxford University Press, 2006.

Souter, Jannelle, and Amanda Zalmanowitz. "Symposium: *Carter v. Canada (Attorney General)*; Introduction and Background to Symposium." *Saskatchewan Law Review* 78, no. 2 (2015): 197–200.

Spiotto, James E. "Search and Seizure: An Empirical Study of the Exclusionary Rule and Its Alternatives." *Journal of Legal Studies* 2 (1973): 243–78.

Stephenson, Scott. "Constitutional Reengineering: Dialogue's Migration from Canada to Australia." *International Journal of Constitutional Law* 11, no. 4 (2013): 870–97.

Stevenson, Garth. *Unfulfilled Union: Canadian Federalism and National Unity*. 5th ed. Montreal and Kingston: McGill-Queen's University Press, 2009.

Stone, Deborah. *Policy Paradox: The Art of Political Decision Making*. New York: W.W. Norton, 2002.

Stone Sweet, Alec. *Governing with Judges: Constitutional Politics in Europe*. Oxford: Oxford University Press, 2000.

Surtees, Doug. "The Authorizing of Physician-Assisted Death in *Carter v. Canada (Attorney General)*." *Saskatchewan Law Review* 78, no. 2 (2015): 225–31.

Sweet, Martin J. *Merely Judgment: Ignoring, Evading, and Trumping the Supreme Court*. Charlottesville: University of Virginia Press, 2010.

Swinton, Katherine. "Federalism under Fire: The Role of the Supreme Court of Canada." *Law and Contemporary Problems* 55, no. 1 (1992): 121–45.

– *The Supreme Court of Canada and Canadian Federalism: The Laskin-Dickson Years*. Toronto: Carswell, 1990.

Tate, C. Neal, and Torbjörn Vallinder, eds. *The Global Expansion of Judicial Power*. New York: New York University Press, 1995.

Thelen, Kathleen. "Historical Institutionalism in Comparative Politics." *Annual Review of Political Science* 2 (1999): 369–404.

– "How Institutions Evolve: Insights from Comparative Historical Analysis." In *Comparative Historical Analysis in the Social Sciences*, edited by James Mahoney and Dietrich Rueschemeyer, 208–40. New York: Cambridge University Press, 2003.

Thériault, Joseph Yvon. *Faire société: Société civile et espaces francophones*. Sudbury: Prise de parole, 2007.

Thobani, Sunera. *Exalted Subjects: Studies in the Making of Race and Nation in Canada*. Toronto: University of Toronto Press, 2007.

Thomas, George C., III, and Richard A. Leo. "The Effects of *Miranda v. Arizona*: 'Embedded' in Our National Culture?" Vol. 29 of *Crime and Justice: A Review of Research*, edited by Michael Tonry, 203–71. Chicago: University of Chicago Press, 2002.

Turner, Dale. "Indigenous Knowledge and the Reconciliation of Section 35(1)." In *From Recognition to Reconciliation: Essays on the Constitutional Entrenchment of Aboriginal and Treaty Rights*, edited by Patrick Macklem and Douglas Sanderson, 175–8. Toronto: University of Toronto Press, 2016.

Turpel, Mary Ellen. "Home/Land." *Canadian Journal of Family Law* 10, no. 1 (1992): 17–40.

Turpel, M.E., and P.A. (Trisha) Monture. "Ode to Elijah: Reflections of Two First Nations Women on the Rekindling of Spirit at the Wake for the Meech Lake Accord." *Queen's Law Journal* 15, no. 2 (1990): 345–59.

Tushnet, Mark. *Taking the Constitution Away from the Courts*. Princeton, NJ: Princeton University Press, 1999.

– *Weak Courts, Strong Rights: Judicial Review and Social Welfare Rights in Comparative Constitutional Law*. Princeton, NJ: Princeton University Press, 2008.

Vanhala, Lisa. "Disability Rights Activists in the Supreme Court of Canada." *Canadian Journal of Political Science* 42 (2009): 981–1002.

– "Legal Opportunity Structures and the Paradox of Legal Mobilization by Environmental Movements in the UK." *Law and Society Review* 46, no. 3 (2012): 523–56.

Vermeule, Adrian. "The Atrophy of Constitutional Powers." *Oxford Journal of Legal Studies* 32, no. 3 (2012): 421–41.

Vipond, Robert C. *Liberty and Community: Canadian Federalism and the Failure of the Constitution*. Albany: State University of New York Press, 1991.

Visser, Max, and Kim Van der Togt. "Learning in Public Sector Organizations: A Theory of Action Approach." *Public Organization Review* 16, no. 2 (2016): 235–49.

von Tigerstrom, Barbara. "Consenting to Physician-Assisted Death: Issues Arising from *Carter v. Canada (Attorney General)*." *Saskatchewan Law Review* 78, no. 2 (2015): 233–9.

Wallner, Jennifer. *Learning to School: Federalism and Public Schooling in Canada*. Toronto: University of Toronto Press, 2014.

Wasby, Stephen L. *The Impact of the United States Supreme Court*. Homewood, IL: Dorsey Press, 1970.

Weiler, Paul. *In the Last Resort: A Critical Study of the Supreme Court of Canada*. Toronto: Carswell-Methuen, 1974.

Weinrib, Lorraine Eisenstat. "The Activist Constitution." In *Judicial Power and Canadian Democracy*, edited by Paul Howe and Peter H. Russell, 80–6. Montreal and Kingston: McGill-Queen's University Press, 2001.

Wells, Paul. *The Longer I'm Prime Minister*. Toronto: Vintage, 2014.

White, Linda A. "Federalism and Equality Rights Implementation in Canada." *Publius* 44, no. 1 (2014): 157–82.

Wilson, Bertha. "We Didn't Volunteer." In *Judicial Power and Canadian Democracy*, edited by Paul Howe and Peter H. Russell, 73–9. Montreal and Kingston: McGill-Queen's University Press, 2001.

Wintemute, Robert. "Sexual Orientation Discrimination as Sex Discrimination: Same-Sex Couples and the *Charter* in *Mossop, Egan* and *Layland*." *McGill Law Journal* 39 (1993–94): 429–78.

Wolfe, Patrick. "Settler Colonialism and the Elimination of the Native." *Journal of Genocide Research* 8, no. 4 (2006): 387–409.

Woo, Grace Li Xiu. *Ghost Dancing with Colonialism: Decolonization and Indigenous Rights at the Supreme Court of Canada*. Vancouver: UBC Press, 2011.

Young, Lisa. "Shaping the Battlefield: Partisan Self-Interest and Election Finance Reform in Canada, 2003–2014." In *The Deregulatory Moment? A Comparative Perspective on Changing Campaign Finance Laws*, edited by Robert G. Boatright, 107–25. Ann Arbor: University of Michigan Press, 2015.

Zahariadis, Nikolaos. "Ambiguity and Multiple Streams." In *Theories of the Policy Process.* 3rd ed., edited by Paul A. Sabatier and Christopher M. Weible, 25–58. Boulder, CO: Westview Press, 2014.

Contributors

Richard Albert, professor, The University of Texas at Austin School of Law

Christopher G. Anderson, associate professor, Department of Political Science, Wilfrid Laurier University

Dennis Baker, associate professor, Department of Political Science, University of Guelph

Stéphanie Chouinard, assistant professor, Department of Political Science, Royal Military College (Kingston) of Canada

Erin Crandall, assistant professor, Department of Politics, Acadia University

Minh Do, doctoral candidate, Department of Political Science, University of Toronto

Megan Gaucher, assistant professor, Department of Law and Legal Studies, Carleton University

Kate Glover Berger, assistant professor, Faculty of Law, Western University

Matthew Hennigar, associate professor, Department of Political Science, Brock University

Janet L. Hiebert, professor, Department of Political Studies, Queen's University

Rachael Johnstone, assistant professor, Department of Political Studies, Bader International Study Centre (Queen's University)

James B. Kelly, professor, Department of Political Science, Concordia University

Kyle Kirkup, assistant professor, Faculty of Law, University of Ottawa

Andrea Lawlor, assistant professor, Department of Political Science, King's University College at Western University

Emmett Macfarlane, associate professor, Department of Political Science, University of Waterloo

Michael McCrossan, assistant professor, Department of History and Politics, University of New Brunswick (Saint John)

Eleni Nicolaides, PhD student, Department of Political Science, University of Guelph

Kate Puddister, assistant professor, Department of Political Science, University of Guelph

Troy Riddell, associate professor, Department of Political Science, University of Guelph

Robert Schertzer, assistant professor, Department of Political Science, University of Toronto

Dave Snow, assistant professor, Department of Political Science, University of Guelph

Dagmar Soennecken, associate professor, School of Public Policy and Administration and Department of Social Science, York University

Marc Zanoni, doctoral candidate, Department of Political Science, University of Guelph

Index

www.ingramcontent.com/pod-product-compliance
Lightning Source LLC
LaVergne TN
LVHW090759070826
844660LV00022B/1026

* 9 7 8 1 4 8 7 5 2 3 1 5 2 *